in Cambridge International AS & A Level

Biology

Second Edition

Richard Fosbery

Helen Shaw Braben
Beverlyn Nathan
Padmajyothi Sripada

Oxford excellence for Cambridge AS & A Level

OXFORD
UNIVERSITY PRESS

Great Clarendon Street, Oxford, OX2 6DP, United Kingdom

Oxford University Press is a department of the University of Oxford.
It furthers the University's objective of excellence in research, scholarship, and education by publishing worldwide. Oxford is a registered trade mark of Oxford University Press in the UK and in
certain other countries

British Library Cataloguing in Publication Data
Data available

9781382005470

1 3 5 7 9 10 8 6 4 2

Paper used in the production of this book is a natural, recyclable product made from wood grown in sustainable forests.
The manufacturing process conforms to the environmental regulations of the country of origin.

Printed in the UK by Bell and Bain Ltd, Glasgow

Acknowledgements

The publisher and authors would like to thank the following for permission to use photographs and other copyright material:

Cover photo courtesy of Subbotina Anna/Shutterstock.

Photos: p10: Richard Fosbery; p11: Louisa Howard, Dartmouth College; p12: Louisa Howard, Dartmouth College; p13: Richard Fosbery; p15: Louisa Howard/Dartmouth EM Facility; p16: Science Photo Library; p18 (tl): Dennis Kunkel Microscopy/Science Photo Library; p18 (tr): Don W. Fawcett/Science Source/Science Photo Library; p18 (b): Louisa Howard, Dartmouth College; p19: AMI Images/Science Photo Library; p50: Adrian Davies/Alamy Stock Photo; p51: Steve Gschmeissner/ Science Photo Library; p62: Richard Fosbery; p63: Richard Fosbery; p64 (bc): Dr Keith Wheeler/Science Photo Library; p64 (bl): Dr Keith Wheeler/Science Photo Library; p65 (tl): Biodisc, Visuals Unlimited/Science Photo Library; p65 (tl): Biodisc, Visuals Unlimited/Science Photo Library; p65 (bl): Richard Fosbery; p65 (br): Richard Fosbery; p66 (l): Richard Fosbery; p66 (r): Dr Keith Wheeler/Science Photo Library; p67 (l): Biodisc/Visuals Unlimited, Inc.; p67 (r): Biodisc/Visuals Unlimited, Inc.; p68 (l): Randy Moore, Visuals Unlimited/Science Photo Library; p68 (r): Dr Keith Wheeler/Science Photo Library; p71: Power and Syred/Science Photo Library; p73 (l): Biophoto Associates/Science Photo Library; p74 (l): Richard Fosbery; p75 (t): Dr Gladden Willis, Visuals Unlimited/Science Photo Library; p75 (bl): Lennart Nilsson, TT/Science Photo Library; p75 (br): Science History Images/Alamy Stock Photo; p80: Don W. Fawcett/Science Source/Science Photo Library; p83 (l): Jose Calvo/Science Photo Library; p83 (r): Kage Mikrofotografie Gbr/Science Photo Library; p101: Cultura Creative Ltd/Alamy Stock Photo; p105: Richard Fosbery; p108: Image Source/Alamy Stock Photo; p117 (b): Steve Gschmeissner/Science Photo Library; p117 (tl): Richard Fosbery; p117 (tr): Richard Fosbery; p118: Sergey Lavrentev/Shutterstock; p126: Patila/Shutterstock; p131: Thomas Deerinck, NCMIR/Science Photo Library; p134: Alfio Scisetti/Alamy Stock Photo; p140: Dr Clare van der Willigen; p141: Nature Picture Library/Alamy Stock Photo; p142 (b): tony mills/Alamy Stock Photo; p142 (c): Cat Edwardes/Alamy Stock Photo; p142 (t): The Natural History Museum/Alamy Stock Photo; p143: Paulo Oliveira/Alamy Stock Photo; p144: Robert Schwemmer, CINMS, NOAA; p150: Reinhard Dirscherl/Science Photo Library; p152: Science History Images/Alamy Stock Photo; p155 (b): schankz/Shutterstock; p155 (t): All Canada Photos/Alamy Stock Photo; p179: RICHARD HUTCHINGS/Science Photo Library; p190: Marek Poplawski/Shutterstock; p191: Nataliia K/Shutterstock; p194: Marek Poplawski/Shutterstock; p180 (bl): Science Pictures Limited/Science Photo Library; p180 (br): Kage Mikrofotografie Gbr/Science Photo Library; p180 (tl): Dr Keith Wheeler/Science Photo Library; p180 (tr): Dr Keith Wheeler/Science Photo Library; p183 (l): Jose Calvo/Science Photo Library; p183 (r): Jose Luis Calvo/Shutterstock; p200: Pexels/Pixabay.

All other artwork by Q2A Media and Aptara.

Every effort has been made to contact copyright holders of material reproduced in this book. Any omissions will be rectified in subsequent printings if notice is given to the publisher.

Contents

Access your support website for the answers to Try this and Exam-style questions here: www.oxfordsecondary.com/caie-al-sci-exam-success

Introduction

Exam Success in Biology will help you to reach your highest potential and achieve the best possible grade. The guide is designed to help you learn the content of the AS & A Level Biology syllabus (9700), to help you develop techniques about how to revise and to answer the questions in the exam papers.

The first part of the syllabus (Units 1 to 11) is examined at AS Level by Papers 1, 2 and 3. You can gain an AS Level qualification in Biology by taking these three papers. The second part of the syllabus (Units 12 to 19) is examined by Papers 4 and 5. You can only gain an A Level qualification in Biology if you take these two papers and the AS papers.

The AS **and** A Level papers can be taken together in the same series. Alternatively, you can follow the staged assessment by taking all three AS papers in one series and the A Level papers in a later series. If your grade for the AS papers was not as good as you hoped, you may retake the papers in another series. However, if you retake you have to take all three papers in the same series.

The table gives a summary of the five examination papers:

Level of assessment	Exam paper	Units	Style of questions	Weighting
AS	Paper 1	1 to 11	40 multiple choice questions (MCQs)	31% of the AS Level 15.5% of the A Level
AS	Paper 2	1 to 11	5 or 6 structured questions	46% of the AS Level 23% of the A Level
AS	Paper 3	1 to 11	2 or 3 questions on practical Biology	23% of the AS Level 11.5% of the A Level
A Level	Paper 4	12 to 19	9 structured questions	38.5% of the A Level
A Level	Paper 5	1 to 19	2 or 3 structured questions	11.5% of the A Level

Assessment objectives

The papers are written to match the three assessment objectives.

*   AO1: Knowledge and understanding
*   AO2: Handling, applying and evaluating information
*   AO3: Experimental skills and investigations

You can find details of these three objectives in the syllabus. You should appreciate that AO1 and AO2 have equal weighting in Papers 1, 2 and 4. In other words, 50% of the marks in those papers are to test what you know (and can recall) and 50% assesses how you can use your knowledge and understanding to analyse and interpret information. AO3 is assessed in Papers 3 and 5.

Know your syllabus

Download the syllabus from the CAIE website (https://www.cambridgeinternational.org) and use it all the time during your course. The subject content of the syllabus is divided into 19 topics. In this book they are known as Units. Each topic is divided into learning outcomes. These tell you exactly what you need to learn and what you should be able to do with the knowledge you acquire.

Command words

Each exam question has a command word. This is usually at the beginning of the question as in '**Explain** how the structure of the heart ensures that blood travels one way'. Sometimes command words are not at the beginning as in 'With reference to the diagram of the respirometer, **suggest** why the bubble moved to the left.'

You can find brief explanations of the command words in the syllabus.

Do your own marking

Mark schemes for the exam-style questions in this book are available on the support website (www.oxfordsecondary.com/caie-al-sci-exam-success). Find out what examiners are looking for by using the mark schemes to mark answers written by your peers. However, do not learn mark schemes in the hope that the same questions will be set when you take the exams. Candidates that try this usually gain very few marks because they are not answering the questions set.

Key features of the book

The following features in the guide will help you develop the skills you need to learn effectively and use your knowledge in unfamiliar contexts.

Knowledge check

This feature recaps the skills and knowledge you should already have before working through the unit.

Worked Example

These give examples of questions, and show you how best to answer them.

Remember

These include key information that you must remember if you are to achieve a high grade.

Link

These show where in the book you can find more information about a topic.

Key terms

These give easy-to-understand definitions of important terms.

Exam tip

These provide advice on how to master your exam technique and help you understand exactly what examiners are looking for.

Try this

These feature gives you an opportunity to test out the skills and knowledge you've learnt with a practice question. Answers to Try this and the end-of-chapter Exam-style questions are available on the OUP support website: www.oxfordsecondary.com/caie-al-sci-exam-success.

Practical Skills

These describe practical skills that you might be tested on and are intended as reminders of work you may have already done in the lab.

Maths Skills

These remind you of the vital mathematical skills that you need in order to answer exam questions in biology.

Raise your grade

Here, you can read model answers that achieved maximum marks, as well as find out how to improve answers where marks were lost and learn how to avoid common errors in exams.

1 Cell structure

The cell

A cell is a basic unit of life composed of cytoplasm surrounded by a cell surface membrane. Some organisms are also surrounded by a cell wall.

There are two types of cellular organisation: **prokaryotes** and **eukaryotes**.

Table 1.1 compares the structure of prokaryotic and eukaryotic cells.

★ **Exam tip**

Make sure you use the syllabus as you read each Unit. Here you need to look at the details of Topic 1: Cell structure.

▼ **Table 1.1** The differences between prokaryotic cells and eukaryotic cells

Feature	Prokaryotic cells	Eukaryotic cells	
		Plant cells	Animal cells
typical size/μm	1–5	40–60	20
capsule/slime layer	found in some	✗	✗
cell wall	✔ (peptidoglycan, not cellulose)	✔ (made of cellulose)	✗

The linear dimensions of plant, animal and bacterial cells are usually stated in micrometres, μm (1/1000th of a mm). The dimensions of the usually much smaller viruses are often stated in nanometres, nm (1/1000th of a μm).

Microscopes are used to study the structure and function of cells. Living cells can be observed using a **light microscope**.

The cells of flowering plants and the cells of mammals are examples of eukaryotic cells. Plant cells are always surrounded by a cellulose cell wall, whereas animal cells do not have cell walls.

The cell surface membrane of eukaryotic cells encloses many different cell structures (sub-cellular structures). These include various distinct organelles and the cytoskeleton (the 'cell skeleton').

Most cell structures can only be seen with an **electron microscope**. You can see from electron micrographs that cells are divided into compartments. Many processes that occur in cells require different conditions, so they are localised into these compartments. For example, lysosomes are required only when a cell needs to break down 'worn out' cell structures and material it has taken in, or when a cell destroys itself. The membrane surrounding lysosomes protects the cell as lysosomes contain enzymes that digest biological molecules and they work best at a pH lower than in the rest of the cell.

Cells carry out various processes and activities to fulfil their specialised functions:

- obtaining energy and converting it into a usable form
- gaining raw materials from their surroundings
- producing biological molecules, such as carbohydrates, lipids, proteins and nucleic acids
- packaging materials so they can be exported from the cell
- excreting waste materials
- storing and using genetic information.

Key terms

Eukaryote: an organism that has cells with true nuclei and membrane-bound **organelles**, such as mitochondria.

Prokaryote: an organism that has cells without nuclei and membrane-bound organelles.

 Link

You can revise the structure and function of cell surface membranes in Unit 4.

 Link

There is more about the function of lysosomes in Unit 11.

💡 **Remember**

To convert:
- millimetres to micrometres multiply by 1000
- micrometres to nanometres multiply by 1000
- nanometres to micrometres divide by 1000
- micrometres to millimetres divide by 1000.

Cell structures work together to carry out these functions in each cell. When a cell makes and secretes a certain protein, it is the nucleus, mitochondria, rough endoplasmic reticulum (RER), Golgi body, Golgi vesicles, microtubules and cell surface membrane that all work together. These cell structures are involved in the different stages between making copies of the gene that codes for the protein and the fusion of secretory vesicles to the cell surface membrane and the release of their contents.

The cell structures can be divided into groups, as shown in Table 1.2.

▼ **Table 1.2** The cell structures of eukaryotic cells that are surrounded by membranes and those that are not made of membranes

Cell structures surrounded by membranes		Cell structures not made of membranes
Single membrane	**Two membranes (double membrane)**	
Golgi body Golgi vesicles lysosome rough endoplasmic reticulum smooth endoplasmic reticulum vacuole of plant cells (surrounded by the tonoplast)	nucleus – surrounded by nuclear envelope chloroplast – surrounded by an envelope of two membranes mitochondrion – surrounded by outer and inner membranes; infoldings of inner membrane are cristae	nucleolus ribosomes cytoskeleton, composed of microtubules and other fibres centrioles (made of microtubules)

The protein-rich liquid in the cytoplasm that surrounds the organelles is called the **cytosol**. Many reactions occur here, such as some of the reactions of respiration.

Viruses are non-cellular as they have no cell structure. They have genetic material (RNA or DNA) surrounded by a protein coat. Some viruses also contain a few enzyme molecules. Viruses typically range in size from 20 to 400 nm. Enveloped viruses (e.g. human immunodeficiency virus, HIV, and the influenza virus) are covered in a phospholipid and protein membrane formed from the cells of their hosts.

→ Try this... 2

Draw a diagram to show the structure of HIV. Label the parts that you have drawn.

Cells need energy

Adenosine triphosphate (ATP) is the energy transfer molecule in cells. Chloroplasts and mitochondria both produce ATP in cells. Some is also made in the cytosol.

ATP produced in chloroplasts is used to make sugars during photosynthesis and is not transferred to the rest of the cell. ATP is made in mitochondria during aerobic respiration. Some of the ATP produced in mitochondria is used within the organelle, for example for protein synthesis, but most is transferred to the rest of the cell for its energy needs. ATP does not travel from cell to cell.

Cells from mesophyll (photosynthetic) tissue and guard cells in leaves have many chloroplasts to maximise the photosynthesis that they can carry out. Cells with high energy demands, such as root hair cells, ciliated epithelial cells (see Unit 9) and plasma cells (see Unit 11) have many mitochondria.

→ Try this... 1

Cilia, plasmodesmata, microvilli and cell wall are missing from Table 1.2. Where would you put them?

🔗 Link

There is more about HIV in Unit 10.

★ Exam tip

Find diagrams and electron micrographs of different types of virus so you get an idea of the variety of shapes and sizes.

🔗 Link

There is more about ATP in Units 6, 12 and 13.

★ Exam tip

Search online for transmission electron micrographs (TEMs) of liver cells as these cells have a high demand for ATP and so have many mitochondria. You can also search for TEMs of mesophyll cells as they have many chloroplasts. These will help you recognise different cell structures.

Making your own learning resources

In biology you have a large amount of information to learn. Learning is an active process, so it helps to spend time organising information into ways that help you remember. Most of us learn more effectively if we work with others, so you can use the six methods described here with another person or as part of a group. You do not have to be in the same room; you can do many of these by communicating electronically. Follow the links to find other ways to organise information to help your learning and revision.

Diagrams

A good way to collect all the information about cell structures is to use diagrams. Figure 1.1 shows a simple labelled diagram of a bacterial cell. Add the information you need to know about prokaryotic cells by *annotating* the diagram. Here there are two annotations about the cell wall – its composition and its function.

Make a large diagram of a plant cell and an animal cell. A3 or poster-sized paper is good for this. Label the diagrams carefully using straight lines made with a ruler (as on Figure 1.1). Highlight the similarities between the two cell types. The structures that you do not highlight are the differences. Annotate your diagrams with information about structural details and functions.

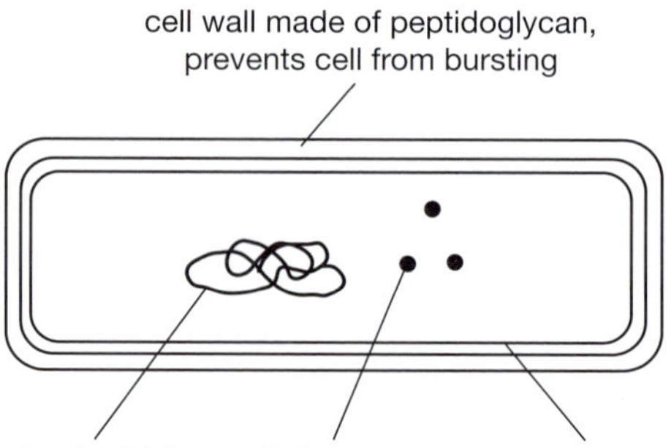

cell wall made of peptidoglycan, prevents cell from bursting

circular DNA   70S ribosome   cell membrane

▲ **Figure 1.1** Copy and complete this diagram by adding any other structures that bacteria can have and annotating all the structures

> Annotate means to add notes to your diagram. These can be as brief and concise as you can make them. Put one idea into each note that you add to the diagram. Each note should relate to a structure you have drawn.

Search on the internet to find some electron micrographs of plant and animal cells and cell structures, such as mitochondria and Golgi bodies. You should be able to find some without labels. Add your own labels and annotate with details about structure and function. This will help you to answer questions that ask for identifications of cell structures from electron micrographs.

Find diagrams or photographs of specialised cells and identify how their structure is related to their function. You could research: red blood cells; phagocytes; lymphocytes; pancreatic acinar cells which secrete enzymes for digestion in the gut; palisade mesophyll cells from a leaf; guard cells from a leaf; phloem sieve tubes; phloem companion cells.

Tables

Use the information you find about specialised cells to make a table (in landscape format) with the following headings: name of cell; tissue; organ; organ system; structural features; function.

Graphic organisers

These are good ways of organising information from your notes and textbooks. Here are three examples.

Figure 1.2 is a partly completed spider diagram for 'cells'. Put the name of the topic in the centre and then try to organise everything you know by thinking of sub-topics and arranging them around the main topic. Keep subdividing as shown in the figure. Keep adding further information as you cover other topics in the syllabus; for example, the person who drew Figure 1.2 could add the names of the specialised cells named in Units 4 to 11.

> ★ **Exam tip**
>
> Use the syllabus to make sure your diagram of a bacterial cell has all the structures listed. You can also add other structures that are found in some bacteria such as *Vibrio cholerae*. See Unit 10 for species of bacteria you should know about.

> ★ **Exam tip**
>
> Use the information in your table to explain how the structure of each cell is related to its function. This is a very common style of question.

> ★ **Exam tip**
>
> Search for 'enchanted learning' and 'thinking maps' for different examples of graphic organisers.

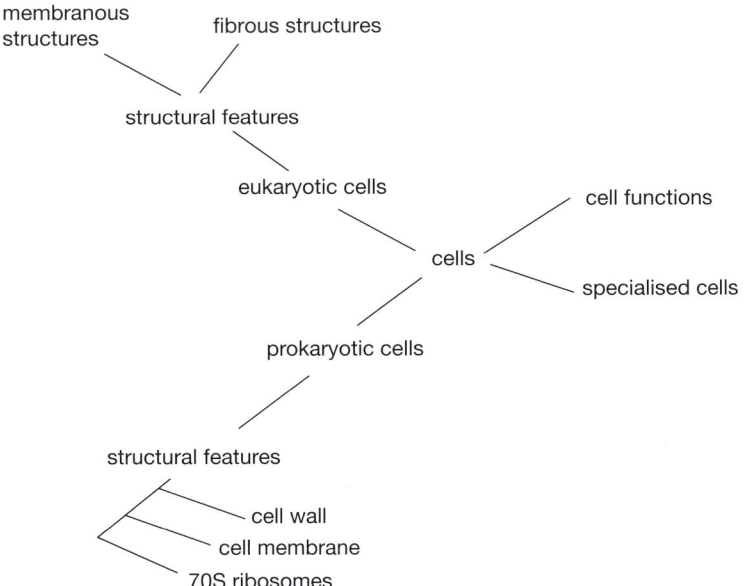

▲ **Figure 1.2** A spider diagram for cells. Try making some of your own spider diagrams for topics in Unit 1.

A common exam question is to ask for similarities and/or differences between structures or processes. You can make tables to show differences, but diagrams like the one in Figure 1.3 are a good way to present similarities and differences in a way that may be easier to remember.

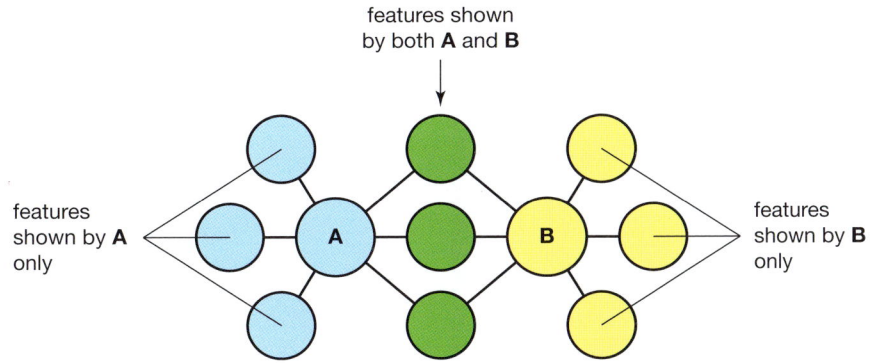

▲ **Figure 1.3** Try this as a way to display the differences and similarities between plant and animal cells. You can have as many circles as you like, but select the main points first.

Flow charts

When describing processes you need to sequence the steps correctly. Often processes are described in textbooks in prose. Use the information to draw flow charts like the one in Figure 1.4. This will help you to learn correct sequences and make it easier for your revision.

Glossary

Make your own glossary of the technical terms in Unit 1. Many text books have glossaries, but it's a good idea to write your own with longer entries. Write sentences using the terms. Test yourself by printing out terms and definitions separately and then matching them together. Or ask a friend to read out the definitions and you call out the terms, then swap. Some terms are very similar, so make sure that you spend time learning how to give precise definitions for them.

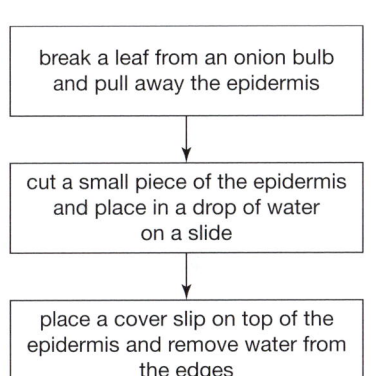

▲ **Figure 1.4** A flow chart to show the steps in making a temporary preparation of onion epidermis cells (see Figure 1.8 on page 13). Adapt this to include the instructions for staining the cells with an iodine solution to show the nuclei.

Use your glossary to write 'mix and match' revision exercises as in Table 1.3 for other students to answer.

▼ **Table 1.3** Write 'mix and match' exercises to prepare yourselves for exam questions that ask you for the meanings of terms or to state the term that matches a description (you can find the answer to this example online)

A	cell surface membrane	1	storage of genetic information
B	Golgi body	2	endocytosis
C	rough endoplasmic reticulum	3	formation of secretory vesicles
D	nucleus	4	formation of proteins
E	lysosome	5	formation of lipids
F	smooth endoplasmic reticulum	6	aerobic respiration
G	nucleolus	7	production of ribosomes
H	mitochondria	8	storage of hydrolytic enzymes

> **✎ Revision strategy**
>
> Make your own glossary and use it to make 'mix and match' exercises like Table 1.3 for all of the Units in the syllabus.

Posters to link topics

Exam questions often test more than one Unit in the syllabus, as in Question 1 on page 17. As part of your learning you should combine information from Unit 1 with other Units. Making posters on large sheets of paper is a good way to do this. Decide what topics you want to link together and then make a list of all the relevant structures and processes. Writing on sticky notes or small pieces of card is a good way to start organising the information and discussing it with others.

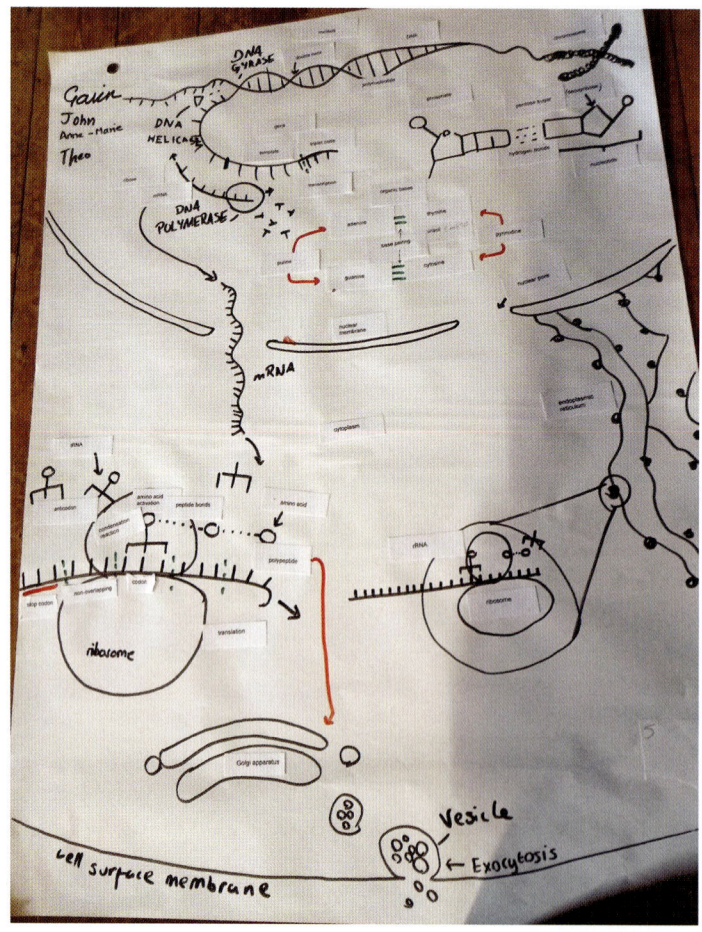

▲ **Figure 1.5** A poster made by a group of students to show how the parts of a cell work together to produce and export a protein. This combines information from Units 1, 4 and 6.

> **★ Exam tip**
>
> The discussions that you have about organising information into a poster are more important than its final appearance. Take the opportunity to learn with others as you work together.

Try this... 3

Figure 1.6 is a drawing made from transmission electron microscope (TEM) images of mammalian cells.

The table shows some functions of the mammalian cell.

(a) Complete the table by indicating the name of the structure that carries out each function and the appropriate label on Figure 1.6. One row has been completed for you.

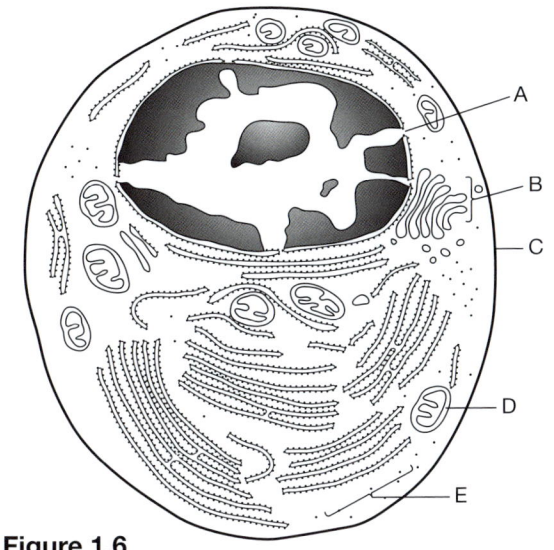

▶ **Figure 1.6**

Function	Name of cell structure	Letter on Figure 1.6
aerobic respiration		
production of polypeptides		
allows movement between nucleus and cytoplasm		
packaging of proteins for export from the cell		
control of movement into and out of the cell	cell surface membrane	C

[4]

(b) Many of the cell structures visible in Figure 1.6 are not visible under a light microscope. Explain why. [2]

Try this... 4

(a) This is a list of structures found in cells:

    70S ribosome   cell wall   mitochondrion   plasmodesmata

    80S ribosome   chloroplast   nucleus

Complete the table to compare prokaryotes and eukaryotes using **only** the structures in the list.

- Each example can be written in **one or more** correct headings.
- All the structures in the list should appear **at least once** in your table.

Prokaryotes	Eukaryotes	
	Plants	Animals

(b) The Golgi body, smooth endoplasmic reticulum and rough endoplasmic reticulum are cellular structures composed of intracellular membranes.

Make drawings to show the appearance of these three structures as they appear in a transmission electron micrograph.

★ **Exam tip**

When making drawings in Papers 2 and 3, follow the rules listed in Unit 20, Practical skills (page 179).

⚙ Practical Skills

Resolution and magnification

The **resolution** of the human eye is about 0.2 mm (200 μm). If two structures are separated by a minimum distance of 0.2 mm, you can see them as two structures; otherwise they appear to you as one structure.

The resolution of the light microscope (LM) is 0.2 μm (200 nm), so anything smaller than this is not visible in the LM and to view them you need to use a device with a resolution *less than* 0.2 μm.

The resolution of TEMs used for many biological images is about 0.5 nm. This means membranes and ribosomes are visible. Anything smaller than 0.5 nm cannot be seen in many electron micrographs of cells.

Resolution determines the highest useful **magnification** that is possible in a microscope. If the resolution is poor it does not matter how much the image is magnified, no further detail is seen. The highest useful magnifications are:

- light microscope: × 1000 to × 1500

- transmission electron microscope: about × 250 000

- scanning electron microscope: × 100 000.

Key terms

Resolution: the ability to distinguish between two structures that are close together.

Magnification: the ratio between the actual size of an object and the size of an image, such as a drawing or a photograph.

💡 **Remember**

Membranes are about 7 nm thick and ribosomes vary in size with a diameter of ≤30 nm. The sizes of these structures are below the resolution of the LM, but they can be resolved in the EM.

⅃ Maths Skills

Calculating magnifications and actual sizes

Scale bars are one way to indicate the real size of an object that is very much smaller than the image. You can use the scale bar in Figure 1.7 to estimate the diameter of the bacterial cell, either by eye or by placing a ruler across the image.

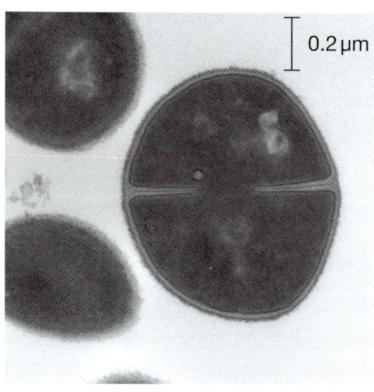
0.2 μm

◀ **Figure 1.7** A transmission electron micrograph of a section through the bacterium *Staphylococcus aureus*. This cell is dividing by binary fission

🔗 **Link**

Some forms of *S. aureus* are causative organisms of infectious (communicable) diseases. You can revise information on the bacteria that cause cholera and tuberculosis in Unit 10.

⭐ **Exam tip**

Look at the unit on the scale bar and make sure that you change your measurement to the same unit. In Figure 1.7, for example, if you have measured in millimetres, multiply by 1000 to give the measurement in micrometres.

To make an accurate measurement, use a ruler to measure the length of the scale bar in millimetres and a linear measurement on the image (e.g. the diameter of the cell in Figure 1.7 at the widest place).

Use this formula to calculate the actual size:

$$\text{actual size} = \frac{\text{distance on image}}{\text{length of scale bar}} \times \text{length given on the scale bar}$$

Worked Example 1

Use the formula to calculate the actual diameter of the cell of *S. aureus* in Figure 1.7.

Distance across cell at widest part = 35 mm = 35 000 µm

$$\text{actual size} = \frac{35\,000\,\mu m}{7\,000\,\mu m} \times 0.2\,\mu m$$

$$= 1.0\,\mu m$$

Images may not have scale bars. Instead the magnification is given. Figure 1.8 shows some plant cells.

Use the magnification from the caption to calculate the actual length of one of the cells:

$$\text{actual length} = \frac{\text{length of image}}{\text{magnification}}$$

 Link

Measurements like this should be given with the degree of uncertainty involved. You can find out what this means and how to determine uncertainty on page 169 in Unit 20, Practical skills.

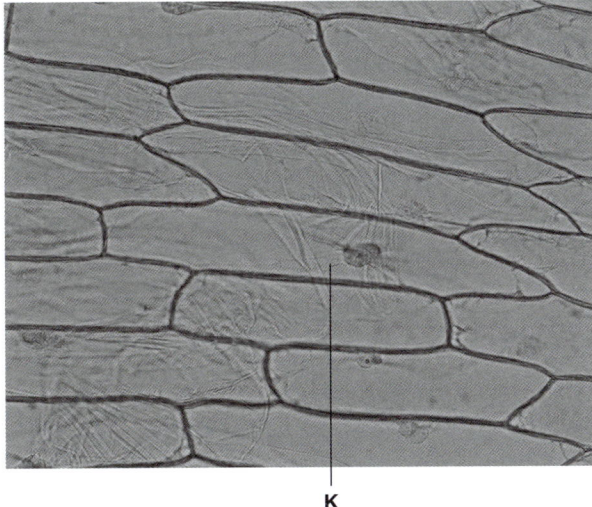

▲ **Figure 1.8** A photomicrograph showing epidermal cells from a scale leaf of an onion bulb (×280)

Worked Example 2

To measure the length of cell **K**, place a ruler to measure the full length of the cell. This should give a measurement of 61 mm. Use the formula:

$$\text{actual length} = \frac{61}{280}\,mm$$

$$\text{actual length} = 0.22\,mm = 220\,\mu m$$

★ **Exam tip**

Always measure images and specimens in millimetres.

★ **Exam tip**

In a calculation question, always check what you are asked to do. You may be asked to give your answer to the nearest whole number and to use certain units. If you are not told which units to use, choose the most appropriate that give answers within the number range 1 to 100.

To calculate the magnification of an image, you need to divide the length of the image by the actual length of the object:

$$\text{magnification} = \frac{\text{length of the image}}{\text{actual length of the object}}$$

Use the triangle in Figure 1.9 to manipulate the formula for magnification.

★ **Exam tip**

Make sure that you use the same units for the numerator (above the line in the calculation) and the denominator (below the line).

image length

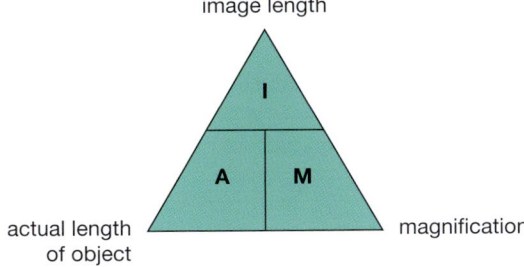

actual length of object   magnification

◀ **Figure 1.9** The 'magnification triangle'. Look at the formula for calculating magnification and the formula for calculating actual size to see how the triangle can help you remember which one to use

Worked Example 3

A student made a temporary preparation of some hairs from the flowers of *Tradescantia*. She then used her smartphone to take some photographs of the cells that make up the hairs. She used the photograph to make a drawing of one of the cells, as shown in Figure 1.10.

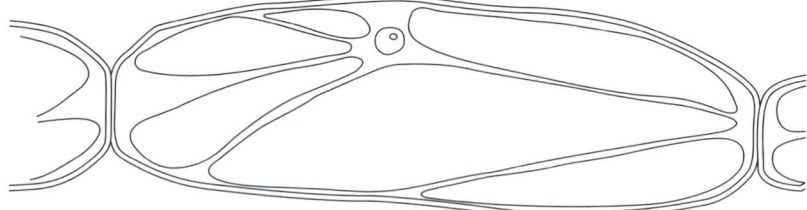

◀ **Figure 1.10**

(a) Add a label line and a label for each of the cell structures:

    A   nucleus

    B   nucleolus

    C   tonoplast

    D   cell wall   [4]

(b) The student observed movement of particles within the cytoplasm of the staminal hairs. State which cell structures are responsible for this movement within the cytoplasm.   [1]

(c) Describe the steps that the student would follow to determine the magnification of her drawing.   [4]

(d) State **two** cell structures, other than those listed in part (a), that would be present in the staminal hair cell shown above that are found in eukaryotic cells, but not in prokaryotic cells.   [2]

Answers

(a)

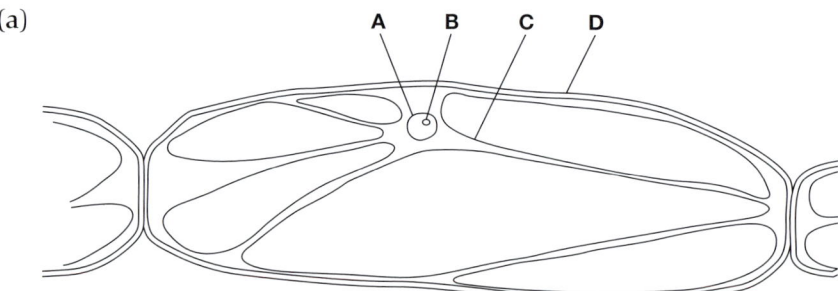

(b) Microtubules.

(c) 1. She would use an eyepiece graticule to measure the length or width of the cell.

    2. She would then convert the measurement in eyepiece units into micrometres.

    3. She would use a ruler to measure the same dimension in the drawing (length or width) in millimetres and convert to micrometres by multiplying by 1000.

    4. The magnification is calculated by dividing the dimension of the drawing (in μm) by the actual dimension (in μm) that she measured in Steps 1 and 2.

> ★ **Exam tip**
>
> Notice that the answer to (c) is presented as a series of numbered points. This is a good way to describe the steps in a procedure, rather than writing continuous prose.

(d) Mitochondria and 80S ribosomes.

How to answer multiple choice questions

The multiple-choice questions (MCQs) in Paper 1 test your recall of knowledge (assessment objective 1 – AO1) and your ability to apply your knowledge to familiar and unfamiliar contexts (assessment objective 2 – AO2).

Each question has four options, A, B, C and D. Only one of these options is the correct answer. The other options are known as distractors. You write your answers on a special answer sheet using a pencil. There is one mark for each question and the paper has 40 questions.

There are many different ways to write multiple choice questions. In Paper 1 only two types of question are used. We will call these Type 1 and Type 2.

The mark for each question is given on the right-hand side of the exam paper. Here the mark is replaced by the assessment objective to help you realise that you are expected to work out answers to some MCQs not simply recall the required information.

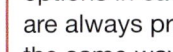 **Exam tip**

In Type 1 multiple choice questions the options A, B, C and D appear directly below the question, the options in each question are always presented in the same way and can be phrases or complete sentences, or presented in a table, graph or diagram. Photographs may also be used.

1   Which cell structure is responsible for moving organelles within cells?

   A   cilia

   B   Golgi body

   C   lysosomes

   D   microtubules   (AO1)

★ **Exam tip**

Read through the question a couple of times before you look at the choices. **D** is the correct answer.

2   There is considerable variation in the diameter of living cells. The diameter of a cell of *Saccharomyces cerevisiae*, a single-celled fungus, is 600 nm. The diameter of a human red blood cell is 7.2 μm.

   How much greater is the diameter of the red blood cell compared with the diameter of *S. cerevisiae*?

   A   0.012

   B   0.12

   C   1.2

   D   12   (AO2)

★ **Exam tip**

Questions 2 and 3 cannot be answered just by knowledge alone. You have to work out the answer from the information given.

The answers to these questions, and all of the other questions in this book, are available on the support website.

3   The photograph shows a virus particle.

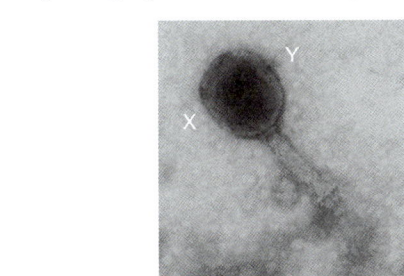

×150 000

What is the diameter of the virus between points **X** and **Y**?

   A   25 nm

   B   25 μm

   C   70 nm

   D   70 μm   (AO2)

★ **Exam tip**

In Type 2 MCQs the options (A, B, C and D) are preceded by terms or statements, usually marked as 1, 2, 3, etc. Each option is a particular combination of the numbered statements (e.g. 1 and 2 only, 3 and 4 only) but only one of the options has the correct combination; the others are distractors.

4   Which are found in the cytoplasm of animal cells?

   1   80S ribosomes

   2   microvilli

   3   centrioles

   A   1 and 2

   B   1 and 3

   C   2 and 3

   D   3 only.   (AO1)

Exam-style questions

1 Which pair of organelles are surrounded by a double membrane?

   A centriole and ribosome

   B chloroplast and nucleus

   C Golgi body and mitochondrion

   D lysosome and rough endoplasmic reticulum

   (AO1)

2 Which of the following organelles does **not** contain DNA?

   A chloroplast

   B mitochondrion

   C nucleus

   D ribosome (AO1)

3 Plasmodesmata connect adjoining plant cells.

   What is the function of plasmodesmata?

   A allow substances to move between cells without crossing membranes

   B hold the cell walls of adjoining cells together

   C allow substances to move through cell surface membranes

   D allow the formation of cell walls during cell division (AO1)

4 Cells can have 70S and 80S ribosomes and circular and linear forms of DNA.

   Which letter in the table below represents a prokaryote?

	70S	80S	Circular DNA	Linear DNA
A	✔	✔	✔	✔
B	✔	✔	✔	
C	✔		✔	
D		✔		✔

   (AO1)

5 The drawing shows an animal cell.

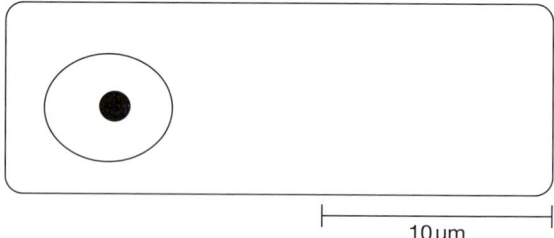

10 μm

   What is the diameter of the nucleolus?

   A 0.45 nm

   B 4.5 μm

   C 1.0 μm

   D 1.3 mm (AO2)

6 The following are structures found in cells.

   1 Golgi body

   2 lysosomes

   3 nucleus

   4 rough endoplasmic reticulum

   5 smooth endoplasmic reticulum

   Which structures are involved in the production of proteins in cells?

   A 1, 3 and 4   B 1, 3 and 5

   C 2 and 4   D 2, 4 and 5   (AO1)

7 The photograph shows a cell of the bacterium *Mycobacterium tuberculosis* in the process of dividing.

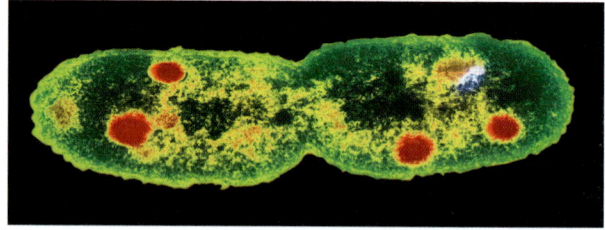

   magnification = × 25 000

   What is the approximate width of the bacterium?

   A 8.0 μm

   B 0.8 μm

   C 0.08 μm

   D 0.008 μm (AO2)

How to answer short-answer questions (SAQs)

The questions in Paper 2 are answered in a different way and involve a variety of different responses:

- completing tables
- matching pairs
- completing sentences
- writing very short answers consisting of a single term or phrase
- writing long answers in continuous prose
- adding labels to a diagram or drawing
- describing a pattern or trend from a table or graph
- interpreting information in the form of text, tables, graphs or diagrams
- giving explanations for biological phenomena.

The questions in Paper 2 will be a mixture of questions to test your recall of knowledge (AO1) and your ability to apply your knowledge (AO2). Most questions include parts that assess both objectives. Most questions test more than one Unit in the AS syllabus. The assessment objective and the Units or Unit tested in each question are included in the answers available on the support website (www.oxfordsecondary.com/caie-al-sci-exam-success).

Read the whole of each question, with all its part questions, before you start writing any answers. This will help you to understand what the question is about and gives you time to think about your answers. Often these questions include information that may be unfamiliar to you. It is a good idea to read the question again slowly and underline or highlight any words or terms that you think are important in understanding what you are being told.

1 Stem cells in bone marrow divide to form progenitor cells that will develop into red blood cells. Erythropoietin (Epo) is a protein released by cells in the kidney that stimulates the division of progenitor cells in bone marrow, but has no effect on their differentiation into mature red blood cells. The surface of each progenitor cell has many erythropoietin receptors (EpoR). The diagram shows the interaction between a molecule of Epo and a receptor molecule.

> ★ **Exam tip**
>
> This paragraph has two terms that will be unfamiliar: erythropoietin and progenitor. The questions may well refer to them so make sure you understand what they are.

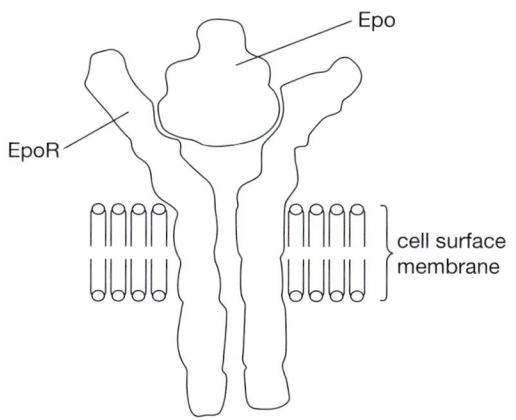

(a) (i) List **three** structures in the cytoplasm of the cells in the kidney that are involved in the production of molecules of EpoR. [3]

(ii) Outline the process of cell signalling involved in stimulating progenitor cells to divide. You should refer to the diagram in your answer. [4]

> ★ **Exam tip**
>
> You should look carefully at any diagrams, drawings, graphs or tables in the same way as you read the text. You can write notes around them that may be helpful in phrasing your answer. Here the shapes of Epo and EpoR might be worth noting in the white space around the diagram.

(b) Once Epo has interacted with EpoR, the complex is taken into the cells and broken down.

Explain how the Epo–EpoR complex is taken into cells and broken down. [4]

> ★ **Exam tip**
>
> 'Taken into the cell' and 'broken down (within the cell)' should be good hints that this is a question about endocytosis (Unit 4) and enzymes (Unit 3). Note that in the text Epo was described as a protein.

(c) Outline the changes that occur as a progenitor cell develops into a mature red blood cell. [3]

> ★ **Exam tip**
>
> This question is asking you to apply your knowledge of the structure of blood cells from Unit 8 to explain how a cell that has just divided can change into a red blood cell.

(d) The quantity of Epo that is released by kidney cells fluctuates.

Suggest why there may be an increase in the release of Epo from kidney cells. [1]

> ★ **Exam tip**
>
> This is an example of an AO2 question where you are expected to give an explanation for something that will not be familiar to you, but there are clues in the question. Think about the function of red blood cells and you will have the answer.

Exam-style questions

1   (a) Draw and label a diagram of a
        mitochondrion that is 50 mm long.   [5]

    (b) Assuming that the actual length of the
        mitochondrion is 3.5 μm, calculate
        the magnification of your drawing.   [1]

    (c) State the function of the mitochondrion
        and explain how this benefits the
        rest of the cell.   [2]

    (d) Explain why:

        (i) some cells have large numbers
             of mitochondria   [2]

        (ii) fertilised eggs without any functional
             mitochondria do not survive.   [2]

2   The image shows part of a cell from the growing
    region at the tip of the plant *Coleus blumei*.

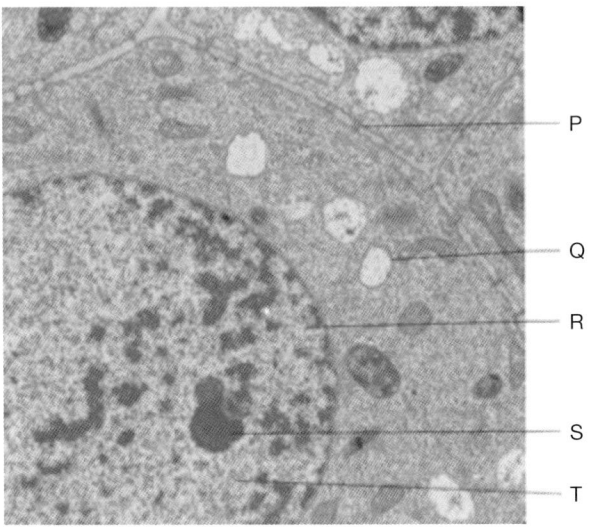

    (a) State the type of microscope that was
        used to make the image and give a reason
        for your answer.   [2]

    (b) Make a table to show the names of the
        structures labelled **P** to **T** and **one** function
        of each structure.   [5]

    (c) State **three** ways in which the structure of
        a prokaryotic cell differs from the structure
        of the cell of *C. blumei* visible in the
        image above.   [3]

3   Microvilli and cilia are found on the surfaces of
    some specialised animal cells. The transmission
    electron micrographs show vertical sections
    through microvilli and cilia.

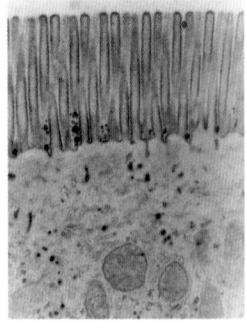   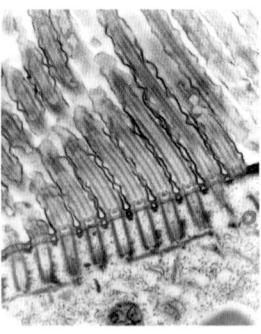

    Microvilli   Cilia

    (a) Describe the differences, visible in the
        transmission electron micrographs,
        between the microvilli and the cilia.   [3]

    (b) Describe the roles of microvilli and cilia. [4]

    (c) Microvilli and cilia are described as intracellular
        structures although they are found on
        the surfaces of cells. State why they
        are **not** extracellular structures.   [1]

    (d) State why microvilli are **not** found
        on the surface of plant cells.   [1]

    (e) Microtubules are found in stem cells in
        animals. Describe the role of microtubules
        during mitotic division of stem cells.   [3]

4   The diagrams show two viruses: tobacco mosaic
    virus (TMV) and human immunodeficiency
    virus (HIV).

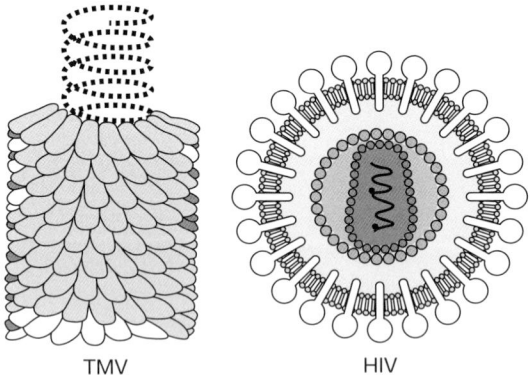

    TMV   HIV

    (a) List three features of **all** viruses that are visible
        in the diagrams.   [3]

    (b) State how the structure of HIV differs
        from the structure of TMV.   [3]

    (c) TMV infects several species of crop plant; HIV
        infects human cells. All viruses are parasitic as
        they rely entirely on the cells of their hosts.

        Explain why all viruses are parasitic.   [3]

↑ Raise your grade

1 (a) Viruses are described as non-cellular. Explain how the structure of a virus differs from the structure of a prokaryotic cell. [3]

> Viruses have no cell wall ✔ and no cytoplasm. ✔

> Correct answers as prokaryotic cells have cell walls and cytoplasm. It is a good idea to give a full comparison and give three structural features not just two.

(b) The electron micrograph (EM) shows a small part of a cell from a young shoot of thale cress, *Arabidopsis thaliana*.

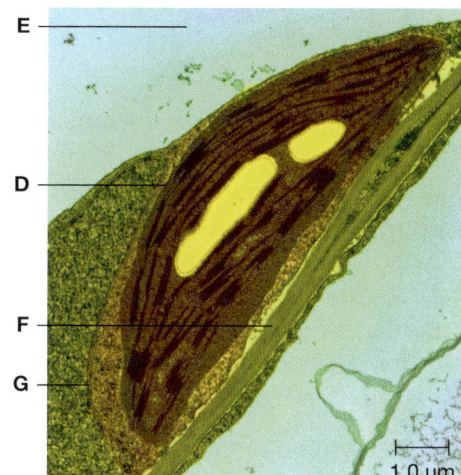

(i) Name the structure labelled **D** and state its function. [2]

> D is a chloroplast ✔ and it carries out photosynthesis. ✔   Both answers are correct.

(ii) Explain the role of the vacuole (**E**) and the cell wall (**F**) in giving support to plant cells. [2]

> The vacuole is full of water and has a hydrostatic pressure that pushes outwards onto the cell wall. ✔ The cell wall is made of cellulose and cannot stretch very much so it stops the vacuole expanding. The cell is turgid. ✔ If all the cells in plant organs (leaf, stem) are like this then the plant is supported and does not wilt.

> The second tick is given for stating that the vacuole is full of water and the cell is turgid.

(iii) The structure labelled **G** is the nuclear envelope. State the evidence visible in the electron micrograph for this identification. [1]

> The nuclear envelope is made of two membranes with a small gap between them. ✔ In the EM you can see this clearly.   Correct answer.

(iv) Explain how you would determine the magnification of the image of the electron micrograph. [2]

> The scale bar is 7 mm long and represents 1.0 μm. This means that the magnification is ×7000. ✗

> The question 'how to calculate the magnification' is not answered. The first step in the answer, stating the length of the scale bar, is correct but the answer must explain that the measurement in millimetres must be multiplied by 1000 to convert to micrometres.

The answer to (iv) shows why it is important to re-read the question after you have written your answer. Make sure that you have answered the question set. Candidates often read too fast and misinterpret questions and so lose marks that they should get.

2 Biological molecules

There are four groups of biological molecules: carbohydrates, lipids, proteins and nucleic acids.

Water is an important constituent of all organisms. As water molecules are polar they interact with other polar molecules and with charged particles (ions). This makes water a good solvent for polar molecules and ions. Water molecules are 'sticky' thanks to the **hydrogen bonds** between them. This **cohesion** between water molecules gives water important properties, for example, in transport in the xylem in plants.

All the major compounds that make up organisms are based on carbon, which forms very strong covalent bonds with itself and with other atoms. In a **covalent bond** a pair of electrons is shared between the atoms in a molecule. It is much stronger than an ionic bond. Many important biological molecules are **macromolecules**, which are large molecules assembled from smaller molecules. **Polymers** are macromolecules that are formed by many **monomers**, which may be identical (as in starch, glycogen and cellulose) or of the same type (as in proteins). **Lipids** are not polymers as they are not composed of repeating monomers.

The sub-unit molecules that are assembled to make macromolecules are formed by **condensation**. The addition of each sub-unit molecule results in the formation of a molecule of water. Macromolecules are broken down by **hydrolysis** – the use of water to break bonds between sub-unit molecules.

Carbohydrates:

- contain the elements C, H and O

- have the general formula $C_x(H_2O)_y$

- include the **monosaccharides** (e.g. glucose), **disaccharides** (e.g. sucrose and maltose) and **polysaccharides** (e.g. starch, glycogen and cellulose)

- monosaccharide molecules are joined together by **glycosidic bonds** to form disaccharides and polysaccharides.

In solution, most glucose is in one of two ring forms:

- α (alpha) glucose has the –OH below the ring at carbon 1

- β (beta) glucose has the –OH above the ring at carbon 1.

All monosaccharides are reducing sugars because they have functional groups that can donate electrons when heated: the aldehyde group on carbon 1 of glucose and the ketone group on carbon 4 of fructose. Sucrose is the most common disaccharide that is a **non-reducing sugar** because these groups on fructose and glucose form the glycosidic bonds between them.

There are three energy storage polysaccharides: amylose, amylopectin and glycogen. All three are polymers of α-glucose. When broken down, glucose molecules are removed from the end of each chain by hydrolysis. Cellulose is a polymer of β-glucose and is a structural molecule, being the main component of plant cell walls. The many hydrogen bonds between cellulose molecules are responsible for the strength of the cell walls.

★ **Exam tip**

Revise the structure of nucleic acids (Unit 6) along with the biological molecules in this Unit and look for similarities and differences between them.

★ **Exam tip**

Remember that hydrogen bonding is the key to explaining the roles of water in living organisms.

★ **Exam tip**

Terms in dark type are given in the syllabus. Make sure you add all the terms in dark type to the glossary you make (see page 9).

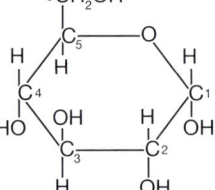

α-glucose   β-glucose

▲ **Figure 2.1** α-Glucose and β-glucose. The numbers refer to the carbon atoms. They are also referred to as C_1, C_2, etc.

★ **Exam tip**

Amylopectin and glycogen are branched molecules with many 'ends' where glucose can be added or removed as required by a cell. Amylose is a straight chain molecule that only has two 'ends'.

Lipids: **triglycerides** have the three-carbon compound glycerol as the main component to which three fatty acids are attached by **ester bonds**.

Phospholipids have two fatty acids and a phosphate group attached to glycerol. There are two different types of fatty acid:

- **saturated fatty acids** with a full complement of hydrogens attached to the carbon chain and no double bonds between carbon atoms in the chain

- **unsaturated fatty acids** with at least one double bond between carbon atoms along the carbon chain so there are fewer hydrogens.

Triglycerides are more efficient for energy storage than polysaccharides as they are highly reduced molecules because of the presence of many hydrogen atoms and far fewer oxygen atoms. When oxidised during respiration, much more energy is released than from the same mass of carbohydrate or protein.

The cell surface membranes that surround cells are mainly composed of phospholipids. Two layers of phospholipids form a phospholipid bilayer with a central hydrophobic region and two hydrophilic regions in contact with water. The hydrophobic core of the membrane forms a barrier for many substances.

Proteins are macromolecules made from one or more chains of amino acids known as **polypeptides**. Polypeptides are unbranched molecules composed of approximately ten or more amino acids linked by **peptide bonds**. Cells use 20 different types of amino acid to make proteins.

All amino acids share the same molecular structure shown in Figure 2.2.

There are four levels of organisation in proteins:

- **primary structure** – sequence of amino acids (determined by the sequence of nucleotide bases in genes)

- **secondary structure** – folding of polypeptide into α-helix and β-pleated sheet

- **tertiary structure** – further folding and coiling of polypeptide to give complex 3D shape

- **quaternary structure** – two or more polypeptides associate together to form a protein.

There are four types of bond that stabilise polypeptides:

- hydrogen bonds between polar groups, such as the dipolar –NH and –CO groups either side of the –C—N– bond of peptide bonds

- ionic bonds between ionised amine ($-NH_3^+$) and carboxyl ($-COO^-$) groups of R-groups

- disulfide bonds between the sulfur-containing R-groups of cysteine residues

- hydrophobic interactions between non-polar R-groups.

Enzymes, antibodies, membrane proteins (e.g. receptors and transport proteins) and **haemoglobin** are all **globular proteins** with complex 3D shapes. Hydrophilic R-groups on their surface form hydrogen bonds with water so the molecules are soluble in water. Internally, amino acids with hydrophobic R-groups exclude water to form a hydrophobic interior. These are metabolic proteins because they carry out a range of functions that contribute to the metabolism of organisms. **Fibrous proteins**, such as **collagen**, are insoluble in water and have simple shapes, such as a helix. They are structural proteins.

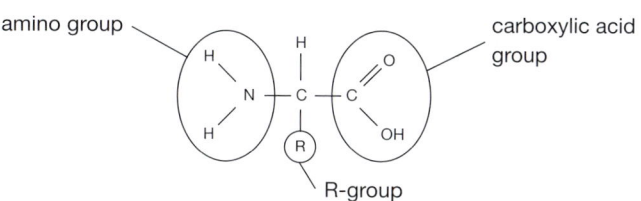

amino group — carboxylic acid group — R-group

▲ **Figure 2.2** A generalised amino acid molecule. Each amino acid has a different R-group, e.g. the R-group of glycine is –H

> 🔗 **Link**
>
> Make drawings of cell surface membranes to show the arrangement of phospholipids in the bilayer (Unit 4). Annotate with information about phospholipid structure to prepare for questions on the role of phospholipids in cells.

> 🔗 **Link**
>
> Protein synthesis is in Unit 6. Make diagrams showing the formation of a peptide bond between two amino acids and annotate with details of where and how this reaction occurs in cells.

> ⭐ **Exam tip**
>
> You could be given information about amino acid sequences in an exam paper. They are often shown using a three-letter code, e.g. gly for glycine.

> ⭐ **Exam tip**
>
> Make tables to show similarities and differences between pairs of biological molecules, e.g. glucose vs starch, proteins vs DNA, collagen vs haemoglobin. Turn the tables into a graphic organiser (Figure 1.3, page 9).

⚙ Practical Skills

Testing for biological molecules

You are likely to be examined on these tests for biological molecules in Paper 3. However, you can also expect questions on these tests in the other papers. You should learn the names of the reagents and the practical steps in each test.

Test for starch: The reagent used in the starch test is **iodine in potassium iodide (KI) solution** (known simply as iodine solution). The substance to be tested may be a solid or a liquid. Place solid samples on a white tile or in a Petri dish and liquid samples into a test-tube.

Use a dropping pipette to add iodine in potassium iodide solution.

> ★ **Exam tip**
>
> The reagent used is iodine in potassium iodide solution (or shortened to iodine in KI solution). 'Iodine solution' may be used but *never* 'iodine'.

Colour change in iodine in potassium iodide solution	Result	Explanation
yellow-orange to blue-black or blue	positive starch present	iodine binds to the centre of the helix of amylose to form a starch–iodine complex which has a blue-black colour
no change; iodine solution remains yellow-orange	negative no starch present	no starch for iodine to bind to

Test for reducing sugars: For solid samples, make a solution in water (can be ground with a pestle and mortar and filtered). Put about $1 \, cm^3$ of the test solution into a test-tube and add an equal volume of Benedict's solution. Heat to about 70–90 °C in a water bath (do not heat directly with a Bunsen burner). Watch carefully for colour changes and the formation of a precipitate.

Colour change on heating with Benedict's solution	Result	Explanation
blue to green/yellow/orange/ (precipitate difficult to see unless allowed to settle) red with a precipitate	positive reducing sugars present (not necessarily glucose)	sugar reduces copper(II) ions (Cu^{2+}) in Benedict's solution to copper(I) ions (Cu^+) to form a precipitate of copper(I) oxide
no change; Benedict's solution remains blue	negative	no reducing sugars present to react with copper(II) ions

Test for non-reducing sugars: The only common non-reducing sugar is sucrose (see page 20). Divide the test solution into two parts, **A** and **B**. Test **A** with Benedict's solution as above. Add a few drops of dilute hydrochloric acid to **B** and boil for at least 3 minutes. Cool the test-tube and add dilute sodium hydroxide solution or solid sodium hydrogen carbonate (beware, the latter will fizz). When neutralised, test with Benedict's solution as above.

Colour change on heating with Benedict's solution	Result	Explanation
A – no change	negative for reducing sugar,	hydrochloric acid acts as a catalyst to hydrolyse sucrose to fructose and glucose, which are both reducing sugars
B – blue to green/yellow/orange/ red precipitate	positive for non-reducing sugar	
A – no change	negative for both reducing and non-reducing sugars	no reducing sugars present even after using hydrochloric acid to hydrolyse any non-reducing sugars
B – no change		

Test for proteins: If the substance to be tested is solid, make a solution in water. Place $1\,cm^3$ of the test solution in a test-tube. Add the same volume of **biuret reagent** and mix by shaking the tube gently from side to side.

Colour change with biuret solution	Result	Explanation
blue to violet/purple/lilac	positive	a coloured complex forms if there are peptide bonds in the test substance
no change to the blue colour	negative	no peptide bonds present

Test for lipids: Lipids are insoluble in water but they are soluble in organic solvents such as ethanol. Crush any solid material to be tested in a pestle and mortar and add some ethanol. If the test substance is a liquid, add some ethanol and shake to dissolve. Pour off the ethanol, which may have dissolved some lipids, into a test-tube of water (do not mix).

Change when adding ethanol to water	Result	Explanation
white cloudy (milky) – an emulsion	positive	the ethanol dissolves the lipid; on addition to water the lipid is dispersed throughout the water as tiny particles – an emulsion
no change	negative	no lipid present to be dispersed

> ★ **Exam tip**
>
> You should carry out these tests for yourself in the lab. Learn all the details. Take photographs of the results to help you remember the practical procedures.

The five tests described so far are qualitative tests. They tell us whether the substance is present or not. They are not quantitative as they do not tell us how much is present. The next test is semi-quantitative as it tells us approximately how much reducing sugar is present in a sample.

Semi-quantitative test for reducing sugars: The final colour change with the Benedict's test indicates how much reducing sugar is present in a test sample. One way to improve this estimate is to make up a series of colour standards using a stock solution of glucose and Benedict's solution.

1. Take $20\,cm^3$ of the stock solution of known concentration, e.g. $100\,g\,dm^{-3}$.

2. Use the stock solution and distilled water to make the following dilutions:

   50.0, 20.0, 10.0, 5.0, 1.0, 0.5, $0.1\,g\,dm^{-3}$.

3. Place equal volumes of the dilutions into labelled test-tubes.

> 💡 **Remember**
>
> Take photographs for a permanent record.

4. Carry out the Benedict's test. Use the same volume of Benedict's solution in each test-tube and heat all the test-tubes for the same length of time.

5. Cool the test-tubes and keep them to use as colour standards, as in the table to the right.

6. Carry out the Benedict's test on a solution of the substance being tested. Use *exactly* the same procedure as when making the colour standards.

7. Cool the test-tube and place next to the colour standards to determine the concentration of reducing sugar; the answer may be a range, e.g. between 1.0 and $5.0\,g\,dm^{-3}$. Place a piece of white card behind the tubes to help match the colours.

Concentration of glucose / g dm⁻³	Result on testing with Benedict's solution
50.0	dark red
20.0	red
10.0	orange
5.0	yellow
1.0	green
0.5	light green
0.1	blue

Worked Example

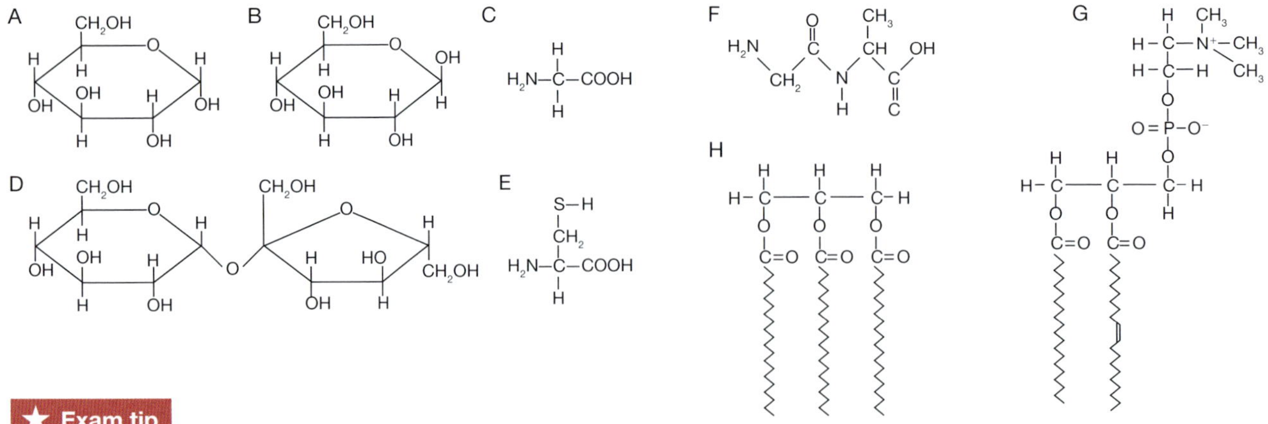

A, B, C, D, E, F, G, H — molecular structures shown.

★ **Exam tip**

Look carefully at the molecular structures and identify them. Circle any significant parts that help you to identify them. Do this before reading the questions.

In each question, choose one of the biological molecules and write down the letter. You may choose each molecule for more than one question. There may be one or more letters that you do not use at all.

(a) an amino acid that is a major constituent of collagen

(b) the disaccharide found in phloem sap

(c) the molecule that is polymerised to form cellulose

(d) a molecule with a peptide bond

(e) a molecule that is hydrolysed to form fatty acids

(f) a molecule with hydrophilic and hydrophobic regions

(g) an amino acid that forms disulfide bonds in proteins [7]

Answers

(a) **C** (glycine) (b) **D** (sucrose) (c) **B** (β-glucose) (d) **F** (dipeptide)

(e) **G** (phospholipid) or **H** (triglyceride) (f) **G** (phospholipid) (g) **E** (cysteine)

→ **Try this... 1**

A student tested some fruit juices with Benedict's solution with the following results:

Fruit juice	Colour after boiling with Benedict's solution
P	orange-red
Q	green
R	blue

(a) Use the table on page 23 to estimate the concentration of reducing sugars in the juices **P**, **Q** and **R**. [3]

(b) Use the results of this investigation to explain the limitations of this method of finding out the actual concentration in any test substance. [3]

(c) State why the Benedict's test cannot show whether or not fructose is in the fruit juices. [1]

→ **Try this... 2**

A student tested some plant and animal tissues to find out which biological molecules they contained. The results of the biochemical tests are shown in the table.

Tissues	Results of biochemical tests			
	Benedict's solution	**Iodine solution**	**Biuret reagent**	**Ethanol and water**
A	red precipitate	yellow-brown	lilac	white emulsion
B	blue	blue-black	blue	no emulsion
C	green	blue-black	lilac	no emulsion
D	yellow precipitate	yellow-brown	lilac	white emulsion
E	blue	yellow-brown	blue	white emulsion

★ **Exam tip**

Look carefully across the rows and down the columns of the table and write some notes to help you identify the biochemicals from the results.

(a) Use the information in the table to state which tissues

   (i) contain starch   [1]

   (ii) did not contain any reducing sugars   [1]

   (iii) contain lipids and proteins.   [1]

(b) State which tissues are likely to be plant in origin and explain your answer.   [2]

(c) What conclusions can be made about the relative concentrations of reducing sugars in the five tissues? Explain your answer.   [3]

→ **Try this... 3**

(a) Plants produce monosaccharides such as glucose. Much of the glucose is converted into the storage compounds amylose and amylopectin.

   (i) State one place where amylose and amylopectin are found in plant cells.   [1]

   (ii) Describe how amylopectin differs from amylose.   [2]

(b) Maltose is the disaccharide produced during the breakdown of starch.

   (i) Complete the diagram below to show the reaction catalysed by maltase.   [3]

   (ii) State the type of reaction that is catalysed by maltase.   [1]

(c) Maltose and glucose are both soluble in water. Explain how water acts as a solvent for molecules such as maltose and glucose.   [3]

✏ **Revision strategy**

Make a glossary of all the terms used in this Unit. Use your glossary to make a 'mix and match' resource for this Unit. You can also use your glossary to make a spider diagram for biological molecules. Add the nucleic acids to your diagram after studying Unit 6.

Choose pairs of compounds from this Unit and make 'bubble' diagrams to show the similarities and differences between the members of each pair. See Figure 1.3 on page 9 to find out how to draw a 'bubble' diagram. Good examples to use are: an amino acid (e.g. glycine) and glucose; haemoglobin and collagen; amylose and amylopectin; protein and triglyceride; triglyceride and phospholipid; collagen and cellulose.

↑ Raise your grade

(a) Triglycerides and phospholipids are similar in structure.

Describe how the structure of phospholipid molecules differs from triglyceride molecules. [3]

Phospholipids have only two fatty acid chains whereas triglycerides have three. ✔

Phospholipids have a hydrophilic phosphate group instead of one of the fatty acids ✔

Phospholipids have hydrophilic heads and hydrophobic tails. ✔

> This answer has three correct differences between these two groups of lipids.

(b) (i) Describe how to carry out a test to show the presence of triglycerides in samples of seeds of different species. [3]

The sample to be tested is put into a test-tube and dissolved in ethanol and shaken. ✔ *The solution is then poured into another test-tube of water.* ✔

> Correct practical details, but the candidate has not stated what to look for if the test is positive. A complete answer would add that a white emulsion would form in the water. A good answer would also state to keep the samples from each species separate and test them separately.

(ii) Explain why the test you describe is a qualitative test. [1]

The result shows you about the quality of the substance tested. ✗

> In this context, it is better to write that a qualitative test identifies the presence or absence of the substance; it is a description of what has been observed. It does not tell us how much of the substance is present. For that we need a quantitative test.

(c) Explain how the structure of triglycerides makes the molecules more suitable for long-term energy storage than glycogen. [3]

Triglycerides have three long fatty acid chains. These chains are composed of carbon and hydrogen. When they are respired they release far more energy than when the glucose from glycogen is respired. ✔

> Not a complete answer. It is necessary to say that more energy for respiration is released from triglycerides (fat) compared with the same *mass* of glycogen. The proportion of carbon–hydrogen bonds in triglycerides is much higher than in glycogen so more energy is released when triglycerides are oxidised in respiration.

(d) Draw a diagram to show the arrangement of four phospholipid molecules in a cell membrane. [2]

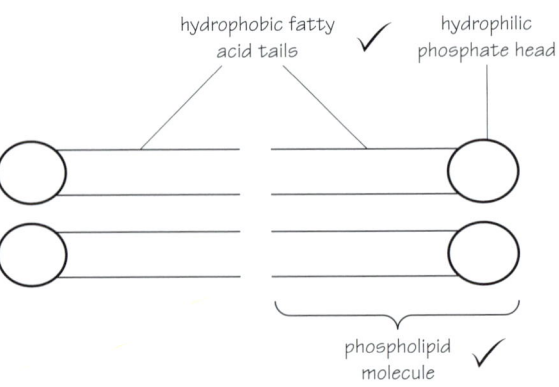

> The four phospholipid molecules are drawn correctly showing how they would appear in a phospholipid bilayer. To make the answer perfectly clear the candidate has labelled a phospholipid and shown the hydrophilic and hydrophobic regions.

Exam-style questions

1 Haemoglobin is an example of a protein with:

A primary structure only

B primary and secondary structure only

C primary, secondary and tertiary structure only

D primary, secondary, tertiary and quaternary structure. [1]

2 Which row shows the correct bond associated with each of the biological molecules shown?

	Disaccharide	Polysaccharide	Protein	Triglyceride
A	hydrogen	glycosidic	ester	peptide
B	peptide	ester	glycosidic	hydrogen
C	glycosidic	glycosidic	peptide	ester
D	glycosidic	peptide	ester	glycosidic

[1]

3 Starch and glycogen are polysaccharides. Which is a feature of starch, but **not** of glycogen?

A starch is made from α-glucose

B starch has an unbranched component

C starch contains 1,6 glycosidic bonds

D starch contains 1,4 glycosidic bonds [1]

4 Some students made three statements about the primary structure of a polypeptide.

1 The primary structure is the sequence of amino acids of the polypeptide.

2 The primary structure is stabilised by hydrogen bonds.

3 The primary structure determines the tertiary structure of the polypeptide.

Which of these statements is/are true?

A **1, 2** and **3**   B **1** and **2** only
C **1** and **3** only   D **1** only [1]

5 Which features is/are found in a phospholipid molecule?

1 ester bonds

2 three fatty acid chains

3 peptide bond

4 hydrophilic group

A **1, 2, 3** and **4**   B **1** and **4** only
C **2** and **3** only   D **4** only [1]

6 (a) The figure shows part of a molecule of cellulose.

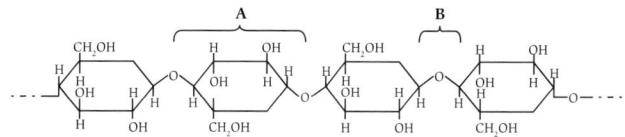

(i) Identify the monomer indicated by **A**. [1]

(ii) State the name of the bond indicated by **B**. [2]

(iii) State the name of the type of reaction that forms the bond labelled **B**. [1]

(b) Describe the properties of cellulose that make it suitable as the main component of the cell walls of plant cells. [5]

(c) Collagen is a fibrous protein.

(i) State **three** ways in which the structure of a collagen molecule differs from the structure of a cellulose molecule. [3]

(ii) Explain how a globular protein differs from a fibrous protein. [2]

7 (a) The figure shows the two amino acids glycine and alanine.

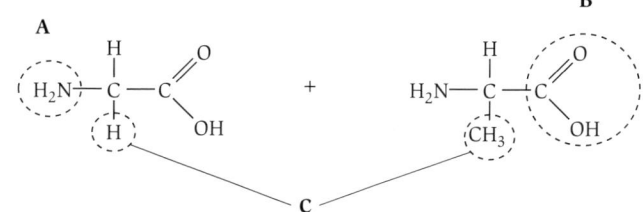

(i) Name the parts of the molecules labelled **A**, **B** and **C**. [3]

(ii) Draw a diagram to show how the two amino acids are joined together by a condensation reaction. [3]

(iii) Name the bond that forms between the two amino acids. [1]

(iv) State the location in the cell where amino acids are joined together in reactions like the one you have drawn. [1]

(b) A protein composed of a single polypeptide has no disulfide bonds. Explain how the tertiary structure of this protein is stabilised. [4]

(c) Explain why haemoglobin is said to have quaternary structure. [1]

3 Enzymes

Knowledge check

You should be able to:

- define the term *enzyme*
- explain why enzymes are important for the survival of organisms.

The mode of action of enzymes

Enzymes are catalysts

In a reaction, **substrate** molecules are converted into molecules of **product**. Most reactions are reversible and **catalysts**, which are effective in very small quantities, speed up both the forward reaction and the reverse reaction:

$$A+B \underset{\longleftarrow}{\overset{\text{catalyst}}{\longrightarrow}} C+D$$

Catalysts cannot change the equilibrium that exists between substrate concentration and product concentration, but they can increase the rate at which the equilibrium is achieved.

Enzymes are biological catalysts. Almost all enzymes are proteins that have a globular structure, which provides an active site where the substrates of the reaction fit together closely, making the reaction more likely to occur.

Enzymes are either:

- **extracellular** – act *outside* cells; for example, in the lumen of the mammalian gut, or
- **intracellular** – act *inside* cells; for example, inside mitochondria.

Enzymes are specific

Two ways in which enzymes catalyse reactions by providing a place for substrates to fit:

- **Lock and key model**: the shape of the **active site** is always **complementary** to the substrate and does not change shape when the substrate enters.
- **Induced fit model**: the shape of the active site is not complementary to the substrate until it binds to the enzyme. It then changes shape to mould itself around the substrate so there is a better fit between the two molecules.

The **specificity** of an enzyme is determined by the shape of its active site, which must be complementary to the shape of the substrate.

Active sites

An active site has a 'pocket', 'depression' or 'groove' shape that is determined by the tertiary structure of the enzyme molecule. The folding of the polypeptide brings specific R-groups of amino acids together to form the appropriate shape for the substrate to fit tightly. The R-groups of some amino acids making the active site are adjacent to each other in the primary sequence, some are not. Substrate molecules are held in place within the active site by hydrogen bonds, ionic bonds or hydrophobic interactions, depending on the type of substrate. The combination of enzyme and substrate is an **enzyme–substrate complex**. When the substrate molecule is bound to the active site, the molecule is put under strain so that bonds are more likely to break or to form.

Link

See Unit 6 for the production of proteins, such as enzymes, and Unit 1 for the role of different cell structures in synthesising and exporting proteins from cells.

In some specialised human cells, for example, liver cells, there are thought to be over a thousand different enzymes that carry out many metabolic reactions.

Remember

The tertiary structure of a polypeptide may consist of α-helices, β-pleated sheets and regions with no distinct secondary structure folded into a specific 3D shape stabilised by hydrogen bonds and other interactions between R-groups.

★ Exam tip

A substrate molecule fits into an active site because it has a complementary shape. Do not write that is has the *same shape* as the active site.

Activation energy

The reactions catalysed by enzymes often involve the formation or breaking of stable covalent bonds, which requires much energy. Enzymes provide a pathway in active sites where substrate molecules are positioned so that the **activation energy** is decreased (Figure 3.1).

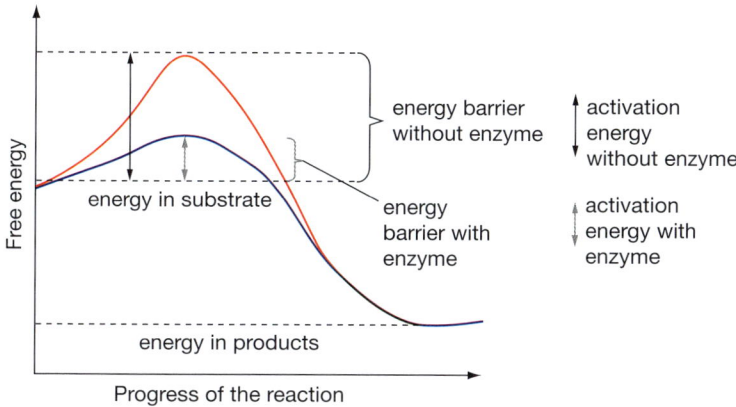

▲ **Figure 3.1** Activation energy for an exothermic reaction

In Figure 3.1, the energy of the substrate is higher than the energy of the products, so the reaction is exothermic as it releases energy. Many of the reactions of respiration are like this. If the energy of the substrate(s) is lower than the energy of the product(s), the reaction is endothermic as energy is required from the surroundings. In many biochemical reactions the energy for these reactions is provided by ATP. Examples are starch and protein synthesis.

Factors that affect the rate of enzyme activity:

- inhibitor concentration
- substrate concentration
- enzyme concentration
- temperature
- pH.

Temperature, substrate concentration and enzyme concentration influence the frequency of collisions between enzyme molecules and substrate molecules.

Temperature, pH and inhibitors affect the stability of enzyme molecules; substrate molecules can only enter active sites if the tertiary structure is not disrupted.

Inhibitors interact with enzymes and reduce their activity.

- **Competitive inhibitors** fit temporarily inside the active site without being changed in a reaction. They compete with the substrate for entry to the active site. If the concentration of the substrate is increased then the effect of the inhibitor can be reduced.

- **Non-competitive inhibitors** do not occupy the active site but bind temporarily to another site on the enzyme, known as an allosteric site. In response, the enzyme molecule changes its overall shape and the active site is no longer complementary to the substrate. Enzyme–substrate complexes cannot form, so the enzyme is inhibited. The effect of non-competitive inhibitors cannot be reduced by increasing the substrate concentration because substrate molecules cannot fit into the active site.

The inhibitors described here are reversible inhibitors. The enzyme is not permanently disabled by the inhibitor. If the inhibitor is removed, then the enzyme becomes active again. You do not need to know about non-reversible inhibitors, but they are sometimes used in practical work.

⚙ Practical Skills

Following the course of enzyme-catalysed reactions

Different enzymes change substrate to product at different rates. The **activity** of an enzyme is determined by finding the rate at which a reaction proceeds. This can be done by following the decrease in concentration of the substrate or the increase in the concentration of the product. During the course of a reaction with fixed quantities of enzyme and substrate, the number of substrate molecules decreases, so the chance of a substrate molecule entering an active site decreases over time. This means that the rate of formation of product molecules also decreases over time.

The breakdown of protein

You can follow the course of an enzyme-catalysed reaction by seeing how long it takes to reach an **end point**, which is something that can be observed or detected. For example, a solution of milk powder is cloudy. Add a protease (e.g. trypsin or pepsin) and the cloudiness gradually disappears because the protease catalyses the hydrolysis of protein in the milk. This reaction can be observed as follows:

> ★ **Exam tip**
>
> Keeping the enzyme solution and substrate solution separate until they are both at the desired temperature for the reaction is called **equilibration**.

1. Add $10\,cm^3$ of a solution of milk powder to test-tube 1.

2. Add $1\,cm^3$ of a protease solution to test-tube 2.

3. Place both test-tubes in a thermostatically controlled water bath at 25 °C for 5 minutes.

4. After 5 minutes, pour the contents of test-tube 2 into test-tube 1, return test-tube 1 to the water bath and start a timer.

5. Observe carefully and time how long it takes for the cloudiness to disappear.

The time taken for the reaction to occur is not the rate of reaction. When there is a fast rate of reaction then the reaction will be completed in a short time. If the rate of reaction is slow, then the reaction will be completed in a long time. The rate of reaction is calculated as the reciprocal of the time taken: $\dfrac{1}{t}$ in which t = the time taken to reach the end point in seconds. The unit is seconds^{-1} (s^{-1}).

The breakdown of hydrogen peroxide

To follow the appearance of a product you can use the enzyme catalase, which catalyses the decomposition of hydrogen peroxide:

$$2H_2O_2 \xrightarrow{\text{catalase}} 2H_2O + O_2$$

A solution of catalase could be used, but usually the enzyme is extracted from plant material, such as potato, celery or lettuce, that contains it. The apparatus can be set up as shown in Figure 3.2. A gas syringe could also be used to collect the oxygen produced.

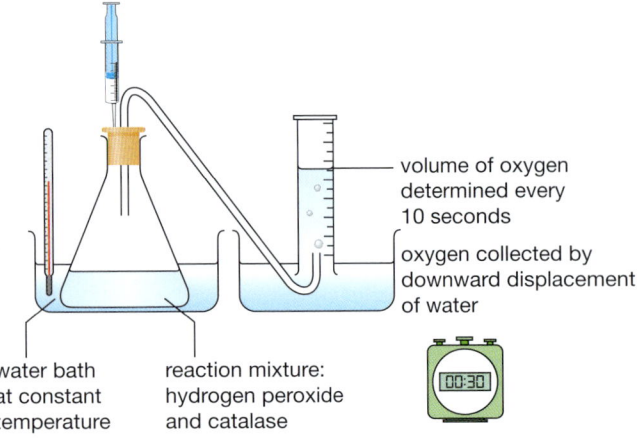

volume of oxygen determined every 10 seconds

oxygen collected by downward displacement of water

water bath at constant temperature

reaction mixture: hydrogen peroxide and catalase

> Hydrogen peroxide is usually provided as a 20 volume solution; '20 volume' means that when $1\,cm^3$ of hydrogen peroxide is decomposed, $20\,cm^3$ of oxygen is produced. A 20 volume solution of hydrogen peroxide has a molarity of $1.67\,mol\,dm^{-3}$.

▲ **Figure 3.2** Apparatus for following the decomposition of hydrogen peroxide to oxygen and water

A set of results obtained for the breakdown of hydrogen peroxide is shown in the table. These have been plotted on a graph (Figure 3.3).

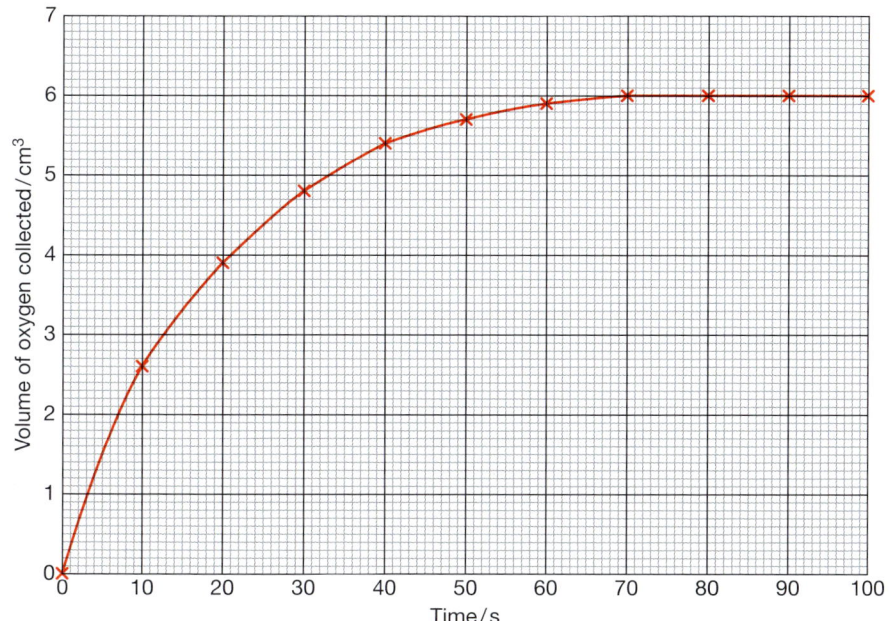

Time / s	Volume of oxygen collected / cm³
0	0.0
10	2.6
20	3.9
30	4.8
40	5.4
50	5.7
60	5.9
70	6.0
80	6.0
90	6.0
100	6.0

▲ **Figure 3.3** The volume of oxygen produced after a solution of catalase is added to hydrogen peroxide

The rate is fastest at the beginning and decreases with time (Figure 3.3) because over time hydrogen peroxide is converted to the products of the reaction and so the concentration of the substrate decreases. When no substrate is left, the reaction stops. The collisions between enzyme molecules and substrate molecules are most frequent at the beginning of the reaction when the enzyme is added to the substrate.

The procedure shown in Figure 3.2 can be used to investigate the effect of **substrate concentration**. The procedure is repeated for each substrate concentration. The results are shown in Figure 3.4.

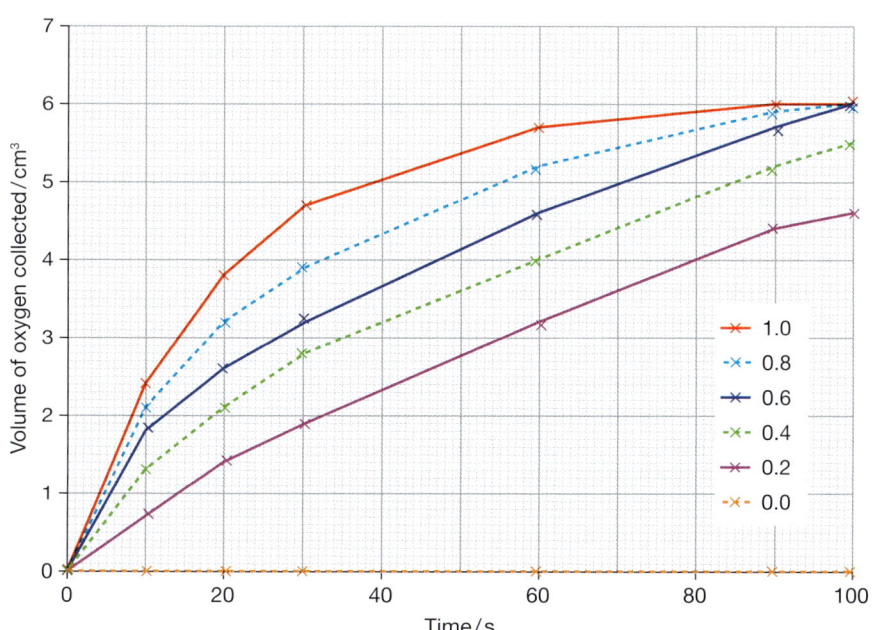

Key (concentrations in mol dm⁻³):
- 1.0
- 0.8
- 0.6
- 0.4
- 0.2
- 0.0

▲ **Figure 3.4** The progress of the reaction with different concentrations of hydrogen peroxide. All variables apart from substrate concentration were kept the same. The key shows the concentrations of hydrogen peroxide in $mol\,dm^{-3}$

🔗 Link

The rules to follow when drawing line graphs are described on page 173. Read the Exam tip on the same page about how to scale the x-axis and the y-axis.

★ Exam tip

Note that it is the *concentration* of hydrogen peroxide that is increased, not the *volume* that is added to each reaction mixture. Avoid using 'amount', which often means 'volume' or quantity. The section headed Working with solutions on page 167 in Unit 20, Practical skills, has more about concentration.

Try this... 1

To determine the initial rate of reaction when the substrate concentration is at its highest, tangents are drawn to the curves.

Draw a tangent to each of the curves in Figure 3.4 and use them to calculate the initial rate of reaction for each substrate concentration.

(a) Show your results in a table and plot a graph to show the effect of increasing substrate concentration on the initial rate of reaction.

(b) Describe the effect of increasing substrate concentration.

(c) Explain the effect that you have described in (b).

(d) Draw a sketch graph to predict the shape of the curve if the investigation is repeated under exactly the same conditions with a range of 0 to 2.0 mol dm^{-3} hydrogen peroxide. Explain the shape of the curve you have drawn.

🔗 **Link**

There is more about determining initial rates of reaction in Unit 20, Practical skills, pages 170–171.

🔗 **Link**

See Figure 20.4 on page 171 to show how to use tangents to determine initial rates of reaction.

★ **Exam tip**

Converting the actual rates of reaction into 'percentage of maximum rate' makes it easier to compare the effect of pH on these three enzymes.

The effect of increasing **enzyme concentration** can be investigated by making a simple dilution of a catalase solution (see page 168). As the enzyme concentration increases, the rate of reaction increases. The rate is directly proportional to the enzyme concentration. If there are more enzyme molecules, there will be more successful collisions per unit time. This assumes that at each concentration of enzyme, the substrate concentration is in excess so that substrate concentration does not limit the rate of reaction.

The activity of enzymes at different **temperatures** can be investigated by placing the reaction mixtures in water baths at a range of temperatures. The substrate and enzyme solutions are equilibrated at the temperatures used, then mixed together and kept at each of those temperatures over the range chosen.

Rates of reaction increase up to a maximum rate at a certain temperature known as the optimum temperature. At temperatures above the optimum, rates of reaction decrease. At high temperatures there is very little or no activity. Optimum temperatures vary greatly. Plant enzymes tend to have low optimum temperatures. Mammalian enzymes have optimum temperatures about 37 °C. Enzymes extracted from organisms that live in habitats at high temperatures have optimum temperatures as high as 100 °C.

Rates increase because there is an increase in kinetic energy and the substrate molecules collide more frequently with the enzyme molecules. As temperatures increase, the enzyme molecules vibrate and the bonds stabilising the tertiary structure begin to break. At the optimum temperature, the number of successful collisions is at its maximum, but above that temperature more and more enzyme molecules become non-functional as they denature. At high temperatures all the enzymes are denatured. The temperature at which this happens varies according to the enzyme concerned.

Look at Figure 3.5 and follow these descriptions:

• each enzyme is active over a range of pH

• as pH increases, the activity of each enzyme increases to a maximum

• maximum activity occurs at the optimum pH for each enzyme

• above the optimum pH, the activity decreases

• there is no activity over certain ranges of pH, e.g. <pH 5 and >pH 9 for catalase.

pH

Reaction mixtures were prepared using buffer solutions. Different ranges of pH were used to investigate three enzymes: pepsin, catalase and alkaline phosphorylase.

The rates of reaction for each enzyme at each pH were determined and then expressed as a percentage of the maximum rate, as shown in Figure 3.5.

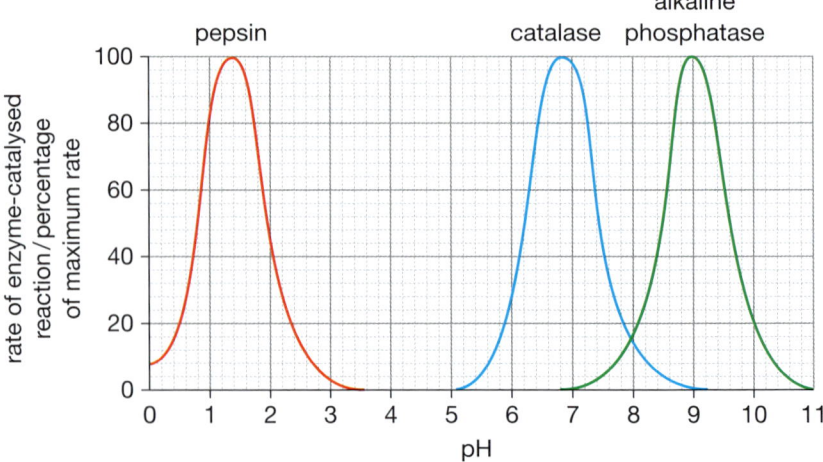

▲ **Figure 3.5** The activity of three enzymes at different values of pH. The reaction mixtures were kept at 20 °C

→ Try this... 2

(a) Use the information in Figure 3.5 to make a table showing, for each enzyme, the range over which it is active and its optimum pH.

(b) Explain the importance of buffer solutions in this investigation.

(c) Suggest a way to measure the pH of each reaction mixture.

(d) The enzyme and substrate solutions were kept at 20 °C before they were mixed together. Explain fully why this was necessary.

(e) Explain the effect of pH on the activity of enzymes.

⚙ Practical Skills

Immobilised enzymes

In many industrial processes when enzymes are used in solution with their substrates, it is difficult to recover them after the reaction they catalyse is finished. If the enzymes are **immobilised** inside gelatinous (jelly-like) beads, it is easy to recover them from reaction mixtures to reduce wastage. Also, the beads can be packed into columns so that substrate solutions are added at the top and product is available at the bottom. One way to immobilise enzymes is within beads of calcium alginate. The substances used to immobilise enzymes and cells are insoluble and inert.

The properties of immobilised enzymes are often different to their properties when they are free in solution. For example, the frequency of collisions between substrate and enzyme decreases as substrate molecules have to diffuse through the beads to the active sites of the enzymes. However, the beads provide protection to the enzymes so they are more stable at higher temperatures and are active over wider ranges of pH. The tertiary structures of enzymes are more stable inside beads than outside if the pH and/or temperature changes.

Making immobilised catalase

A solution of an enzyme is mixed with an equal volume of sodium alginate solution. The mixture is added to a calcium chloride solution. When the sodium alginate comes into contact with calcium chloride it forms a gel enclosing the molecules of enzyme in small beads.

Catalase can be immobilised in calcium alginate beads by following this procedure.

1. Pour about 100 cm³ of calcium chloride solution into a measuring cylinder.

2. Using a fine pipette drip approximately 10 cm³ of a catalase and sodium alginate mixture from a height of about 20 mm above the top of the cylinder. Maintain a gentle pressure on the pipette to avoid introducing air bubbles into the mixture.

3. As soon as the drops of mixture enter the calcium chloride solution they form into beads. When you have made enough beads, pour off the calcium chloride solution and transfer the beads to a small beaker. Place the beads into a beaker of water until required.

4. The beads can be placed into test-tubes of hydrogen peroxide solution. They usually sink and then rise again to the surface when bubbles collect around the beads.

The beads can be used in investigations to find out the effect of temperature, pH, substrate concentration and, by making several batches of beads with different volumes of catalase added to sodium alginate, enzyme concentration. The effect of immobilising catalase can be investigated by making a solution of the enzyme *at the same concentration* and seeing how the rates of reaction compare.

Cells can also be immobilised in calcium alginate beads. Immobilised yeast can be used as a source of catalase and sucrase in practical investigations, as shown in Figure 3.6.

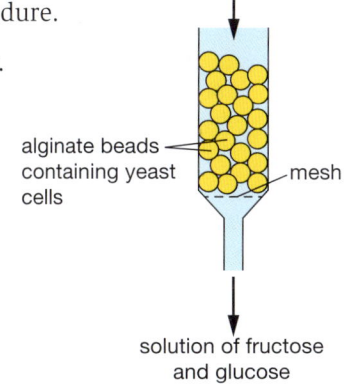

▲ **Figure 3.6** Yeast produces sucrase, which hydrolyses sucrose to glucose and fructose. Benedict's solution is used to detect the presence of reducing sugars in the product that is collected

🔗 **Link**

Exam-style question 5 is about immobilised enzymes.

Maths Skills

Rates of reaction and the Michaelis–Menten constant

Different enzymes have different affinities for their substrates. The term **affinity** in this context means the ease with which the substrate fits into the active site. The **Michaelis–Menten constant (K_m)** is a measure of this affinity. The K_m for any enzyme is determined by measuring the rate of reaction at different concentrations of substrate. As we have seen, at a certain concentration the rate remains constant because enzyme concentration becomes the limiting factor (see Try this... 1, page 32). This maximum rate is known as the V_{max} in which V represents velocity (speed) of the rate of reaction. The Michaelis–Menten constant (K_m) is determined by calculating the substrate concentration at half the value of V_{max}. You can see this for two enzymes in Figure 3.7.

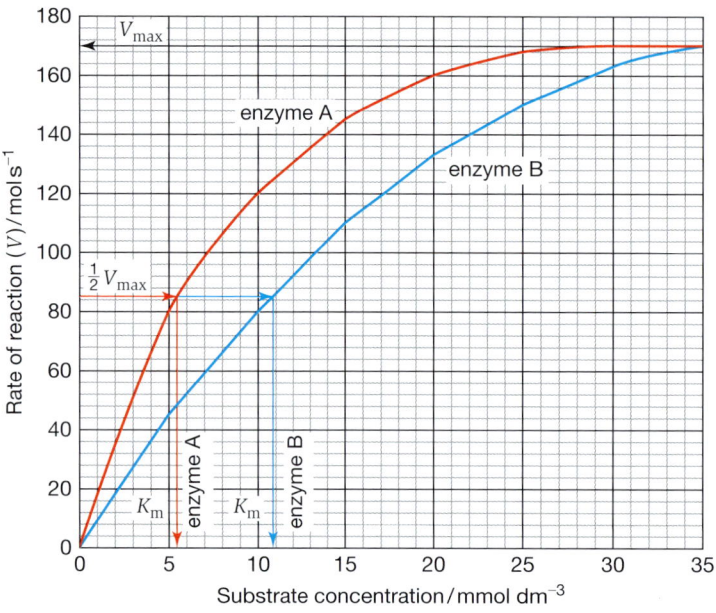

▲ **Figure 3.7** Determining the Michaelis–Menten constant (K_m) for two enzymes, A and B. V is the reaction velocity (rate of reaction per unit time) and V_{max} is the maximum velocity of the reaction

Remember that the graph in Figure 3.7 is a plot of the *initial rates of reaction* for different concentrations of substrate. In the example, the range of concentrations is 0–35 mmol dm^{-3}. At the maximum rate, every active site is constantly being filled as the reaction proceeds. This is the *maximum number of enzyme–substrate* complexes (ESCs) that can be formed by the enzyme under the conditions of the reaction.

Enzyme A reaches V_{max} at a lower concentration than enzyme B. Enzyme A forms the maximum number of ESCs at a *lower substrate concentration* than enzyme B. This means that A has a *higher affinity* for the substrate than enzyme B. Enzymes with high affinity for their substrate have a low value for K_m while enzymes with a low affinity have a high value for K_m.

A low value for K_m indicates that the enzyme requires only a small amount of substrate for their active sites to become saturated. Hence, the maximum velocity is reached at relatively low substrate concentrations. A high value for K_m indicates the need for high substrate concentrations to achieve maximum reaction velocity.

Worked Example

Competitive inhibitors and non-competitive inhibitors have different effects on enzyme activity. They differ in their effects on the maximum velocity of an enzyme-catalysed reaction (V_{max}) and on the Michaelis–Menten constant (K_m).

(a) Sketch a graph to show the effect of a competitive inhibitor on the activity of an enzyme.

(b) Use your sketch graph to show the effect of the competitive inhibitor on V_{max} and K_m.

(c) Sketch a second graph to show the effect of a non-competitive inhibitor on the activity of an enzyme.

(d) Use your sketch graph to show the effect of the non-competitive inhibitor on V_{max} and K_m.

Answers

(a)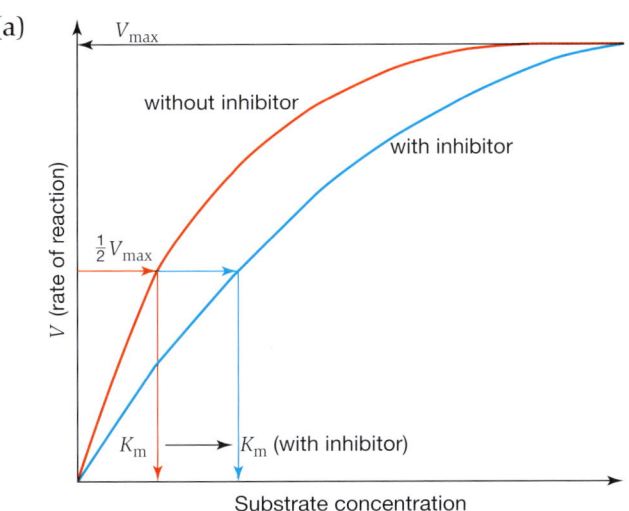

Marks are awarded for putting the substrate concentration on the x-axis and the rate of reaction or velocity (V) on the y-axis; for both lines (with and without inhibitor) reaching the same maximum rate; and for the line showing the effect of the inhibitor being to the right of the line for 'without inhibitor'.

(b) Marks are given for showing that the competitive inhibitor has no effect on V_{max} but it increases the K_m so that the enzyme has a lower affinity for its substrate when the inhibitor is present. (This is because the inhibitor molecules occupy the active site so that substrate molecules cannot enter. The effect of this competition is overcome as the substrate concentration is increased.)

(c)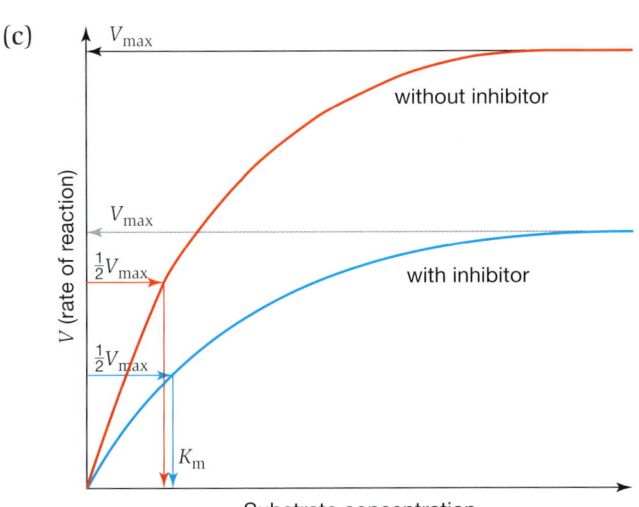

Marks are awarded for putting the substrate concentration on the x-axis and the rate of reaction or velocity (V) on the y-axis; for the line for 'without inhibitor' reaching a higher maximum rate than the line for 'with inhibitor'; and for the lines having the same shape.

(d) Marks are awarded for showing that the non-competitive inhibitor reduces V_{max} but the K_m remains the same.

↑ Raise your grade

Dopa oxidase catalyses a reaction that gives a colour change. The effect of an inhibitor on the rate of reaction at different substrate concentrations was investigated. The graph shows the results.

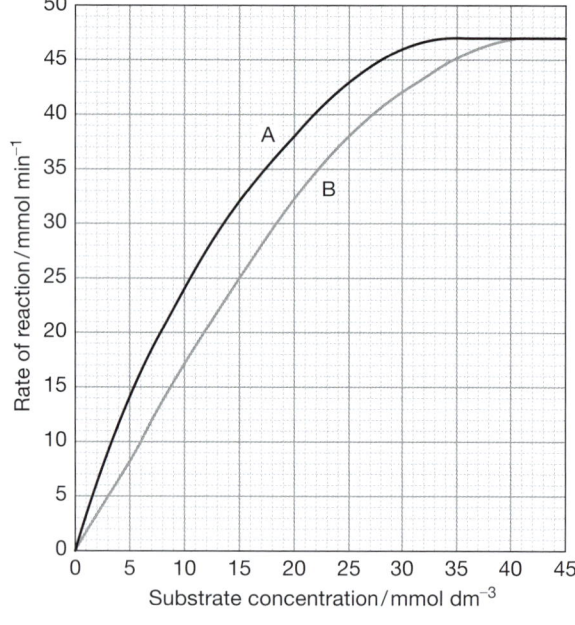

(a) Use the graph to determine:

(i) the maximum rate of reaction (V_{max}) for line A. [1]

47 mmol min⁻¹. ✔

(ii) the Michaelis–Menten constant (K_m) for line A. [1]

10 mmol dm⁻³ ✔

(iii) the effect of the inhibitor on K_m of this enzyme. [1]

The K_m is increased to 14.0 mmol dm⁻³ ✔

(iv) the effect of the inhibitor on V_{max}. [1]

V_{max} is unchanged ✔   Correct answers to all parts of (a).

(b) A different enzyme has a much higher K_m than dopa oxidase. What does this tell you about the two enzymes? [1]

The enzyme with the higher K_m has a lower affinity for its substrate than dopa oxidase. ✔

Correct answer.

(c) Identify the type of inhibitor and use the graph to give a reason for your answer. [2]

The inhibitor is competitive. ✔ This is because it competes with the substrate for the active site. ✗

No reason given based on the evidence in the graph. The answer should state that at high concentrations the substrate competes effectively with the inhibitor so V_{max} is the same as in the reactions without the inhibitor.

Exam-style questions

1   An intracellular protease acts on cell proteins that are no longer required by a cell.

Which bonds are broken by this protease?

A   disulfide   B   ester

C   glycosidic   D   peptide   [1]

2   A student investigated the effect of amylase on the breakdown of starch. Three steps were included in the procedure.

1   The amylase solution and the starch solution were kept at 25 °C for 5 minutes before mixing.

2   Samples were removed from the reaction mixture and tested with iodine in KI solution at 30 s intervals.

3   The reaction mixture was stirred throughout.

Which step or steps ensured that variables were controlled?

A   1, 2 and 3   B   1 and 2 only

C   2 and 3 only   D   1 only   [1]

3   A student prepared some test-tubes with solutions as follows:

Test-tube	Contents
1	starch and α-amylase
2	glucose and sucrase
3	glycogen and α-amylase
4	starch and sucrase
5	sucrose and amylase

All the test-tubes were kept at 40 °C for 15 minutes. In which test-tubes would reducing sugar be detected after 15 minutes?

A   1, 4 and 5   B   1, 2 and 3

C   1, 3 and 5   D   1, 3 and 4   [1]

4   The fungus *Aspergillus niger* is the source of the extracellular enzyme β-galactosidase that is used commercially.

(a) (i) State what is meant by an extracellular enzyme.   [1]

(ii) Explain why each enzyme is specific to one reaction.   [3]

β-galactosidase catalyses a reaction in which the disaccharide lactose is hydrolysed into glucose and galactose. Some students investigated the effect of increasing the concentration of β-galactosidase on its activity. The students prepared a solution of lactose and different concentrations of β-galactosidase. The lactose solution and enzyme solutions were kept separately at pH 7 and 20 °C for five minutes before mixing them. The initial rate of each reaction mixture was determined. The results are plotted on the graph.

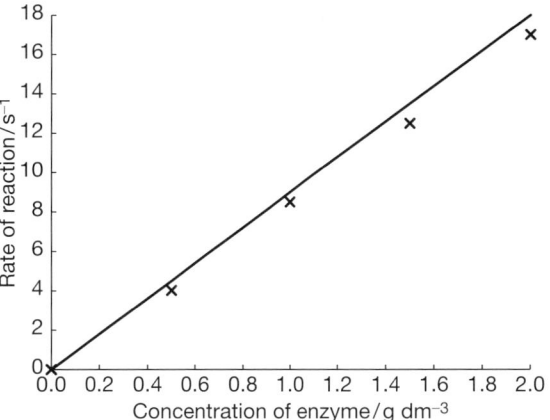

(b) (i) State two other variables that should be kept constant when setting up the reaction mixtures.   [2]

(ii) Explain why it is important to determine the initial rate in an investigation like this.   [2]

(c) Explain the results shown in the graph.   [5]

(d) Predict the results that are likely to be obtained if the enzyme concentration is increased above 2.0 g dm^{-3}. Explain your answer.   [2]

Questions in style of Paper 3

5   A student is set the task of planning an investigation into the effect of substrate concentration on the activity of immobilised catalase. The student was provided with a 20 vol hydrogen peroxide solution.

(a) State the independent variable and the dependent variable for this investigation   [2]

(b) Explain how you will change the independent variable.   [3]

(c) Explain how you will measure the dependent variable.   [2]

(d) Explain how you will process and present the results.   [3]

The fluid mosaic membrane

A eukaryotic cell has a **cell surface membrane** (plasma membrane) that separates the contents of the cell from its surroundings. Cell surface membranes are partially permeable as they allow some substances and prevent others from moving in and out of cells. **Intracellular membranes** within cells form cell structures, such as mitochondria, endoplasmic reticulum, chloroplasts and Golgi bodies (see Unit 1).

Cell membranes are fluid because the phospholipids form a liquid layer in which individual molecules can move laterally (Figure 4.1). Proteins in the membranes also move, forming a scattered pattern resembling a mosaic.

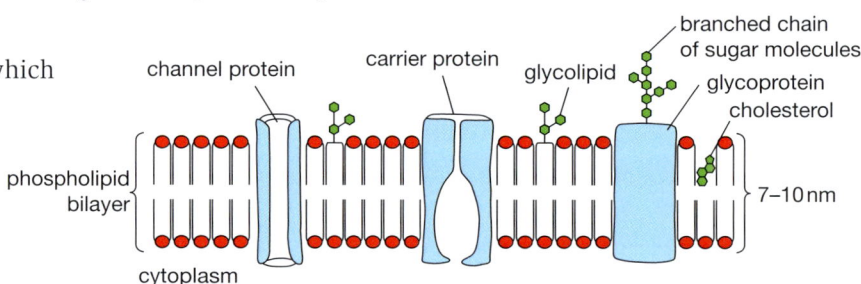

▲ **Figure 4.1** The fluid mosaic structure of a cell surface membrane. The sugar chains of glycoproteins and glycolipids are only found on the outer side

▼ **Table 4.1** The components of cell surface membranes and their functions

Component of cell surface membranes	Function
phospholipids (see Unit 2 for structure)	• form a bilayer that acts as a barrier between the cytoplasm and the surroundings of cells and is fluid so proteins can move about • hydrophilic region so can interact with aqueous cytosol and the surroundings, e.g. tissue fluid in mammals • hydrophobic region that forms the hydrophobic core of the bilayer, which is permeable to non-polar molecules and impermeable to ions and large polar molecules
proteins	• transmembrane proteins form channels and carriers • enzymes that catalyse reactions on external or internal surfaces of membranes
cholesterol	• stabilises the phospholipid bilayer by binding to polar 'heads' and non-polar 'tails' of phospholipid molecules (see page 26) • controls fluidity by preventing the phospholipid bilayer from solidifying at low temperatures and becoming too fluid at high temperatures • prevents passage of ions and polar molecules (e.g. water and glucose)

▼ **Table 4.1** continued

Component of cell surface membranes	Function
glycoproteins – proteins with short chains of sugars (often branched) attached on exterior (outer) side	• receptors for signalling molecules, e.g. hormones and neurotransmitters • promote adhesion between similar cells to form tissues during development • cell 'markers' that are recognised by antibodies and lymphocytes (also known as cell surface antigens)
glycolipids – lipids consisting of glycerol, 2 fatty acids with one or more sugars attached on exterior side	

Functions of membranes at cell surfaces

▼ **Table 4.2** Some functions of cell surface membranes

Function	Comments
barrier	many water-soluble substances cannot pass across; large molecules that are required in the cell, such as proteins, cannot leave
permeability	partially permeable as some substances can pass through the phospholipid bilayer and others through transmembrane proteins; many substances cannot pass through membranes
absorption through membrane	different cell membranes are folded to different extents to increase the surface area for absorption through the phospholipid bilayer and transmembrane proteins
movement by bulk flow	substances that cannot pass through the bilayer or transmembrane proteins are taken into the cell in vesicles or vacuoles formed by the cell surface membrane; when these substances are removed from a cell, they are carried to the cell surface in vesicles or vacuoles; see endocytosis and exocytosis on page 44
recognition	receptors have binding sites for cell signalling molecules such as hormones and growth factors recognising cells that must form links during tissue and organ development cell surface antigens, which identify cells to the immune system

★ **Exam tip**

Diagrams of cell surface membranes are usually based on animal cell membranes. A lot of cholesterol is found in the cell surface membranes of animal cells, much less is found in plant cell membranes, but none is found in prokaryote membranes.

💡 **Remember**

Proteins are made of amino acids, some of which have non-polar R-groups. The hydrophobic regions of transmembrane proteins are made of these amino acids.

★ **Exam tip**

Do not confuse cell membranes with cell walls. Membranes are made of phospholipids and proteins; cellulose is the major component of plant cell walls. Plants, fungi and prokaryotes have cell walls that surround cell membranes; animal cells do not have cell walls.

Channel and **carrier proteins** are transmembrane proteins. Channel proteins are used in facilitated diffusion; carrier proteins are used in facilitated diffusion and active transport (page 44).

Channel proteins have a central space running through them lined with polar R-groups that allow ions and polar molecules to pass through the membrane. Channel proteins can remain open all the time or open and close in response to certain stimuli.

Carrier proteins change shape (conformational change) to move ions and polar molecules, such as glucose, across membranes. In facilitated diffusion the substance concerned binds to the protein and this prompts a change in shape so that the substance is moved through the membrane. When the ion or polar molecule is deposited on the opposite side, the carrier protein returns to its original shape ready for another ion or molecule to bind.

💡 **Remember**

The conformational changes are like the change in shape that occurs in the induced fit model of enzyme action. They are reversible changes in the tertiary structure of the protein.

Functions of intracellular membranes

Eukaryotic cells have membrane around their nuclei and often have large quantities of membrane inside the cytoplasm. These membranes fulfill many functions, as described in Table 4.3.

▼ **Table 4.3** Some functions of intracellular membranes

Function	Examples
form compartments	• isolation of hydrolytic enzymes in lysosomes so they do not harm the cell • concentration of substances, e.g. enzymes and their substrates • provision of areas with different pH, e.g. interiors of chloroplasts and mitochondria have a different pH from the rest of the cytoplasm
provide large surface area	• chloroplasts and mitochondria have membranes for forming ATP • chloroplasts have membranes for many pigment molecules, such as chlorophyll • rough endoplasmic reticulum (RER) has a large surface for ribosomes
intracellular transport	• vacuoles and vesicles move substances from cell surface membrane into the cell, from RER to Golgi body and Golgi body to cell surface membrane • the endoplasmic reticulum provides an extensive transport system separated from the cytosol by ER membranes

Movement across membranes

Movement across membranes is either by passive mechanisms or by active mechanisms. The latter require metabolic energy, which cells must provide by making ATP in respiration.

Passive mechanisms

Molecules cross membranes by **diffusion** down their concentration gradient as a result of their own kinetic energy. The cell does not need to use metabolic energy to move the molecules.

Simple diffusion. Molecules pass through the phospholipid bilayer. Small, uncharged molecules, such as oxygen and carbon dioxide, pass readily through the phospholipid bilayer. Lipid (fat)-soluble substances, such as steroids and fatty acids, can also pass easily by simple diffusion.

Facilitated diffusion. Unless they are very small, polar molecules cannot pass through the phospholipid bilayer so they move through channel proteins and carrier proteins. Water molecules are polar and they cannot easily pass through the bilayer. Cells have aquaporins, which are channel proteins specialised for the transport of water across membranes (see Figure 4.2).

Factors that influence the rate of diffusion

The rate of diffusion can be determined by finding out how much of a particular substance moves from one place to another in a fixed time. This may involve determining the rate of movement in or out of cells or movement across one or more layers of cells. For example, in the lungs, oxygen and carbon dioxide diffuse across a barrier of cells that is about 0.5 µm across (see Unit 9).

The factors that influence the rate of diffusion are:

• steepness of the concentration gradient between two areas

• surface area that the ions or molecules can diffuse through

• distance from one area to another

• type of ion or molecule

• size of ion or molecule

• type of cell surface membrane

• temperature.

★ **Exam tip**

Diffusion is a topic that you will find throughout the syllabus. Make sure that you learn the differences between these two types of diffusion and be prepared to apply this knowledge to the topics in other units.

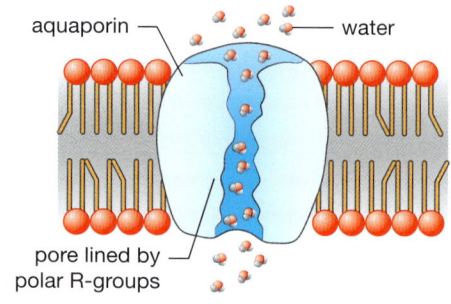

▲ **Figure 4.2** An aquaporin

⚙ **Practical Skills**

The effect of some of these factors can be investigated with non-living materials, such as Visking tubing and agar. Practical investigations using Visking tubing or agar are set in Paper 3. These require careful manipulation of apparatus and materials. They also require good skills of timing and observation. See page 184 for an example.

Osmosis

Osmosis is the passive movement of water through a partially permeable membrane from a place with a higher water potential to a place with a lower water potential. In cells that have aquaporins, most of the water that travels through membranes passes through these channel proteins, which are specialised for the movement of water (not all cells need aquaporins).

Water potential

Water potential is the tendency of water to move from one place to another and is determined by:

- the free energy of water present

- the concentration of solutes, such as ions and sugars

- the pressure exerted by the cell wall that resists any increase in volume (in plant cells and prokaryotes, not in animal cells).

Water molecules are in constant motion and therefore have kinetic energy. This free energy of water can be changed. It can be:

- *decreased* by the addition of solutes, such as sucrose and sodium chloride, because water molecules form clusters around ions and polar molecules resulting in negative water potentials

- *increased* if an external pressure is applied.

Pure water (with no solutes) has a water potential of zero. The addition of a solute decreases the free energy of water so that the solution formed has a negative water potential. This means that:

- solutions with low concentrations of solute molecules have negative water potentials just below zero

- solutions with high concentrations of solute molecules have much lower (more negative) water potentials

- water moves from a place with a high water potential (high free energy) to a place with a low water potential (low free energy).

Cytoplasm and the cell sap inside plant vacuoles contain many solutes, such as proteins, sugars and ions.

When cells are placed:

- in distilled water, more water molecules move into the cell down the water potential gradient than move out; the *net* movement of water is into the cell

- in solutions with high concentrations of solutes (e.g. of sucrose or sodium chloride), more water molecules move out of cells down the water potential gradient than move in; the *net* movement of water is out of the cells.

> **→ Try this... 1**
>
> Make copies of the graphs on page 43, 46 and 47. Use the information in this Unit and in the answers to the questions to annotate the graphs to explain the trends in each graph. This is good practice for answering questions on graphs that start with the phrase: 'With reference to ...'

⚙ Practical Skills

A quantitative investigation using plant tissue

Choose a suitable plant tissue such as European potato (*Solanum tuberosum*), sweet potato (*Ipomoea batatas*) or yam (*Dioscorea alata*). The part of these plants that you eat is storage tissue.

1. Use a cork borer or a chip-making machine to cut the tissue into cylinders or 'chips'.

2. Cut all the pieces to the same length and make sure that the ends are square. Use paper towel to surface dry the pieces of potato.

3. Weigh the pieces and record their individual masses.

4. Place the pieces into separate test-tubes containing solutions of sucrose as shown in Table 4.4.

5. After 12 hours reweigh the pieces and record the results.

In this investigation, it is necessary to calculate the percentage change in mass because the initial masses of the pieces are likely to be different.

The percentage change in mass is the **derived variable**.

★ **Exam tip**

As you read a procedure like this, identify the independent and dependent variables. The independent variable in this investigation is the concentration of the sucrose solution and the dependent variable is the change in mass.

🔗 **Link**

For more on variables see Unit 20, Practical skills.

★ **Exam tip**

Calculations involving percentage changes are often asked in examinations. Questions may involve taking figures from a graph.

📐 Maths Skills

Percentage change

Percentage change is calculated as follows:

$$\text{percentage change} = \frac{\text{change in mass}}{\text{original mass}} \times 100.$$

Concentration of sucrose solution / mol dm⁻³	Initial mass / g	Final mass / g	Change in mass / g	Percentage change in mass	Mean percentage change in mass
0.0	1.26	1.49	0.23	18.3	
	1.26	1.51	0.25	19.8	19.3
	1.22	1.46	0.24	19.7	
0.2	1.22	1.31	0.09	7.4	
	1.27	1.32	0.05	3.9	5.4
	1.25	1.31	0.06	4.8	
0.4	1.43	1.29	−0.14	−9.8	
	1.32	1.26	−0.06	−4.5	−7.7
	1.37	1.25	−0.12	−8.8	
0.6	1.32	1.10	−0.22	−16.7	
	1.26	1.07	−0.19	−15.1	−15.2
	1.22	1.05	−0.17	−13.9	
0.8	1.28	0.98	−0.30	−23.4	
	1.25	1.01	−0.24	−19.2	−21.2
	1.23	0.97	−0.26	−21.1	
1.0	1.31	0.96	−0.35	−26.7	
	1.27	1.00	−0.27	−21.3	−23.3
	1.23	0.96	−0.27	−22.0	

◀ **Table 4.4** The effect of immersion in different concentrations of sucrose solution on the mass of pieces of storage tissue of European potato

Table 4.5 shows the water potentials of the six solutions of sucrose.

Concentration of sucrose solution / mol dm⁻³	Water potential / kPa
0.00	0
0.20	−540
0.40	−1120
0.60	−1800
0.80	−2580
1.00	−3500

◀ **Table 4.5** The water potentials of six sucrose solutions

Three pieces of plant tissue are used for each concentration to see how much variation there is in the results. If there is little variation in the results for each concentration then you can say that the results are repeatable. The three pieces of potato cannot be labelled so they are put into separate test-tubes rather than all in the same container.

You can plot these results on a graph (Figure 4.3).

Where the curve on the graph passes through the horizontal line at 0% there is no change in mass. You can use the graph to estimate the concentration at which there is no change in mass. Here the intercept at 0% is 0.28 mol dm⁻³. You can draw a graph of the water potentials of different sucrose solutions from Table 4.5 and use it to find the water potential in kPa of this concentration of sucrose.

These changes in mass are the result of movement of water by osmosis between the cells and the sucrose solution. In a solution:

- more concentrated than 0.28 mol dm⁻³, water moves from the cells into the solution; pieces of tissue decrease in size

- less concentrated than 0.28 mol dm⁻³, water moves from the surrounding solution into the cells; pieces of tissue increase in size

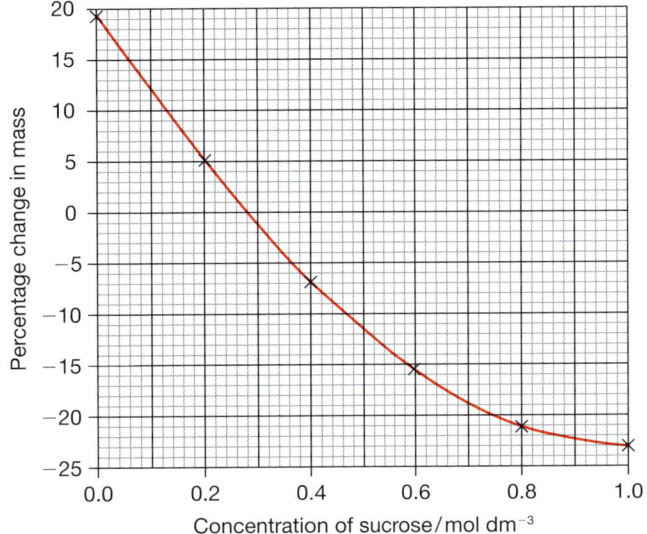

▲ **Figure 4.3** The effect of immersion of potato storage tissue in different solutions of sucrose

- in which there is no change in mass, there is no net movement of water; water molecules still move in and out of cells through cell surface membranes, which remain permeable.

The effects of gain and loss of water on plant cells are investigated by immersing epidermal tissue from an onion in solutions with different water potentials. Cells immersed in distilled water are **fully turgid**. Water enters the cells and increases the volume of the vacuole, which pushes the cytoplasm and cell surface membrane against the cell wall. The pressure potential exerted by the cellulose cell wall withstands this turgor pressure. Cells immersed in a solution with a very low water potential are **plasmolysed**. Water diffuses out of the cells by osmosis. Most of the water comes from the vacuole that decreases in volume, pulling the cytoplasm and cell membrane away from the cell wall. The space between the cell wall and the cell surface membrane fills with the external solution. Cells can recover from plasmolysis if they receive sufficient water.

★ **Exam tip**

When there is no overall movement of water, it is best to write that there is no net movement of water by osmosis.

Active mechanisms

Active mechanisms require metabolic energy. There are two types: active transport and bulk flow.

Active transport. This is used to move substances required inside cells that are present in very low concentrations outside. They cannot be absorbed by passive transport mechanisms. Active transport (Figure 4.4) happens in root cells that absorb ions, such as magnesium and phosphate ions, from soil water.

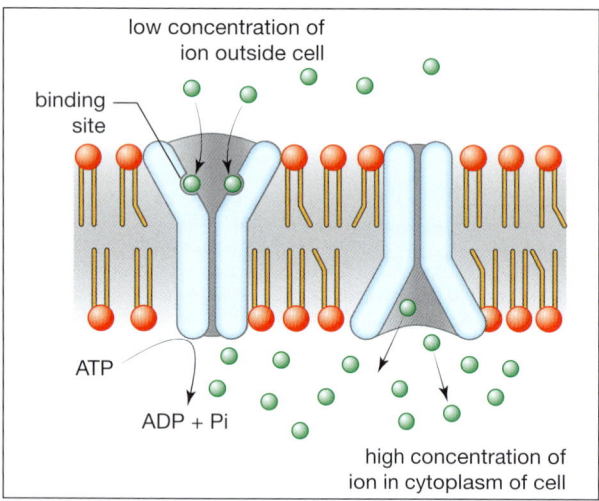

▲ **Figure 4.4** A carrier protein using ATP to provide energy to move ions across a cell surface membrane into the cyto-plasm against a concentration gradient

Active transport is also used to move substances out of cells. Most cells have carrier proteins that move sodium ions out of their cytoplasm, which maintains a lower concentration of sodium ions inside compared with outside. This helps to reduce their water potential so they absorb less water than if the sodium ions remained in the cells.

Bulk transport. Cells take in particles or liquids from their surroundings by **endocytosis**. For example, phagocytic white blood cells take in bacteria by **phagocytosis**. Bacteria are much too large to pass through the transmembrane proteins or through the bilayer. So the bacteria are enclosed in a vacuole formed from the cell surface membrane. Each time membrane is used in endocytosis, the quantity of cell surface membrane is reduced, so more phospholipids and proteins must be added to replace it.

Cells in the pancreas make inactive enzymes that are packaged into vesicles by Golgi bodies. These vesicles travel through the cytoplasm to fuse with the cell surface membrane to release their contents by **exocytosis**.

> ★ **Exam tip**
>
> The carrier protein changes shape each time it moves molecules across the membrane. This change in shape is a conformational change in the protein.

> 🔗 **Link**
>
> There is more about the carrier proteins that move sodium and potassium ions by active transport in nerve cells in Unit 15.

> **Key terms**
>
> **Bulk transport**: the movement of large quantities of particles and liquids across cell membranes by endocytosis or exocytosis.
>
> **Endocytosis**: the movement of particles and liquids into a cell by the infolding of the cell surface membrane to form vacuoles or vesicles.
>
> **Exocytosis**: the movement of substances out of a cell by means of vesicles that fuse with cell surface membrane to release the contents to the outside.

> → **Try this... 2**
>
> (a) State **three** factors that influence the rate of diffusion of small polar molecules through cell surface membranes.
>
> (b) Explain the difference between each of the following: (i) carrier protein and channel protein; (ii) simple diffusion and facilitated diffusion across membranes; (iii) passive and active transport across membranes; (iv) signalling protein and receptor protein; (v) exocytosis and endocytosis.
>
> (c) Plants such as sea lavender and mangrove live in very salty soils that have very low water potentials. Outline how you would find the water potential of the root tissue of these plants.

> ★ **Exam tip**
>
> Part (**b**) is a comparison question requiring short answers. Part (**c**) requires an extended response with ideas written in a logical and sequential manner.

Cell signalling

Many proteins and glycoproteins on cell surfaces are receptors for chemical signals sent between cells. In animals, these chemicals can be hormones, neurotransmitters and growth factors. Some are:

- lipid-soluble (e.g. the steroid hormones testosterone and oestrogen), they diffuse through the phospholipid bilayer into the cytoplasm and possibly into the nucleus, and are detected inside the cell

- water-soluble (e.g. the protein hormones insulin and glucagon) and they do not cross membranes. There are specific receptors on the cell surface for these two hormones and for others, such as adrenaline and many peptide hormones like antidiuretic hormone (ADH) (see Unit 14).

The only cells that can respond to the signalling molecules are those with appropriate receptors. These cells are known as **target cells**.

The receptors on the surface of target cells bind with the signalling molecule because their shapes are complementary. The two fit together in the same way that substrate molecules fit into the active sites of enzymes.

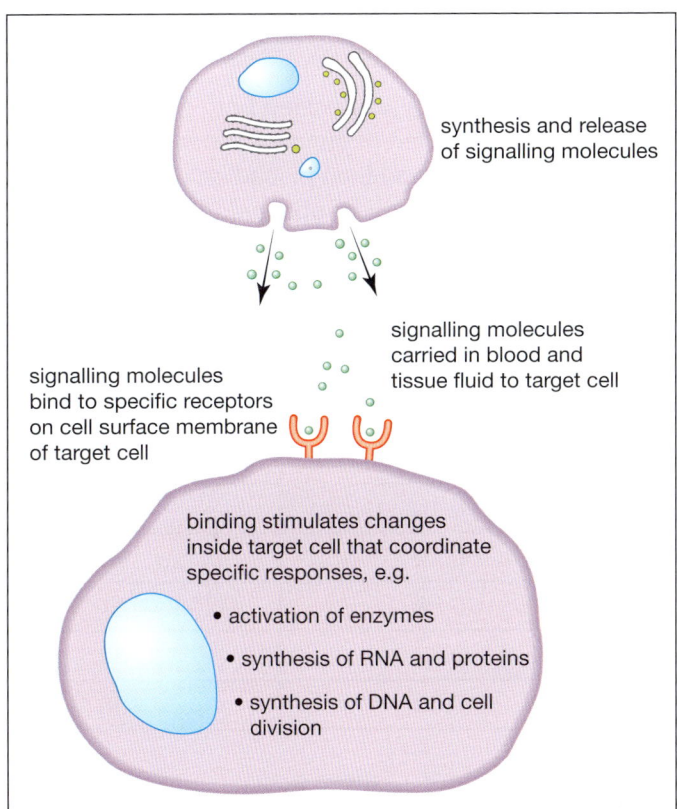

synthesis and release of signalling molecules

signalling molecules carried in blood and tissue fluid to target cell

signalling molecules bind to specific receptors on cell surface membrane of target cell

binding stimulates changes inside target cell that coordinate specific responses, e.g.

- activation of enzymes
- synthesis of RNA and proteins
- synthesis of DNA and cell division

▲ **Figure 4.5** Cell signalling by a protein hormone in an animal (not drawn to scale)

Cell signalling also occurs in plants, which have a very complex form of chemical communication involving the use of hormones, such as auxins, gibberellins and abscisic acid (ABA).

Worked Example

Asthma is a disease in which muscle in the airways contracts to reduce the flow of air deep into the lungs. Salbutamol is one drug taken (often by inhaler) to treat asthma. It binds to β2 adrenergic receptors, which stimulates enzymes in the membrane to convert ATP into cyclic AMP. When the concentration of cyclic AMP increases inside the muscle cells lining the airways, the cells relax allowing the airways to widen.

Adrenaline is the hormone that β2 adrenergic receptors normally detect. Salbutamol is described as an agonist of adrenaline as it mimics the action of this hormone.

(a) Explain how salbutamol is able to mimic adrenaline in its action on the airways of people with asthma.

(b) One consequence of salbutamol cell signalling is a decrease in the intracellular concentration of calcium ions in smooth muscle cells. Suggest a way in which the concentration of calcium ions in the cell is reduced.

Answers

(a) Salbutamol has a similar shape to adrenaline. This shape is complementary to the shape of the β2 adrenergic receptor on smooth muscle cells.

(b) Calcium ions are pumped out of the smooth muscle cells against their concentration gradient by active transport

★ **Exam tip**

Salbutamol is an example of a drug that acts in a cell signalling pathway. You may never have heard of salbutamol and you are unlikely to be taught about it. This question tests your ability to apply your knowledge of biological principles to new and unfamiliar situations.

⬆ Raise your grade

Some epidermis was peeled from onion scale leaves, cut into pieces and placed in solutions of different concentrations of sodium chloride. The pieces were immersed for 10 minutes and then placed on microscope slides in the same solutions. The epidermal pieces were observed under high power. In each case, 100 cells were chosen at random and the number of these that were plasmolysed was recorded. The results are shown in the following table.

Concentration of sodium chloride solution / mol dm⁻³	Percentage of plasmolysed cells
0.00	0
0.10	7
0.20	43
0.30	67
0.40	87
0.50	100

(a) Plot a graph of these results. [5]

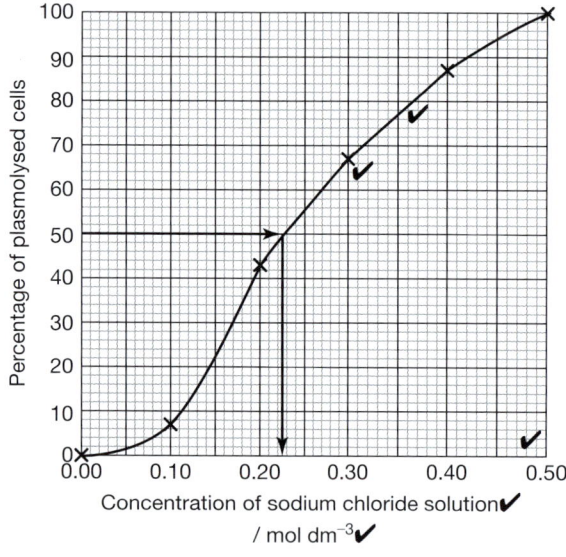

Correct graph: axes are correct with the independent variable (concentration) on the x-axis and the dependent variable (percentage of plasmolysed cells) on the y-axis; both scaled correctly; x-axis labelled with the correct units; points plotted accurately; suitable line of best fit drawn.

(b) State the concentration of sodium chloride in which 50% of the cells should be plasmolysed. [1]

Water potential = 0.225 mol dm⁻³ ✔

The candidate has used a ruler to draw lines on the graph to show the intercept at 50% plasmolysis to find the correct answer.

(c) Explain how plant cells become plasmolysed. [4]

The water potential of the surrounding solution is lower than the water potential of the cell. ✔ Water moves out of the cell by osmosis down the water potential gradient. ✔ The cytoplasm and the vacuole decrease in size ✔ and the cell surface membrane is pulled away from the cell wall. ✔   Good answer that uses the correct terms.

Exam-style questions

1   Cell surface (plasma) membranes in mammalian cells include the following compounds.

1 cholesterol   **2** glycolipids
3 phospholipids   **4** glycoproteins

Which compound is involved in each of these functions of cell surface membranes?

	A	B	C	D
Cell recognition by lymphocytes	1	2	3	4
Allowing diffusion of non-polar substances into the cell	4	3	1	2
Detection of hormones, such as insulin	3	4	2	1
Maintaining the fluidity of membrane	2	1	4	3

[1]

2   Epidermal growth factor (EGF) is a signalling molecule made of protein. The response of cells to this signalling molecule is the synthesis of DNA.

Which describes the receptor for EGF?

A   a channel protein with a hydrophilic pore specific to EGF

B   a glycolipid with a hydrophobic region exposed to tissue fluid

C   a protein situated on a chromosome in the nucleus

D   a cell membrane protein with a complementary shape to EGF   [1]

3   An agar block has the following dimensions:

length = 4 mm; width = 4 mm; height = 2 mm

Which is the surface area : volume ratio for this agar block?

A   1:1   B   2:1

C   3:1   D   4:1   [1]

4   Haemolysis occurs when red blood cells absorb water and burst releasing their cell contents into their surroundings.

A student investigated the effect of immersing red blood cells in solutions of sodium chloride. The student took three samples from each solution and used a cell counter to determine the number of intact red blood cells in each sample.

The mean numbers of red blood cells for each concentration were expressed as a percentage of the cell count obtained in a sample of blood diluted with the same volume of artificial blood plasma. The percentages are shown in the graph.

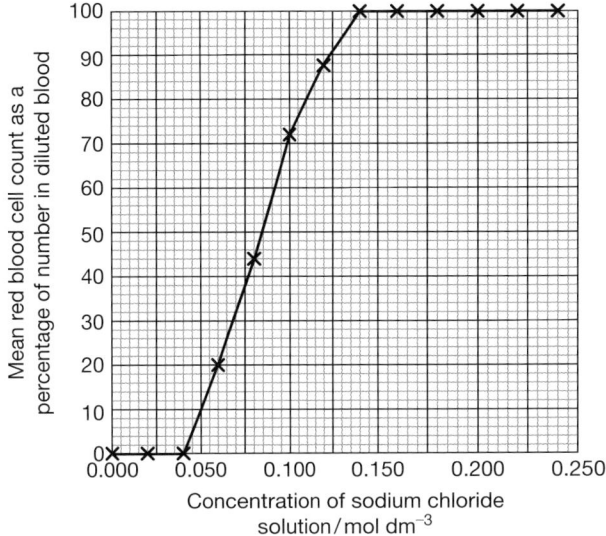

(a) Explain why the student took three samples from each test-tube.   [2]

(b) Use the graph to predict the concentration of sodium chloride in which 50% of the cells are destroyed by haemolysis.   [1]

(c) Explain the results shown in the graph.   [5]

(d) The student repeated the investigation using a culture of a single-celled alga.

State and explain how the results with this alga would differ from those shown in the graph.   [4]

5   (a) (i)   Make a labelled diagram to show the structure of a cell surface membrane. Indicate on your diagram the external surface of the membrane.   [5]

      (ii)   State the width of the membrane.   [1]

   (b) Suggest why the term *fluid mosaic* is used to describe the structure of membranes.   [2]

   (c) Explain how polar molecules pass across cell surface membranes.   [3]

Chromosomes

Eukaryotic cells have nuclei that you can see clearly with the light microscope. Some areas within nuclei stain more darkly than others. This is even more obvious in the electron microscope. The material inside nuclei is **chromatin**.

A long molecule of DNA is wound around **histone** proteins to form a chromosome. In heterochromatin, the lengths of DNA and histones are much more tightly coiled than in euchromatin.

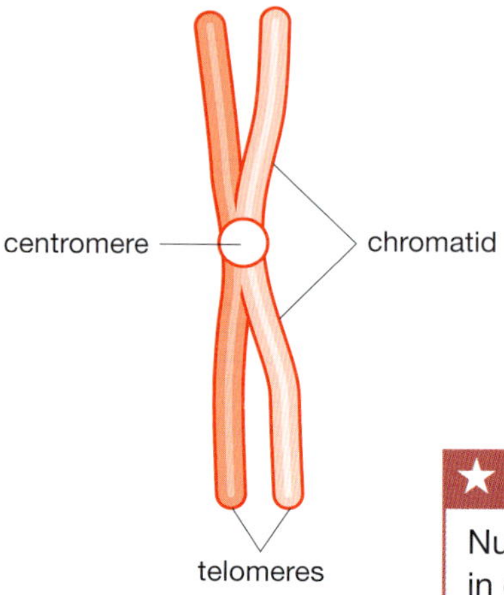

Chromosomes are visible as separate structures only during cell division when they are highly condensed with DNA and histones packed tightly together. At this time, each chromosome consists of two molecules of DNA joined together at the **centromere**. Each molecule of DNA and its associated histones is known as a **chromatid**. In dividing cells, chromosomes are first visible as separate thread-like structures when the cell begins the process of division. All the DNA is in the form of tightly packed heterochromatin, which makes it possible to move the chromosomes around the cell without them becoming tangled.

During cell division it is possible to count the number of chromosomes. In body cells the number is the **diploid** number (abbreviated to 2n). In gametes, the number is the **haploid** number (n). In humans 2n = 46 and n = 23.

In multicellular organisms, mitosis is involved in:

- growth
- repair of tissues following wounding or other damage
- replacement of cells and tissues
- asexual reproduction
- cloning lymphocytes in the immune response.

The cell cycle

During the **mitotic cell cycle** the nucleus divides first to form two daughter nuclei, usually followed by the division of the cytoplasm to give two daughter cells, each with its own nucleus. Sometimes nuclear division is not followed by cytoplasmic division, as happens in many fungi that have hyphae (long thin threads) that are not subdivided into cells.

centromere — chromatid

telomeres

◀ **Figure 5.1** A chromosome composed of two **sister chromatids** joined together at the centromere. The ends of the DNA molecules that make up each chromatid are **telomeres**

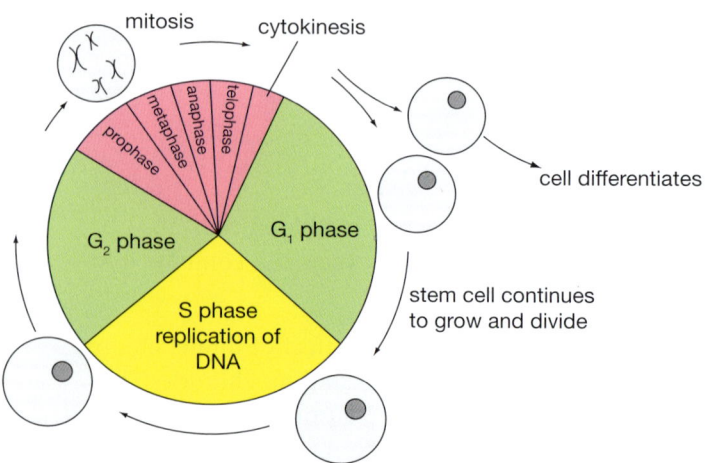

▲ **Figure 5.2** The mitotic cell cycle. The proportion of time a cell spends in mitosis is very short. The longest stage is interphase, which comprises the G_1 phase, the S phase and the G_2 phase

After a new cell is formed, the following events occur in this sequence:

- **growth** of cytoplasm (G_1) – molecules such as nucleoside triphosphates (activated nucleotides) are made in preparation for replication and protein synthesis (transcription and translation); amino acids are synthesised and attached to tRNA ready for translation (see Unit 6)

- **synthesis** phase (S) – **DNA replication**

- **growth** of cytoplasm (G_2) – organelles such as chloroplasts and mitochondria divide, more membrane is formed and polysaccharides and triglycerides are stored for energy

- mitosis (division of the nucleus)

- cytokinesis (division of the whole cell).

Replication almost always results in identical DNA, so the genetic information inherited by the two daughter cells is identical to that of the parent cell. If replication is not like this, then the cells may differ genetically and not function together in a tissue. When a genetically different cell begins to express different proteins on its cell surface, the immune system eliminates it. If it does not, the cell may divide and grow to form a **tumour**.

Cell division

Almost immediately after fertilisation, a mammalian zygote divides into two **genetically identical cells**. Growth by cell division continues until a hollow ball of cells is formed. This embryo is about the same size as the zygote but is now composed of many cells. Each time a cell divides, its nucleus divides first and then the cytoplasm divides to give two new cells, each with a nucleus. **Mitosis** is the nuclear division that occurs as cells increase in number like this. The nuclei that are produced are genetically identical to each other and to the parent nucleus. This maintains **genetic stability** throughout the life of an organism.

Later in development, the cells in the embryo gain nutrients and grow. Cells cannot grow indefinitely. When a cell reaches a certain size, it is unable to support itself as the area of the cell surface membrane is too small to absorb enough oxygen and to lose carbon dioxide fast enough to support the increase in the volume of **protoplasm** (cytoplasm plus nucleus) – the surface area:volume ratio becomes smaller. This is one reason why cells divide into two after growing for a while.

> ★ **Exam tip**
>
> You can recall the sequence of stages of mitosis by the first letter of each phase – PMAT. Remember that interphase is not a stage of mitosis, but it is a stage of the cell cycle so IPMAT is correct for learning the whole cell cycle.

> ★ **Exam tip**
>
> DNA replication, the synthesis of biological molecules and the formation of membranes and organelles that all occur during interphase are highly active processes. Therefore, do not call interphase a 'resting stage'.

Worked Example

The DNA content of cells changes throughout the cell cycle. This graph shows the changes that occur.

(a) Outline what happens at each stage of the cell cycle to bring about the changes in the quantity of DNA shown in the graph.

(b) Explain briefly how mutations of the genes that control the cell cycle lead to the formation of tumours.

(c) The enzyme that catalyses the formation of DNA during replication is unable to copy the ends of each chromosome. Outline how cells avoid the progressive loss of genes from the ends of chromosomes with every cell cycle.

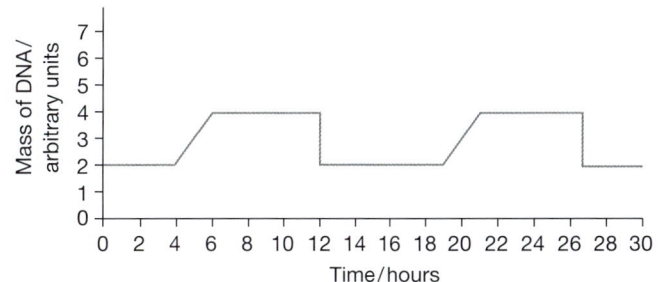

▲ **Figure 5.3** Changes in DNA content in a cell during two mitotic cell cycles

Answers

(a) The cell is in the G_1 stage for the first 4 hours. The quantity of DNA increases during the S phase (4–6 hours) because this is when DNA replication occurs so that each chromosome has two molecules of DNA. In the G_2 phase, after the S phase, there is twice as much DNA as in the G_1 phase. During cytokinesis (at 12 hours) the mass of DNA halves as the cell divides into two and each cell gets a complete set of single-stranded chromosomes from the original parent cell. Each chromosome has one DNA molecule. Between 12 and 19 hours the quantity remains constant in G_1 of the next cycle as no replication occurs in this stage.

(b) The cell cycle is not controlled properly. Cells with these mutations divide uncontrollably to produce many cells that form a tumour. These cells do not respond to signals that tell normal cells not to divide.

(c) There are telomeres at the ends of each chromosome. Each telomere is made of a short sequence of nucleotides that is repeated many times. Telomeres are copied by another enzyme, telomerase, so that they can be synthesised during replication. This makes sure chromosomes do not become shorter during each S phase of the cell cycle and prevents the loss of genes that would otherwise happen.

Mitosis ensures that each new cell has exactly the same genetic information as its parent cell. All the cells in the body (except for gametes) have identical genetic information so that they can all work together efficiently.

As a result of mitosis:

- two daughter nuclei are produced

- the two daughter nuclei have the same number of chromosomes as each other and the same as the parent nucleus

- genetic stability is maintained throughout the life of an individual because the genetic information is the same in the daughter cells as in the parent cell

- there is no genetic variation between cells.

In multicellular organisms, cells produced by cell division often remain together to form tissues and differentiate to become specialised to carry out specific functions.

Other undifferentiated cells can continue dividing by mitosis to produce more and more cells, which can specialise.

In animals these are **stem cells**, which divide:

- to form new cells that specialise to form new tissues, to replace worn out tissues or to repair damaged tissues with replacement cells

- in the bone marrow – to replace red and white blood cells, which have a limited life span

- at the base of the epidermis in the skin – to replace the cells at the surface that are constantly rubbed off and to form cells to cover wounds and replace the damaged cells when the skin is cut.

In plants, these are **meristematic cells**, which are found in areas called **meristems**; for example, root tips (see page 51), shoot tips, and the cambium, which gives rise to xylem and phloem tissues (see Unit 7).

Mitosis is also involved in asexual reproduction of multicellular organisms. This happens in fungi, in some animals and in many plant species (Figure 5.4).

★ **Exam tip**

Do not confuse mitosis with meiosis, the other form of nuclear division (see Unit 16). In mitosis, the chromosome number stays the same and daughter nuclei are genetically identical. In meiosis, daughter nuclei have half the chromosome number of the parent cell and are genetically different.

▲ **Figure 5.4** These plantlets are formed from meristematic cells that divide at the edge of the leaves of the Mexican hat plant, *Bryophyllum daigremontianum*; this is an example of vegetative (asexual) reproduction

★ **Exam tip**

A common error is to write 'repair of cells' as a function of mitosis. A cell cannot be repaired by dividing into two. It can, however, be destroyed and *replaced* by cells formed by the division of stem cells.

⚙ Practical Skills

Observing the mitotic cell cycle

You can see the stages of mitosis for yourself if you make a temporary preparation of the cells from the root tips of onion or garlic. You can use the following procedure with cloves of garlic (*Allium sativum*).

1. Score the underside of a clove of garlic with a sharp knife and suspend the garlic over water so the base just touches the water surface.

2. After several days, remove some intact roots.

3. Cut off 10–20 mm of the root tips. Put in a small volume of ethanoic acid on a watch glass (or other shallow dish) for 10 minutes.

4. Heat 10–25 cm³ of 1 mol dm⁻³ hydrochloric acid to 60 °C in a water bath. (The acid hydrolyses the middle lamella that holds plant cells together.)

5. Wash the root tips in cold water for 4–5 minutes and dry on filter paper.

6. Use a mounted needle to transfer the root tips to the hot hydrochloric acid and leave for 5 minutes.

7. Wash the root tips again in cold water for 4–5 minutes and dry on filter paper.

8. Use the mounted needle to remove two root tips onto a clean microscope slide.

9. Use a scalpel to remove all the tissue except for 2 mm from the growing root tip. Discard the rest, but keep the tips.

10. Add a small drop of ethano-orcein (acetic-orcein) stain or toluidine blue stain and leave for 2 minutes.

11. Break up the tissue with a mounted needle.

12. Place a cover slip over the root tips. Place filter paper over the cover slip and press gently to spread the cells. Alternatively tap the surface of the cover slip gently with the blunt end of a mounted needle or pencil.

13. Use the low power of the microscope to search the slide for cells like those in the photomicrograph.

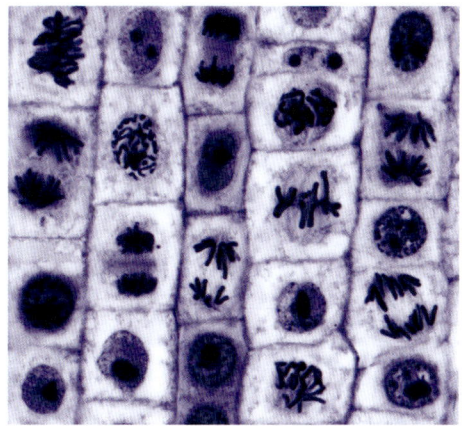

▲ **Figure 5.5** A stained section of a root tip meristem of garlic. There are cells here in various stages of the cell cycle.

➡ Try this... 1

Search online for a photomicrograph showing stages of mitosis in root tip cells.

(a) Label one example of a cell in each of the four stages of mitosis.

(b) Label one example of a cell in interphase.

(c) Explain how the cell cycle in root cells differs from the cell cycle in animal cells.

➡ Try this... 2

The table shows the number of cells in each stage of the cell cycle in sections of the root tip meristem of onion, *Allium cepa*. It takes 13 hours at 25 °C to complete the cell cycle in this species.

Stage of cell cycle	Number of cells	Percentage of cells in each stage	Length of time of each stage / min
interphase	254	73.6	574
prophase	45		
metaphase	16	4.6	36
anaphase	7	2.0	16
telophase	23		
total	345	100.0	780

(a) Complete the table by (i) calculating the number of cells in prophase and telophase as a percentage of the total number counted, and (ii) calculating the length of time of each of these stages.

(b) Suggest the conclusions that the student could make about the relative length of time of each stage in the cell cycle.

(c) Describe what happens to a root tip cell during and immediately after telophase.

↑ Raise your grade

1 (a) Outline the processes that occur to prepare a cell for division and explain why these
processes need to occur. [5]

> It is important that more DNA is produced by semi-conservative replication. ✔ Each
> molecule of DNA in every chromosome is copied so there are two copies for when the cell
> divides into two. It is also important that the cell grows and makes new organelles. ✔ The
> new cells need enough mitochondria to make ATP so more of them need to be made. ✔
> More membrane also needs to be made so there is enough for the two new cells when they
> divide in cytokinesis. ✔

> The second sentence is too vague to gain a mark for any detail about replication or chromatids.
> Instead of writing 'two copies of DNA', it is better to refer to the two strands or polynucleotides as in
> Unit 6 page 54.

(b) Name the stage of mitosis in which each of the following occurs:

   (i)   sister chromatids are separated when centromeres split apart; anaphase ✔

   (ii) chromosomes condense; prophase ✔

   (iii) sister chromatids move to opposite poles; telophase ✗

   (iv) nuclear envelope reforms; interphase ✗

   (v)   chromosomes assemble at the equator of the cell. metaphase ✔ [5]

> Telophase is incorrect for **(iii)**, sister chromatids move to opposite poles during *anaphase*.
> However, telophase is the correct response to **(iv)**, *not* interphase.

(c) Explain the role of mitosis in the growth of animals and plants. [3]

> The daughter cells produced by mitosis are genetically identical. ✔ This means that they all
> have the same DNA and identical genes and all the cells in an animal or a plant can work
> together. If any of the cells were genetically different they might be attacked by other cells
> (e.g. by the immune system in animals) ✔ or divide uncontrollably to form tumours, which
> could harm the organism.

> It is better to say that the daughter cells have identical alleles of all the genes in the organism.
> This is because all individuals of the same species have the same genes. If you need to be
> reminded about genes and alleles see Unit 16.

(d) State **three** roles of mitosis in animals and plants other than growth. [3]

> Asexual reproduction, ✔ cell replacement ✔ and repair of tissues. ✔   Correct answer.

(e) Suggest what might happen to the daughter cells at the end of one mitotic cell cycle. [2]

> Both daughter cells may grow and divide again. ✔ Both cells may change into specialised
> cells and so do not divide again. ✔

> Good answer. The candidate has noticed that there are 2 marks for this question and has
> given two different suggestions. Another suggestion is to use Figure 5.2 and say that one cell
> remains to divide and the other becomes specialised and stops dividing.

Exam-style questions

1   In root tip cells the formation of the cell plate that begins the separation of daughter cells occurs. In which stage of the cell cycle do daughter cells separate from each other?

A   anaphase

B   cytokinesis

C   interphase

D   prophase   [1]

2   Which row shows the stages of mitosis when DNA is replicated, the nuclear envelope forms and sister chromatids separate?

	DNA replication	Formation of nuclear envelope	Separation of sister chromatids
A	anaphase	interphase	prophase
B	cytokinesis	metaphase	telophase
C	interphase	telophase	anaphase
D	prophase	cytokinesis	metaphase

[1]

3   The graph shows the distance between the centromeres of sister chromatids and the distance between centromeres and the poles during mitosis.

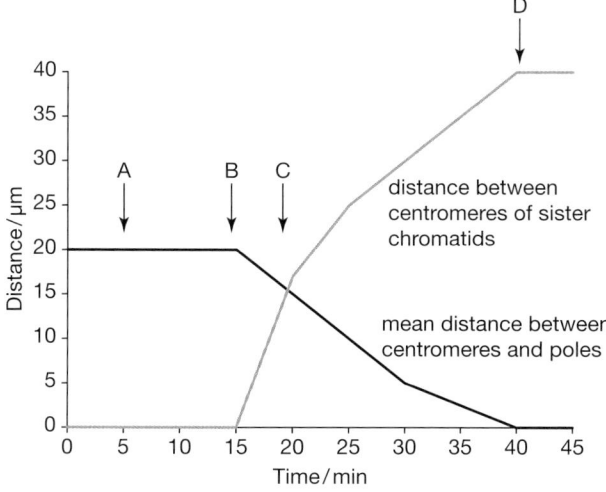

Which shows the beginning of anaphase?   [1]

4   Which shows the role of telomeres?

A   stimulate the decondensing of chromosomes during telophase

B   attach chromatids to the spindle at metaphase

C   prevent shortening of DNA at the ends of chromosomes

D   provide support for the DNA molecule in each chromosome   [1]

5   The yellow fever mosquito, *Aedes aegypti*, has a diploid number of 6.

The drawing is made from a photograph of the chromosomes taken at metaphase of mitosis.

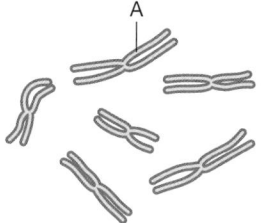

(a) The length of chromosome **A** is 8.4 µm. Calculate the magnification of the drawing:

  • write out the formula that you will use

  • use the formula to calculate the magnification

  • give your answer to two significant figures   [3]

(b) (i) Draw a diagram to show the arrangement of any two of the chromosomes of *Aedes aegypti* in the middle of anaphase of mitosis.   [3]

   (ii) On your diagram label a centromere and indicate the position of the poles of the spindle apparatus.   [2]

(c) Describe what happens to the nuclear envelope and the cell surface membrane during the cell division of a cell of an animal, such as *A. aegypti*.   [4]

(d) At either end of each chromosome shown in the drawing are telomeres.

   Outline the role of telomeres.   [3]

(e) Explain the advantages of using a light microscope to study the behaviour of chromosomes rather than the electron microscope.   [3]

Polynucleotides

The two nucleic acids are: deoxyribonucleic acid (DNA) and ribonucleic acid (RNA).

These polymers are built up from **nucleotide** monomers (Figure 6.1). DNA is a large, stable molecule that is a long-term store of genetic information. Three types of RNA use the information from DNA in the synthesis of polypeptides:

- messenger RNA (mRNA)
- ribosomal RNA (rRNA)
- transfer RNA (tRNA).

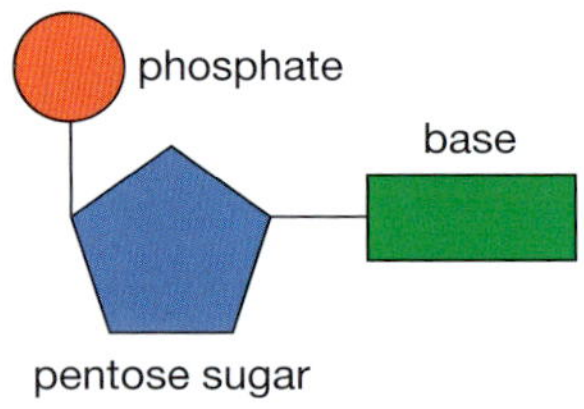

There are five different organic bases: **pyrimidine** bases have one ring composed of carbon and nitrogen atoms and the **purine** bases have two rings. Nucleotides join together to make polynucleotides by forming **phosphodiester bonds** between the phosphate group of one nucleotide and the pentose sugar of the next.

★ **Exam tip**

Do not confuse the structure of DNA with the structure of proteins. The monomers of DNA are nucleotides; the monomers of proteins are amino acids.

phosphate

base

pentose sugar

◀ **Figure 6.1** A simple diagram of a nucleotide. Different shapes are used to show the five different bases found in nucleic acids, DNA and RNA

ATP is a phosphorylated nucleotide

Adenosine triphosphate (ATP) is a phosphorylated nucleotide, which means it has a structure like that shown in Figure 6.1 with the addition of two more phosphate groups. The base is adenine and the pentose sugar is ribose (see page 59 for a diagram of ATP).

★ **Exam tip**

In RNA 'U replaces T'. Remember this as you work through the next few pages. DNA has thymine, RNA has uracil instead.

DNA and RNA

A molecule of DNA is a double helix consisting of two polynucleotides (double-stranded) that are held together by **hydrogen bonds**. The deoxyribose sugars and phosphates make up the sugar–phosphate 'backbone' of each polynucleotide with the bases projecting inwards and forming hydrogen bonds with the bases of the other polynucleotide. DNA is double-stranded in eukaryotes and prokaryotes. Some viruses have single-stranded DNA. mRNA is a single-stranded molecule. tRNA and rRNA are mostly single-stranded and have some regions with **base pairing**. The two strands shown in Figure 6.2 are **antiparallel**. The deoxyribose sugars in one strand are arranged in a 3′ to 5′ direction and in the other in a 5′ to 3′ direction.

★ **Exam tip**

ATP is the main molecule used in energy transfer in all organisms. It is also used as one of the monomers to form RNA.

💡 **Remember**

Look back at Unit 2 to revise hydrogen bonding.

★ **Exam tip**

You can expect to be asked to compare DNA and RNA and also to discuss the significance of the differences between them.

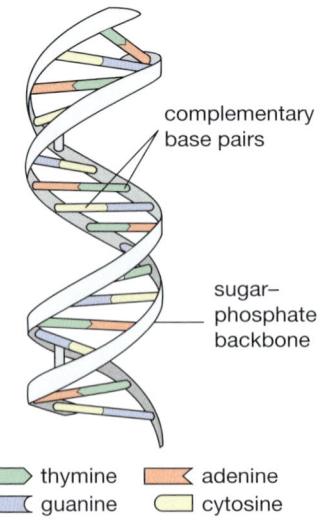

complementary base pairs

sugar–phosphate backbone

▢ thymine   ▱ adenine
▢ guanine   ▱ cytosine

▲ **Figure 6.2** The double helix structure of DNA

DNA replication

Templates and base pairing

DNA is a store of genetic information and is passed on to new cells in growth and to new generations of organisms in asexual and sexual reproduction.

The double polynucleotide structure is ideal for replication because each polynucleotide acts as a template for making a new one. This is called **semi-conservative replication**. The term template means that a copy is made by pairing nucleotide bases against an already existing strand. Each polynucleotide has a sequence of bases and within DNA you know that adenine always pairs with thymine and cytosine always pairs with guanine. The enzyme DNA polymerase joins together nucleotides that are complementary to the template strand, one at a time. This results in a a new polynucleotide with a sequence of bases complementary to the template polynucleotide. The nucleotides are joined together by phosphodiester bonds and the bases form hydrogen bonds with the template polynucleotide. There are two hydrogen bonds between base pair A–T and three between base pair C–G (Figure 6.3). Each hydrogen bond is weak, but collectively they provide stability for each molecule of DNA because the two strands are not easily separated.

Revision strategy

Make a diagram that shows the antiparallel structure of DNA. Find diagrams that show replication forks where DNA is split apart. From this, you can see how DNA polymerase that travels in the 3′ to 5′ direction along the template strand can make the leading strand as one continuous polynucleotide, but makes the lagging strand in separate fragments.

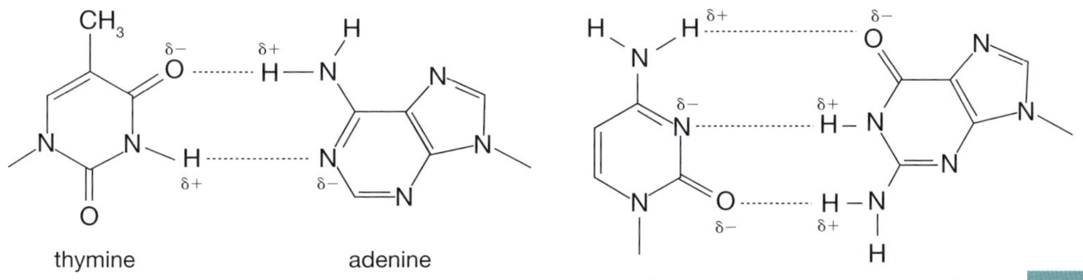

▲ **Figure 6.3** There are two hydrogen bonds between adenine (A) and thymine (T) and three between cytosine (C) and guanine (G) in DNA

Link

You can follow animations of replication at www.johnkyrk.com and at www.dnaftb.org/20.

DNA polymerase can only travel in one direction (3′ to 5′) along the template strand. This means that it makes one of the new polynucleotides (the leading strand) in one piece, but makes the other new polynucleotide (the lagging strand) in the opposite direction in separate pieces. These pieces, known as Okazaki fragments, are joined together by the enzyme DNA ligase before replication is complete.

Replication ensures that the sequence of base pairs always remains the same, although occasionally mistakes occur. These mistakes are mutations.

Protein synthesis

Protein synthesis involves the following processes:

- **transcription** of DNA in the nucleus to produce mRNA

- modification of mRNA transcripts in the nucleus by removal of introns

- activation of amino acids which involves attaching them to tRNA molecules – this occurs in the cytoplasm

- **translation** of mRNA on ribosomes to form polypeptides

- post-translational modification inside the RER and in the Golgi body.

Key terms

Protein synthesis: production of proteins in cells involving **transcription** of DNA to produce mRNA, **translation** of mRNA in ribosomes to produce **polypeptides** and post-translational changes to polypeptides to form **proteins**.

Transcription: production of mRNA by assembly of **nucleotides** on a template **polynucleotide** of DNA.

Translation: the assembly of amino acids on ribosomes using sequences of codons in mRNA to determine the sequence of amino acids in a polypeptide.

Remember

See Unit 1 to remind yourself about the cell structures that are involved in protein synthesis: ribosomes, RER and the Golgi body.

Genetic code

DNA is a store of genetic information for the synthesis of polypeptides. The sequence of bases in a length of DNA codes for the assembly of amino acids to make polypeptides. Each triplet of bases is a DNA **codon**. On mRNA each triplet is an RNA codon. There are four bases in DNA (A, T, C and G) and four in RNA (A, U, C and G) so it is possible to make 64 different codons.

There are codons for each of the 20 amino acids. Methione (Met) has only one codon (AUG), while most have two or more (see Figure 6.4). There are three triplets that do not code for any amino acid; these codons are 'stop' codons that indicate the end of a sequence of codons for a polypeptide.

The sequences of the bases in the two DNA polynucleotides relate to the sequence in mRNA (Figure 6.5). The polynucleotide along which the sequence of RNA nucleotides is assembled is the **template strand** (or transcribed strand) for transcription; the complementary polynucleotide is the non-template (non-transcribed) strand. The non-template strand has a sequence of bases, which is the same as that of the mRNA produced except that U replaces T. Figure 6.5 shows part of the base sequence of a gene and the mRNA transcript. The first sequence is part of the non-template strand of the gene, the second sequence is part of the template strand and the third sequence is part of the mRNA made during transcription.

Why 64 codons? You can count the number in the RNA wheel in Figure 6.4 or calculate it as 4^3 ($4 \times 4 \times 4$).

> ★ **Exam tip**
>
> A two-base code only specifies $4^2 = 16$ amino acids; a three-base code has $4^3 = 64$ triplets, which is many more than needed hence the description *degenerate*.

> 💡 **Remember**
>
> The genetic code is all the codons you can see in the RNA wheel. The genetic code is *not* the sequence of bases in DNA or RNA that determines the sequence of amino acids in a protein.

> ★ **Exam tip**
>
> You do not need to remember any of these codons, but you should be able to use the genetic code to find the amino acid that is coded by each codon and also the codons for any given amino acid.

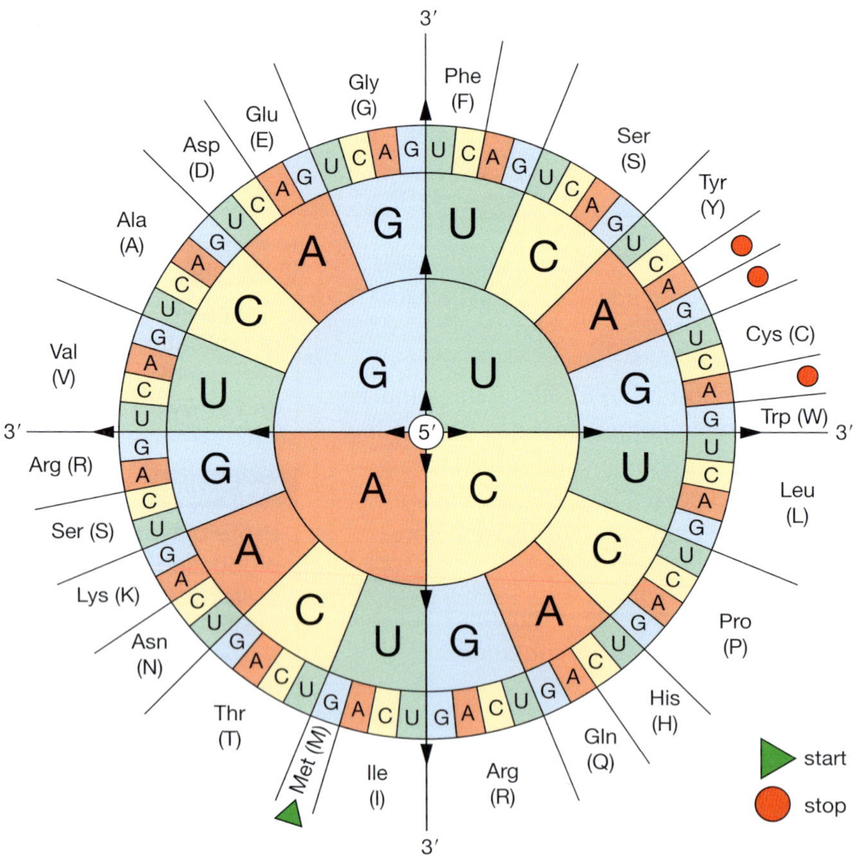

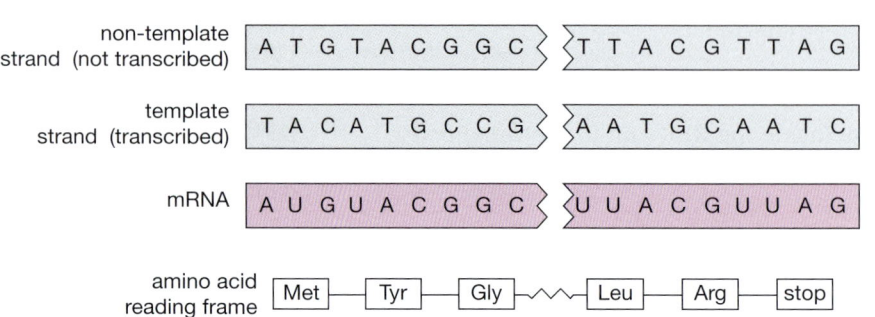

◀ **Figure 6.4** The mRNA wheel. This shows the genetic code in the form of mRNA codons (e.g. GGG for glycine (Gly)). The amino acids are identified by their three-letter and one-letter codes. When using this to find out the amino acids coded for by DNA codons on the strand that is not transcribed (non-template strand), change U to T

◀ **Figure 6.5** Follow the sequence of bases in the two polynucleotide strands of DNA and in the single mRNA polynucleotide

To use the RNA wheel, find the first base, for example, U, then the second, for example, A, and then the third, for example, C. This mRNA codon (UAC) codes for the amino acid tyrosine (Tyr). The DNA codon in the non-template strand is the same as in mRNA – TAC. Now find the complementary base sequence in the template strand of DNA – this will be ATG (remember T is used in DNA, not U).

> **As you read this paragraph** look carefully at Figure 6.5. The RNA codon UAC is the second triplet.

 **Try this... 1**

> The genetic code is described as a universal code. Explain what this means and use Figures 6.4 and 6.5 to list all the features of the code that you can. You can use your list to help answer many of the other questions in this Unit.

Transcription

Transcription occurs in the nucleus of eukaryotic cells. For transcription to occur only the section of the DNA corresponding to the gene must uncoil and the hydrogen bonds must break so that the template strand is exposed.

The enzyme **RNA polymerase** moves along the template (transcribed) strand in the 3′–5′ direction to synthesise a molecule of mRNA. The enzyme ensures that complementary base pairing occurs between the free nucleotides and the bases on the template strand so that mRNA has the same base sequence as the non-template (non-transcribed) strand. RNA polymerase catalyses the formation of phosphodiester bonds to form the sugar–phosphate backbone of mRNA.

The end product of transcription is an mRNA primary transcript. These molecules of mRNA are modified by the removal of lengths of nucleotides at intervals. These nucleotides that are not translated are called **introns**. The lengths of nucleotides that are translated are **exons**. As there are many ribosomes, the cell is able to synthesise many copies of the polypeptide at the same time, so mRNA polymerase catalyses the synthesis of many mRNA molecules from the gene. These modified mRNA transcripts travel from the nucleus, through nuclear pores and into the cytoplasm.

mRNA molecules are short-lived. A cell's requirements change from minute to minute, so the cytoplasm contains ribonuclease enzymes that catalyse the hydrolysis of phosphodiester bonds in mRNA molecules. This releases nucleotides that can be reused for synthesis of RNA.

Once in the cytoplasm, mRNA can be translated into the primary sequence of a polypeptide. Amino acids have first to be 'identified' or 'labelled' using the same three-base code. As amino acid molecules do not have bases, they are attached to molecules of tRNA in the process of **amino acid activation**.

Amino acid activation

Enzymes in the cytoplasm have active sites that accept specific amino acids and specific tRNA molecules. The enzymes recognise the specific tRNA molecule for each type of amino acid. Energy is required for the attachment of an amino acid to its tRNA molecule. This is the only stage in protein synthesis in which the identity of the amino acid is important as after this it is identified by its tRNA molecule (Figure 6.6). tRNA molecules have a shape resembling a clover leaf with:

- a site where amino acids are attached – always with the base sequence –CCA

- two 'loops' of nucleotides formed by some base pairing

- a 'loop' with an **anticodon** – the combination of three bases that identifies the amino acid.

> **Link**
>
> Transcription factors bind to the region of DNA in front of the gene known as the promoter sequence. Transcription factors 'switch on' genes during cell differentiation.

> **Try this... 2**
>
> Make a table to summarise the similarities and differences between replication and transcription.

> **Remember**
>
> This is a good place to look back to Unit 2 page 21 to remind yourself of the structure of an amino acid.

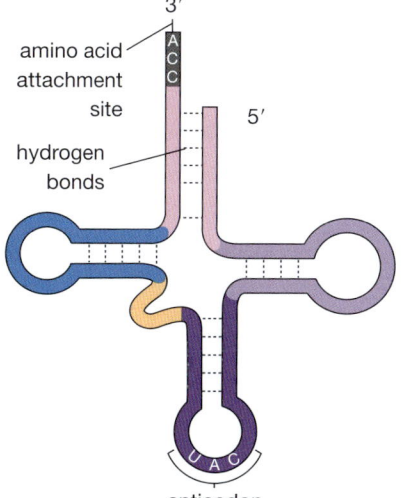

▲ **Figure 6.6** The tRNA molecule that carries methionine to ribosomes. The anticodon UAC pairs with the codon AUG on mRNA to start translation of all polypeptides

Translation

mRNA combines with the small sub-unit of a ribosome and then the large sub-unit joins so there is a 'groove' between the two. Two parts of the 'groove' allow amino acids to be brought close enough for a peptide bond to form between them:

- the A (amino-acyl) site accepts the tRNA–amino acid complex
- the P (peptidyl) site holds the lengthening polypeptide.

As you read the text, follow the stages of translation in Figure 6.7.

> ★ **Exam tip**
>
> A and P sites. A stands for amino-acyl and P for peptidyl. It is acceptable to know them as A and P sites.

To start the process, a tRNA–methionine complex enters the P site. The first codon (AUG) is the start codon and only a tRNA molecule with the anticodon UAC will form complementary base pairs with it and therefore occupy the site. The A site is now exposed and another tRNA-amino acid complex enters the site. In Figure 6.7 the tRNA carries serine. If, by chance, another tRNA–amino acid complex enters the A site, then it does not pair and does not remain in place. Now that both sites are full, the enzyme peptidyl transferase in the ribosome catalyses the formation of a peptide bond between the C-terminal of methionine and the N-terminal of serine to join the two amino acids together.

Now the ribosome moves to the third codon. The first tRNA molecule leaves the ribosome and the second one carrying the dipeptide (Met–Ser) occupies the P site. A tRNA with the anticodon UGG occupies the now empty A site and another peptide bond forms between the dipeptide and glycine.

This process continues until the ribosome reaches a stop codon. There is no tRNA with an anticodon for this, so translation stops.

After translation on ribosomes on the rough endoplasmic reticulum (RER), polypeptides move through the lumen of the RER to the Golgi body. Polypeptides are modified while inside the RER and the Golgi body. They are folded into complex tertiary structures and may be combined with other polypeptides to form proteins with quaternary structure. Polypeptides often have sugar molecules attached to form glycoproteins.

Mutation

Mutation refers to changes in DNA. A change occurs in a single cell and is passed to all the descendants of that cell by DNA replication and mitosis. **Gene mutations** occur during DNA replication during interphase of the cell cycle; these are changes to the number or sequence of base pairs.

Three ways in which the nucleotide sequence in the DNA of a gene can change:

- deletion – loss of one or more nucleotide pairs
- insertion – addition of one or more nucleotide pairs
- substitution – exchange of one or more nucleotide pairs in DNA.

> → **Try this... 3**
>
> Use Figures 6.4 and 6.5 to make diagrams to show how the deletion, addition and substitution of nucleotide pairs can change the primary structure of a peptide with seven amino acids.

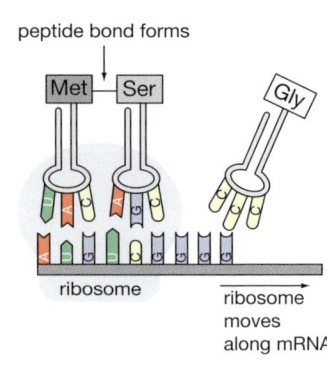

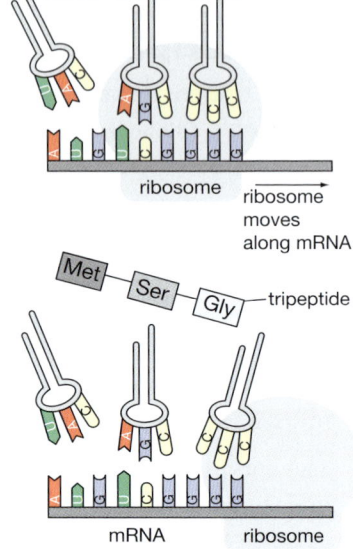

▲ **Figure 6.7** Translation

> 💡 **Remember**
>
> A codon is a three nucleotide sequence of DNA or RNA that codes for a specific amino acid. The sequence of codons in a specific gene determines the sequence of amino acids in the polypeptide that is translated.

> 🔗 **Link**
>
> Watch animations of translation, such as those at www.johnkyrk.com and www.dnaftb.org or on YouTube.

Worked Example

(a) (i) ATP is described as a phosphorylated nucleotide.

Make a simple labelled diagram of ATP.

(ii) State how ATP differs from the nucleotides in a molecule of DNA.

(b) Explain why a stable DNA molecule needs four different bases and not three.

(c) State a structural difference between each of the following pairs: ribose and deoxyribose; pyrimidine and purine; polynucleotide and polypeptide.

Answers

(a) (i)

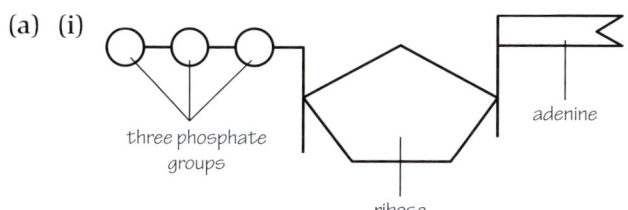

(ii) ATP has ribose and three phosphate groups whereas a nucleotide in DNA has deoxyribose and one phosphate group.

(b) DNA consists of two polynucleotide strands joined together by hydrogen bonding between complementary bases. The pairs of bases that fit together between the two backbones of the polynucleotides are A–T and C–G. The genetic code is composed of different arrangements of the four bases. If there were only three different bases then it would not be possible to pair the bases to keep the same distance between the polynucleotides along the whole molecule of DNA.

(c) Ribose has an –OH group on carbon 3; deoxyribose has –H on carbon 3. Pyrimidines have one ring whereas purines have two rings. A polynucleotide is a polymer made of nucleotide monomers; a polypeptide is a polymer made of amino acid monomers.

➜ Try this... 4

(a) State three ways in which transcription differs from replication.

The table shows the modes of action of three drugs that inhibit replication and protein synthesis.

Drug	Mode of action
A aphidicolin	inhibits DNA polymerase
R rifampicin (rifampin)	inhibits RNA polymerase
T tetracycline	prevents the attachment of t-RNA to the A site of ribosomes

(b) Explain the effect that (i) drug **A** has on replication, and (ii) drugs **R** and **T** have on protein synthesis.

(c) Drugs **R** and **T** only affect bacteria. Suggest why these drugs do not affect eukaryotic cells.

➜ Try this... 5

The enzyme RNase breaks down molecules of mRNA. The diagram shows:

• the base pairs for part of the gene that codes for RNase in the region where there is a cysteine residue (from codon 178 to codon 187)

• the corresponding sequence of amino acids in the enzyme.

GTT	ATC	CCT	AAG	ATC	CAA	TGT	CTT	CCC	CCC
CAA	TAG	GGA	TTC	TAG	GTT	ACA	GAA	GGG	GGG
V	I	P	K	I	Q	C	L	P	P

Use information from Figure 6.4 to help with your answers.

(a) With reference to the sequences above, explain why only one polynucleotide of this gene is transcribed and not both.

(b) One substitution mutation that occurs in gene *RNASET2* changes the first base of the seventh codon in the diagram from T to C.

State and explain the effects of this mutation on the enzyme RNaseT2.

⬆ Raise your grade

This question is similar to a real Paper 2 question as it deals with topics from several Units rather than just one. This is why it is important in your revision to make links between different topics.

(a) DNA and polypeptides are both polymers.

State two ways in which a molecule of DNA differs from a polypeptide. [2]

DNA is a double helix, ✔ but a polypeptide has only one 'strand' not two ✔ and it may have a helix shape but it cannot be a double helix.

> Good attempt at explaining the difference between the whole molecules. It might be easier to state the differences in the monomers (nucleotides vs amino acids) and the chemical composition (DNA has phosphate but the polypeptide does not).

(b) A length of DNA with a specific nucleotide sequence codes for a polypeptide that is part of the receptor protein for the hormone insulin. The receptor protein is a glycoprotein found in the cell surface membrane of cells in the liver, muscles and fat storage tissue.

(i) State the name given to a length of DNA that codes for a polypeptide. [1]

gene ✔

(ii) Outline how a sequence of nucleotides in DNA leads to the production of the polypeptide that is part of the receptor for insulin. [6]

The sequence of nucleotides is transcribed by RNA polymerase to form mRNA. ✔ This travels through the nuclear pores into the cytoplasm. mRNA combines with a ribosome and translation occurs. ✔ tRNA molecules bring amino acids to the ribosome and anticodons pair with complementary codons on the mRNA, ✔ e.g. the anticodon AAA pairs with the codon UUU. ✔ The amino acids are reacted together by a condensation reaction to form peptide bonds. ✔ A polypeptide forms and moves via the ER to the Golgi body ✔ where it is modified by glycosylation so it has sugars attached to some of the amino acids.

> Good answer that gives a brief overview of the whole process. The inclusion of an example of anticodon–codon binding was a good idea.

(c) Receptors for hormones such as testosterone are in the nucleus rather than on the cell surface membrane.

Suggest why the receptor for insulin is on the cell surface, but the receptor for testosterone is in the nucleus. [3]

Insulin is a globular protein and therefore water soluble as it is transported in the blood plasma, which is mostly water. ✔ Insulin cannot pass through the phospholipid bilayer and there is no channel or carrier protein for it. ✔ Therefore, cells have cell surface receptors for insulin. Testosterone is a steroid (a type of lipid) so can pass through the phospholipid bilayer by simple diffusion. ✔

> The candidate has given a very thorough answer.

Exam-style questions

1 During transcription nucleotides are assembled along the template strand of DNA to form mRNA.

In a DNA molecule, the triplet CAG on the template strand codes for the amino acid valine.

What is the base sequence of the anticodon on the tRNA to which valine becomes attached?

A CAG   B CUG

C GTC   D GUC   [1]

2 A DNA molecule is replicated to form two molecules of DNA. Which statement about the polynucleotides of the newly replicated DNA molecule is correct?

A both polynucleotides are made of newly polymerised nucleotides

B both polynucleotides contain bases from the original molecule

C one polynucleotide is new and the other was part of the original molecule

D the base pairs are conserved and have new sugar–phosphate backbones   [1]

3 The proportion of guanine in a sample of DNA is 22%. What proportion of the bases are adenine?

A 22%   B 28%

C 44%   D 56%   [1]

4 Which describes a codon?

A a part of DNA or mRNA that codes for a specific amino acid

B a part of DNA that codes for a particular polypeptide

C a part of mRNA that codes for three amino acids

D a part of a tRNA molecule that binds to mRNA   [1]

5 Some cells that secrete proteins were given the amino acid methionine labelled with ^{35}S, which is a radioactive isotope of sulfur. Which is the sequence of cell structures that would be labelled with radioactivity?

A cell surface membrane, Golgi vesicles, ribosomes

B Golgi body, lysosomes, cell surface membrane

C nucleus, rough endoplasmic reticulum, Golgi body

D ribosomes, rough endoplasmic reticulum, Golgi vesicles   [1]

6 The diagram shows the part of the process of protein synthesis that occurs in the cytoplasm of eukaryotic cells.

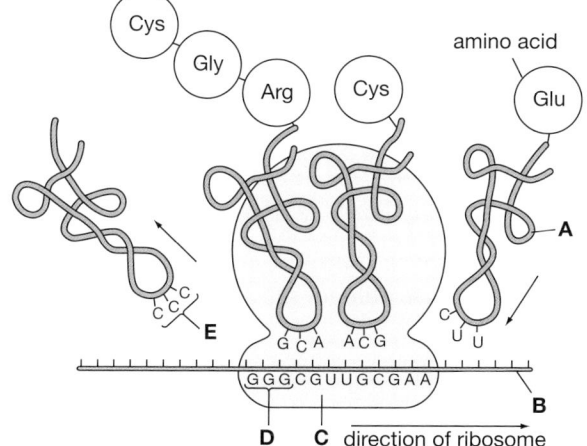

(a) Name the types of RNA labelled **A**, **B** and **C**.   [3]

(b) State the terms used to describe the groups of nucleotide bases at **D** and **E**.   [2]

(c) Explain how amino acids become arranged into the correct sequence in the primary structure of the protein. (You may refer to the diagram above to help you with your answer.)   [5]

(d) Describe three features of a polypeptide molecule that are **not** found in a DNA molecule.   [3]

7 (a) State **three** ways in which the structure of a molecule of mRNA differs from a molecule of DNA.   [3]

(b) Explain why RNA polymerase travels along a region of DNA many times in a short period of time, while DNA polymerase only travels along a region of DNA once per cell cycle.   [3]

(c) Explain the role of DNA ligase during the replication of DNA.   [3]

Knowledge check

You should be able to:

- state that xylem and phloem are tissues composed of specialised cells

- outline the roles of xylem and phloem in the life of plants

Transport of water and ions in plants

There are four aspects to transport in plants:

- absorption of water and ions from the soil

- movement of water and ions over short distances within organs (roots, stems and leaves), for example, from root hairs to xylem and from xylem to mesophyll cells in leaves

- long distance transport of xylem sap from roots to all other parts of a plant and phloem sap from leaves and storage organs to the rest of the plant

- loss of water vapour from leaves to the atmosphere.

Roots have epidermal cells with root hairs that increase the surface area for absorption.

Root hairs are near the root tips where the epidermis is permeable. They are very thin so they can extend between soil particles; they have thin cellulose cell walls and there is no cuticle, so diffusion distances are short. The cell surface membranes of root hair cells have carrier proteins and channel proteins for absorption of ions; they also have many **aquaporins**.

The concentration of ions in the soil is very low, so plants use active transport to absorb them.

Water moves from the soil down a water potential gradient by osmosis into the root hair cells mainly through the aquaporins in the cell surface membranes.

The pathway taken by water and ions from root hair cells to the xylem in the centre of the root is the one of least resistance. There are plenty of cell walls and intercellular spaces through which water and ions can pass without having to go across cell surface membranes – **apoplastic pathway**. Some water and ions will enter cells and pass from cell to cell through the interconnecting **plasmodesmata – symplastic pathway**. Some water may also travel through the tonoplast into the vacuole of each cell on its way across the cortex of the root. This **vacuolar pathway** is part of the symplastic pathway.

The central vascular tissue in roots is surrounded by the **endodermis**, a single layer of cells of the cortex that controls the movement of ions from the cortex to the xylem. The cell walls contain **suberin**, which is an impermeable, waxy substance that does not allow water and ions to flow *between* the cells. Instead, everything has to travel *through* the cytoplasm of the cells. In young roots, this suberinised band is visible in cross-sections of the root and is known as the **Casparian strip**. This allows cells of the endodermis to control what passes into the central vascular tissue.

▲ **Figure 7.1** Root hairs of thyme, *Thymus* sp. (×30)

 Link

Aquaporins, the special channel proteins for water, are described in Unit 4 (see page 40).

Remember

Facilitated diffusion and active transport both use carrier proteins. Remind yourself about these methods of movement across cell membranes in Unit 4.

Remember

At this point you should revise osmosis and water potential gradients from Unit 4.

Remember

Do *not* confuse plasmodesmata with channel proteins in cell membranes, such as aquaporins.

Movement in the stems to the leaves and the air

The gas exchange surfaces within leaves are the surfaces of the palisade and spongy mesophyll cells that are in contact with air. They are moist because water diffuses into them from the interior of cells and because water moves directly through cell walls from the xylem. Water evaporates from the water films in the cell walls. This makes the air spaces throughout the leaves fully saturated with water vapour. The relative humidity inside the air spaces is always 100%. If the atmosphere has a lower relative humidity, then water vapour will diffuse out through the stomata. This loss of water vapour from plants is **transpiration**.

Transpiration leads to the loss of large quantities of water vapour because of the extensive gas exchange surface inside leaves. When stomata are open, water vapour can easily diffuse into the atmosphere.

Transpiration pull

Loss of water vapour from the aerial surfaces of a plant causes water movement through the plant – the energy to evaporate water comes from the Sun. Transport in the xylem by **transpiration pull** is a passive process for the plant.

Water evaporates from the cell walls of mesophyll cells into the air spaces. This results in water moving out of mesophyll cells into cell walls. Cellulose is hydrophilic and attracts water by hydrogen bonding. This attraction of water to a surface where water is in contact with the air exerts a pulling action on water into the cell and through the apoplast all the way to the xylem in the leaf. This is because of the forces of cohesion between water molecules – the result of hydrogen bonding. The 'pull' from the leaves driven by the evaporation of water and the cohesive forces between water molecules is the **cohesion-tension** mechanism that results in transpiration pull.

Water molecules 'stick' together by cohesion and they also 'stick' to the cellulose lining the walls of xylem vessels by **adhesion**. Both are important in maintaining a flow of water in the narrow xylem vessels and in pulling water across the small spaces in the cell walls between xylem and other tissues.

You can explain the mechanism of water transport in xylem in steps:

- Loss of water *vapour* by diffusion, mainly through stomata although there is some loss through the cuticle (cuticular transpiration).

- Evaporation of water from the cell walls of mesophyll cells.

- Cohesion-tension acts to pull water across the apoplastic pathway from the xylem in the leaf. Water may also move down the water potential gradient from the cells to the cell surfaces. This decreases the water potential of the cells, helping to move water from the apoplast.

- Cohesion-tension acts to pull water upwards in the xylem vessels.

> **→ Try this... 2**
>
> Xerophytes are plants that are adapted to living in places where there is a shortage of water. Their leaves have various adaptations to reduce water loss.
>
> Make a list of structural features of the leaves of xerophytes. Explain how each feature helps the plants to reduce water loss. Use the terms transpiration, water potential, gradients, water vapour and diffusion in your answers.

> **→ Try this... 1**
>
> Make a flow chart to show the pathway taken from the soil, through a plant and into the atmosphere.

> **💡 Remember**
>
> This is a good place to remind yourself about hydrogen bonding from Unit 2.

Flowering plants have three organs: stem, root and leaf. All other organs are modifications of these three. **Dicotyledonous** plants have two cotyledons or 'seed leaves'. **Herbaceous** plants do not have wood in their roots and stems.

> **🔗 Link**
>
> There is more about stomata and the way they control the diffusion of gases into and out of leaves in Unit 14 page 120.

▲ **Figure 7.2** Rolling like this reduces the loss of water vapour from inside the leaves

⚙ Practical Skills

Plan diagrams of plant organs

You must be able to recognise the cross-sections of roots, stems and leaves of herbaceous dicotyledons. You are expected to draw plan diagrams to show the distribution of tissues in these sections. Microscope slides and/or photomicrographs in Paper 3 could be other species that you have not seen before.

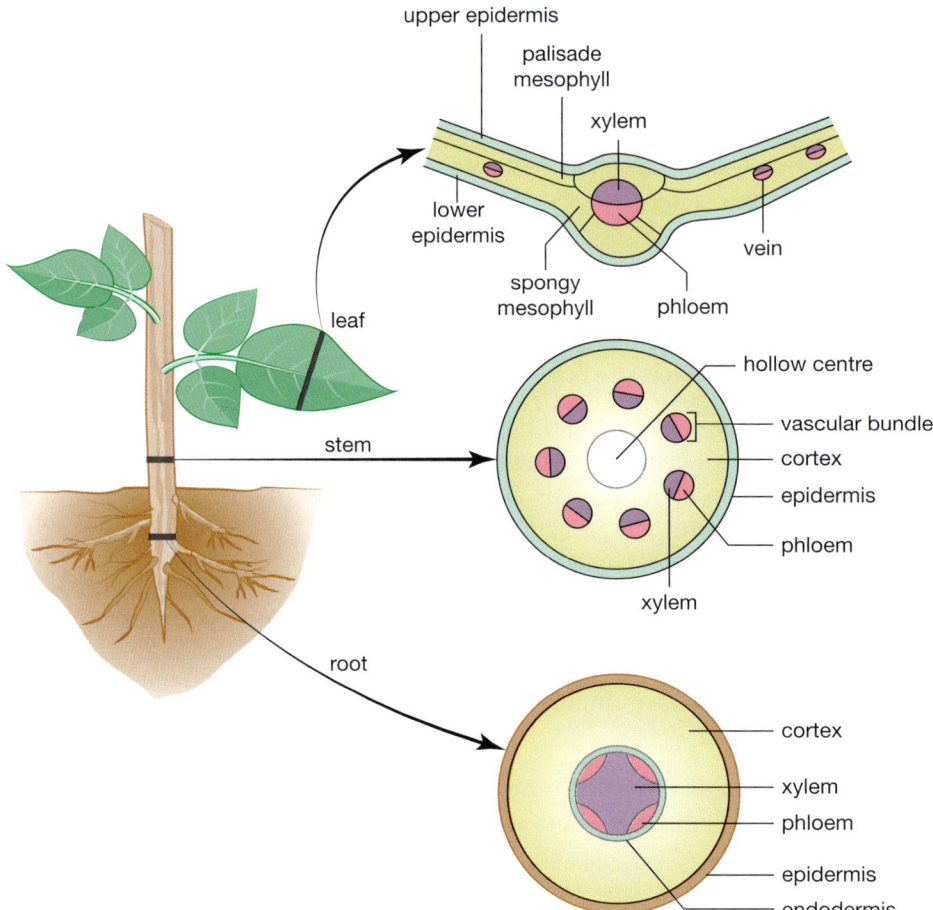

▲ **Figure 7.3** Simple plan diagrams showing the distribution of tissues in the root, stem and leaf of a herbaceous dicotyledonous plant

Exam tip

Expect to see plan diagrams in Paper 1 or Paper 2 and expect to name the different tissues shown in Figure 7.3. Do *not* draw plan diagrams like these in Paper 3 – draw what you see in the slides or photomicrographs as in Figures 7.5, 7.9 and 7.12.

🔗 Link

Plan diagrams show the distribution and relative proportions of the different tissues in organs. They never show any cells. In Unit 20, Practical skills (page 179), you will find some advice about how to draw plan diagrams.

Root

The central vascular tissue (**xylem** and **phloem**) in roots is in the centre of the root; in young roots, the xylem in the centre has a cross-like or star-like appearance.

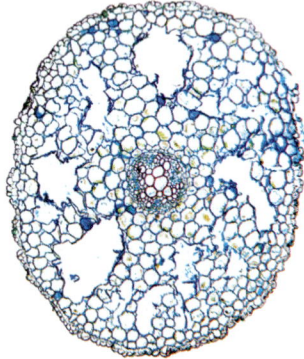

▲ **Figure 7.4** A Photomicrograph of a cross-section of a root of buttercup, *R. repens* (×25)

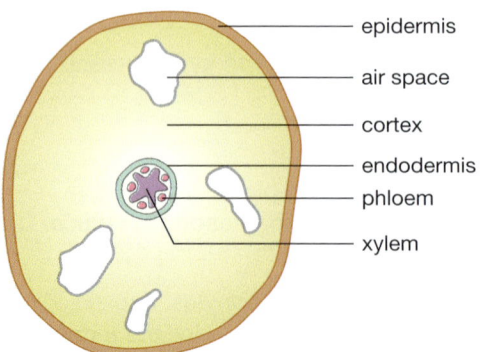

▲ **Figure 7.5** A plan diagram of the cross-sections in Figures 7.4 and 7.6 (×25)

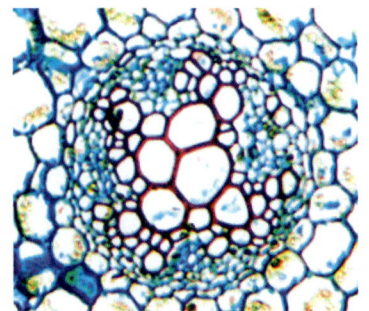

▲ **Figure 7.6** A cross-section of the central region of a root of buttercup, *R. repens* (×150)

Stem

The vascular tissue in stems is arranged into vascular bundles that are between the central pith and the outer cortex (Figures 7.7 and 7.8). Xylem is always nearer to the central part of the stem relative to the phloem. (Figure 7.9).

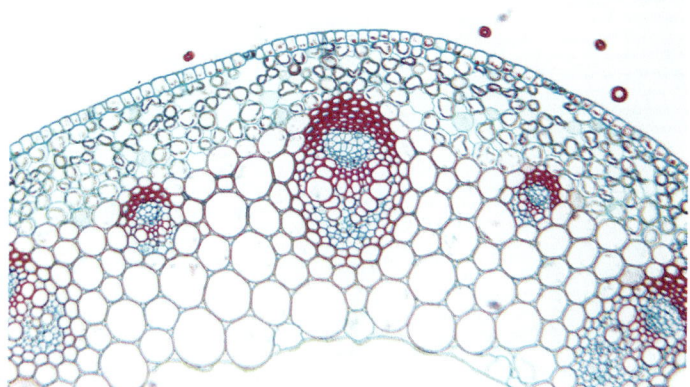

▲ **Figure 7.7** Part of a cross-section of a stem of buttercup, *R. repens*. Five vascular bundles are visible (×40)

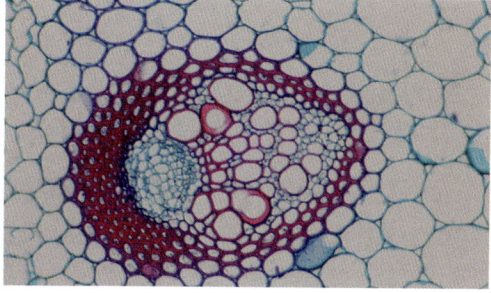

▲ **Figure 7.8** A cross-section of a vascular bundle of buttercup, *R. repens* (×80)

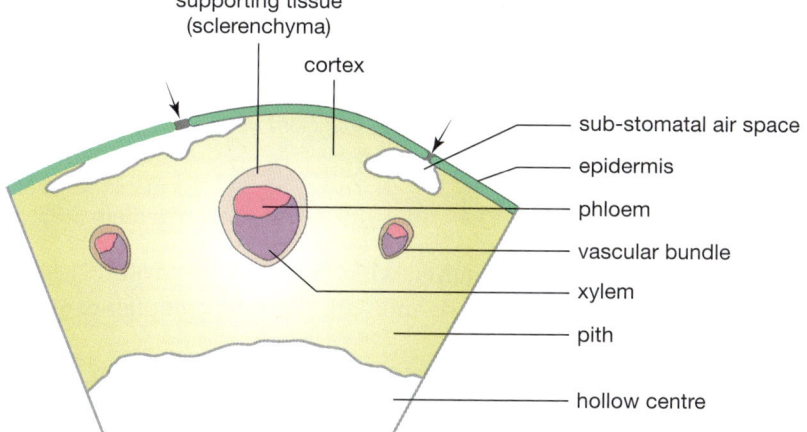

supporting tissue (sclerenchyma)

cortex

sub-stomatal air space

epidermis

phloem

vascular bundle

xylem

pith

hollow centre

▲ **Figure 7.9** A plan diagram of the cross-section in Figure 7.7. The arrows indicate the positions of stomata (×30)

Leaf

The vascular tissue in leaves is arranged into vascular bundles that are within the spongy mesophyll. The xylem is always nearer to the upper leaf surface than the phloem.

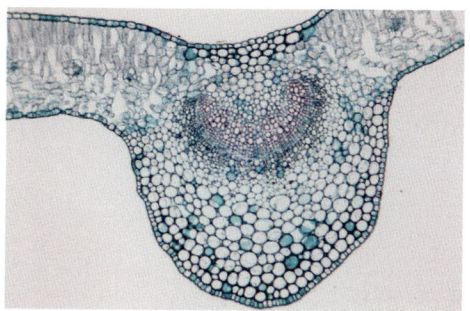

▲ **Figure 7.10** A cross-section of the central part of a leaf of privet, *Ligustrum* sp. This shows the main vein that forms the midrib – the central part of the leaf (×10)

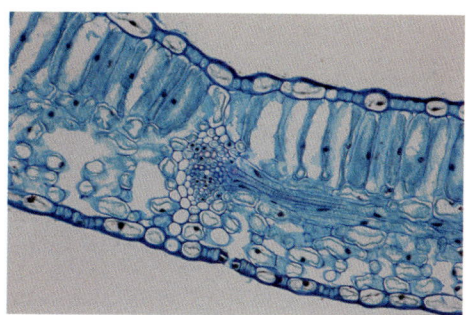

▲ **Figure 7.11** A cross-section of a leaf of *Helleborus*. The section has cut along a vein at a point where it branches. Some xylem vessels are visible to the right of the cross-section of the vein. There is an open stoma on the lower surface with the two guard cells on either side (×40)

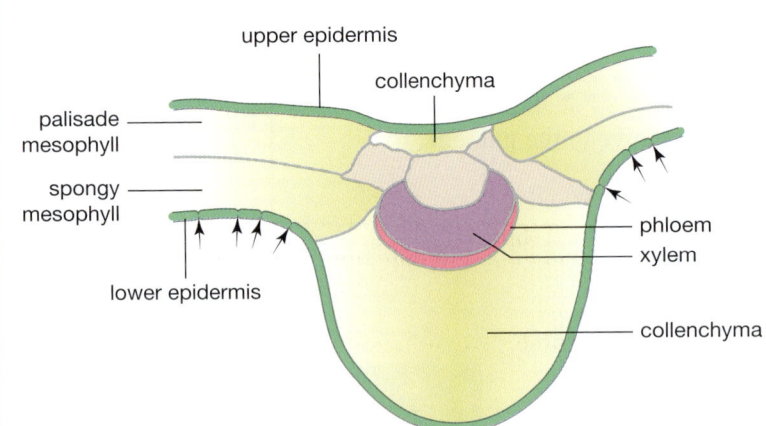

▲ **Figure 7.12** A plan diagram of the cross-section in Figure 7.10. The arrows indicate the positions of stomata (×12)

The structure of xylem vessels

You can recognise xylem vessels as they have thick cell walls, wide cells and no cell contents (Figures 7.13 and 7.14). In sections prepared for the microscope they are often stained to locate the cells with lignin. Their cell walls are often stained red or bright blue.

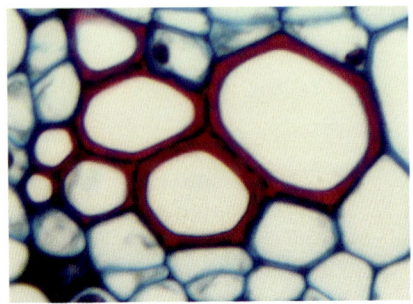

◀ **Figure 7.13** Xylem vessels from the central vascular tissue of a root in cross-section (×400)

◀ **Figure 7.14** Xylem vessels with spiral thickening in the centre of a longitudinal section of a stem (×25)

Xylem vessels are made of specialised cells, **xylem vessel elements**, which differentiate from meristematic cells. These cells thicken the side walls with cellulose and with lignin, a complex compound that waterproofs the walls and gives them strength.

The end walls are not thickened. When water starts to flow through the column of these cells, the end walls break apart to form a continuous column without any cytoplasm or end walls to create resistance. As xylem vessels are dead and have no cell contents and no cell surface membranes, they are part of the apoplastic pathway.

Adaptations of xylem vessels

Feature that makes cell walls impermeable to water so it remains in the xylem vessels:

- walls impregnated with lignin.

Features that allow flow of water throughout the plant:

- xylem vessel elements are arranged in columns, forming 'tubes' that extend from roots to leaves

- cellulose walls are hydrophilic so water molecules can form hydrogen bonds to them so that columns of water are supported.

Features that give a low resistance to the flow of water in the xylem vessels:

- wide lumen, up to 0.7 mm

- no cell contents – no membranes, cytoplasm or nucleus

- no end walls separating the xylem vessel elements

- xylem vessels are continuous columns.

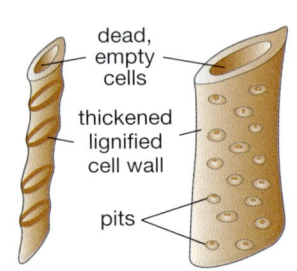

dead, empty cells

thickened lignified cell wall

pits

▲ **Figure 7.15** The adaptive features of xylem vessels

Worked Example

Figures **K1** and **K2** are photomicrographs of stained transverse sections of parts of the leaves of two different plants.

This question is based on questions in Paper 3.

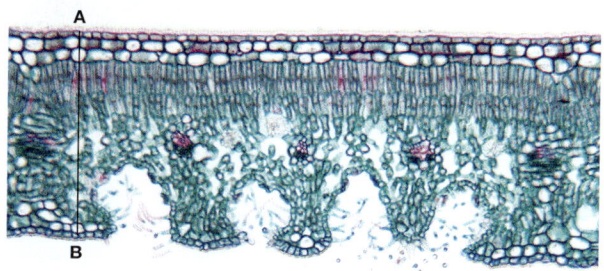

▲ **Figure K1** ×37

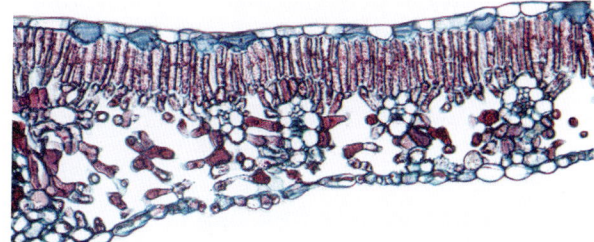

▲ **Figure K2** ×125

(a) (i) Draw a large plan diagram of the leaf shown in Figure **K1**.

   (ii) Use ruled label lines and labels to identify the upper epidermis, lower epidermis, palisade mesophyll and spongy mesophyll.

   (iii) Calculate the actual distance between the upper and lower surfaces of the leaf across the line **A–B**. Show all your working and express your answer with an appropriate unit

(b) Compare the structure of the leaves shown in Figures **K1** and **K2**.

   (i) Make a table to record **four** differences between the structure of the two leaves as visible in the photomicrographs.

   (ii) The leaf shown in Figure **K1** was taken from a plant that grows in a habitat where the supply of water is limited. Explain how **three** features of the leaf visible in Figure **K1** help the plant survive where water supply is limited.

Answers

(a) (i) and (ii)

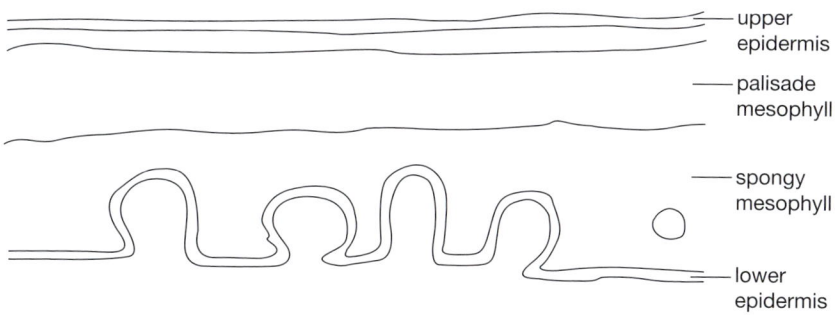

   (iii) Length of A–B on Figure **K1** = 24 mm

   Magnification = × 37

   Actual length of A–B = 24 ÷ 37 = 0.65 mm (= 650 μm)

(b) (i) An example of a suitable table.

Feature	K1	K2
infoldings on lower surface of leaf	present	absent
hairs (trichomes) on lower epidermis	present	absent
layers of cells in the palisade mesophyll	4	2
layers of cells between upper epidermis and palisade mesophyll	2	none

(ii) The three layers of thick-walled cells at the top of the leaf increase the distance for water to diffuse from the centre of the leaf to the cuticle. This reduces the movement of water and the loss by transpiration through the cuticle.

The infoldings or grooves in the lower part of the leaf create areas of high humidity. This reduces the water potential gradient between the intercellular air spaces in the leaf and the atmosphere outside the leaf. This reduces the loss of water vapour from the stomata into the air.

The hairs on the lower epidermis reduce the air movement near the stomata, which are inside the grooves. This creates a layer of still air so reducing the movement of water vapour away from the leaf.

⚙ Practical Skills

You can recognise phloem sieve tubes as their cell walls are not as thick as xylem cell walls and they are usually adjacent to the much smaller companion cell. Some sections have sieve plates (see Figure 7.16 and Figure 7.17).

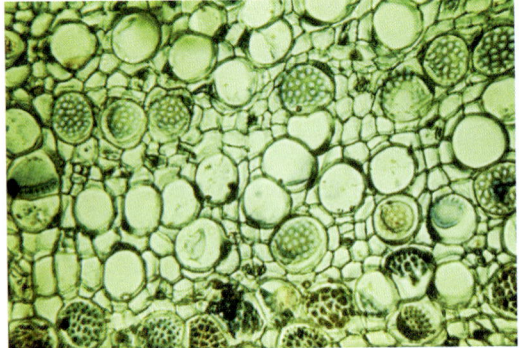

▲ **Figure 7.16** A cross-section of phloem tissue from a vascular bundle in a stem of a squash plant, *Cucurbita pepo*, showing phloem sieve tubes (×350)

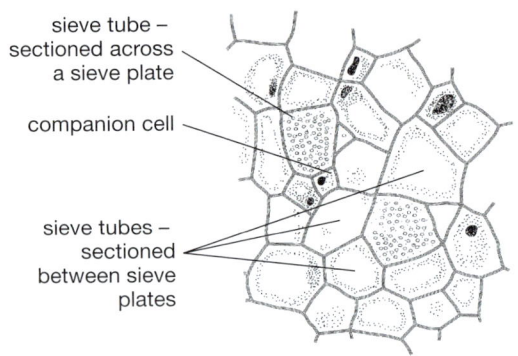

▲ **Figure 7.17** A drawing of the phloem tissue showing the position of sieve tube elements, sieve pores and companion cells (×400)

Sieve plates are perforated end walls that are thought to prevent sieve tubes expanding because of the high hydrostatic pressures that develop within them. There are many plasmodesmata between sieve tubes and companion cells in sources and sinks where assimilates, such as sucrose, are loaded and unloaded.

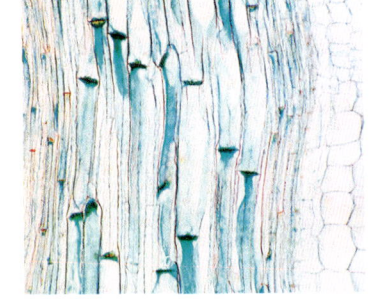

▶ **Figure 7.18** A longitudinal section of phloem tissue from *Cucurbita pepo* showing sieve tubes with sieve plates (×30)

Movement in the phloem

The movement of phloem sap from **source** to **sink** is known as **translocation** (meaning from one place to another). Phloem transports **assimilates**, which are compounds produced by the metabolism of a plant. Sucrose and amino acids are produced in mesophyll cells and transported across the leaf into the nearest fine endings of the phloem sieve tubes.

Phloem transports assimilates produced by mature, photosynthesising leaves to regions where growth occurs in roots, stems, flowers, fruits and seeds and also to storage organs, such as root and stem tubers. Storage organs store energy as starch for survival over very dry or very cold periods. When growth begins again, these stores are mobilised and sucrose and amino acids are sent to new shoots and young leaves that are not yet photosynthesising. Some organs can be both sources and sinks in phloem transport at different times in the growth of a plant.

Key terms

Source: any plant organ that makes substances and loads them into phloem, e.g. leaves.

Sink: any plant organ that unloads substances from the phloem and uses them in its metabolism, e.g. storage organs.

Assimilates: substances produced by a plant's metabolism, e.g. sucrose and amino acids.

The conducting cells in phloem form **sieve tubes**, which are made from specialised cells known as **sieve tube elements**. These cells differentiate from meristematic cells that divide longitudinally to form two cells of different sizes. The larger cells are sieve tube elements and the smaller cells are companion cells. Sieve tube elements lose their nuclei and much of the cytoplasm, but companion cells retain their nuclei and have a dense cytoplasm with many mitochondria to provide energy.

Adaptations of phloem sieve tubes

Sieve tube elements have:

- cell surface membranes that retain sucrose and other assimilates within the cells

- few cell contents to reduce resistance to flow of phloem sap

- sieve plates to hold sieve tubes together and resist any internal pressure

- sieve pores to allow ease of flow between sieve tube elements.

Companion cells have:

- many mitochondria to provide energy to move solutions into the sieve tubes

- many plasmodesmata to allow easy movement of phloem sap into and out of the sieve tubes

- pump proteins and cotransporter proteins in the cell surface membranes for absorption of sucrose from the apoplast pathway from mesophyll cells

- some plasmodesmata shared with mesophyll cells for transport of sucrose via the symplast pathway (in some species).

Mechanism of translocation

Phloem sap may move in either direction in a plant. For example, on a hot, bright day that has good conditions for photosynthesis, phloem sap moves downwards from leaves to roots and also upwards from leaves to growing points, flowers, seeds and fruits. Xylem sap moves only in one direction as it is pulled upwards by transpiration. During the life of a plant, phloem sap may travel in both directions through an individual sieve tube. When a leaf starts to grow, it is not photosynthesising but using sucrose imported from other leaves to provide its cells with energy. Later, when the leaf is photosynthesising, it becomes a net exporter of sucrose, which will then flow through sieve tubes in the opposite direction to that at the start.

There are three main principles involved with transport in the phloem:

- Sucrose and other assimilates are loaded at the source where there is a build up of hydrostatic pressure.

- A pressure gradient is responsible for movement of phloem sap through sieve tubes from source to a sink.

- Sucrose and other assimilates are unloaded at the sink so forming a low hydrostatic pressure.

The mechanism for phloem transport is **mass flow** (or **pressure flow**), which is achieved by hydrostatic pressure gradients between sources and sinks.

Key terms

Phloem sieve tube: a long column of **sieve tube elements** that transport organic compounds in plants.

Phloem sieve tube element: a cell that forms part of a sieve tube.

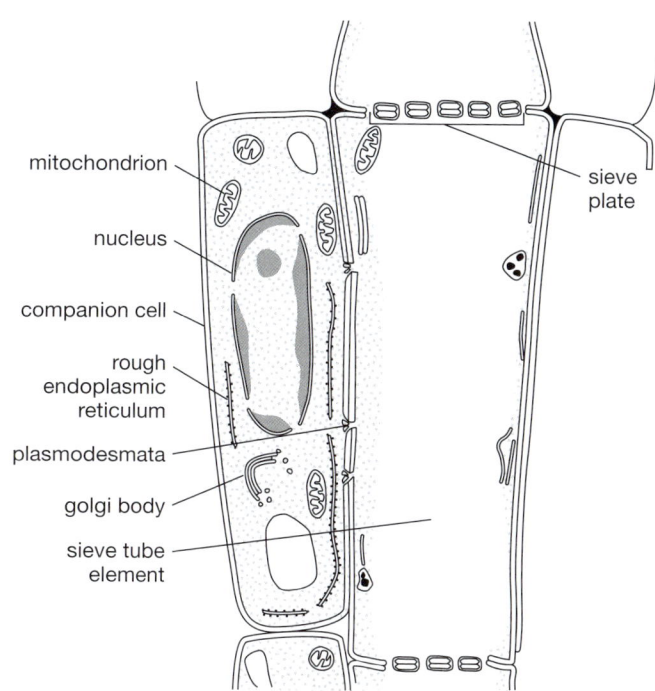

mitochondrion

nucleus

companion cell

rough endoplasmic reticulum

plasmodesmata

golgi body

sieve tube element

sieve plate

▲ **Figure 7.19** This drawing was made from transmission electron micrographs. It shows a sieve tube and a companion cell in longitudinal section

★ Exam tip

Make sure you fully understand how osmosis and water potential gradients are involved in phloem transport. Osmosis is essential for the creation of the pressure gradient between source and sink.

Key term

Mass flow: the movement of a fluid in a transport system. The fluid moves in one direction within vessels (e.g. xylem vessels and phloem sieve tubes in flowering plants).

⬆ Raise your grade

Aphids and spittlebugs (froghoppers) are small insects that have mouthparts adapted for sucking liquids. Aphids feed on phloem sap and spittlebugs feed on xylem sap.

(a) Suggest why aphids are likely to show faster growth rates than spittlebugs.   [3]

> *Aphids feed on phloem sap, which contains sucrose and amino acids.* ✔ *The sucrose provides energy to the aphids and the amino acids are used to make proteins so the aphids can grow.* ✔

> The right idea, but the candidate has not explained why spittlebugs do not grow as fast. To gain full marks the answer needs to include that xylem contains very few organic compounds to provide energy or materials for making proteins, carbohydrates, fats and nucleic acids.

(b) Ringing (also known as girdling) is used to investigate the movement of solutes in stems. A complete ring of tissue external to the xylem is removed.

The concentrations of sucrose were determined in several parts of a stem that were ringed. Samples were also taken from the same positions on the stem of an unringed control plant. The results are shown in the table.

Part of the plant where phloem sap sample taken	Concentration of sucrose / arbitrary units	
	Ringed plant	**Unringed (control) plant**
in the stem above the ring	0.60	0.43
in the stem below the ring	0.00	0.41
in the roots	0.03	0.30

(i) With reference to the table, describe the effect of ringing.   [3]

> *All the sucrose remains above the ring rather than moving downwards.* ✗

> Incorrect answer. The question implies that answers should make use of the results either by quoting them or carrying out one or more calculations with the data. The candidate could have stated that there is no sucrose below the ring, whereas in the control the concentration was 0.41 au.

(ii) Explain the effect of ringing on the distribution of sucrose.   [2]

> *Ringing removes the phloem tissue* ✔ *so sucrose does not move from the leaves (source) to the roots (sink).* ✔ *This is why there is a high concentration above the ring.*

> Correct answer that explains why there is no sucrose below the ring

(c) Explain how the radioisotope, ^{14}C, applied to leaves became incorporated into nectar in flowers and in starch grains in the roots of a plant.   [4]

> *The radioactive carbon dioxide was used by the leaves to make sugars and then sucrose,* ✔ *which is transported in the phloem.* ✔ *The sucrose passes from the leaves to the flowers to make nectar. It also passes down the phloem to the roots* ✔ *and is converted into starch and stored in starch* ✔ *grains.*

> This answer explains that phloem transports sucrose in both directions in the stem. The conversion of carbon dioxide into sucrose also gains a mark.

Exam-style questions

1 Where is the Casparian strip located in a plant?

   A   endodermis in roots

   B   epidermis in leaves

   C   xylem in stems

   D   phloem in leaves   [1]

2 The table shows the water potentials of four plant tissues.

Tissue	Water potential / MPa
A	−0.01
B	−1.07
C	−2.60
D	−3.67

   Which tissue will show very little change in mass when immersed in distilled water?   [1]

3 Companion cells in phloem tissue have carrier molecules that act as cotransporters.

   Which describes the action of this cotransporter mechanism?

   A   moving glucose into the companion cell

   B   moving hydrogen out of the companion cell

   C   moving sodium out of the companion cell

   D   moving sucrose into the companion cell   [1]

4 Which process is involved in the active loading of sucrose from mesophyll cells into phloem tissue?

   A   facilitated diffusion from companion cells to sieve tube elements

   B   active transport of potassium ions into companion cells

   C   cotransport of sucrose and hydrogen ions into companion cells

   D   exocytosis of assimilates from mesophyll cells into intercellular spaces

5 A fine glass tube was inserted into a phloem sieve tube. Phloem sap continued to drip from the glass tube for several hours. Which is responsible for this?

   A   active transport

   B   hydrostatic pressure

   C   mass flow

   D   transpiration pull

6 (a) Explain why all flowering plants that live on land lose water by transpiration.   [2]

   (b) Describe the role of endodermal cells in the root in the transport of water.   [3]

   (c) The scanning electron micrograph shows some xylem vessels.

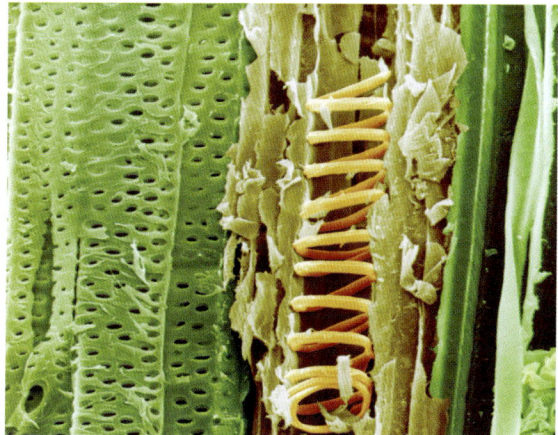

   Explain how features of xylem vessels, **visible in the SEM**, are adaptations for the movement of water over long distances.   [4]

7 (a) Flowering plants are multicellular. Explain why they need a transport system.   [3]

   (b) A molecule of sucrose moves from a mesophyll cell in a leaf to a cell in the root tuber of a sweet potato plant.

      Explain the mechanisms involved in the movement of sucrose:

      (i) from a mesophyll cell in a leaf into a companion cell   [4]

      (ii) from a sieve tube in a leaf to the root tuber.   [5]

   (c) (i) Explain the terms source and sink as applied to transport in plants.   [3]

       (ii) State two examples of sources and two examples of sinks.   [2]

   (d) Explain how transport in the phloem differs from transport in the xylem.   [3]

8 Transport in mammals

The circulatory system of mammals

The circulatory system of a mammal is a **closed double circulation** consisting of the heart, blood vessels and blood.

The heart is the pump that keeps the blood flowing through the circulation.

The double circulation has two circuits:

- **Pulmonary circulation** – blood flows from the heart to the lungs in the pulmonary arteries and returns to the heart in the pulmonary veins.

- **Systemic circulation** – blood is pumped by the heart into the aorta and then through arteries to all the organs, except the lungs; blood returns to the heart in veins which empty into the vena cava, which is the body's main vein leading into the heart.

The advantage of a double circulation is that blood is sent to different parts of the body at different pressures. Blood flows through the lungs at a much lower pressure than that in the systemic circulation, which prevents damage to the delicate capillaries in the lungs. A high pressure in the aorta means that blood is delivered to other organs at high pressures so there is an efficient supply of oxygen and nutrients.

Blood and tissue fluid

All exchanges between blood and cells occur through **tissue fluid**. These include:

- oxygen diffusing out of the blood into tissue fluid

- carbon dioxide diffusing from tissue fluid into the blood

- water and some solutes forced into tissue fluid by the pressure of the blood.

Water and substances are forced out of the blood because the pressure of the blood is higher than the pressure of the tissue fluid. This is called **pressure filtration**. Blood flows at high pressure from arteries into arterioles, which reduce the pressure so as not to damage the delicate capillaries. As blood flows through the capillaries its pressure decreases even more, which makes it possible for water to pass back into the blood plasma by osmosis. Blood contains solutes, such as albumen, which give the blood plasma a lower water potential than the tissue fluid. Albumen is a large protein molecule that cannot easily leave the blood through the capillary walls. Blood leaving capillaries enters venules and then flows into veins. Tissue fluid that does not return to the blood is drained away by the lymphatic system (Figure 8.1).

Key terms

Closed circulation: blood flows around the body within vessels.

Double circulation: blood flows through the heart twice in one complete circulation of the body.

★ Exam tip

Think of the heart as a double pump: pumping blood through the pulmonary circulation for gas exchange in the lungs and pumping blood through the systemic circulation to supply all the other organs with oxygen, nutrients, hormones and to remove waste substances, such as urea and carbon dioxide. Do not confuse a double pump with a double circulation.

★ Exam tip

Make a large diagram to show the circulatory system of a mammal. Then follow the pathway of a blood cell as it travels through organs such as the liver, intestines and kidney. This will help you to explain what is meant by a *closed double circulation*.

Key term

Tissue fluid: the extracellular fluid around all the cells of the body. It is formed by pressure filtration from the blood and removed by reabsorption into the blood and by drainage into the lymphatic system.

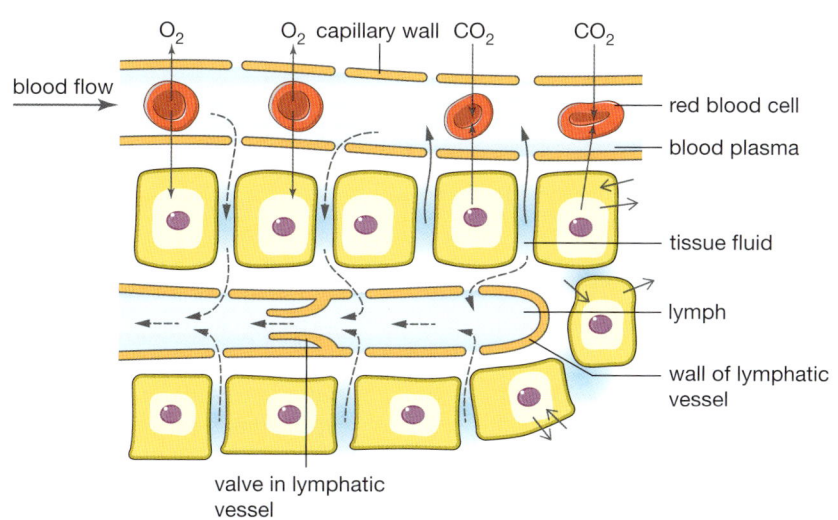

◀ **Figure 8.1** The relationship between three body fluids: blood, tissue fluid and lymph. Blood plasma is the liquid part of the blood

⟶ diffusion of O_2 and CO_2

┈▶ flow of water and solutes from blood plasma, through tissue fluid to lymph

⟶ flow of water into blood plasma by osmosis

⟶ movement of substances into and out of cells

⚙ Practical Skills

Blood cells

Take a prepared slide of mammalian blood and look carefully under low power to find the faint red or pink layer. Focus carefully, turn to high power and refocus. Take care to keep the objective lens above the cover slip while you search and focus under high power (Figure 8.2).

The nuclei of white blood cells are often stained blue. Find the three different types of white blood cell by searching across the slide. Red blood cells have no nuclei and are usually pink, often with an almost clear centre.

> ★ **Exam tip**
>
> White blood cells vary in size. If you are asked to identify these cells from a photo or a drawing, always look at the shape of their nuclei rather than their size.

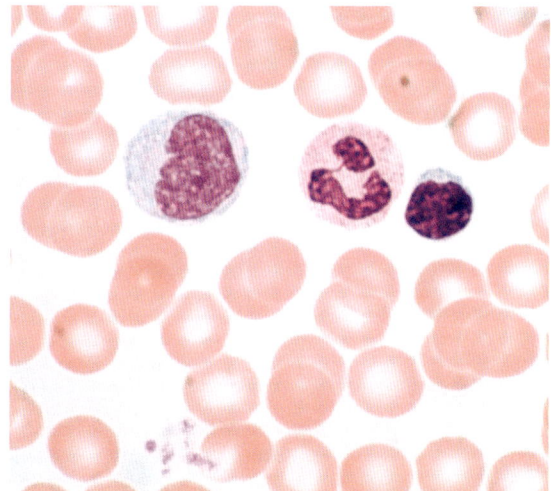

▲ **Figure 8.2** Blood cells photographed using the high power of a microscope. The nucleated cells are (from left to right) a monocyte, a neutrophil and a lymphocyte (×800)

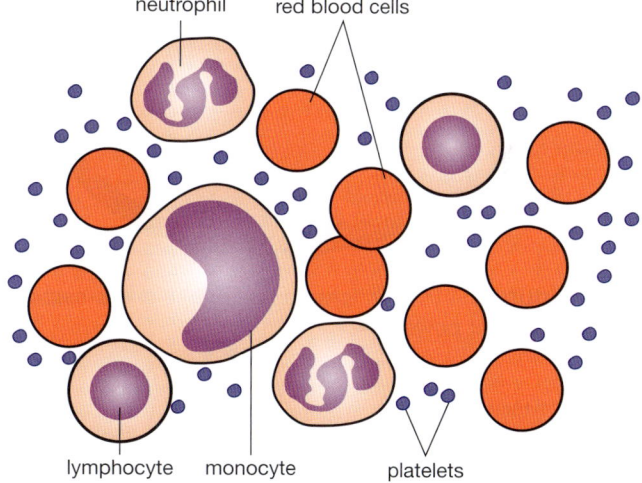

▲ **Figure 8.3** The types of blood cells shown in Figure 8.2. You should be able to recognise these in slides of blood and in photomicrographs and electron micrographs

→ **Try this... 1**

Prepare some tables to help your revision.

- Make a table to compare the four types of blood cell shown in Figures 8.2 and 8.3. You could use five columns – the first for the features you are comparing and one each for the cell types. See Table 1.1 on page 6 for the layout to use.

- Make a table to compare the composition and functions of blood and tissue fluid. For this table you need three columns headed 'features', 'blood' and 'tissue fluid'.

⚙ Practical Skills

Looking at blood vessels

You should look at microscope slides and images of the three types of blood vessels and make plan diagrams to show the tissues within their walls.

Capillaries are best viewed as photomicrographs and electron micrographs (see Figures 8.8 and 8.9).

The walls of arteries and veins have three regions:

Tunica intima (also known as tunica interna) is a single layer of endothelial cells and some elastic tissue. In images of arteries, the tunica intima often has a corrugated (or crinkly) appearance which is a result of the loss of blood pressure during the preparation of microscope slides. When filled with blood, the walls of arteries are round in cross section and smooth, and the elastic tissue is stretched.

Tunica media is formed of smooth muscle tissue, elastic fibres and collagen fibres. In arteries this is the thickest of the three regions.

Tunica adventitia (tunica externa) is the outer region composed mostly of collagen fibres with some elastic fibres.

> **★ Exam tip**
>
> Use a calibrated eyepiece graticule so your drawings have the same proportions as the structures you are studying. In Paper 3, you may have to take measurements of the blood vessels and calculate magnifications of your drawings.

Structure of arteries

There are two types of artery: elastic artery and muscular artery. Elastic arteries, such as the aorta, are close to the heart and muscular arteries are further away, delivering blood into organs. You only need to know about the structure of muscular arteries (Figures 8.4 and 8.5).

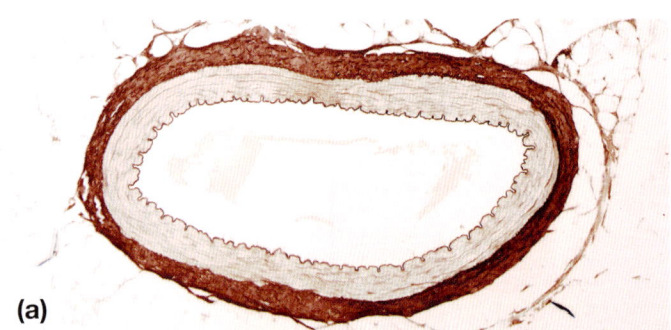 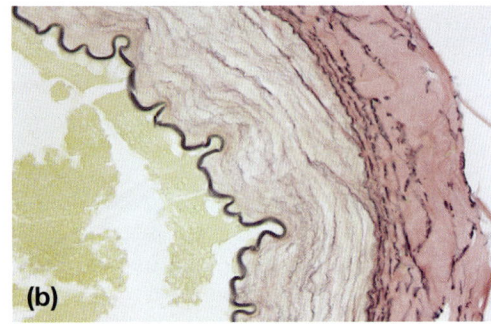

(a) **(b)**

▲ **Figure 8.4** Photomicrographs of **(a)** a cross-section of a muscular artery at low power (×12) and **(b)** detail of the wall at higher power (×40)

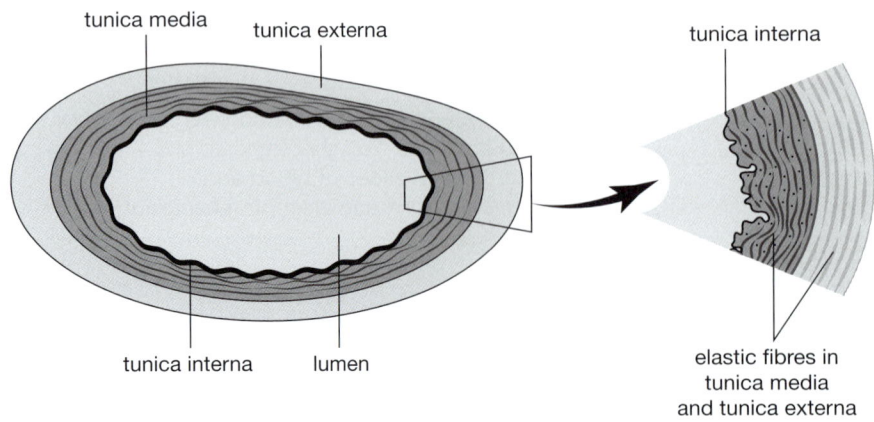

> **★ Exam tip**
>
> If you are asked to add annotations to a plan diagram, you should use them to describe what you can see. This could include the relative proportions of the layers and details of the staining or the appearance of the tissues. Do not shade your diagram and draw the lines with a sharp pencil.

▲ **Figure 8.5** Drawings of the muscular artery in Figure 8.4

Structure of veins

The blood pressure in veins is much less than in arteries so the walls are much thinner as there is far less smooth muscle and elastic tissue. Notice that veins rarely have regular shapes when prepared for the microscope, so make sure that you draw the shape that you see as carefully as possible.

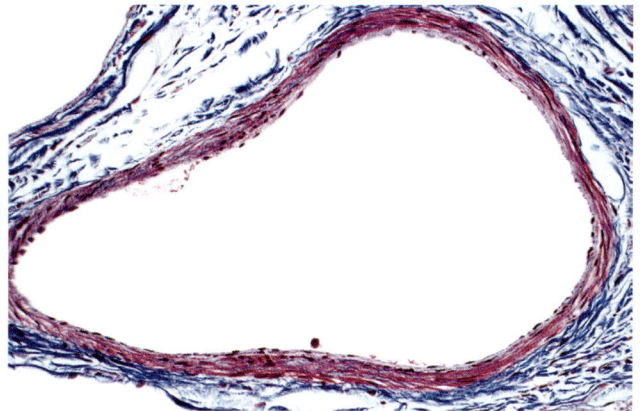

▲ **Figure 8.6** A cross-section of a vein at low power (×150)

▲ **Figure 8.7** A plan diagram of the vein in Figure 8.6

Structure of capillaries

The blood pressure in capillaries is low so that the delicate walls made of a single layer of endothelium are not damaged. The pressure at the arterial end is sufficiently high to cause water and solutes to pass from the blood into tissue fluid. The movement of water and solutes, such as glucose and amino acids, is made easier by the small pores between the endothelial cells. Oxygen and carbon dioxide pass through these pores, but can diffuse through the endothelial cells.

> ★ **Exam tip**
>
> Capillary walls are formed of endothelial cells; it is not correct to say that they have cell walls, as that is confusing them with plants.

> ★ **Exam tip**
>
> You are expected to be able to make a drawing of a capillary and it is best to practise drawing one from a TEM such as the one in Figure 8.9. See pages 180–181 for examples of drawings made from photographs.

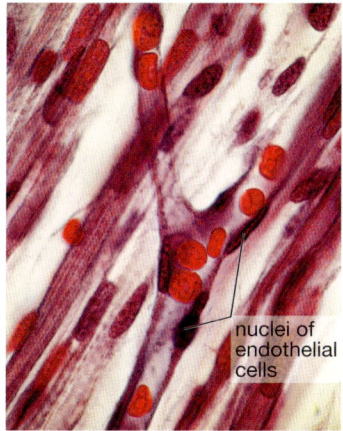

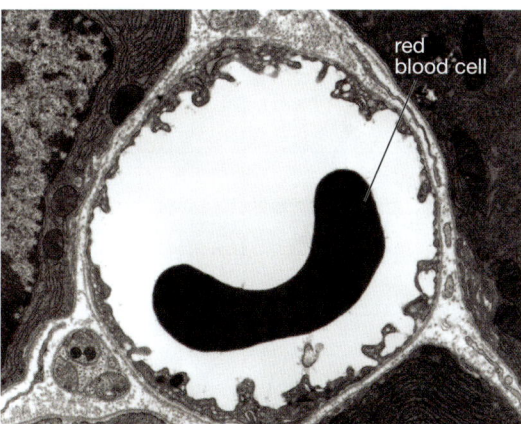

▲ **Figure 8.8** A photomicro-graph showing red blood cells moving in single file inside a capillary (×550)

▲ **Figure 8.9** TEM of a cross-section of a capillary. The diameter is about the same as that of a red blood cell (×6000)

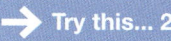 **Try this... 2**

Make a table to show how the structure of arteries, veins and capillaries is related to their functions.

Haemoglobin and the transport of oxygen

Haemoglobin is a conjugated protein with quaternary structure. The four parts of the molecule are two α-globin polypeptides and two β-globin polypeptides. Each globin is associated with a haem group. Oxygen combines loosely with the iron in the haem group. When this happens, the whole molecule changes shape, making it easier for haemoglobin to accept more oxygen. Each haemoglobin molecule can transport four molecules of oxygen to form oxyhaemoglobin:

$$Hb + 4O_2 \rightarrow HbO_8$$

The binding of one molecule of oxygen to haemoglobin makes it easier to bind another; once the second one has bound, it makes it easier to bind the third and so on. This **cooperative binding** is responsible for the results obtained from investigations into the ability of haemoglobin to take up and supply oxygen.

Partial pressure is the pressure exerted by one gas as part of a gas mixture. The concentration of oxygen in different parts of the body can be equated with partial pressures in the atmosphere. The concentrations of oxygen in tissues are much lower as the oxygen is being used in respiration.

Tissues	Partial pressure of oxygen (pO_2)/kPa
alveolar air in the lungs	13.5
resting muscle	5.0
active muscle, e.g. during strenuous exercise	3.5

◀ **Table 8.1** Partial pressures of oxygen in three places in the mammalian body

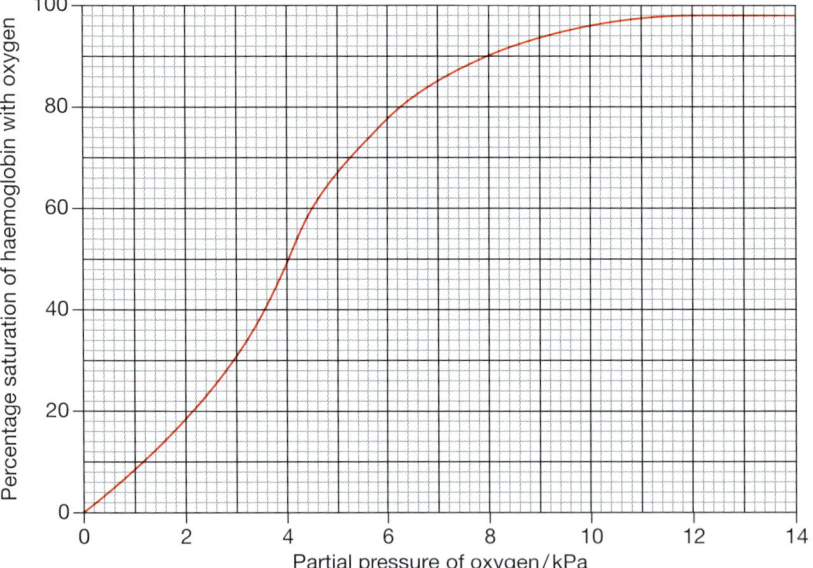

◀ **Figure 8.10** An oxygen–haemoglobin dissociation curve. Think of the x-axis as the 'availability of oxygen' and the y-axis as the 'affinity of haemoglobin for oxygen'

You need to know how changes in the availability of oxygen influence the oxygen-carrying capacity of haemoglobin in the blood.

Figure 8.10 is an oxygen–haemoglobin *dissociation* curve because you start at the right with loading of blood with oxygen in the lungs and move to the left with unloading of oxygen from the blood in the tissues. From right to left, oxygen *dissociates* from haemoglobin. The graph shows the results of an experiment to investigate the response of haemoglobin to different concentrations of oxygen. The steep part of the line coincides with the partial pressures of oxygen in respiring tissues where oxyhaemoglobin dissociates to provide them with oxygen (5.0 kPa down to about 3.5 kPa). A slight decrease in the pO_2 in the tissues stimulates much dissociation, so oxyhaemoglobin gives its oxygen to the tissues.

Link

Search online for 'haemoglobin animated images' to help understand the structure and function of this protein.

Link

See Unit 9 for details of gas exchange in the lungs.

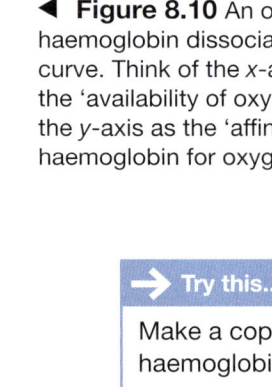

Try this... 3

Make a copy of the oxygen–haemoglobin dissociation curve on a piece of graph paper. You can annotate your graph to show which part is equivalent to loading in the lungs (about 13.3 kPa) and which part is equivalent to unloading in the tissues (5.0–3.5 kPa). Use it to practise using this graph to read off percentage saturations at specific partial pressures of oxygen.

Exam tip

Carbon dioxide must pass through five cell surface membranes to move from red blood cells to the alveoli.

Haemoglobin and the transport of carbon dioxide

Carbon dioxide diffuses into blood plasma from respiring cells. It is highly soluble in water and about 5% of carbon dioxide transported in the blood dissolves in the plasma. Some also reacts with water in the plasma to form hydrogen carbonate ions, but this is a slow reaction as it is not catalysed by an enzyme. Most of the carbon dioxide diffuses down its concentration gradient into red blood cells.

About 10% of the carbon dioxide in the blood enters red blood cells and combines with the $-NH_2$ terminals of the polypeptides that make up haemoglobin to form **carbaminohaemoglobin**.

Red blood cells contain the enzyme **carbonic anhydrase** which catalyses the following reaction to form carbonic acid which then dissociates:

$$CO_2 + H_2O \xrightarrow{\text{carbonic anhydrase}} H_2CO_3 \rightarrow H^+ + HCO_3^-$$

- **Hydrogen carbonate ions** (HCO_3^-): these ions accumulate inside the cytoplasm of the red blood cells as they travel along capillaries in respiring tissues. Their concentration is greater than that in the plasma so they diffuse out of the cells through specialised channel proteins into the plasma. About 85% of the carbon dioxide transported in the blood is carried as hydrogencarbonate ions in the plasma, where they associate with sodium ions and form part of the buffer system that maintains the blood at a constant pH.

- **Hydrogen ions:** to prevent accumulation of these ions in red blood cells – which would lower the pH and decrease the activity of enzymes – haemoglobin absorbs hydrogen ions to form **haemoglobinic acid** (often written as HHb) and this helps to maintain a constant pH. This lowers the affinity of haemoglobin for oxygen and promotes the dissociation of oxyhaemoglobin. This is key to understanding the effect that carbon dioxide has on the unloading of oxygen from oxyhaemoglobin in respiring tissues. When the rate of respiration increases – as it does in muscle tissue during exercise – there are more hydrogen ions produced in the red blood cells, more are absorbed by haemoglobin so more oxygen is released. The increase in carbon dioxide in the blood stimulates:

  - the release of *more* oxygen, which allows
  - *more* aerobic respiration to occur.

Unloading carbon dioxide from the blood

When the blood reaches the lungs, all the events described above go into reverse. There is a low concentration of carbon dioxide in the alveoli so some carbon dioxide starts diffusing out of the blood. Also, there is a high concentration of oxygen in the alveoli and this diffuses into the red blood cells. At high concentrations of oxygen, haemoglobin has a higher affinity for oxygen than hydrogen ions, so these leave HHb and provide a substrate for the reaction catalysed by carbonic anhydrase:

$$H^+ + HCO_3^- \xrightarrow{\text{carbonic anhydrase}} H_2CO_3 \rightarrow H_2O + CO_2$$

The carbon dioxide diffuses down its concentration gradient out of the red blood cells and into the alveoli.

★ **Exam tip**

Carbonic anhydrase is one of the fastest acting enzymes. Its turnover number is $600\,000\,s^{-1}$ which means it can process 600 000 molecules of carbon dioxide in one second.

★ **Exam tip**

Look carefully at the oxygen dissociation curves in Question 5 on page 81 and re-read the paragraphs about loading blood with carbon dioxide. Notice where the word more is used. Oxyhaemoglobin unloads oxygen in tissues because of the low pO_2, but if the pCO_2 in the tissues increases, this stimulates it to unload even more. Use the word 'more' when explaining this effect.

★ **Exam tip**

This extra dissociation of oxyhaemoglobin reduces the reliance on anaerobic respiration, which would lead to production of lactate and eventually to fatigue.

The effect of carbon dioxide on the saturation of haemoglobin with oxygen can be seen in the graph on page 81. The curve is shifted to the right. This effect is known as the **Bohr effect**. Use a ruler to study this graph more carefully. You can see that the result of increasing the pCO_2 from 2.7 to 10.7 kPa is to shift the curve to the right. But the important point about this is the difference between the saturation at *each* partial pressure of oxygen. To see this, put a ruler at a partial pressure of oxygen corresponding to that in the tissues. You could choose any partial pressure between 3 and 5 kPa on the x-axis. Put your ruler vertically and read off the values from the y-axis. The saturation with oxygen is less when more carbon dioxide is present. This means that oxyhaemoglobin unloads *more* oxygen than when the pCO_2 is less.

The heart

The heart consists of two pumps working in series. Deoxygenated blood flows into the right side of the heart, which pumps it into the pulmonary circulation; oxygenated blood returns from the lungs to the left side of the heart where it is pumped into the systemic circulation. The two sides contract and relax together at the same time.

Watch an animation of the heart showing what happens as it beats. You should see the events of **systole**, the contraction phase, and **diastole**, the relaxation phase.

> **Chloride shift**
>
> When hydrogen carbonate ions diffuse out of red blood cells, chloride ions diffuse in to maintain ionic equilibrium. When hydrogen carbonate ions diffuse into red blood cells, chloride ions diffuse out.

> ★ **Exam tip**
>
> It is a good idea to dissect a heart, or watch one being dissected, so you can see what the structures look like and to appreciate how the heart works.

Worked Example 1

The volume of blood pumped out by each ventricle is the **stroke volume**. This is between 60 and 80 cm³ at rest increasing to 200 cm³ during strenuous exercise. The **cardiac output** is the volume of blood pumped out by the left ventricle per minute.

(a) A person has a stroke volume at rest of 70 cm³. The heart rate is 75 beats per minute. Calculate the cardiac output.

(b) The cardiac output for a man doing strenuous exercise is 25 dm³ min⁻¹.

Calculate the stroke volume if the heart rate is 120 beats min⁻¹.

(c) Suggest why (i) the volumes of blood ejected by the left and right ventricles are always the same at any one time and (ii) these volumes increase during exercise.

Answers

(a) Cardiac output = (70 × 75) = 5.3 dm³ min⁻¹ (2 s.f.)

(b) Stroke volume = $\left(\dfrac{25}{120}\right)$ = 210 cm³ (2 s.f.)

(c) (i) The volume of blood pumped out by the right ventricle passes via the pulmonary circulation to the left ventricle. The same volume must be pumped by both ventricles at the same time otherwise some blood will remain in the lungs.

(ii) The total volume of oxygen delivered to the organs, especially the muscles, needs to increase to maintain aerobic respiration that supplies energy for muscle contraction. More blood is pumped by the heart to the lungs to be oxygenated and more is pumped to the rest of the body to supply oxygen. There is also increased delivery of glucose and increased removal of carbon dioxide from respiring tissues.

The cardiac cycle

Use a diagram of the circulatory system to trace the pathway taken by blood through the heart and the pulmonary and systemic circulations. Do not confuse the pathway taken by blood in the heart with the cardiac cycle, which is the changes that occur within the heart during one heartbeat.

The biggest changes in pressure occur on the left side of the heart so it is usually the left that is used to show the cardiac cycle.

> → **Try this... 4**
>
> Draw a flow chart to show the pathway taken by blood cells as they travel from the hepatic vein, that drains blood from the liver, to the hepatic artery. Annotate to show the functions of the parts of the circulatory system in the flow chart.

Worked Example 2

The graph in Figure 8.11 shows changes in blood pressure in the left side of the heart during one heartbeat. Follow the changes by putting a ruler vertically against the *y*-axis and moving it to the right.

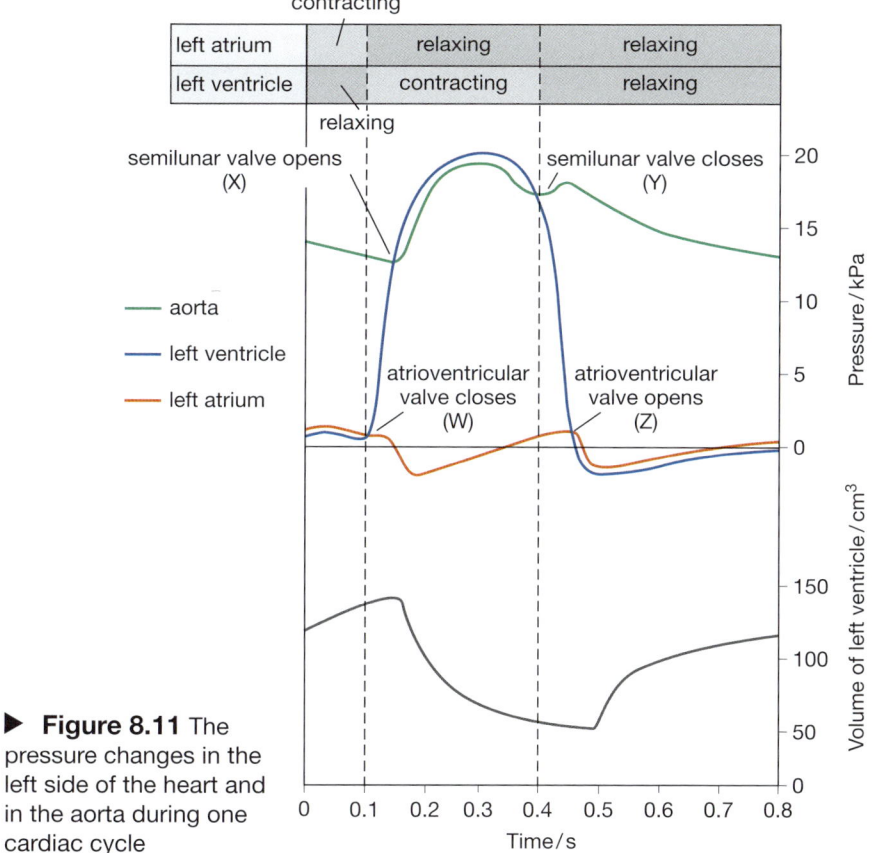

▶ **Figure 8.11** The pressure changes in the left side of the heart and in the aorta during one cardiac cycle

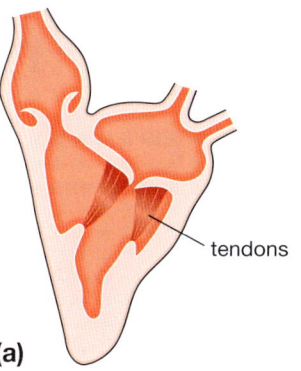

(a)

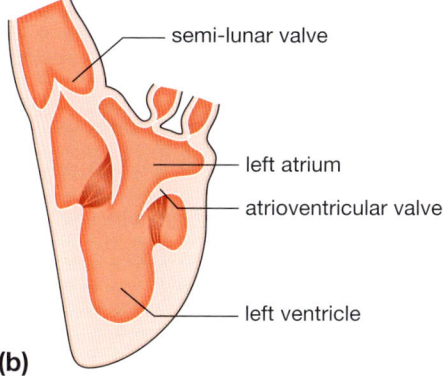

(b)

▲ **Figure 8.12** The left side of the heart at two different stages of the cardiac cycle: **(a)** ventricular systole and **(b)** atrial systole

Use Figure 8.11 to explain how changes in pressure within the heart bring about the opening and closing of the valves indicated at **W**, **X**, **Y** and **Z**.

Answers

At **W**, the pressure in the left ventricle increases above that in the left atrium. This forces the atrioventricular valve to close (Figure 8.12(a)). The blood moves under the 'flaps' of the valve and the valve tendons prevent the valve 'blowing back' into the left atrium.

At **X**, the pressure in the left ventricle increases so that it is above that of the aorta. This causes the semi-lunar valves to open so that blood flows into the aorta (Figure 8.12(a)).

At **Y**, the left ventricle is relaxing and expanding. The blood pressure decreases so that it is lower than that of blood in the aorta. The blood from the aorta fills the 'pockets' of the semi-lunar valves and they close (Figure 8.12(b)).

At **Z**, the blood pressure of the ventricle decreases to below that of blood in the left atrium so the atrioventricular valve opens (Figure 8.12(b)).

★ **Exam tip**

You should be able to interpret this graph. Try searching online for 'cardiac cycle animation' to find something to help you follow the changes in the heart. Notice how the volume of the left ventricle changes during the cycle. The volume decreases during systole and increases during diastole.

★ **Exam tip**

The graph shows that:

- at **W** and **Z** the pressures in the left ventricle and the left atrium are the same

- at **X** and **Y** the pressures in the left ventricle and the aorta are the same.

These are sometimes called 'the crossing points' in this graph of the cardiac cycle.

→ **Try this... 5**

Make a graphic organiser that will help you revise the structure and function of the heart. This could be a large annotated diagram.

→ **Try this... 6**

Make an annotated diagram of the internal structure of the heart to show how the cardiac cycle is coordinated by the SAN, AVN and Purkyne tissue.

↑ Raise your grade

(a) Mammals have a closed, double circulation.

Explain how the structure of the heart enables it to pump blood into two circulations at different pressures. [4]

> The heart is divided into two halves, separated by the septum, ✔ so that deoxygenated blood and oxygenated blood are kept separate. ✔ The pressure of blood leaving the heart is caused by the thickness of the cardiac muscle. The thicker the muscle the greater the pressure. The left ventricle has a thicker wall ✔ and pumps blood at a much higher pressure into the systemic circulation than the right ventricle, ✔ which pumps blood into the pulmonary circulation.

> Correct answer. The candidate has answered each aspect of the circulation given in the question. It was a good idea to start by explaining the role of the septum.

(b) The drawing on the left was made from a photomicrograph of mammalian blood. The drawing shows two white blood cells and some red blood cells. On the right is a TEM of a neutrophil.

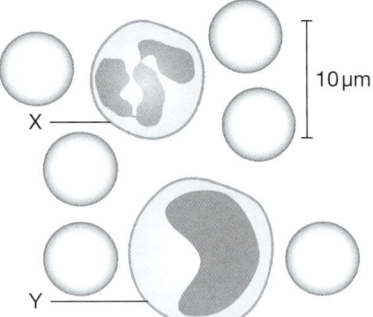
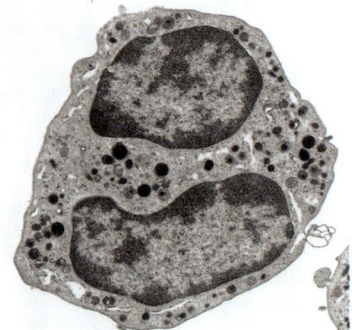

(i) Calculate the magnification of the drawing. Show your working and express your answer to the nearest whole number. [2]

> The length of the scale bar is 1.5 cm. This = 1500 μm. ✘ The magnification = $\frac{1500}{10}$ = ×150 ✔

> The candidate measured the length of the scale bar in centimetres and incorrectly multiplied by 1000 to give micrometres (there are 10 000 μm in a cm). It is much better to measure in millimetres, not in centimetres. The actual magnification = ×1500. One mark has been awarded for showing that the measurement made from the image should be divided by the actual measurement from the scale bar.

(ii) Suggest why the nucleus in the TEM of the neutrophil has a different appearance to the nucleus in cell **X** in the drawing. [2]

> Specimens for the TEM are cut so they are very thin. The drawing has been made from a blood sample put on a slide for the light microscope. ✔ In **X** you can see the links between the three parts of the nucleus (neutrophils have lobed nuclei) but they are not present in the thin section for the TEM. ✔ The resolution of the TEM is also greater than the LM so you can see more detail.

> A good answer that makes use of information from Unit 1 on microscopy.

(iii) State the names of the cells labelled X and Y and give a reason for each of your answers. [4]

> The cells are white blood cells and they protect the body against infections. They have nuclei unlike the surrounding red blood cells.

> The candidate has misread the question. There are two cells to be named: Cell **X** is a neutrophil and Cell **Y** is a monocyte. This is because **X** has a lobed nucleus, **Y** has a kidney bean-shaped nucleus.

Exam-style questions

1 The following are found in the walls of blood vessels.

   1   collagen fibres

   2   elastic fibres

   3   endothelial cells

   4   smooth muscle cells   [1]

  Which are found in the walls of veins?

  A **1, 2, 3** and **4**

  B **1** and **2** only

  C **3** and **4** only

  D **1** and **4** only   [1]

2 During which stage in the cardiac cycle do semi-lunar valves at the base of the pulmonary artery open?

  A atrial diastole

  B atrial systole

  C ventricular diastole

  D ventricular systole   [1]

3 Which describes the enzyme carbonic anhydrase?

	Site of action	Substrate	Product(s)
A	blood plasma	carbon dioxide and water	hydrogen carbonate ions
B	blood plasma	haemoglobin and oxygen	oxyhaemoglobin
C	cytoplasm of red blood cells	carbon dioxide and water	carbonic acid
D	cytoplasm of red blood cells	haemoglobin and carbon dioxide	carbaminohaemo-globin

      [1]

4 Which part of the circulation contains oxygenated blood?

  A pulmonary arteries

  B right atrium

  C pulmonary veins

  D vena cava   [1]

5 (a) Explain why haemoglobin is described as a protein with quaternary structure.   [2]

  (b) One of the functions of blood is to transport carbon dioxide.

     Outline what happens to carbon dioxide when it enters the blood from respiring cells so that it can be transported to the lungs.   [5]

  (c) The graph shows the effect of two partial pressures of carbon dioxide on the oxygen dissociation curve for haemoglobin.

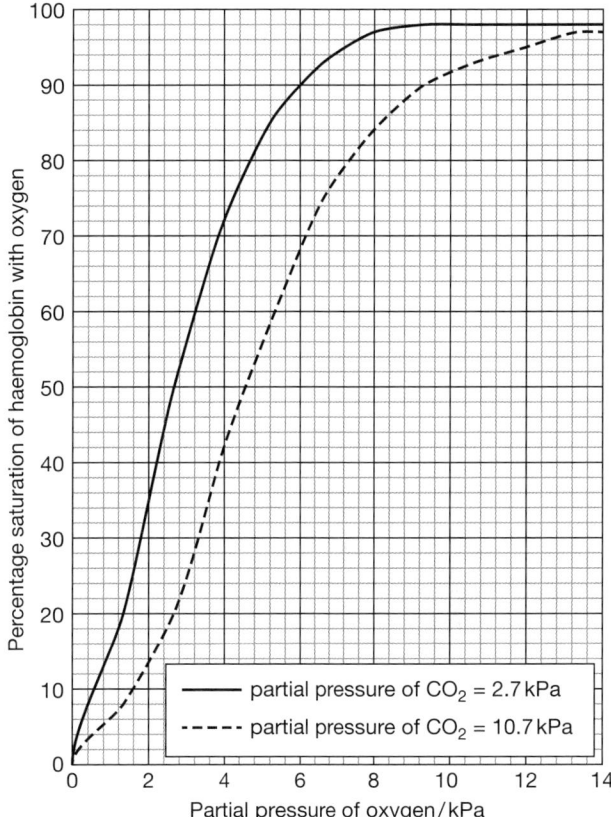

     State the percentage saturation of haemoglobin with oxygen at a pO_2 of 4.0 kPa at the two partial pressures of carbon dioxide, 2.7 kPa and 10.7 kPa.   [1]

  (d) (i) State the name of the effect of increasing pCO_2 on the saturation of haemoglobin with oxygen.   [1]

      (ii) Explain how the effect you have named in (i) ensures efficient delivery of oxygen to tissues during exercise.   [4]

9 Gas exchange

The gas exchange system

You should be able to locate the organs that comprise the gas exchange system. Make sure that you can do this by using diagrams from text books and web sites.

The trachea, the two bronchi entering the lungs and the bronchioles form the airways of the gas exchange system. The trachea branches to form two bronchi. Bronchi have a similar structure to the trachea, but the cartilage is in blocks in the walls of the bronchi instead of in rings as it is in the trachea. Bronchioles have no cartilage.

The airways allow the uninterrupted flow of air into and out of the lungs. To do this they must be kept open and be able to respond to demands for an increased oxygen supply by widening when necessary.

The airways also protect the gas exchange surface. The lining of the airways is formed by ciliated epithelium that contains goblet cells. Beneath the epithelium there are mucous glands. Goblet cells and mucous glands secrete mucus onto the surface of the epithelium to trap any small particles – including pathogens, such as bacteria, viruses and fungal spores – that have passed the hairs in the nose.

> **→ Try this... 1**
>
> Make a large copy of the diagram in Question 5 on page 85 in the middle of a large piece of paper. Add labels to the diagram. Annotate the diagram to explain how gas exchange occurs in the lungs.

> **→ Try this... 2**
>
> Make a list of all the cell types in the mammalian gas exchange system. Describe the distribution of these cells. State the function of each cell type. Explain how these cells are adapted to the functions they perform in this system. You could present all your information in a table or as a large chart.

Gas exchange in the alveolus

Alveoli are tiny air-filled sacs, adapted for the efficient exchange of gases by diffusion between the air and blood capillaries. This requires a **short diffusion distance** (less than $0.3\,\mu m$), a **large surface area** and a **steep concentration gradient**.

Breathing ventilates the alveoli, maintaining near constant concentrations of oxygen and carbon dioxide in alveolar air. Blood flows through capillaries in the lungs, bringing a constant supply of deoxygenated blood. Ventilation and blood flow combine to maintain a steep concentration gradient for oxygen between the blood and alveolar air. The same is also true for carbon dioxide, although the concentration gradient is not as steep as it is for oxygen.

> **★ Exam tip**
>
> In this Unit, you do not need to know how the breathing movements ventilate the lungs.

> **★ Exam tip**
>
> Do not confuse breathing and gas exchange with respiration, which is the chemical processes that occur inside cells to transfer energy from molecules such as glucose and fat to ATP.

> **🔗 Link**
>
> See Unit 10 for the different types of pathogen and the ways in which they are transmitted from person to person. The pathogen that causes TB is transmitted through the air in droplets of water.

> **💡 Remember**
>
> In the lungs, oxygen diffuses into the blood, carbon dioxide diffuses out of the blood.

⚙ Practical Skills

Making plan diagrams of the trachea and lungs

Study prepared slides and images of the trachea and the lungs. In sections of a lung look for sections through a bronchus, bronchioles, alveoli, arteries, veins and capillaries. Using the high power of your microscope find all the cells and tissues in the list you made for *Try this... 2* (page 82).

You should be able to make plan diagrams of:

- the trachea, to show the distribution of the tissues

- the lungs, to show bronchi, bronchioles, branches of the pulmonary artery and vein, and the alveoli.

You must be able to recognise the different cells and tissues. Always draw what you see, not what you remember drawing or seeing in a book.

Make drawings of representative areas in the wall of the trachea or bronchus seen with the high power of your microscope. Recognise and identify the different cell types and describe their appearance, for example, the colours that they are stained.

> ⭐ **Exam tip**
>
> When making these plan diagrams, you should not draw any cells, as explained in Unit 20, Practical skills, page 179.

> ⭐ **Exam tip**
>
> Make a list of tissues and cells that you are expected to recognise and write a description of each one. Search online for web sites that have images of human tissues and organs. You could start with 'histology guide Leeds University', although there are many to choose from.

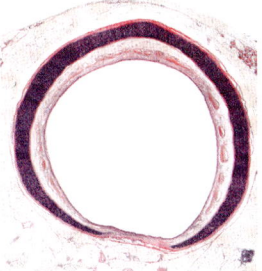

▲ **Figure 9.1** A photomicrograph of a cross section of the trachea of a small mammal

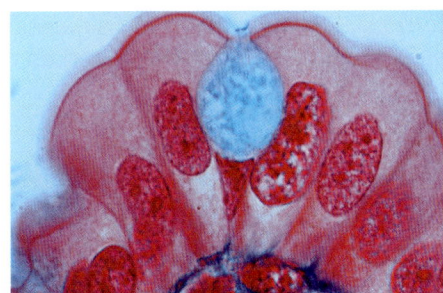

▲ **Figure 9.2** A photomicrograph showing a goblet cell from a ciliated epithelium of the bronchus

Worked Example

(a) Make a plan diagram of the cross-section of the photomicrograph of the trachea in Figure 9.1. Label the tissues shown in your drawing.

This question is based on questions in Paper 3.

(b) The actual distance across the lumen of the trachea is 3.5 mm. Calculate the magnification of your plan diagram and add this information to your drawing. Show your working.

(c) Make a drawing of the goblet cell and the two adjacent cells visible in Figure 9.2. Show on your answer to (a) the region of the trachea where goblet cells are found.

Answers

(a)

- cartilage
- ciliated epithelium with goblet cells
- fibrous tissue with mucous glands
- smooth muscle

(c)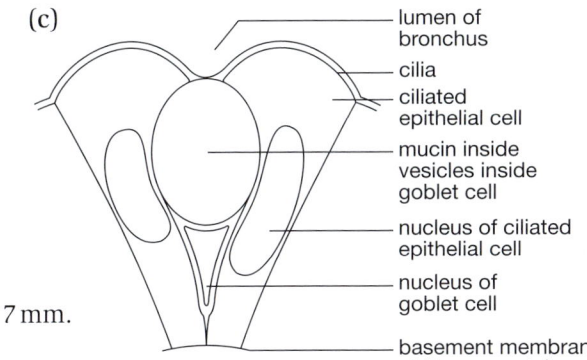

- lumen of bronchus
- cilia
- ciliated epithelial cell
- mucin inside vesicles inside goblet cell
- nucleus of ciliated epithelial cell
- nucleus of goblet cell
- basement membrane of fibrous proteins

(b) Distance across the trachea in the plan diagram is 17 mm.

$$\text{Magnification} = \frac{17}{3.5} = \times 4.9$$

↑ Raise your grade

(a) (i) Describe the structure of the tissue that forms the lining of the bronchus. [2]

The lining is made from a ciliated epithelium. ✔ This has many cells with cilia facing into the lumen. In between these cells are goblet cells that make mucus and release it onto the surface. ✔ The mucus is sticky and any small particles in the air attach to it.

> Correct answer that starts well naming the tissue and stating that goblet cells are present. This is enough to gain full marks. The function of mucus is not relevant to the question so the extra detail does not gain marks.

(ii) Explain how the distribution of cartilage in the lining of the bronchus differs from the distribution in the trachea. [2]

The cartilage in the trachea forms rings that are arranged at intervals down the length of the organ. There are no rings in the bronchus, just pieces of cartilage not organised into rings. ✔

> The candidate correctly identified the main difference between the trachea and the bronchus. However, the rings are not described as C-shaped or incomplete rings.

(b) Explain **two** ways in which the structure of an alveolus is adapted for gas exchange. [2]

1. Alveoli are lined by squamous epithelial cells which are very thin (only about 2–3 μm thick) to allow a short distance for oxygen and carbon dioxide to diffuse. ✔

2. Elastic fibres around the epithelium recoil when breathing out. Recoiling removes air so alveoli can fill with atmospheric air to maintain the gradient for oxygen. ✔

> This question asks for explanations. Answers that just state 'thin epithelial cells' and 'elastic fibres stretch and recoil' would not gain any marks. It would be better to write 'concentration gradient for oxygen'.

(c) During exercise, changes occur in the bronchi and in the arteries that supply leg muscles. Outline the changes that occur in both of these structures. [6]

The trachea widens during exercise so that more air can reach the lungs. More blood flows in an artery during exercise. This is because the muscle contracts much more to move the blood.

> The candidate has answered the question about the trachea rather than the bronchi. Even though the principle is the same, no marks are awarded. 'More air' and 'more blood' should be more precise. The candidate could refer to a greater volume per minute or to a greater speed of flow. Blood is pumped into arteries by the ventricles. The smooth muscle in arteries does *not* contract to move blood along. No marks are awarded for the answer.

(d) Macrophages and neutrophils are found within lung tissue. State the differences between these two cells. [4]

Both cells are phagocytes. Macrophages are found in tissues and are larger cells with bean-shaped nuclei. ✔ Neutrophils are found in the blood and are smaller cells with lobed nuclei ✔ (see drawing below).

nucleus

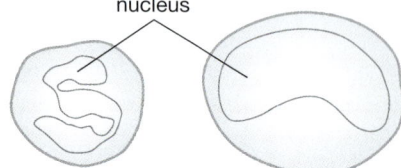

> It is a good idea to include drawings and diagrams in your answers if you can to help make it clear what you want to say.

Exam-style questions

1 The gas exchange system contains these cells and tissues:

1 cartilage

2 ciliated epithelium

3 elastic fibres

4 goblet cells

Which are found in the wall of the trachea?

A 1, 2, 3 and 4   B 1 and 3 only

C 2, 3 and 4 only   D 2 and 4 only   [1]

2 Carbon dioxide is transported in the blood in a variety of ways. Some of it is transported inside red blood cells.

How is carbon dioxide transported in red blood cells?

A carbonic acid

B carbaminohaemoglobin

C carboxyhaemoglobin

D haemoglobinic acid   [1]

3 The drawing was made from an electron micrograph of a goblet cell.

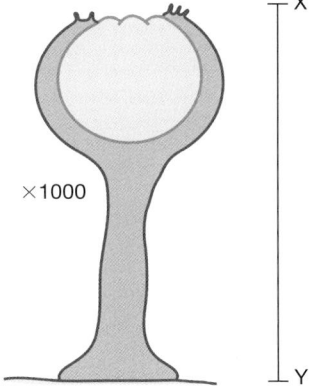

What is the actual length of the goblet cell from X to Y?

A 4.5 mm   B 4.5 µm

C 45.0 µm   D 450.0 nm   [1]

4 Which feature of the mammalian gas exchange surface is an adaptation for reducing the diffusion distance between air and blood?

A many capillaries

B moist surface

C elastic fibres

D squamous epithelial cells   [1]

5 (a) Gas exchange in mammals occurs in the alveoli. The drawing shows an alveolus and surrounding structures.

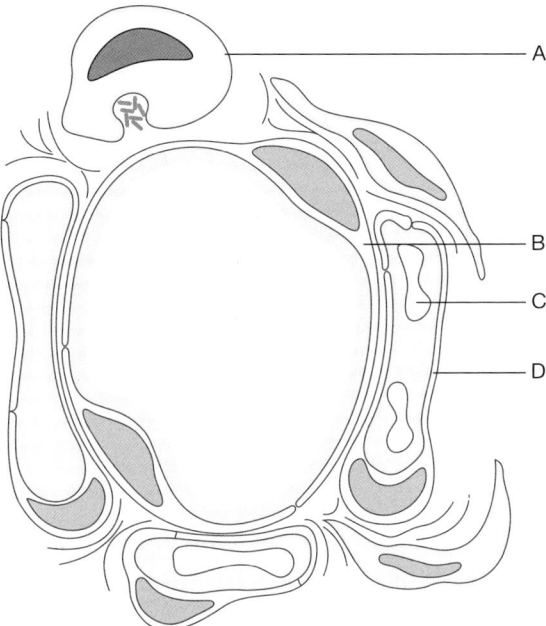

The table shows some details of four cells that are labelled in the drawing. Complete the table by:

• naming the cells

• stating the function of each cell

• stating the letter that identifies each cell.

Name of cell	Function of cell	Letter on drawing
	phagocytosis	
		B
red blood cell		
	forms the wall of the capillary	

[4]

(b) State four structural features of the trachea that are adaptations for its function. Explain how each feature is an adaptation.   [4]

Knowledge check

You should be able to:

- define the term *disease*
- state the structural features of prokaryotic cells
- state that antibiotics are a type of medicinal drug

Infectious diseases are caused by a disease-causing organism or **pathogen**. Most human pathogens are microorganisms belonging to three main types. In order of size, these are:

- viruses
- bacteria
- protoctists

Viruses are non-cellular. Bacteria are prokaryotic organisms. **Protoctists** are eukaryotic organisms. Table 10.1 lists the four infectious diseases that you need to know about.

Transmission refers to the way in which a pathogen is transferred from an **infected host** to an **uninfected host**. This is also known as the **transmission cycle** as it continues from host to host. Some pathogens only have one method of transmission, others have several methods. The factors that put most people at risk of infectious diseases are poverty and poor housing.

> ★ **Exam tip**
>
> The names of the causative organisms in Table 10.1 must be spelt correctly in exam answers.

> 💡 **Remember**
>
> This is a good opportunity to revise the similarities and differences between prokaryotes and eukaryotes. Exam questions often cover two or more units, such as Units 1 and 10.

▼ **Table 10.1**

Disease	Causative organism (pathogen)		Main method of transmission
	Type	**Name**	
malaria	protoctist	several species of *Plasmodium*, e.g. *P. falciparum, P. malariae, P. ovale, P. vivax*	insect vector – female *Anopheles* mosquito
cholera	bacterium	*Vibrio cholerae*	faecal–oral route, i.e., bacteria passed out in faeces to contaminate food and drinking water
tuberculosis (TB)	bacterium	*Mycobacterium tuberculosis*	airborne droplets of water, i.e., infected people breathe out bacteria in droplets of water which are breathed in by uninfected people
		Mycobacterium bovis	transmitted from infected cattle in unpasteurised milk
HIV/AIDS	virus	Human Immunodeficiency Virus	body fluid contact, e.g. transmitted in semen during sexual intercourse (vaginal and anal sex)

> ★ **Exam tip**
>
> Malaria is caused by several species of *Plasmodium*, for example, *P. falciparum*. The pathogens that cause malaria are transmitted by mosquitoes. Malaria is *not* caused by mosquitoes.

Worked Example 1

A risk factor is any factor that increases the chance that a person will develop a disease.

(a) Explain why cholera is categorised as an infectious disease but lung cancer is not.

(b) (i) State **two** risk factors associated with cholera.

(ii) Explain what is meant by the term *transmission* as applied to infectious diseases.

Answers

(a) Infectious diseases, such as cholera, are caused by pathogens that enter the body. Non-infectious diseases are not caused by pathogens. The cause of many cases of lung cancer is tobacco smoking.

(b) (i) No or very poor sanitation; drinking water contaminated by human faeces.

(ii) The movement of a pathogen from an infected person to a non-infected person.

The prevention and control of infectious diseases

Disease prevention uses methods that stop the transmission of pathogens to uninfected people. These methods prevent the spread of infectious diseases by breaking the transmission cycle. Vaccination is the most successful method of prevention.

Disease control uses methods that reduce the number of people who are infected, for example, during an epidemic. This also involves breaking the transmission cycle but concentrates on reducing the transfer of pathogens from people who are infected, for example, using insecticides to kill insect vectors, such as *Anopheles*.

→ Try this... 1

Use the web sites of the following organisations to compile a list of the ways in which the impact of the four infectious diseases in this unit can be reduced.

WHO; CDC; TB Alert; UNAIDS; Avert; End malaria.

Summarise the information you find as a poster, graphic organiser or electronic presentation.

Antibiotics

Antibiotics are substances produced by microorganisms (or synthesised chemically) that are used as drugs for the treatment of infectious diseases. Many antibiotics are semi-synthetic because they are modified chemically after production by microorganisms in fermenters, or they are produced entirely by chemical synthesis (although they may have been originally discovered in organisms).

Antibiotics act on bacteria in one of three ways:

- kill bacteria by causing them to burst (lysis)
- kill bacteria without causing them to burst
- stop bacteria reproducing without killing them

Antibiotics are effective against bacteria and also some fungi. They are not effective against viruses. Antibiotics have their effects by interfering in cell processes, such as replication and protein synthesis, that occur in bacteria, but *not* in viruses. Antibiotics inhibit processes that do not occur in human cells. For example, penicillin inhibits the formation of cell walls in bacteria while they are growing. Penicillin cannot act on humans as our cells do not have cell walls. **Broad spectrum antibiotics** act on a wide range of bacteria. **Narrow spectrum antibiotics** only work on a few.

★ Exam tip

You may know the terms bacteriolytic, bactericidal and bacteriostatic for these three ways. You could use technical terms, like these, in your answers if you are sure they are relevant to the questions.

💡 Remember

Recall from Unit 1 that viruses do not have the cell structures, such as ribosomes and cell wall, that are targeted by antibiotics.

Antibiotic resistance

Antibiotics are not equally effective against all bacteria. Doctors select the most effective antibiotic for each disease that they treat. Some antibiotics have no effect at all on some bacteria, others may be effective but it is best to find out before prescribing. A sample of bacteria may be taken from a patient and incubated with different antibiotics to find the most effective one to use for treatment. Alternatively, bacteria are tested to see if they have genes coding for proteins that in some way give them resistance to antibiotics.

Bacteria become resistant to antibiotics because of random mutations in DNA. Normally these mutant bacteria do not compete well with the non-mutant ('normal') forms. The normal forms are susceptible to being destroyed by antibiotics.

When someone takes an antibiotic for a bacterial infection, bacteria that are susceptible will die. In most cases, if a doctor's instructions are followed correctly, this will be all the bacteria. However, if the instructions are not followed, perhaps because people stop taking the antibiotic when they feel slightly better, then some susceptible bacteria survive and if any mutations occur these might give resistance. The next time there is an infection of this strain of bacteria, the antibiotic may not work as there are some resistant bacteria among those that have infected the body.

Antibiotic resistance is a serious problem as some bacteria, such as *M. tuberculosis*, show resistance to the drugs, including antibiotics, that are used in treatment. As bacteria become resistant, this makes treating disease very difficult. Antibiotics have been used for over 70 years, so now there are many resistant strains of pathogenic bacteria.

An alarming number of human pathogens have acquired genes to combat all the antibiotics that are presently used. This includes vancomycin, which is used as an antibiotic of 'last resort' to treat infections that cannot be cured by other antibiotics. Vancomycin resistance took 30 years to develop from its introduction. These multidrug-resistant strains are particularly common in hospitals where antibiotic use is heavy, and the patients often have weakened immune systems. One of these is methicillin-resistant *Staphylococcus aureus* or MRSA. This has caused deaths in hospital of patients with suppressed immune systems, for example, people taking immunosuppressive drugs following organ transplants.

To combat antibiotic resistance, it is important that people follow the instructions from their doctor to ensure no pathogenic bacteria are left in their bodies. Antibiotics should not be overused; for example, for treating mild complaints and some should be kept 'as a last resort' when all others have failed.

Do not confuse the resistance of bacteria to antibiotics with immunity. Bacteria become resistant to antibiotics, they do not become immune. As you will see in Unit 11, immunity involves specialised cells working together to recognise and destroy a pathogenic organism. Also note that people do not become resistant or immune to antibiotics. Some people are allergic to some antibiotics and, if so, they should not be prescribed those antibiotics.

> **Remember**
>
> Mutations in bacteria occur by changes to the base sequences of their DNA (see Unit 6 page 58).

> ★ **Exam tip**
>
> Use the index of this book to find information about transcription, translation and DNA replication. As part of your revision use the topic of *Infectious disease* to revise other areas of the syllabus for Papers 1 and 2.

> ★ **Exam tip**
>
> Anti-viral drugs are not antibiotics. Zidovudine, which is used for treatment of HIV/AIDS, and acyclovir, which is used to treat herpes, are examples of anti-viral drugs.

> ★ **Exam tip**
>
> There are more ways to reduce the impact of antibiotic resistance than given here. Search the web sites of the World Health Organization (WHO) and the Centers for Disease Control and Prevention (CDC) in the USA for more information.

→ Try this... 2

Outline how the antibiotic penicillin acts on bacteria.

Explain why antibiotics are of no use in treating viral diseases.

Suggest **three** steps that can be taken to reduce the impact of antibiotic resistance.

Worked Example 2

(a) Describe the ways in which HIV is transmitted.

Figure 10.1 shows the changes in the estimated number of people infected with HIV in the WHO Caribbean region from 1990 to 2010.

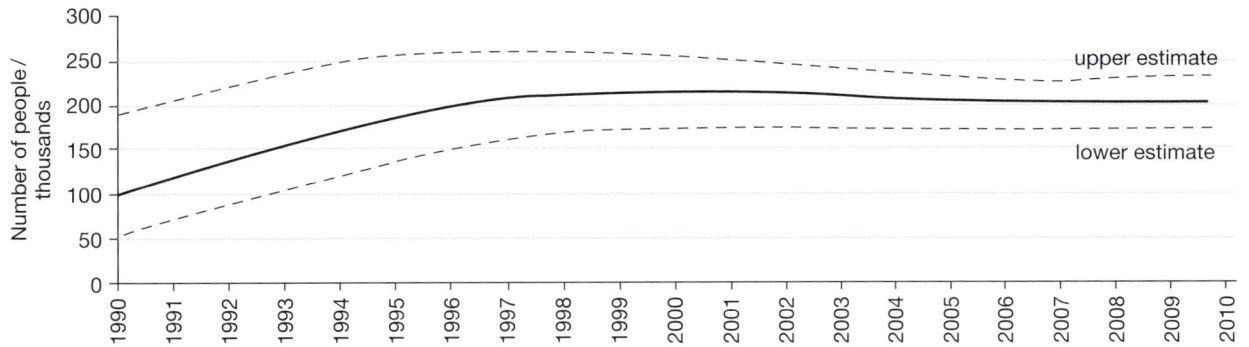

▲ **Figure 10.1**

Use Figure 10.1 to help you answer these questions.

(b) (i) Describe the changes in the estimated numbers of people with HIV infection in the Caribbean region between 1990 and 2010.

(ii) Suggest reasons for the pattern you have described.

(c) Explain why the upper and lower estimates for HIV infection have been included in the graph.

> ★ **Exam tip**
>
> This question is an example of the type of question that tests your ability to use your knowledge to analyse and interpret unfamiliar information and data.

(d) The mortality (death) rate for HIV/AIDS in the Caribbean reached a peak around 2005 and has fallen since. Suggest why the trend for mortality differs from that for prevalence shown in Figure 10.1.

(e) Discuss the problems in controlling the global spread of HIV/AIDS.

Answers

(a) HIV is transmitted by unprotected sex (vaginal and anal) and by sharing needles (e.g. by intravenous drug users). It can also be transmitted at birth from a mother to her baby when blood comes into contact.

(b) (i) The number increases from 100 000 people in 1990 to 210 000 in 1998–99 and decreases to 200 000 in 2005.

(ii) The increase could be due to increased transmission of HIV or it could be due to better diagnosis of people who are HIV positive (HIV +) or people who had been infected with HIV many years before beginning to show symptoms of infection. There is often a period of up to 10 years or more before symptoms of AIDS appear.

(c) It is difficult to find out how many people in the population of a region are HIV +. Health services differ in their success at diagnosing people who are HIV +. The numbers collected by different countries may be the result of samples of the population, for example, people who attend health clinics or hospitals. Many people who are HIV + do not show any symptoms so they may not be known to the health services.

(d) Mortality rates have fallen while the number of people living with HIV has remained constant could be due to better health care. People with HIV can be treated with drugs that prevent the decrease in number of helper T-lymphocytes so that they are not susceptible to opportunistic diseases that are likely to kill them, such as cancers, pneumonia and TB.

> ★ **Exam tip**
>
> The answer to part **(d)** includes some information from Unit 11, which is required for a complete answer.

(e) Some problems with preventing the transmission of HIV are:

Providing enough condoms for those who should use them, especially if they are poor. Educating people to use condoms and realising the dangers of not using them. Discouraging the sharing of needles between drug addicts. Countries not having enough resources to provide drugs to treat people living with HIV.

⬆ Raise your grade

The 'Roll Back Malaria' partnership is a global programme for restricting the spread of malaria established in 1998. Malaria is particularly important in Africa where trials of vaccines are currently being conducted. The genome of *Plasmodium* has been sequenced and this has made it easier to develop vaccines and drugs for controlling malaria.

The figure shows the changes in mortality from malaria between 1900 and 2014 in Africa and in the rest of the world.

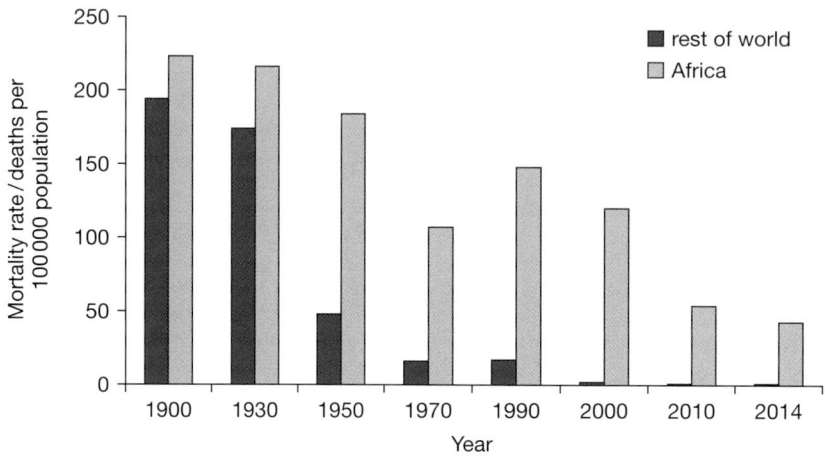

(a) Describe the trends in mortality from malaria in Africa and the rest of the world between 1900 and 2014. [4]

> Deaths from malaria have decreased greatly in the rest of the world from about 195 per 100 000 in 1900 to almost nothing in the 2000s. ✔ The mortality rate has always been higher in Africa, decreasing from over 220 to 110 per 100 000 in 1970, ✔ then it increased again to 150 in 1990 ✔ and decreased again to 40 in 2014. ✔

> Correct answer. The candidate has used words like 'increase' and 'decrease' to describe the trends rather than just stating the data, which would not be an acceptable response.

(b) Explain the trends that you have described in **(a)**. [4]

> Malaria was controlled in many countries by using insecticides to kill mosquitoes and by removing the places where mosquitoes breed. ✔ These control programmes that targeted the vector were very effective in North America and in Mediterranean countries. ✔ After about 1970, mosquitoes became resistant to insecticides and control programmes were less effective, especially in Africa where there were many wars. *Plasmodium* has also become resistant to the drugs used to control it like chloroquine. ✔ There are now drugs available based on artemisinin that are used successfully to treat cases of malaria. These are used in South-East Asia and have reduced the death rates from malaria. ✔

> Good answer. If you are asked to 'explain' you should give reasons. When there are several marks (four in this question) then you should give at least the same number of different points. Some can be further detail (e.g. chloroquine in this answer) that will often gain marks.

Exam-style questions

1 What is the name of the pathogen that causes cholera?

   A *Vibro cholera*   B *Vibro cholerae*

   C *Vibrio cholera*   D *Vibrio cholerae*   [1]

2 Four infectious diseases are:

   1   cholera

   2   HIV/AIDS

   3   malaria

   4   tuberculosis

   Which are caused by bacteria?

   A **1, 2** and **3**   B **1** and **4** only

   C **2** and **4** only   D **3** only   [1]

3 A patient in hospital had a bacterial infection that was proving difficult to treat.

A medical technician collected a sample of bacteria from the patient. The bacteria were spread over the surface of an agar plate. Six paper discs, each soaked in a solution of a different antibiotic (**1** to **6**), were placed on the agar plate. The figure shows the growth of the bacteria on the plate after 24 hours.

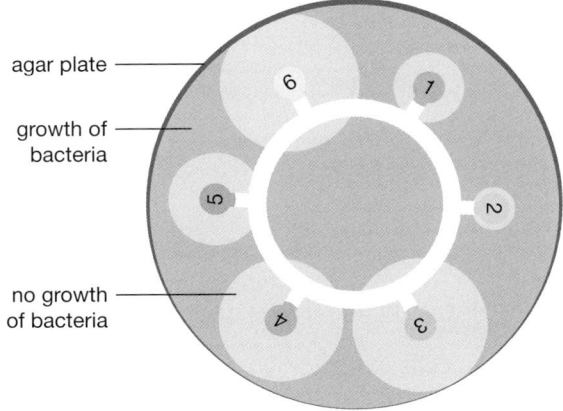

agar plate

growth of bacteria

no growth of bacteria

Which combination of antibiotics is most likely to be effective in treating the bacterial infection?

   A **1, 4** and **5**

   B **1, 2** and **6**

   C **2, 3** and **5**

   D **3, 4** and **6**   [1]

4 What is most likely to increase the risk of antibiotic resistance spreading in a population of humans?

   A an increase in the incidence of viral diseases

   B an increase in the recruitment of doctors

   C overuse of antibiotics by the population

   D successful vaccination campaigns   [1]

5 (a) State **three** ways in which the structure of *Mycobacterium tuberculosis* differs from the structure of human white blood cells.   [3]

   (b) Describe how *M. tuberculosis* is transmitted.   [2]

Drug resistance is a problem in treating TB, especially the forms of *M. tuberculosis* that are resistant to two or more of the front-line drugs. There are two forms:

* multiple drug resistant strains of tuberculosis (MDR-TB) are resistant to at least the two main drugs used to treat TB – isoniazid and rifampicin

* extensively (or extreme) drug-resistant tuberculosis (XDR-TB) has also emerged as a very serious threat to health, especially of those people who are HIV + ; these strains are resistant to first-line drugs and the drugs used to treat MDR-TB

These resistant strains of TB do not respond to the standard 6-month treatment with first-line anti-bacterial drugs and can take 2 years or more to treat with drugs that are less potent and much more expensive.

In 2019, 206 030 people with multidrug- or rifampicin-resistant TB (MDR/RR-TB) were recorded by the World Health Organization, a 10% increase from 186 883 in 2018. It is estimated that about 6 to 10% of these cases were XDR-TB, although many are unreported.

   (c) Outline how bacteria can become resistant to antibiotics.   [3]

   (d) Suggest why TB and many other infectious diseases are treated with combination therapy not a single antibiotic.   [2]

   (e) Outline the consequences of drug resistance in combating tuberculosis.   [3]

11 Immunity

The mode of action of phagocytes

Neutrophils and macrophages are phagocytes that engulf pathogens and other foreign particles by endocytosis.

→ **Try this... 1**

Figure 11.1 shows a phagocyte in action. Research the function of phagocytes. Copy the drawings and add notes about what happens at each stage. Use your knowledge from Units 1 and 10.

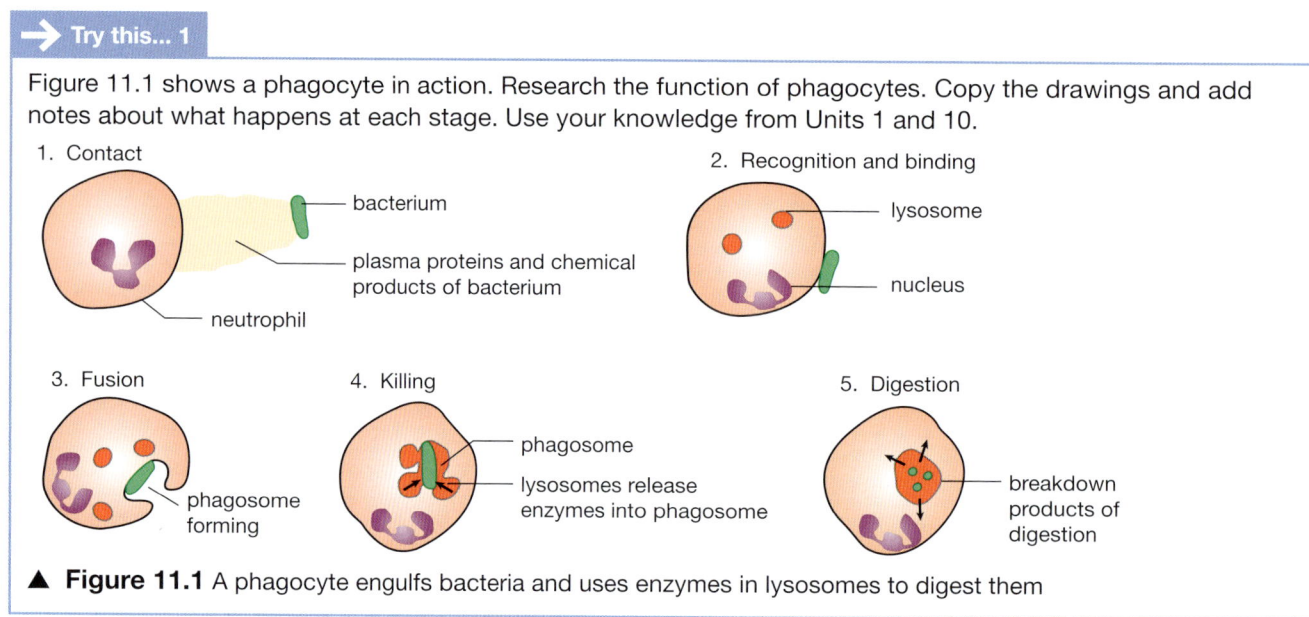

1. Contact
   - bacterium
   - plasma proteins and chemical products of bacterium
   - neutrophil

2. Recognition and binding
   - lysosome
   - nucleus

3. Fusion
   - phagosome forming

4. Killing
   - phagosome
   - lysosomes release enzymes into phagosome

5. Digestion
   - breakdown products of digestion

▲ **Figure 11.1** A phagocyte engulfs bacteria and uses enzymes in lysosomes to digest them

The number of neutrophils in the blood increases rapidly during an infection as they leave the bone marrow, circulate in the blood and then pass through capillary walls into tissues. They do not live long after engulfing and digesting bacteria. More are produced and released from bone marrow to replace those that die. This explains why the number of white blood cells in the blood increases during infections. Macrophages are long-lived cells that are found in many tissues of the body.

Antigens and antibodies

Pathogens are surrounded by large molecules, such as proteins, glycoproteins and polysaccharides. The molecules are recognised as 'foreign' and stimulate the immune system to produce **antibodies**. Any foreign substance that has this effect is an **antigen**.

Self and non-self

Macromolecules that belong to the body are known as '**self**' antigens. Although they do not stimulate an **immune response** in the body, they can act as antigens in stimulating antibody production if removed and inserted into an animal or into another person. Any macromolecule that is not recognised as 'self' is known as '**non-self**'. The antigens on the surface of pathogens are an example. The entry of 'non-self' antigens stimulates an immune response.

★ **Exam tip**

Macrophages add antigenic material from pathogens to proteins on their cell surface – see antigen presentation on page 94.

Key terms

Antibody: protein that is secreted by plasma cells (active B-cells) in response to the presence of an antigen.

Antigen: any macromolecule, e.g. polysaccharide or protein, that stimulates the production of antibodies.

Immune response: series of events that occur in the immune system in response to the presence of a non-self antigen in the body.

▼ Table 11.1 The functions of B-lymphocytes and two types of T-lymphocyte

Lymphocyte	Function
B-lymphocytes (B-cells)	• differentiate into **plasma cells** that secrete antibodies • production of memory B-lymphocytes
T-helper cells (helper T-lymphocytes)	• respond to non-self antigens presented on the surface of macrophages • secrete cytokines (cell signalling molecules) to stimulate B-cells, T-killer cells and macrophages • production of memory T-lymphocytes
T-killer cells (cytotoxic T-lymphocytes)	• respond to non-self antigens on the surface of many body cells • attach to cells infected with intracellular pathogens and kill them • attach to cancer cells and cells in transplanted tissues and kill them • production of memory T-lymphocytes

➡ **Try this... 2**

Search online for a transmission electron micrograph of a plasma cell. Make a labelled diagram of the cell. Annotate your diagram to show how it is adapted for protein synthesis. Your annotations will help your revision of many aspects of Units 1, 2, 6 and 11 for Papers 1 and 2.

Immune responses

Immune responses involve the activation of clones of lymphocytes by the presentation of antigens. When a pathogen enters the body for the first time there are very few lymphocytes with the specific membrane receptors that have a complementary shape to a particular antigen on the surface of the pathogen.

Each small group of lymphocytes is a clone as they all express the same membrane receptor. The activation of clones of lymphocytes that have membrane receptors complementary to a particular antigen is **clonal selection**. To be effective, many more cells need to be produced. In **clonal expansion**, the activated lymphocytes divide by mitosis to form many more identical cells, all with the same specificity.

One type of immune response involves the production of antibodies. After clonal expansion, B-cells differentiate into plasma cells, which quickly produce antibodies. After a short while they die. Other cells in each clone do not become active, but remain in the body, often for many years. These cells are **memory B-lymphocytes (memory B-cells)** and they represent a long-term increase in the number of cells in the original clone.

When antibodies combine with antigens they form antigen–antibody complexes, which phagocytes can then engulf and destroy. Antibodies are very effective against pathogens while they are in the blood, lymph and between cells within tissues. They are of limited use in protecting against intracellular pathogens as, being protein, they cannot cross cell membranes.

➡ **Try this... 3**

Make a flow chart to show the stages of an immune response in which B-cells are activated to make antibodies against a pathogen. Add notes about what happens in each stage. When you have read about T-helper cells on the next page you can add information about them to your flow chart.

The role of T-lymphocytes in immune responses

Pathogens are ingested by phagocytes and are partly digested. Their antigens are presented on the surface of macrophages and other antigen presenting cells (APCs). T-helper cells with membrane receptor proteins complementary to the antigens bind to the cell surface of these APCs. This interaction stimulates the T-helper cells to secrete cytokines, which activate specific B-cells to divide and differentiate into plasma cells. They also stimulate macrophages to be more effective at killing the pathogens within them. The clone of T-helper cells also divides by mitosis, so that there are more of these cells to increase their stimulatory effect on macrophages and many also remain in the body as memory T-helper cells.

Another type of immune response involves T-killer cells, which are the most important defence against intracellular pathogens. B-cells and antibodies are not involved in this type of immune response. These pathogens give away their presence within cells as some of their antigens appear in the cell membranes of host cells. For example, during processing in the Golgi body, viral proteins attach to membrane proteins and are exposed at the cell surface when Golgi vesicles fuse with the cell surface membrane. This is another example of **antigen presentation**. The antigen is detected by patrolling T-killer cells with the specific membrane receptor protein.

Once activated, T-killer cells attach to the surface of the infected cells and release perforins, which are proteins that make holes in the cell surface membranes of infected cells. Toxins, such as hydrogen peroxide, pass from the cytotoxic cells into the infected cells and kill them. This is the only way to remove intracellular pathogens, such as viruses and some bacteria. It also prevents reproduction of the pathogen and the spread of pathogens to other cells in the body.

Immunological memory

Infection by the measles virus tends to give long-term immunity to reinfection by the same pathogen. This is because in the first infection, during the clonal expansion stage, memory B-cells and memory T-cells are produced in addition to plasma cells, activated T-helper cells and activated T-killer cells. Memory cells do not differentiate, but continue to circulate in the blood and lymph often for years, possibly a lifetime. If these cells contact the same antigens, then there is another immune response in which these memory cells divide and differentiate. Memory B-cells form plasma cells; memory T-helper cells form active T-helper cells and memory T-killer cells form active T-killer cells.

Memory cells belong to a much larger clone of cells than existed before the first infection so they can respond much faster during second and subsequent infections (see Figure 11.2).

Vaccination

A vaccine is the equivalent of the first encounter with an antigen that stimulates an immune response without people being ill. This is equivalent to the primary response. A secondary response occurs in a vaccinated person when they encounter the pathogen for the first time, so they are protected against the disease.

Vaccination programmes are an important part of the health protection offered by governments to their citizens. Infants and children are vaccinated against diseases that used to be common in populations and were responsible for much ill health and many deaths.

Key term

Antigen presentation: the display of antigens on the surface of antigen presenting cells, e.g. macrophages act as APCs to activate to T-lymphocytes.

→ Try this... 4

Make another flow chart to show the events that occur during an immune response to make T-killer cells against a pathogen that invades host cells. Show how these T-cells kill the infected host cells. Add notes explaining the importance of each stage.

★ Exam tip

Memory cells are produced during the first (primary) response to a specific antigen (see Figure 11.2).

Key terms

Active immunity: protection against disease gained following contact with an antigen by infection (natural) or by vaccination (artificial).

Passive immunity: protection against disease gained by transfer of antibodies from mother (natural) or by injection (artificial).

★ Exam tip

Use information from Worked Example 2 on page 96 and your own research to make a table comparing the two types of active immunity with the two types of passive immunity.

Antibody structure and function

Antibodies are glycoproteins known as immunoglobulins (Ig for short). The simplest form of antibody molecule (Ig class G or IgG), and the only one you have to know about, is composed of four polypeptides.

Each IgG molecule is composed of two identical long polypeptides (heavy chains) and two identical short polypeptides (light chains).

In order to bind to its specific antigen, each type of antibody molecule has an antigen-binding site that has a specific shape complementary to the antigen. It is possible for different antibodies to have different-shaped binding sites because amino acids can be arranged in different sequences to give different three-dimensional shapes. Because these binding sites vary, these regions are also called **variable regions**.

We need many antibodies with different variable regions to 'fit around' different antigens. The better the 'fit' between antigen and antibody, the more efficient the response to infection.

Antibodies have many roles, including causing bacteria to clump together so preventing their spread through the body and coating pathogens to facilitate phagocytosis. Antibodies that attach to bacteria help to 'mark' them for destruction by phagocytes. Antitoxins are the antibodies that form complexes with toxins to make them harmless. They are important in the defence against tetanus and diphtheria.

During the **primary immune response** it takes a while for the specific antibody molecules to appear in the plasma following the presentation of antigen (Figure 11.2). Antigen presentation, clonal selection and clonal expansion have to take place before there are plasma cells able to secrete the appropriate antibody. The concentration increases to a maximum and then decreases as the antibody molecules are removed from circulation.

When a second presentation of the identical antigen occurs, the antibody concentration increases almost immediately in the **secondary immune response**. This happens because there are many more cells (memory cells) of the appropriate B-cell clone to differentiate into plasma cells.

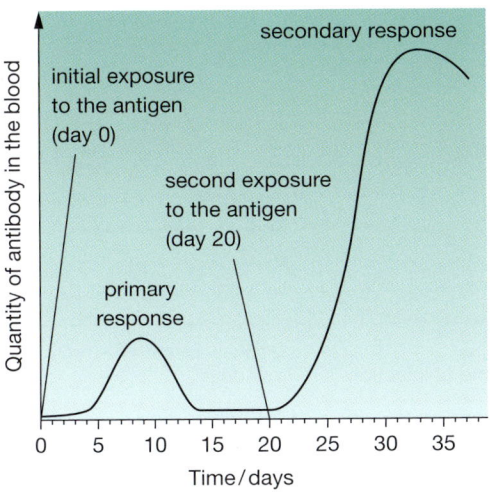

◀ **Figure 11.2** Primary and secondary immune responses

Worked Example 1

Figure 11.3 shows an antibody molecule.

(a) Name the type of cell that produces antibodies.

(b) State one function for each of the component parts of the antibody that are labelled on the diagram.

(c) Explain why the part of the antibody molecule incorporating the binding site is also known as the variable region.

Answers

(a) Plasma cell.

(b) Variable region – binds to antigens. Constant region – binds to receptors on phagocytes.

(c) Different antibodies have different antigen binding sites as they bind to different antigens. These different sites have different shapes so that they are complementary to their antigens. The sequences of amino acids gives them these different shapes and as they vary so much they are called variable regions.

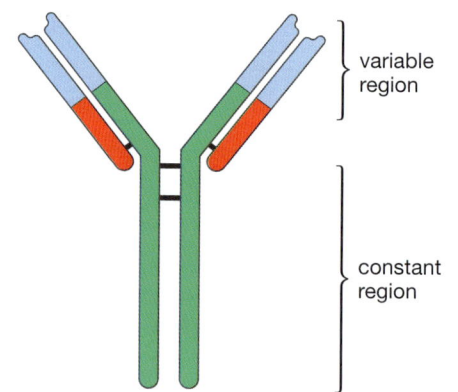

▲ **Figure 11.3**

★ **Exam tip**

Note that the two variable regions on each antibody molecule are identical, so they both bind to the same antigen.

Worked Example 2

Tetanus is a disease caused by a bacterium that lives in soil. A young man is involved in a serious car accident and is transferred to hospital. The team in the Accident and Emergency department decides that he is at risk of tetanus as he has got soil into his wounds. He is given an injection of anti-tetanus antibodies. He cannot remember whether he has been vaccinated against tetanus, so is given the vaccine as a precaution.

The health workers decide to check that he has enough of the antibodies in his blood so they take blood samples at regular intervals while he is in hospital. The results are shown in Figures 11.4a and b.

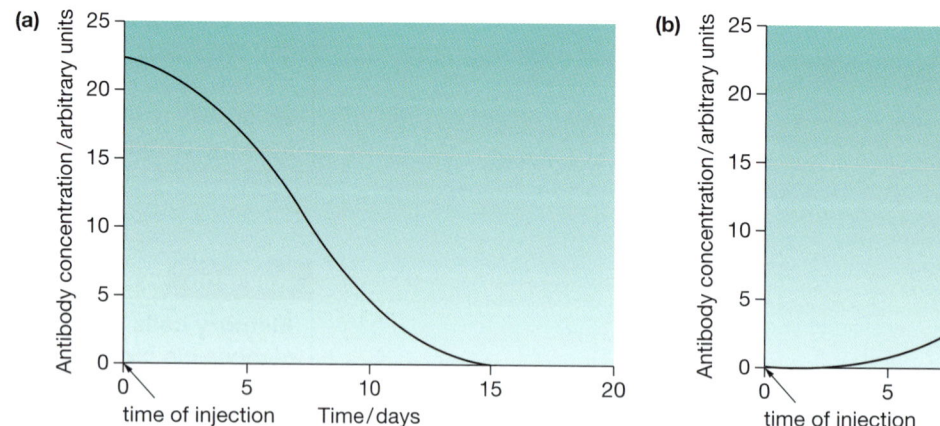

▲ **Figure 11.4** Changes in antibody concentration in the blood following an injection of **(a)** antibodies and **(b)** vaccine to protect against tetanus

(a) Describe the differences between antibody concentrations as shown in the two graphs. [4]

(b) Explain why injecting a vaccine has a different response to that following the injection of antibodies. [5]

★ **Exam tip**

Read the caption to the two graphs very carefully and then move a ruler vertically across each graph from left to right and note the changes in the two types of antibody.

(c) Hospitals in countries with venomous snakes hold supplies of antivenom antibodies. Suggest how this anti-venom is produced. [3]

(d) Explain why the secondary response to an antigen is much faster than the primary response. [5]

Answers

(a) In Figure 11.4a the concentration of antibodies is very high at time zero when the injection of antibodies is given. The concentration gradually decreases to zero by day 15. In Figure 11.4b, the antibody concentration following the injection of the tetanus vaccine only starts to increase by day 3. There is a gradual increase which then peaks at day 15 and then decreases.

(b) Figure 11.4a shows artificial passive immunity and Figure 11.4b shows artificial active immunity following an injection of the vaccine.

Vaccines contain antigens, **not** antibodies. The antigen stimulates an immune response that takes time to produce antibodies. Antigen presentation, clonal selection and clonal expansion have to occur before plasma cells start to secrete antibodies. An immune response does not happen in artificial passive immunity. There are no plasma cells so antibodies are not continually produced; the only antibodies in the body that will act on the pathogen concerned are those in the injection. They are gradually removed from the blood over time and not replaced.

(c) A very low concentration of the venom is injected into a large animal, such as a horse. Molecules in the venom act as antigens in the immune response in the animal. After several weeks blood is taken from the animal. The plasma will contain antibodies against molecules in the venom. The blood is treated to remove all the blood cells, platelets and some clotting agents in the plasma to make the anti-venom.

(d) A primary immune response occurs when an antigen enters the body for the first time. There is a time lag between the entry of the antigen (e.g. when a pathogen invades the body or a vaccine is given) and the appearance of antibodies in the blood plasma. This is because the processes of antigen presentation, clonal selection and clonal expansion have to the place before antibodies are released by plasma cells. During a primary response many memory cells are formed. These are identical to the original cells that responded, but they do not make antibody. When the identical antigen enters the body again, memory B-cells respond and become plasma cells, which is why the antibody concentration increases much faster in a secondary response because there are so many of them.

Worked Example 3

(a) Explain what is meant by the term monoclonal antibody.

(b) Explain why monoclonal antibodies are produced by a process that involves cell fusion.

(c) Outline the advantages of using monoclonal antibodies in diagnosis and treatment.

Answers

(a) An antibody that is produced by a single clone of hybridoma cells. All the antibodies in any sample of a monoclonal antibody have identical variable regions and so form antigen–antibody complexes with only one type of antigen. They are highly antigen-specific.

(b) Antibodies are produced by plasma cells (activated B-lymphocytes). Each clone of plasma cells produces antibody molecules that are all identical. But plasma cells cannot be grown in culture. To make monoclonal antibodies, plasma cells are first fused with myeloma cells that have the ability to grow in culture and keep on dividing.

(c) Each type of monoclonal antibody (Mab) is specific to one antigen so can be used to detect the presence of antigens associated with pathogens or with cancer cells. Mabs can also detect very small quantities of antigens so are good for early diagnosis and treatment. In diagnosis and treatment monoclonal antibodies can be injected into the body and will collect at the site of an infection or tumour, so are good for detecting their location in the body and for delivering drugs or radiation treatment.

⬆ Raise your grade

(a) State the difference between antigens and antibodies. [2]

> An antigen is any compound that stimulates the production of antibodies. ✔ An antibody is a protein molecule produced by plasma cells (activated B-lymphocytes) during an immune response. ✔

> Correct answer that distinguishes carefully between these two terms.

(b) Outline the roles of T-lymphocytes in immune responses. [5]

> There are two types of T-lymphocyte: T-helper cells and T-killer cells. T-helper cells respond to antigens releasing chemicals that stimulate B-cells to divide, become plasma cells and produce antibodies. ✔ T-killer cells have a different role. They respond to antigens that are on the surfaces of cells. If they recognise the antigen as non-self ✔ then the cells must have a pathogen inside. ✔ These T-cells attach to the infected cells and kill them.

> A further mark could be gained by describing how cytotoxic T-cells kill infected host cells. The term cytokine should be used in the second sentence to gain a mark.

(c) Describe the hybridoma method of producing monoclonal antibodies. [5]

> Inject a solution of antigens into a mouth. ✘ After several weeks remove some B-lymphocytes from the spleen ✔ of the mouth. These B-lymphocytes will be plasma cells that make antibodies. They are then fused with tumour cells ✔ that divide by mitsosis when kept in culture dishes with nutrients. The fused cells are called hybridomas ✔ and they have chromosomes from both cells.

> The first sentence should read 'Inject a solution of an antigen into a mouse'. Later mitosis has been misspelt, but this can be ignored and the mark given for identifying the spleen as the source of plasma cells. 'Mitsosis' cannot be confused with anything other than mitosis, so the examiner may award a mark. However, it is easy to misspell mitosis so it looks like meiosis, in which case no mark would be awarded. This shows how important it is to reread answers to check for errors.

(d) Measles is a highly infectious viral disease. Children are at high risk of infection with this virus when there is an outbreak of this disease. Outline how children under 1 year of age may gain passive immunity **and** artificial active immunity to measles. [2]

> - Passive immunity – the child gains antibodies against measles across the placenta before birth and in breast milk. ✔
> - Active immunity – the child is vaccinated and the measles antigens stimulate an immune response to give long-term immunity (but it needs bossters). ✔

> There is no need to use bullet points in answering this question, but it is a way to make sure that **both** parts of the question are answered. Note that there is no point in vaccinating a child against measles while there are still maternal antibodies in the child's body. It would be useless as the maternal antibodies will form complexes with the antigens and there would be no immune response to give active immunity. Boosters (not 'bossters') are given as part of the vaccination programme for measles.

Exam-style questions

1 Which row shows correct examples of artificial active immunity and natural passive immunity?

	Example of artificial active immunity	Example of natural passive immunity
A	immunity to meningitis after infection	receiving antibodies to polio in breast milk
B	immunity to meningitis after vaccination	receiving antibodies to measles in breast milk
C	immunity to polio after infection	receiving antibodies to tetanus by injection
D	immunity to polio after vaccination	receiving antibodies to tetanus by injection

[1]

2 These cells are part of the body's defence system:

1 B-lymphocytes

2 macrophages

3 T-lymphocytes

Which of these cells produce memory cells?

A 1, 2 and 3   B 1 and 2

C 1 and 3   D 2 and 3   [1]

3 Which of these events happen during clonal expansion during an immune response?

1 cytokinesis

2 DNA replication

3 mitosis

A 1, 2 and 3   B 1 and 2

C 1 and 3   D 2 and 3   [1]

4 The diagram shows the antigens on the surface of a virus and receptors on four clones of B-lymphocytes. Which clone responds when the pathogen enters the body?

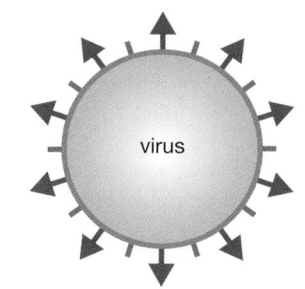

5 A student discovered that there are four ways in which a person can become immune:

1 being injected with a vaccine containing isolated antigens from a pathogen

2 being injected with specific antibodies

3 receiving breast milk

4 catching a new strain of a disease

Which of these ways are examples of passive immunity?

A 1, 2, 3 and 4

B 1, 2 and 4

C 2 and 3

D 3 and 4   [1]

6 Soon after a pathogen enters the human body for the first time, the blood contains many different antibody molecules, each produced by a different group of cells.

(a) Distinguish between the terms *pathogen* and *antigen*. [2]

(b) Explain why the response is a *polyclonal response*. [3]

(c) State why these antibodies are present in the blood much sooner following a subsequent infection by the same pathogen. [2]

(d) Monoclonal antibodies are produced for diagnosis and treatment.

Suggest and explain how monoclonal antibodies are used in the treatment of cancer. [5]

7 (a) (i) Draw a diagram of an antibody molecule. [3]

(ii) Label your diagram to show where the antibody molecule binds to antigens. [1]

(b) Explain why only some B-cells respond when a particular type of pathogen enters the body. [3]

(c) Outline the changes that occur to B-cells during a primary immune response. [4]

(d) Explain why the secondary response to an antigen is much faster than the primary response. [5]

Energy and respiration

Units 12 (Energy and respiration) and 13 (Photosynthesis) are all about energy. All the time you learn and revise each of these units keep asking yourself the question 'what is this process for?' Remember that both are energy transfer processes:

- photosynthesis – transfer of light energy to chemical energy in the bonds of biochemical molecules especially carbohydrates, lipids and proteins

- respiration – transfer of energy in the bonds of biochemical molecules to energy in the bonds of ATP.

ATP is often known as the 'universal energy currency'. Figure 12.1 shows the role of ATP in cells. The bonds between the phosphate groups of ATP are unstable and break easily so ATP can be considered an 'immediate' source of energy. The hydrolysis of an ATP molecule supplies enough energy for an individual step in most anabolic reactions.

ATP synthesis using energy from:
- oxidation of carbohydrates, proteins and fats in respiration (substrate-linked phosphorylation and oxidative phosphorylation)
- light in photosynthesis (photophosphorylation)

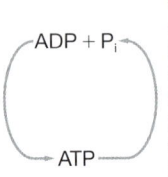

$ADP + P_i$

hydrolysis of ATP to provide energy for biosynthesis, movement, active transport, etc.

ATP

This equation shows the type of reaction that occurs in substrate-linked phosphorylation:

enzyme

$$XP + ADP \rightarrow X + ATP$$

▲ **Figure 12.1** ATP is hydrolysed when it is used to form ADP and phosphate. When reformed, a condensation reaction occurs between ADP and a phosphate ion (P_i). Enzymes catalyse the formation of ATP

There are two ways in which ATP is produced.

Substrate-linked phosphorylation. ADP and a phosphorylated compound are substrates that occupy the active site of certain enzymes. A phosphate group transfers from the compound (shown by XP) to ADP. Production of ATP occurs like this in glycolysis and the Krebs cycle during cellular respiration.

Phosphorylation by chemiosmosis. Most ATP in cells is produced in mitochondria using a hydrogen ion (proton) gradient across the inner mitochondrial membrane (Figure 12.2). This gradient is established by pumping protons from one side of a membrane to the other side. The energy for this comes from energetic electrons that release energy as they flow along

> **Remember**
>
> Unit 12 is about *cellular* respiration; it is not about breathing and gas exchange.

> ★ **Exam tip**
>
> Make a list of the processes that occur in plant, animal and bacterial cells that require energy from the hydrolysis of ATP.

> **Remember**
>
> Remember what you learnt in Unit 3 about active sites. ATP fits into the active sites of many enzymes. Remember also that anabolic reactions are those that make larger molecules, such as protein from amino acids, starch from glucose or nucleic acids from nucleotides.

> ★ **Exam tip**
>
> This is a good time to remind yourself of the biochemistry you learnt in Unit 2 and the structure and function of enzymes from Unit 3.

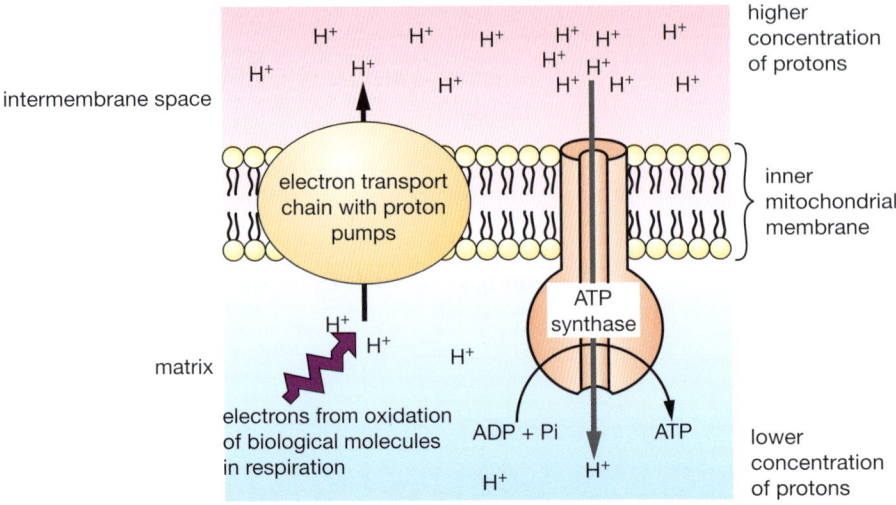

intermembrane space

H⁺ ... (higher concentration of protons)

electron transport chain with proton pumps

inner mitochondrial membrane

ATP synthase

matrix

electrons from oxidation of biological molecules in respiration

$ADP + Pi$ ATP

lower concentration of protons

◀ **Figure 12.2** Chemiosmosis is the movement of protons down a concentration gradient through molecules of ATP synthase across inner mitochondrial membranes. It is a form of facilitated diffusion

the electron transport chain (ETC). The oxidation of reduced coenzymes (NAD and FAD) is the immediate source of energy for the flow of electrons. Chemiosmosis occurs when the protons move down an electrochemical gradient by facilitated diffusion through the large membrane protein ATP synthase, which catalyses the phosphorylation of ADP to form ATP.

Coenzymes

Some enzymes do not function unless they are combined with a *cofactor*. Cofactors may be ions or complex organic substances that occupy the active site and take part in the reaction or are involved in other ways. Most coenzymes are mobile and travel back and forth between enzymes.

Respiration in aerobic respiration

Cells respire carbohydrates, fats and proteins. You need to know how glucose is respired. There are four stages involved in the aerobic respiration of glucose:

1. glycolysis (see Worked Example 1 and Exam-style question 3(a))

2. link reaction (see Exam-style questions 2(c) and 4)

3. Krebs cycle (see Exam-style question 3(b))

4. oxidative phosphorylation (see Try this ... 3).

Make your own diagrams of these four stages on large sheets of paper. Highlight the first substance in each pathway and the end products of each pathway. Make sure that your diagrams include all the information required by the syllabus, including these processes:

lysis (splitting), oxidation, reduction of coenzymes, substrate-linked phosphorylation, dehydrogenation, decarboxylation, chemiosmosis.

Use diagrams and TEMs (see Figure 12.3) to make a large, labelled diagram of a mitochondrion and annotate it to show how it gains the substances it needs for stages 2, 3 and 4 and how its structure is related to its functions in respiration.

Respiration in anaerobic conditions

During vigorous exercise the heart and lungs cannot supply sufficient oxygen to maintain high rates of aerobic respiration to provide the ATP required in muscle tissue. Muscle cells adapt to this by using an additional pathway – lactate fermentation, which recycles NAD so that glycolysis can continue to produce ATP. Lactate is the end product. Yeast can survive in anaerobic conditions by using a pathway that involves recycling NAD and the decarboxylation of pyruvate to produce ethanol and carbon dioxide. These two pathways are efficient at converting pyruvate, but in glycolysis the yield of ATP per molecule of glucose is low (see Table 12.1) so they are wasteful of glucose. Mammals can respire lactate (in heart muscle and in the liver) so energy is not lost. Yeast cannot metabolise ethanol so excretes it.

> ★ **Exam tip**
>
> This is a good opportunity to look back at Unit 4 for the movement of substances through channel and carrier proteins in membranes.

> ★ **Exam tip**
>
> Make a table or chart to show the roles of these coenzymes in respiration:
>
> coenzyme A, FAD and NAD.

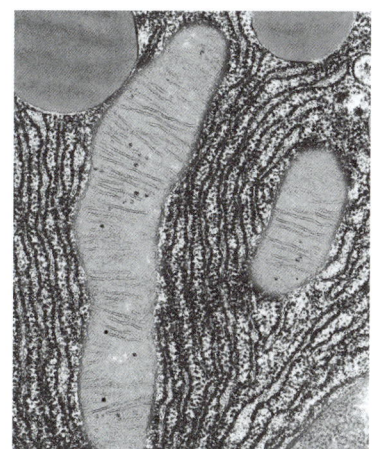

▲ **Figure 12.3** A TEM of mitochondria from a pancreatic cell. Cell structure (Unit 1) provides a foundation for Units 12, 13, 14 and 15

> ★ **Exam tip**
>
> Plants can also use the ethanol fermentation pathway. Rice, *Oryza sativa*, growing in flooded fields is a good example.

▼ **Table 12.1** Respiration in aerobic and anaerobic conditions

Feature	Type of respiration		
	Respiration in aerobic conditions	Respiration in anaerobic conditions	
		Ethanol fermentation in yeast and plants (e.g. rice)	Lactate fermentation in mammals
decarboxylation	yes	yes	no
oxidation of reduced NAD	yes – in mitochondria using ETC	yes – in cytosol by using ethanal as hydrogen acceptor	yes – in cytosol using pyruvate as hydrogen acceptor
products per molecule of glucose	$6 \times H_2O$, $6 \times CO_2$ 32 ATP	$2 \times$ ethanol, $2 \times CO_2$ 4 ATP	$2 \times$ lactate 4 ATP
net gain of ATP	30*	2	2

*The actual net gain of ATP in aerobic respiration varies for several reasons. Remember that it is about 30, so aerobic respiration is about 15 times more efficient in producing ATP compared with ethanol fermentation or lactate fermentation.

⚙ Practical Skills

Using redox dyes to investigate respiration

Methylene blue is a redox dye. It is reduced to a colourless form, which can be readily oxidised back to the blue-coloured form:

reduction

coloured form of methylene blue ⇌ colourless form of methylene blue

oxidation

When added to yeast suspensions, methylene blue changes colour as it accepts some of the hydrogen ions and electrons that normally reduce NAD in glycolysis. Methylene blue can be used to investigate the factors that influence respiration in yeast. This procedure uses it to investigate the effect of temperature.

1. Use a syringe to place 10 cm³ of 10% glucose solution into six test-tubes labelled **A** to **F**.

2. Use a 1 cm³ syringe to add 1 cm³ 0.005% methylene blue solution to each test-tube.

3. Use a glass rod to stir the contents of each tube so the blue dye is spread evenly.

4. Place the test-tubes into water baths maintained at the following temperatures:
    10 °C (**A**), 20 °C (**B**), 30 °C (**C**), 40 °C (**D**), 50 °C (**E**) and 60 °C (**F**).

5. Use a syringe to put 1 cm³ of a 20% yeast suspension into six test-tubes labelled **1** to **6**.
    Place test-tube **1** in the same water bath with test-tube **A**, **2** with **B** and so on.

6. Start a timer and leave it running throughout the investigation.

7. After 5 minutes, pour the 1 cm³ yeast suspension in test-tube **1** into the glucose solution
    in test-tube **A** and return test-tube **A** to the water bath at 10 °C. Note the time from the timer.

8. Use the glass rod to stir the contents of the test-tube **A**.

9. Repeat steps 7 and 8 with the remaining pairs of test-tubes.

10. Observe the colour of the tubes and record the time when the contents of each test-tube
    no longer has a blue colour.

11. If there is no change in colour after 20 minutes, record 'no change'.

▼ **Table 12.2** Results from a student investigation

Test-tube	Temperature / °C	Time taken for methylene blue to be decolourised / s	Rate of respiration (1000/t) / s⁻¹
A	10	1080	0.93
B	20	330	3.03
C	30	267	3.75
D	40	187	5.35
E	50	94	10.64
F	60	no change	0.00

The rate of respiration was determined by calculating the reciprocal of the time taken for methylene blue to be decolourised.

➜ Try this... 1

(a) Draw a graph of the results. [5]

(b) Explain the results. [4]

(c) Suggest two limitations of the method, explain the effect they have on the quality of the data and suggest an improvement for each limitation. [9]

(d) Suggest and explain two control experiments that should be included to ensure the method is a valid way to investigate rates of respiration. [4]

 **Practical Skills**

Using a simple respirometer to measure rates of respiration and to determine RQ

The simple respirometer shown in Figure 12.4 is set up to measure the uptake of oxygen by some germinating seeds. The carbon dioxide absorbent reacts with carbon dioxide to form calcium carbonate. As carbon dioxide is absorbed from the air inside the syringe barrel, the meniscus moves towards the syringe. The volume of oxygen absorbed is calculated using the distance travelled by the meniscus (*h*) and the radius of the capillary tubing (*r*):

$$\text{volume of oxygen absorbed} = \pi r^2 h$$

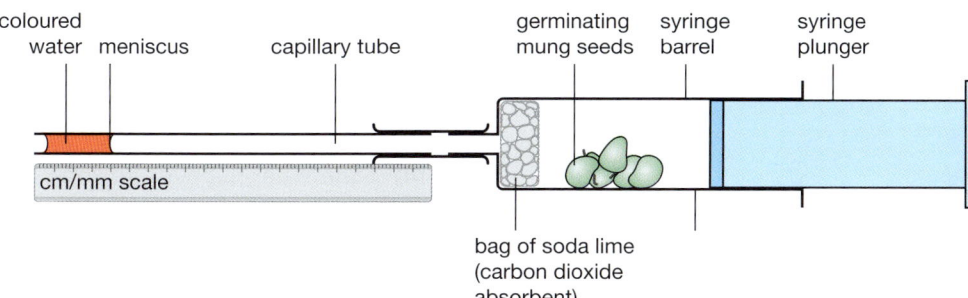

◀ **Figure 12.4**
A respirometer set up to measure the rate of respiration of germinating mung bean seeds. The internal diameter of the capillary tubing is 0.4 mm

To determine the respiratory quotient (RQ), follow these instructions:

1. Set up the respirometer as shown in Figure 12.4. Mark the start position of the meniscus on the capillary tubing and then again after a known length of time. Record the distance travelled by the meniscus and the time taken. Repeat the experiment at least twice with the same batch of seeds so you can calculate a mean volume of oxygen absorbed per unit mass of seeds.

2. Remove the syringe plunger, the seeds and the bag of soda lime. Wipe out the inside of the barrel with a paper towel. Put in some inert material (e.g. small beads) with same volume as the soda lime.

3. Replace the seeds in the syringe. Replace the plunger and put the respirometer on the bench for at least 2 minutes.

4. Draw up the liquid into the capillary tubing and record the position of the meniscus. The meniscus will either move towards the seeds, move away from the seeds or remain in the same place.

5. Take repeat readings and use them to calculate the mean volume of carbon dioxide produced over the same length of time.

To calculate the volume of carbon dioxide produced it helps to know what is happening when there is no soda lime in the respirometer.

*   If the meniscus stays in the same place the volume of carbon dioxide produced is exactly the same as the volume of oxygen absorbed (and the RQ is 1).

*   If the meniscus moves towards the seeds the volume of carbon dioxide produced is *less* than the volume of oxygen absorbed (and the RQ is less than 1).

*   If the meniscus moves away from the seeds the volume of carbon dioxide produced is *more* than the volume of oxygen absorbed (and the RQ is more than 1).

The movement of the meniscus in the simple respirometer could be due to a change in temperature. If the air heats up and expands in the syringe then this will cause the meniscus to move away from the syringe and if it cools and contracts then the meniscus will move towards the syringe.

With this design of respirometer it is difficult to keep the temperature constant, so another design replaces the syringe with a boiling tube in a water bath (see Exam-style question 5).

A control tube should be set up in exactly the same way as shown in Figure 12.4 but some inert material of the same mass replaces the beans. Small glass beads are suitable. If there is any movement of the droplet in this control respirometer, then this needs to be taken account of when calculating movement of fluid in the experimental tube, before calculating rates of oxygen uptake and carbon dioxide produced.

RQ values are useful as they tell us whether respiration is aerobic or not, and the type of substrate that is respired (e.g. carbohydrate, lipid or protein) or the likely mix of substrates.

Worked Example 1

The diagram shows the stages of glycolysis in a mammalian cell.

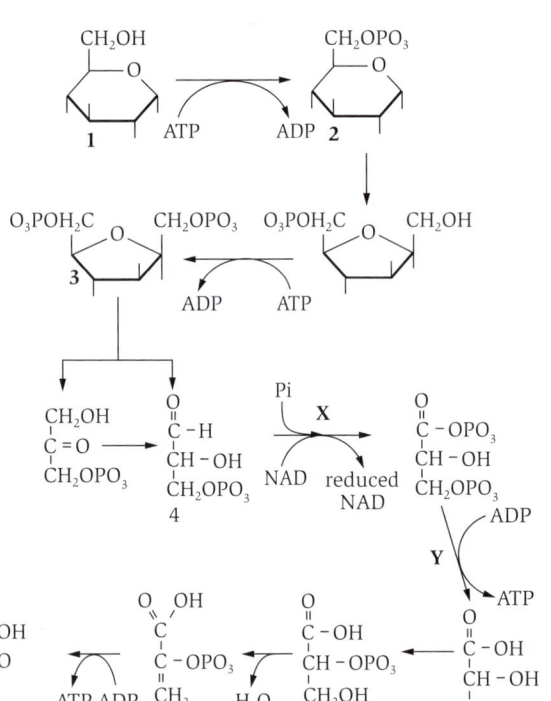

★ **Exam tip**

Look carefully at the diagram stage by stage before you read the questions.

(a) (i) Name the molecules labelled **2, 3, 4** and **6**. [4]

(ii) State a possible source of substance **1**. [1]

(iii) State what happens at stage **Y**. [1]

(iv) State what happens to the reduced NAD. [2]

(b) (i) Discuss the importance of the reaction that occurs at **X**. [2]

(ii) State the immediate fate of the molecule labelled **6** under aerobic conditions in the mammalian cell. [2]

Answers

(a) (i) **2** glucose phosphate   **4** triose phosphate

       3 fructose 1, 6-bisphosphate   **6** pyruvate

(ii) Glucose is formed from the breakdown of glycogen.

(iii) ADP is phosphorylated in substrate-linked phosphorylation.

(iv) NAD is a hydrogen carrier that delivers hydrogen for use in oxidative phosphorylation. The reduced NAD is oxidised to transfer electrons to the electron transport chain and transfer protons for proton pumping in the mitochondrion.

(b) (i) This reaction conserves energy as a phosphorylated compound. This energy would otherwise be transferred to the cell as heat and so not available to the cell as ATP.

(ii) Pyruvate diffuses into the matrix of mitochondria. Pyruvate is the substrate for the link reaction where it is decarboxylated and combines with coenzyme A to form acetyl coenzyme A. The acetyl group then enters the Krebs cycle.

➡ Try this... 2

A student used a simple respirometer to determine the RQ of a sample of some germinating mung seeds. The internal diameter of the capillary tubing was 0.4 mm. The student's results are in the table.

(a) Plot a graph of the results and use them to calculate the volume of oxygen absorbed and the volume of carbon dioxide produced. [5]

(b) Calculate the RQ for the germinating mung seeds. Show all your working. [4]

(c) Sunflower seeds are rich in lipids. Explain the advantage of storing lipid in seeds. [3]

(d) The RQ of sunflower seeds in early germination is determined as 0.69. The RQ of sunflower seedlings that have fully expanded leaves is 0.92.

Explain why the RQ of sunflower seedlings differs from the RQ of germinating seeds. [4]

Time / s	Distance moved by meniscus / mm	
	With soda lime	Without soda lime
0	0.0	0.0
30	12.5	0.5
60	21.5	1.0
90	33.0	1.5
120	42.5	2.0
150	54.0	2.5
180	64.0	3.5
210	71.5	4.0
240	79.5	5.0
270	88.5	6.3

→ Try this... 3

(a) Which of the following is reduced during oxidative phosphorylation?
NAD, FAD, oxygen, water [1]

(b) Describe the role of each of the following in oxidative phosphorylation:

    (i) electron transport chain [3]   (ii) proton gradient. [4]

(c) (i) Explain the role of oxygen in respiration. [4]   (ii) List the products of oxidative phosphorylation. [2]

(d) An experiment was carried out using three inhibitors of the ETC in mitochondria, **P**, **Q** and **R**. The state of four electron carriers, **A** to **D**, after the addition of each inhibitor is shown in the table.

Inhibitor	Name			
	A	**B**	**C**	**D**
A	oxidised	reduced	reduced	oxidised
Q	oxidised	oxidised	reduced	oxidised
R	reduced	reduced	reduced	oxidised

State the sequence of electron carriers in this ETC and explain your answer. [6]

→ Try this... 4

Plan a method to investigate the effect of changing the concentration of glucose on the rate of respiration in yeast using the redox dye, methylene blue.

You are provided with the following apparatus and materials:

a stirring rod, a water bath, a thermometer, a timer, an unlimited supply of: test-tubes and syringes, 10% glucose solution, 20% yeast suspension, 0.005% methylene blue solution.

Read pages 185 and 186 before you start writing an answer to this question

Make a word bank. Make a glossary of all the technical terms in this Unit. You will be surprised how many there are. Group the terms into three categories: substances (e.g. triose phosphate), processes (e.g. phosphorylation, chemiosmosis) and cell structures, including those that need a supply of ATP, (e.g. cilia). Use the list of substances and processes to make flow charts to show the metabolic pathways in aerobic and anaerobic respiration. Remember that respiration occurs in plants, protoctists, fungi and bacteria as well as in animals!

Animations. Search online for animations of the stages of cellular respiration. Try those at http://www.johnkyrk.com.

▲ **Figure 12.5** Technical terms written on cards or sticky notes can be used in many ways to help you revise. You may need more than three categories to group all the terms

↑ Raise your grade

Most of the ATP produced in an animal cell is formed in mitochondria.

(a) (i) Describe the structure of ATP. [1]

ATP is composed of a nitrogenous base, ribose sugar and three phosphate
groups arranged as I have drawn here:

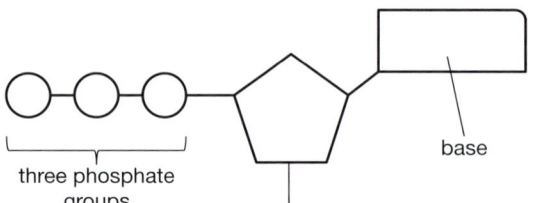

three phosphate groups — ribose — base

Including a diagram is a good idea, but no mark can be awarded as the base has not been named as **adenine.**

(ii) Explain how ATP is suitable as the universal energy currency in organisms. [3]

ATP is a small, water-soluble molecule so can diffuse through cells easily. ✔ ✔ The
hydrolysis of the terminal phosphate released enough energy (30 kJ mol⁻¹) for most
reactions. ✔ The adenine and ribose 'handle' of ATP fits into many protein molecules
(e.g. active site of enzymes). ✔

A good answer that easily scores the marks.

(iii) Explain how the ATP that is **not** produced in the mitochondria of animal cells is formed. [3]

ATP is formed during glycolysis ✔ by the movement of a phosphate group from a 3C
compound to ADP. This occurs in the active site of an enzyme and is called substrate-
linked phosphorylation. ✔ It occurs four times for every molecule of glucose that is
respired. ✔ This makes four molecules of ATP, but two molecules are used in the first
stage of glycolysis so the net gain is two.

Good answer but the last sentence is unnecessary.

(b) Describe how the structure of a mitochondrion enables aerobic respiration to occur efficiently. You may use a labelled and annotated diagram to help your answer. [4]

Mitochondria have an envelope made of two membranes. The outer membrane has carrier
proteins for the transfer of substrates and products of aerobic respiration to pass in and
and out. ✔ Pyruvate and ADP pass through these proteins. The inner membrane is
folded to form cristae. ✔ This gives a large surface for the protein complexes of the
ETC and for the enzyme ATP synthase. ✔ Inside the mitochondria is the matrix that has
all the enzymes of the Krebs cycle and link reaction (and other metabolic processes). ✔

A good description.

(c) There are no mitochondria in red blood cells.

Suggest and explain how they respire. [2]

They respire by carrying out glycolysis to make the ATP they need.

This is not enough for the mark. When *only* glycolysis occurs there is no recycling of NAD to keep respiration going. The candidate needs to state that the pyruvate produced in glycolysis is converted to lactate and it is this reaction that recycles NAD for respiration.

Exam-style questions

Structured questions (Paper 4)

1   An investigation was carried out into the production of ATP in mitochondria. A suspension of mitochondria was prepared. To this was added ADP, phosphate ions and plenty of pyruvate and oxygen. The concentrations of these four substances were determined at intervals.

(a) Explain why pyruvate was used as the substrate rather than glucose. [1]

(b) State what you would expect to happen to the concentrations of the four substances added to the suspension and give detailed explanations for your answer. [4]

(c) The experiment was repeated but no phosphate ions were added.

Predict what would happen to the concentration of oxygen in the suspension and explain your answer. [3]

2   NAD and coenzyme A are coenzymes involved in respiration.

The concentration of NAD in muscle is very limited, about $0.8\,\mu\text{mol}\,g^{-1}$ of tissue.

(a) Outline how reduced NAD is formed during respiration. [2]

(b) Explain how reduced NAD is recycled in muscle tissue when oxygen is available, and when it is not available. [4]

(c) Describe the role of coenzyme A in respiration. [2]

3   (a) Glycolysis is the first stage of respiration.
    (i) State precisely where glycolysis occurs in cells. [1]

    (ii) Outline the changes that occur to glucose during glycolysis. [6]

(b) State three roles of the Krebs cycle in respiration. [4]

(c) Explain how rice plants survive when they are submerged in water. [6]

4   (a) State the precise site of the link reaction. [1]

(b) Using the link reaction as an example, distinguish between dehydrogenation and decarboxylation. [4]

(c) Suggest why pyruvate goes through carrier proteins, rather than go through the phospholipid bilayer, when entering the mitochondrion. [2]

(d) Suggest what happens to the ATP produced in the Krebs cycle. [3]

Data analysis and evaluation (Paper 5)

5   The apparatus in the diagram was used to compare the rates of respiration of germinating seeds of pinto beans, *Phaseolus vulgaris*, with the respiration of leaves of the same species.

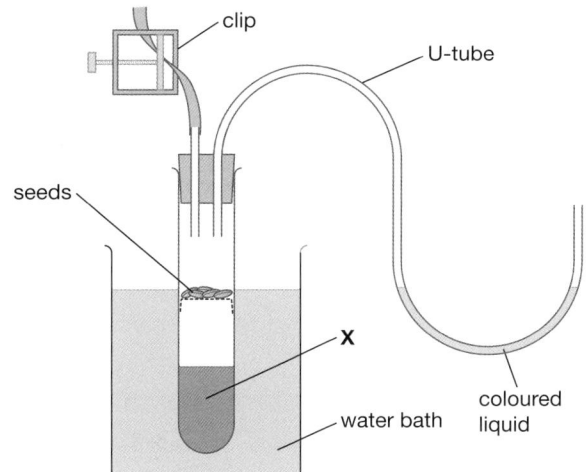

(a) Name a suitable chemical to use as **X** and explain why it is used. [3]

The apparatus was put into a water bath at 27 °C with the clip open. After 10 minutes the clip was closed and the position of the coloured liquid recorded over time. The results are shown in the table.

Time / minutes	0	5	10	15	20	25	30	35
Position of coloured liquid / mm	0	0	0	31	65	95	130	162

(b) Explain **(i)** why a water bath is used, and **(ii)** why the apparatus is left for 10 minutes before closing the clip. [2]

(c) The diameter of the capillary tube is 0.8 mm. Use the results in the table to calculate the rate of oxygen uptake in mm^3 per hour. Show your working. [3]

(d) Explain how the results would differ if the investigation was repeated at 17 °C. [2]

(e) Suggest a suitable control experiment for this investigation and explain why it is necessary. [2]

(f) State how the apparatus would be used to find the rate of respiration of the leaves to make a valid comparison with the beans. Explain your answer. [3]

13 Photosynthesis

Photosynthesis in outline

The process of photosynthesis may be *summarised* by this equation:

$$nCO_2 + nH_2O \xrightarrow[\text{chlorophyll and enzymes}]{\text{light energy}} (CH_2O)n + nO_2$$

Photosynthesis occurs in two stages in the chloroplasts (Figure 13.1):

- **Light-dependent stage** in which light energy is absorbed and there is energy transfer with the formation of ATP and reduced NADP.

- **Light-independent stage** in which carbon dioxide is fixed to make carbohydrates.

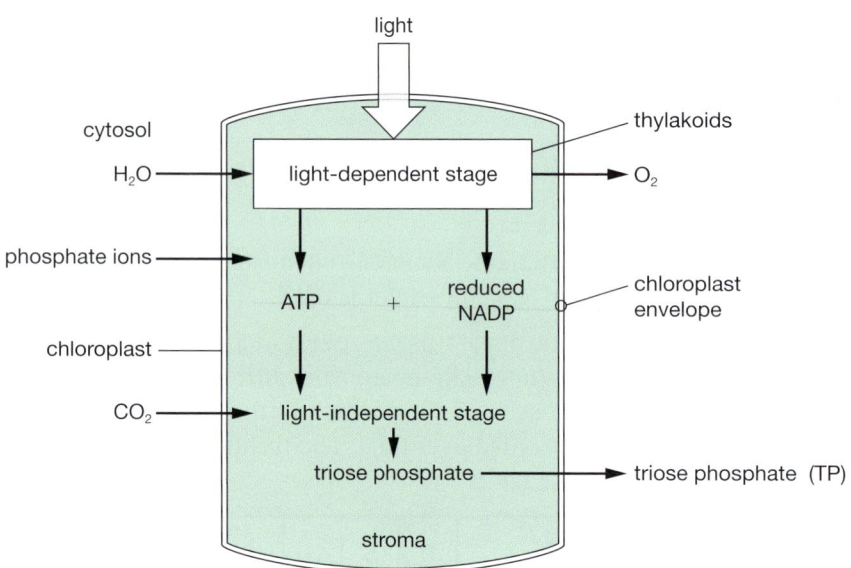

▲ **Figure 13.1** The sites of the two stages of photosynthesis within the chloroplast and exchanges that occur between them and the rest of the cell

Light energy is absorbed in the light-dependent stage. The fixing of carbon dioxide occurs in the light-independent stage. This metabolic pathway – the **Calvin cycle** – is cyclic as the acceptor substance is recycled from the products of carbon fixation.

Chloroplast pigments

Chloroplasts contain coloured compounds (pigments) that absorb light. Plants absorb light in the visual part of the electromagnetic spectrum between the wavelengths of 400 and 700 nm. The pigments absorb most strongly at either end of this range – in the blue-violet and red regions of the spectrum. When white light is shone onto a suspension of chloroplasts made from a leaf, light in these regions is absorbed and light in the green region is reflected or passes through.

> **→ Try this... 1**
>
> Make a table to show the composition and functions of the structures that compose a chloroplast beginning with the outer envelope (double membrane).

★ **Exam tip**

Do *not* use the terms 'light reaction' and 'dark reaction' for the two stages of photosynthesis. Use the terms 'light-dependent stage' and 'light-independent stage' instead.

🔗 **Link**

Both stages of photosynthesis occur in chloroplasts. Compare them with mitochondria – see Unit 12.

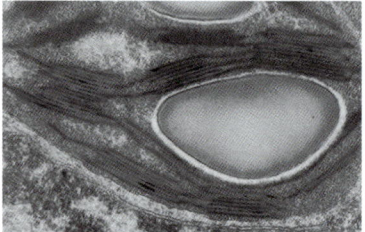

▲ **Figure 13.2** Transmission electron micrograph of a chloroplast

★ **Exam tip**

Make a large, labelled drawing of a chloroplast and annotate it with information about the two stages of photosynthesis. Use your annotated drawing to help your revision of this topic.

★ **Exam tip**

Compare the structures and functions of chloroplasts with those of mitochondria. Make a list of the similarities and differences.

★ **Exam tip**

Find information about the electromagnetic spectrum to find the wavelengths between the ultraviolet and infrared regions.

▼ **Table 13.1** The chloroplast pigments

Pigment	Colour	Function in photosynthesis
chlorophyll *a*	yellow-green	absorbs red and blue-violet light
chlorophyll *b*	blue-green	absorbs red and blue-violet light
β-carotene	orange	absorb blue-violet light
xanthophylls	yellow	may also protect chlorophylls from damage from light and oxygen
		absorb wavelengths that chlorophylls are poor at absorbing

The light-dependent stage

The pigments in the chloroplast are arranged into **photosystems**. There are two of these photosystems; each one consists of **accessory pigments** and proteins arranged around a **reaction centre** containing a pair of chlorophyll *a* molecules:

- **Photosystem 1** (PSI) – reaction centre (a type of chlorophyll *a* known as P700) with a peak absorbance of light at a wavelength of 700 nm.

- **Photosystem 2** (PSII) – reaction centre (a type of chlorophyll *a* known as P680) with peak absorbance of light at a wavelength of 680 nm.

The accessory pigments absorb light of many wavelengths and the energy is transferred to the pair of chlorophyll *a* molecules in the reaction centres of PSI and PSII.

The energy excites electrons in each chlorophyll *a* molecule.

Non-cyclic photophosphorylation: involves photolysis of water and production of reduced NADP and ATP. Electrons travel from PSII to PSI and then to NADP.

Cyclic photophosphorylation: involves production of ATP without photolysis of water or production of reduced NADP. Electrons travel from PSI but instead of reaching NADP they return to PSI.

The light-independent stage

The three main processes that occur in the Calvin cycle are:

- **carboxylation** – fixation of carbon dioxide by reaction with the acceptor compound, ribulose bisphosphate (RuBP)

- **reduction** – to form carbohydrates

- **regeneration** – of RuBP using ATP, so completing the cycle.

Limiting factors

There are three environmental factors that have most influence on the rate of photosynthesis.

Light provides energy for photosynthesis. As the light intensity increases so does the supply of energy that can be absorbed by chloroplast pigments in the thylakoids.

Carbon dioxide is one of the raw materials for photosynthesis. As the carbon dioxide concentration increases so does the supply of carbon to be fixed in the light-independent stage. Water is the other raw material.

Temperature influences the activity of enzymes so an increase leads to an increase in enzyme activity up to an optimum temperature. Both light-dependent and light-independent stages involve enzymes, but temperature has a much greater effect on the light-independent stage.

💡 **Remember**

Thylakoids are like cristae that have split from the inner mitochondrial membrane. The direction in which protons are pumped is the same – from the matrix into the intermembrane space in mitochondria and from the stroma into the thylakoid space in chloroplasts.

★ **Exam tip**

Rubisco is the most abundant and most important enzyme on Earth. Remember, it is responsible for fixing carbon dioxide so plants can make energy-rich compounds that can provide energy, be used for long-term storage and be converted into all the biochemicals, including proteins and nucleic acids.

★ **Exam tip**

It is most important that you use **light intensity** and **carbon dioxide concentration** when writing about these limiting factors; 'light' and 'carbon dioxide' unqualified are not correct.

→ **Try this... 2**

Make a word bank. Make a glossary of all the technical terms in this Unit. Group the terms into three categories: substances (e.g. xanthophyll and ribulose bisphosphate), processes (e.g. cyclic photophosphorylation, reduction) and parts of the chloroplast. Do not forget the source of energy for photosynthesis, the raw materials, the products and the limiting factors. Use the list of substances and processes to make flow charts to show the pathways in the two stages of photosynthesis.

⚙ Practical Skills

Separating chloroplast pigments by chromatography

Chromatography is a technique for separating, identifying and measuring the quantities of substances extracted from biological material.

Figure 13.3 shows a procedure for separating chloroplast pigments using thin layer chromatography (TLC). It is a good idea to run pure substances alongside the extract, for example β-carotene and lutein (a xanthophyll) to help with identification.

The extraction solvent is propanone (acetone). The running solvent is petroleum ether and propanone in proportions of 2:1.

The solvent front moves up the TLC plate. The plate should be removed when it is about 10 mm from the stopper. The solvent front should be marked immediately with a pencil line. It is a good idea to photograph the chromatogram as the colours fade quickly.

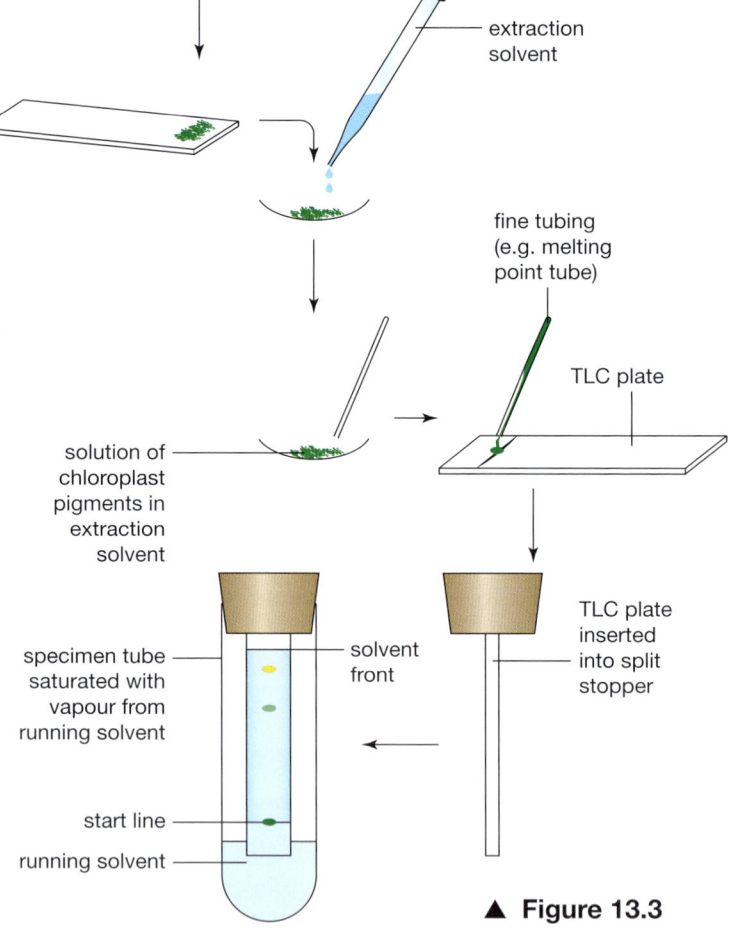

▲ **Figure 13.3**

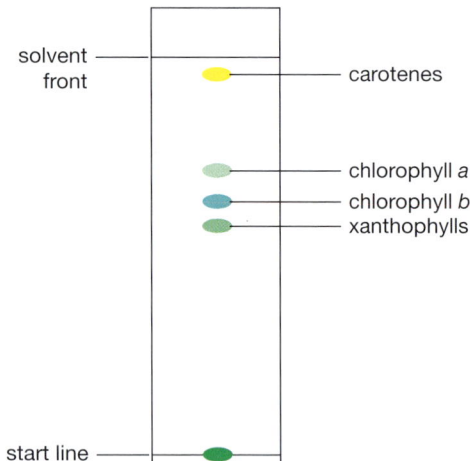

▲ **Figure 13.4** A chromatogram of chloroplast pigments. The exact position of each pigment (and its R_f value) may vary according to the solvents used

The R_f value (retention factor) is the ratio between the distance travelled by a substance and the distance travelled by the solvent front. It is independent of the length of the chromatogram or the length travelled by the solvent front.

$$R_f = \frac{\text{distance travelled by substance}}{\text{distance travelled by solvent front}}$$

★ **Exam tip**

R_f (retention) values do not have units and are expressed as a single number: $R_f = 0$, substance insoluble in the solvent; $R_f = 1$, completely soluble.

⚙ Practical Skills

Investigating factors that influence the rate of photosynthesis

Rates of photosynthesis can be measured by:

- detecting the activity of the light-dependent stage using redox dyes, such as methylene blue and DCPIP

- measuring the production of oxygen in the light-dependent stage by collecting the gas (as oxygen is not very soluble in water).

Experimental work on photosynthesis often uses suspensions of the single-celled alga *Chlorella* or chloroplasts isolated from the leaves of plants such as lettuce and spinach. Chloroplasts are organelles so have no cell walls. They are suspended in a sucrose solution with the same water potential as cytoplasm to prevent them bursting.

Rates of photosynthesis using a redox indicator

The transfer of electrons and hydrogen ions to NADP occurs during the light-dependent stage. DCPIP, a blue indicator, acts as a hydrogen acceptor, turning colourless as it is reduced during the light-dependent stage. DCPIP is used instead of NADP so that visual results can be obtained.

electrons and hydrogen ions from water + DCPIP → reduced DCPIP
(blue)   (colourless)

In this procedure, chloroplast suspensions with added DCPIP are exposed to different **wavelengths of light**.

> 💡 **Remember**
>
> In Unit 12, methylene blue was used as a redox indicator to investigate the rate of respiration.

1. Put $5\,cm^3$ of the chloroplast suspension into a test-tube and add $1\,cm^3$ of water. This tube is a colour standard to help decide when the redox indicator has become colourless.

2. Label five test-tubes **A** to **E**. Wrap each test-tube in foil to exclude light.

3. Put $5\,cm^3$ of the chloroplast suspension into each test-tube and cover with a foil cap or a stopper.

4. Add $1\,cm^3$ of the medium containing DCPIP to each test-tube.

5. Start a timer and turn on a light source, such as a bench lamp. Make sure there are no other light sources.

6. Remove the foil from test-tube **A**, wrap a purple filter around the front of the test-tube facing the light source and secure with an elastic band. Put the test-tube in a rack and note the time.

7. Repeat Step 6 with the other test-tubes using blue, green, orange and red filters for these tubes.

8. Record the time when the colour of the suspension in each tube matches the colour standard.

9. The rate of photosynthesis can be determined by calculating the reciprocal of the time taken for the indicator to become colourless.

Colour of filter	Wavelength / nm	Time taken for DCPIP to decolourise / s	Rate of photosynthesis (×1000) / s⁻¹
purple	425	38	26.3
blue	450	83	12.0
green	525	485	2.1
orange	625	46	21.7
red	675	51	19.6

➡ Try this... 3

(a) Draw a graph of the results.   [5]

(b) (i) Explain why the graph is an action spectrum for the *Chlorella* suspension.   [1]

    (ii) Predict how an absorption spectrum for a suspension of *Chlorella* would compare with the graph you have drawn.   [3]

(c) Plan a method using the redox indicator DCPIP to investigate the effect of different light intensities on the rate of photosynthesis of a suspension of *Chlorella*. Explain how the results will be processed.   [10]

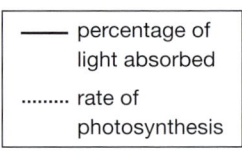

Worked Example 1

(a) State the role of the light-dependent stage of photosynthesis. [2]

Light of different wavelengths was passed through a flask containing a suspension of the unicellular alga, *Chlorella*. A light sensor was placed behind the flask to measure the light transmitted through the suspension. A sensor was placed in the middle of the suspension to detect changes in the oxygen concentration. Data from the sensors were recorded by a data logger and used to plot an absorption spectrum and an action spectrum as shown in Figure 13.5.

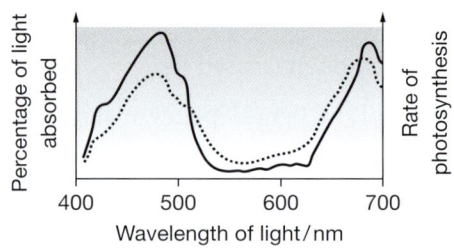

▲ **Figure 13.5**

(b) State what is meant by the terms absorption spectrum and action spectrum. [2]

(c) The transmission of light through a flask of water was 100%. Suggest how the figures for the absorption spectrum were calculated from the readings from the light sensor. [1]

(d) Explain how results from the oxygen sensor were used to plot the action spectrum. [2]

(e) State the conclusions that can be made from the absorption spectrum and the action spectrum for *Chlorella*. [2]

Answers

(a) Energy transfer from light energy to chemical energy with the formation of ATP and reduced NADP. These two end products of the light-dependent stage provide the energy for the fixation of carbon dioxide and the production of the carbon acceptor substance, RuBP.

(b) An absorption spectrum shows how much light energy is absorbed at different wavelengths. An action spectrum shows how much photosynthesis occurs at each wavelength.

(c) The readings from the light sensor were subtracted from 100.

(d) The oxygen concentration indicates the rate of photosynthesis. A high oxygen concentration indicates a high rate of photosynthesis. The rate can be determined by calculating the increase in oxygen concentration over a period of time.

(e) The absorption spectrum and the action spectrum show the same pattern with the highest rates of photosynthesis occurring at the same wavelengths as the highest absorption of light, in the blue regions (about 475 nm) and the red regions (about 675 nm) of the spectrum.

→ Try this... 4

The relative concentrations of three intermediate compounds in the Calvin cycle (GP, TP and RuBP) were determined. The effects of changes in light intensity and carbon dioxide concentration on the relative concentrations of these compounds were investigated. The results are shown in Figure 13.6.

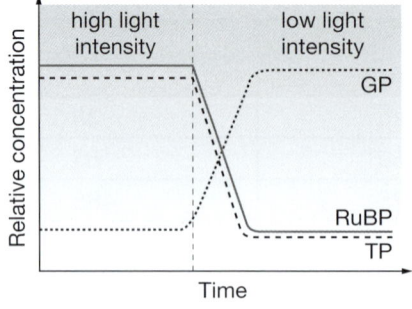

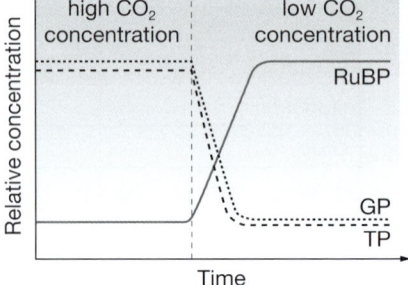

▲ **Figure 13.6**

Explain the changes in the concentrations of GP, TP and RuBP shown in Figure 13.6: (a) as the light intensity changes [4] (b) as the carbon dioxide concentration changes. [4]

→ **Try this... 5**

A student investigated the effect of light intensity on the rate of photosynthesis of an aquatic plant by collecting the gas produced in a capillary tube with an internal diameter of 0.4 mm. The student began with the lamp at 50 mm from the plant, moving the lamp further away after each result was taken. The results are shown in Table 13.2.

Distance from lamp to plant / mm	Length of gas in capillary tubing / mm	Length of time for gas to collect / s
50	65	180
75	43	120
100	50	200
150	28	210
200	10	200
250	5	250

▲ **Table 13.2**

(a)   Use the results in Table 13.2 to present a new table of data that shows the light intensity (as $1/d^2$), the volumes of gas collected and the rates of photosynthesis (in $mm^3\,min^{-1}$). [5]

(b)   Use the data in your table to plot a graph to show the effect of light intensity on the rate of photosynthesis. [5]

(c)   Suggest three limitations of the procedure as described above. [3]

→ **Try this... 6**

The diagram in Figure 13.7 summarises the process of non-cyclic photophosphorylation in the light-dependent stage of photosynthesis, which occurs across thylakoid membranes inside chloroplasts.

(a)   State the names of the components of the light-dependent stage shown in Figure 13.7:

(i)   the pigment complexes at **A** and at **B**

(ii)   the type of chloroplast pigment shown by P680 and P700

(iii) the type of molecule shown by **C**

(iv) the reaction that occurs at **D**

(v)   the enzyme shown by **E**.   [5]

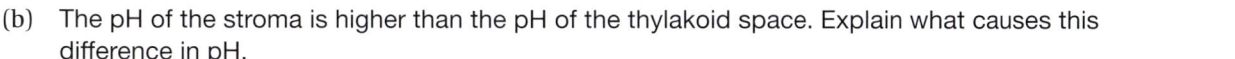

▲ **Figure 13.7**

(b)   The pH of the stroma is higher than the pH of the thylakoid space. Explain what causes this difference in pH. [3]

(c)   Explain the role of the pH gradient between the thylakoid space and the stroma. [3]

(d)   Describe the uses of ATP and reduced NADP in photosynthesis. [4]

(e)   Explain how low light intensities act as a limiting factor of photosynthesis. [4]

→ **Try this... 7**

(a) Outline the processes that occur in photosynthesis during:

(i) the light-dependent stage [6]

(ii) the light-independent stage. [6]

(b) Discuss the roles of the following in photosynthesis:

(i)   ATP   (ii)   NADP   (iii)   chlorophyll *a*   (iv)   carotene

(v)   carbon dioxide   (vi)   RuBP   (vii) rubisco   (viii) ATP synthase

(ix)   proton pumps. [18]

↑ Raise your grade

(a) The figure shows the formation of ATP in a palisade cell.

(i) Explain the term *phosphorylation*. [2]

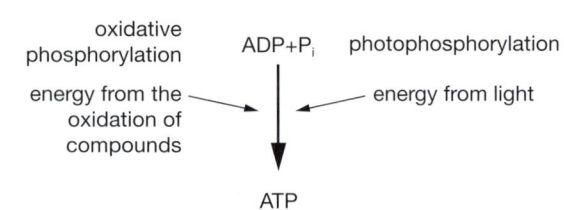

> It is the addition of a phosphate group to a compound, ✔ e.g. ADP gains a phosphate group from an intermediate compound during glycolysis ✔ to become ATP in substrate-linked phosphorylation. | This is a good answer.

(ii) State the precise sites in a plant cell of the two types of phosphorylation. [2]

> Oxidative happens in mitochondria; ✗ photophosphorylation in chloroplasts. ✗

> This is not precise enough to gain either of the marks. The answers are inner mitochondrial membranes and thylakoid membranes in chloroplasts.

(iii) State three similarities *and* three differences between photophosphorylation and oxidative phosphorylation, *other than* where they occur. [6]

> Both processes use the ETC, ✔ ATP synthase is in both organelles to produce ATP ✔ and both have proton pumps to make a high concentration of protons (in the intermembrane space and in the thylakoid space). ✔

> These answers are correct but the candidate has forgotten to give any differences.

(b) Describe the role of photolysis in the light-dependent stage of photosynthesis. [4]

> The splitting of water provides protons and electrons ✔. The protons accumulate in the thylakoid spaces to give the proton gradient. Electrons are provided to chlorophyll a in the reaction centre of PS2 ✔ so more can pass to the electron transport chain ✔. Protons and electrons react with NADP to form reduced NADP ✔ for the Calvin cycle.

> A good answer. There is no need to mention oxygen (the by-product of photosynthesis) as it is not used in the light-dependent stage.

(c) State five uses of ATP in a plant cell. [5]

> DNA replication, ✔ absorbing ions by active transport ✔ and activating amino acids for protein synthesis. ✔ | The candidate has only given three uses, not five.

(d) Describe how a chloroplast is adapted to carry out photosynthesis efficiently. [5]

> Chloroplasts have thylakoid membranes that are stacked into grana. ✔ These give a large surface area for absorbing light. ✔ The light-independent reactions occur on the thylakoids ✗ to make ATP and reduced NADP, which are used in the Calvin cycle. The rest of the chloroplast is made up of the matrix that has no membrane in it. Here there are enzymes of the Calvin cycle where glucose is made. Some is stored in starch grains.

> The candidate has written 'independent' rather than 'dependent' in the third sentence. An easy mistake to make. Always re-read your answers before the end of the exam looking specifically for these mistakes. The rest of the answer lacks the A Level detail on the two stages of photosynthesis. For example, there is nothing about chloroplast pigments, proton pumps or ATP synthase in the description of thylakoids. There is no detail about the enzymes of the Calvin cycle, for example, rubisco, and the fixation of carbon dioxide in the light-independent stage.

Exam-style questions

Structured questions (Paper 4)

1 The figure shows the Calvin cycle.

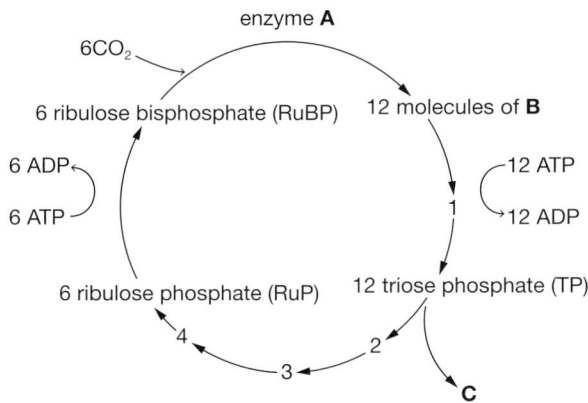

(a) (i) Name enzyme **A**, substance **B** and one of the substances formed at **C**. [3]

(ii) State the source of ATP. [1]

(iii) Name the precise site of the reactions of the Calvin cycle. [1]

(iv) State the number of carbon atoms in ribulose bisphosphate. [1]

(b) Explain the advantage of the reactions forming a cycle, as shown in the diagram. [2]

(c) Discuss the roles of pigments and electron carriers in photosynthesis. [6]

2 (a) Describe the role of cyclic photophosphorylation. [4]

Scientists investigated the effect of light intensity on the rate of photosynthesis of barley plants. The table shows the net uptake of carbon dioxide at different light intensities, measured in PAR*.

PAR / $W\,m^{-2}$	Net uptake of carbon dioxide / $g\,m^{-2}$ leaf h^{-1}
0	−0.3
50	0.8
100	1.4
200	1.6
300	1.6

*PAR = photosynthetically active radiation: the wavelengths of light absorbed by plants (400–700 nm).

(b) Explain the result for $0\,W\,m^{-2}$. [3]

(c) Explain the effect of increasing the light intensity on carbon dioxide uptake. [6]

Data analysis and evaluation (Paper 5)

3 Hydrogencarbonate indicator solution is sensitive to changes in pH. The diagram shows the range of colours obtained when treated with buffer solutions of different pH.

pH	7.6	8.0	8.4	8.8	9.2
colour	yellow	orange	red	magenta	purple

When atmospheric air is bubbled through the indicator solution it becomes red.

A concentrated culture of the unicellular alga *Scenedesmus quadricauda* was immobilised in small beads of calcium alginate, which were then placed into six test-tubes of the red hydrogencarbonate solution. The test-tubes were placed into different light intensities for one hour and the colours recorded. The beads were removed and the absorbance of the indicator solution was determined using a colorimeter with a green filter. The results are shown in the table.

Relative light intensity	Hydrogencarbonate indicator solution after 1 hour	
	Colour	Absorbance
0 (darkness)	yellow	0.33
0.06	yellow	0.43
0.16	orange	0.50
0.40	red	0.57
0.80	magenta	0.67
1.60	purple	0.73

(a) Suggest the advantage of using immobilised algae in this investigation, rather than using a suspension of the algae. [2]

(b) Suggest three variables that should be controlled in this investigation. [3]

(c) Explain the results shown in the table. [7]

(d) (i) Explain the advantage of using a colorimeter for taking the results. [2]

(ii) Suggest how this investigation could be improved. [2]

Planning question (Paper 5)

4 The rate of photosynthesis can be determined by measuring oxygen production by aquatic plants.

(a) Plan a method to determine the effect of changing the carbon dioxide concentration on the rate of photosynthesis of an aquatic plant. [10]

(b) Explain how the results will be collected and how rates of photosynthesis will be calculated and presented on a graph. [5]

(c) Draw a sketch graph to show the results you predict for this investigation. [3]

(d) Explain the effect of increasing the carbon dioxide concentration on the rate of photosynthesis. [4]

14 Homeostasis

Scientists ask questions all the time. One technique you can practise while learning the topics in this syllabus is to rephrase the learning outcomes as questions. You can then set about answering them. Try telling your answers (without notes) to someone else and see if they are convinced by what you tell them.

The next four pages are presented in the form of questions and answers. You can apply this technique to other Units in the course. The numbers in brackets refer to the learning outcomes. Look at the syllabus for the details of each learning outcome.

Why is homeostasis important to mammals? (14.1.1)

You will recall from Unit 3 that enzymes work efficiently if kept at an optimum temperature and pH. Changes in these two factors away from the optimum cause the rates of enzyme-catalysed reactions to change. If the temperature is too high or the pH change too extreme, it is likely that enzymes will become denatured and the reactions they catalyse will slow down or stop. Most enzymes work inside cells, which have mechanisms to keep some conditions constant. However, in a multicellular organism there is a limit to what each cell can achieve and the actions of different specialised cells need to be coordinated by the nervous system and by the endocrine system.

What are the main principles of homeostasis? (14.1.2)

Homeostasis involves keeping conditions within narrow limits. To do this each system needs:

- receptors that detect internal and/or external stimuli

- a control centre, such as the hypothalamus in the brain

- one or more effector organs to bring about corrective actions; examples are the muscles, kidneys and liver

- the nervous system and/or endocrine system for coordinating the tissues and organs involved.

Each homeostatic system uses the principle of negative feedback.

What is negative feedback? (14.1.2 and 14.1.10)

A good example of homeostasis that you may know is the control of body temperature. This is controlled by *negative* feedback because the responses stimulated by the hypothalamus always counteract the change in body temperature. This negative feedback system is always attempting to *reduce* the difference between the actual body temperature and the ideal body temperature or set point. The corrective actions are 'switched off' when the blood temperature returns to normal.

What is excretion? (14.1.3 and 14.1.6)

Excretion is the removal from the body of toxic substances, the waste products of metabolism and substances that are in excess of requirements. All substances that are excreted have passed through the blood at some stage. Urea and carbon dioxide are the main excretory products of mammals. Amino acids cannot be stored. Any that are in excess as they are not needed to make proteins are deaminated to form ammonia and keto acids. Ammonia is converted to urea and excreted through the kidneys. Keto acids can be respired via the Krebs cycle. The production and excretion of carbon dioxide is described in Units 12 and 9.

★ **Exam tip**

The questions on these pages are written as direct questions. Questions like this start with words like 'why' and 'how'. Exam questions in Papers 4 and 5 are not like this. They use the command words which you can find listed on page 45 of the syllabus.

★ **Exam tip**

Research the answers to the questions on pages 116 to 121 and see if you can improve the answers. Write your own answers and then use them to explain these topics to someone else – *without looking at any notes or presentation slides*.

★ **Exam tip**

When you write about homeostasis, use the terms listed here: set point, narrow limits, stimulus, receptor, monitor, control centre, effector, negative feedback and corrective action.

🔗 **Link**

Cell signalling is essential for coordination in homeostasis. Read page 45 and take the principle further by answering *Try this... 6* on page 120.

💡 **Remember**

Keto acids are organic compounds that have a carboxylic acid group and a ketone group. Pyruvate and oxaloacetate are examples.

Try this... 1

What can you identify in photographic images of the kidney? (14.1.5)

Look carefully at Figures 14.1 and 14.2. Make a sketch of the structures that you can see and identify them.

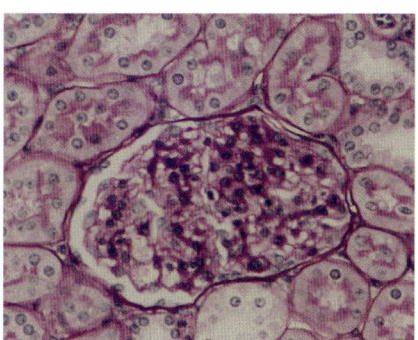 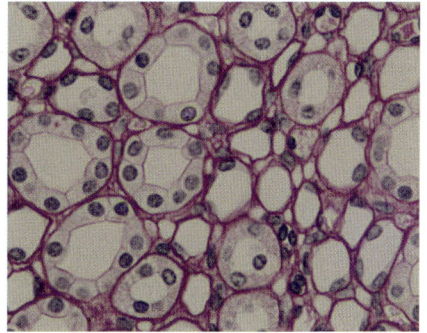

▲ **Figure 14.1** A section through the cortex of the kidney

▲ **Figure 14.2** A section through the medulla of the kidney

What are the processes that occur in the kidney to produce urine? (14.1.6 and 14.1.7)

There are three that you should know about:

- ultrafiltration producing filtrate in Bowman's capsules

- selective reabsorption in the proximal convoluted tubules

- control of the reabsorption of water in the collecting ducts.

How does ultrafiltration take place in the kidney? (14.1.6)

Blood flows into the glomerulus through branches of the renal artery. Pressure filtration occurs in all capillaries, but the capillaries that make up the glomerulus and the podocytes that form the inner epithelium that lines Bowman's capsule are adapted for efficient ultrafiltration.

- Blood pressure is high as the kidneys are near the heart. The efferent arterioles are narrower than the afferent arterioles, which builds up a head of pressure in the glomerulus.

- The capillaries have numerous pores in their walls which are at least 4 nm in diameter. These capillaries have more pores than capillaries elsewhere in the body.

- Around each capillary is a basement membrane that is made of fibrous proteins and acts like a molecular sieve to allow everything with a relative molecular mass (RMM) of less than 69 000 through into the Bowman's capsule. This is the only barrier between blood and the filtrate.

Try this... 2

Make a sketch of the cells visible in Figure 14.3. Label the features of these PCT cells that are adaptations for the movement of solutes from the filtrate into the blood. Use your drawing to add notes about selective reabsorption.

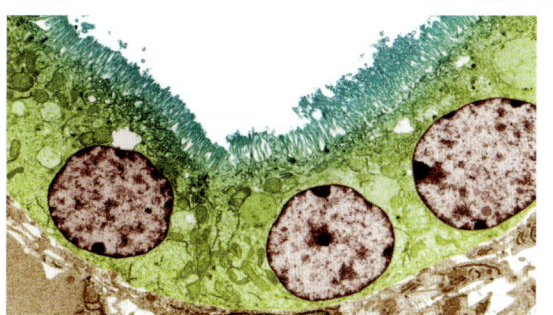

▲ **Figure 14.3** A TEM of some cells that form the lining of a proximal convoluted tubule

Key terms

Set point: the value for a physiological factor maintained as part of homeostatic equilibrium.

Stimulus: any change in the environment or inside the body that leads to a response.

Receptor: a cell or sensory neurone acting as a transducer to convert the energy of a stimulus into electrical impulses that travel along a neurone.

Effector: muscle or gland that carries out an action when stimulated by a nerve impulse or hormone.

Negative feedback: control mechanism that always returns a physiological factor to its set point to maintain homeostatic equilibrium.

Corrective action: a change in the body that restores the value for a physiological factor to its set point.

★ **Exam tip**

Looking at plenty of diagrams of the kidney and animations of ultrafiltration and selective reabsorption will help to improve your understanding of the structure and function of the kidney.

★ **Exam tip**

Search online for scanning electron micrographs of nephrons, especially the glomerulus, so that you can see how it is adapted for ultrafiltration. Make a model of a glomerular capillary with podocytes wrapped around it. This will show you how the structure of podocytes facilitates ultrafiltration.

Why is it important to keep the water potential and glucose concentration of the blood constant? (14.1.1)

Water potential: when the water potential decreases *below* the set point, the blood plasma becomes too concentrated and water passes out of cells by osmosis from the tissues, which become dehydrated and function less efficiently. If the water potential increases *above* the set point, the blood plasma becomes too dilute and water passes into cells by osmosis. This causes them to swell and function less efficiently. If the water potential increases too much the cells may burst.

Blood glucose concentration: glucose is an important respiratory substrate. Some cells rely entirely on glucose and cannot respire anything else. If the concentration decreases below a certain level, then people are likely to go into a coma. Above a certain concentration and the water potential of the plasma becomes too low and water passes out of cells.

How is negative feedback involved in osmoregulation? (14.1.2 and 14.1.8)

Just beneath the hypothalamus is the pituitary gland. Receptor cells (sometimes known as 'osmostats') in the hypothalamus send impulses down neurones that end within the posterior pituitary gland. These neurones make the peptide hormone ADH, which they release into capillaries in the pituitary so that it can be distributed throughout the body in the blood. The target cells of ADH are the epithelial cells of the DCT and the collecting ducts in the kidneys.

ADH interacts with receptors on the cell surface membranes of the DCT and CD cells, leading to the movement of vesicles containing aquaporins. These vesicles move towards the luminal membranes of the epithelial cells where they fuse with the cell surface membrane. Putting aquaporins into the membrane makes it much easier for water to flow from the urine into the cells. Other aquaporins are in the basal and lateral membranes of the epithelial cells to let water move out of the cells and into the blood. Sodium ions, chloride ions and urea are the solutes that contribute to the low water potential in the tissue fluid in the medulla.

The water that is reabsorbed enters the capillaries in the medulla. These vessels have the same shape as the loops of Henle. This parallel arrangement of loops and the blood vessels, known as vasa recta, in the medulla helps to maintain the high solute concentration (low water potential) in the tissue fluid.

When water potential is restored to the set point, ADH secretion stops. ADH has a short half-life (10–30 minutes) so its concentration in the blood decreases fairly quickly. Without the stimulation by ADH, the DCT and CD cells remove the aquaporins from the luminal surface and the permeability to water of these cells decreases. Water is not reabsorbed so dilute urine is produced. This removes excess water from the body.

Test strips and biosensors are used to measure the concentration of glucose in urine and blood. How do they work? (14.1.11)

Test strips for glucose use two enzymes:

- glucose oxidase catalyses this reaction:

  glucose + oxygen → gluconic acid + hydrogen peroxide

- peroxidase catalyses a reaction between hydrogen peroxide and a chromogen, which is a compound in the pad that changes colour:

  hydrogen peroxide + chromogen → oxidised chromogen + water

  (colourless)   (coloured)

The colour is matched against a colour chart to determine the concentration of glucose if the test is positive (Figure 14.4).

🔗 Link

This is a good opportunity to revise your knowledge and understanding of water potential and osmosis from Unit 4.

★ Exam tip

The 'concentration' of the body fluids is rarely given in text books and web sites as a water potential. You may find osmotic potential, osmotic pressure, osmolarity and osmolality. At A Level your response should be in terms of water potential as you learnt in Unit 4.

★ Exam tip

You can show the fluctuations that occur in water potential by drawing a sine wave on a pair of axes. The horizontal axis is time and the vertical axis is water potential. As you read this section, relate what happens to the increases and decreases shown on your graph.

→ Try this... 3

Answer question 2 on page 123 and then draw a feedback loop to show what happens when the water potential of the blood increases above normal (the blood plasma becomes less concentrated).

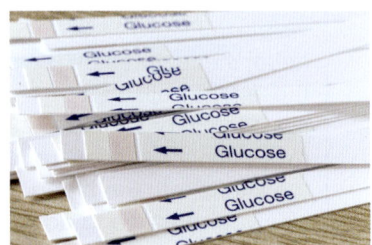

▲ **Figure 14.4** Test strips for glucose. The enzymes are immobilised in the coloured pad at the end of the strip

→ Try this... 4

The table shows the concentrations of glucose and insulin in the blood plasma at different times in the life of a teenager who often went without meals.

	Glucose concentration in the plasma / mg 100 cm^{-3}	Insulin concentration in the plasma / arbitrary units
during an overnight fast	80	9
during a large breakfast	160	70
after the absorption of a meal is complete	70	10
during prolonged fasting	60	6

(a) Describe the relationship between the concentrations of glucose and insulin in the blood plasma as given in the table. [2]

(b) Explain the changes in the concentrations of glucose and insulin in the blood during a meal and when the glucose is absorbed. [5]

(c) Explain how the concentration of glucose in the plasma is maintained during periods of prolonged fasting. [3]

→ Try this... 5

Biosensors are used by people with diabetes to measure the concentration of glucose in their blood.

Figure 14.5 shows how a glucose biosensor works to give a digital reading of the glucose concentration.

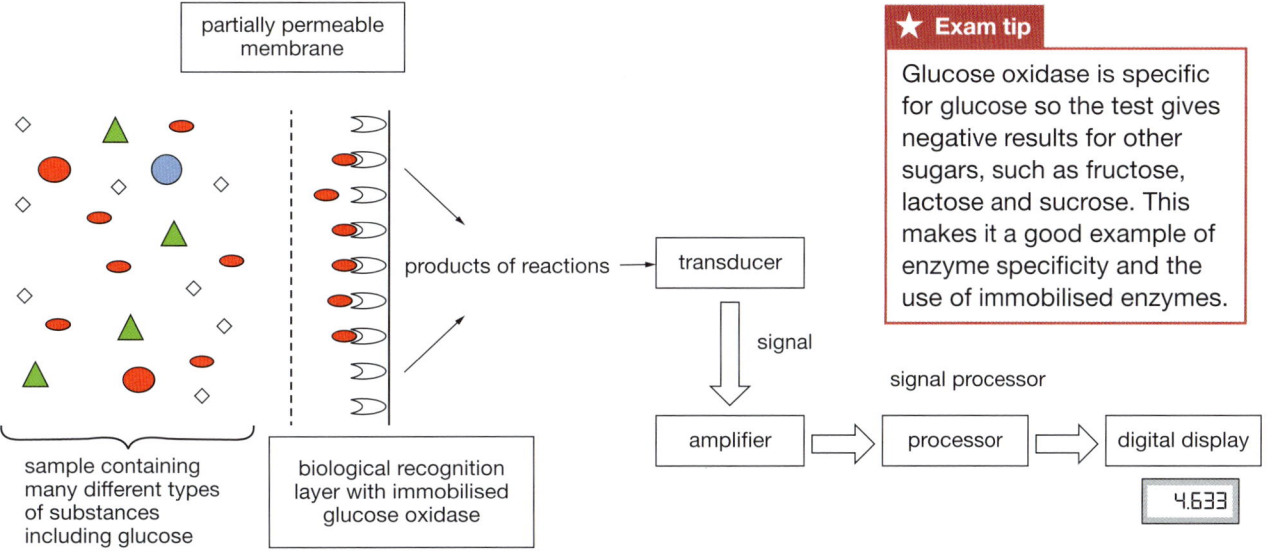

★ **Exam tip**

Glucose oxidase is specific for glucose so the test gives negative results for other sugars, such as fructose, lactose and sucrose. This makes it a good example of enzyme specificity and the use of immobilised enzymes.

▲ **Figure 14.5**

(a) (i) Write out the word equation to show the reaction that is catalysed by glucose oxidase. [2]

(ii) Explain how the design of the biosensor ensures that only glucose molecules give a positive reading when a blood sample is tested. [2]

(iii) Outline how the reaction that occurs at the biological recognition layer result in a digital reading. [3]

(iv) Some glucose biosensors give results as 'glucose concentration in blood' and others as 'glucose concentration in blood plasma'. Suggest and explain which gives the higher concentration for the same sample of blood. [2]

(b) Discuss the advantages for diabetics of using a biosensor, like that shown in Figure 14.5, rather than urinalysis using test strips. [4]

→ **Try this... 6**

Use syllabus statement 14.1.9 to extend your knowledge of cell signalling. Figure 14.6 shows what happens when glucagon arrives at the surface of a liver cell with the production of the second messenger, cyclic AMP.

Copy Figure 14.6 and show the events that occur inside the liver cell that lead to the production of glucose which then diffuses into the blood.

Annotate your diagram to show the enzyme cascade and how the original stimulus from glucagon at the cell surface is amplified so that the liver cell can give a rapid response.

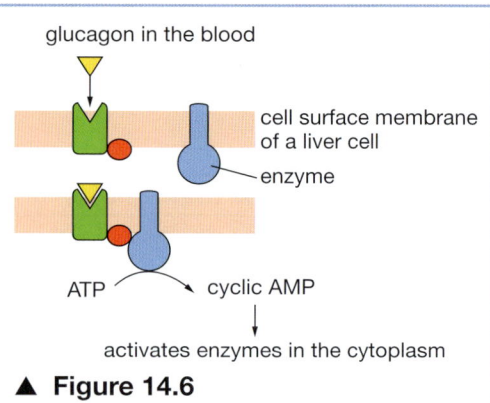

glucagon in the blood

cell surface membrane of a liver cell

enzyme

ATP   cyclic AMP

activates enzymes in the cytoplasm

▲ **Figure 14.6**

Homeostasis in plants: what's that all about? (14.2.1)

Plants respond to changes in their environment to maintain internal conditions. The most obvious of these involves maintaining carbon dioxide concentrations inside leaves for photosynthesis. Plants open stomata to allow the diffusion of carbon dioxide into internal air spaces. These air spaces are fully saturated with water vapour, which in most conditions diffuses out. If the water cannot be replaced quickly enough because rates of transpiration are higher than rates of water absorption, plants often wilt. This moves the leaves out of the direct rays of the sun and is a homeostatic mechanism. Often a few cells at the base of the leaf become flaccid and this is enough to lower the leaf and reduce water loss. Often the stomata close as well to reduce rates of transpiration.

How do stomata work? (14.2.3)

Rates of transpiration are dependent on the size of the stomatal pores, which is controlled by guard cells (Figure 14.7). These cells are sensitive to light intensity, humidity, temperature and carbon dioxide concentrations inside leaves. They are also sensitive to signalling chemicals released by the plants when water is in short supply. Stomata tend to be closed at night and open during the day, although there are some species where this rhythm is reversed.

🔗 **Link**

This is a good opportunity to revise transport of water in plants and transpiration from Unit 7.

✏ **Revision strategy**

As you read this section on stomata make a flow chart diagram to summarise the changes that occur when stomata open and close.

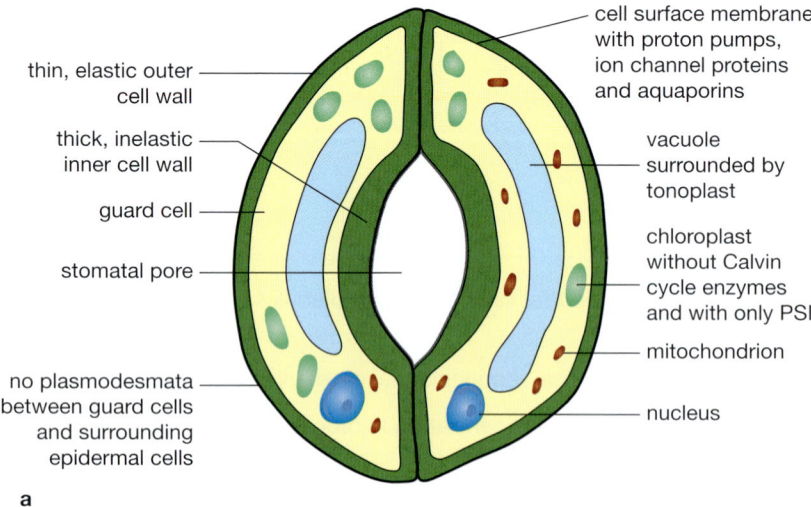

thin, elastic outer cell wall

thick, inelastic inner cell wall

guard cell

stomatal pore

no plasmodesmata between guard cells and surrounding epidermal cells

cell surface membrane with proton pumps, ion channel proteins and aquaporins

vacuole surrounded by tonoplast

chloroplast without Calvin cycle enzymes and with only PSI

mitochondrion

nucleus

a

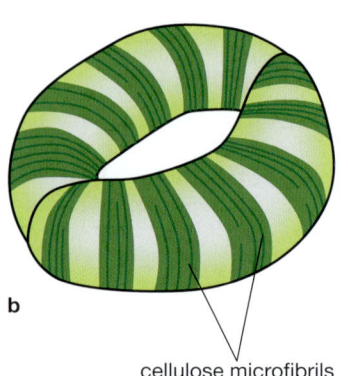

b

cellulose microfibrils

▲ **Figure 14.7**

Stomatal opening is dependent on the detection of blue light by phototropin molecules in the cytoplasm of guard cells. Phototropins are pigment molecules that respond to light by activating proton pumps in the cell surface membranes.

Proton pumps move protons *out* of the cell using ATP as their source of energy. This makes the inside of the cell more negative, a change that stimulates K^+ ion influx channel proteins to open. Potassium ions diffuse into the guard cells. Other ion channels open allowing the diffusion of negatively charged ions (chloride and nitrate) to maintain electroneutrality. Starch is converted to malate, which also increases the concentration of solutes in the guard cells so decreasing the water potential. Water enters the cell through aquaporins. The cells become turgid and expand. Cellulose microfibrils in the cell walls prevent guard cells becoming any wider. As each guard cell enlarges it lengthens, pushing against the other guard cell at either end; both cells bow outwards so opening the pore between them (Figure 14.7).

In the dark, proton pumps stop functioning as there is now no stimulation from phototropins. The inside of the cell becomes less negatively charged and potassium ion influx channel proteins close. Other channel proteins open to allow potassium ions to diffuse out. Other ions also diffuse out and malate is converted back into starch. The decrease in solute concentration causes an increase in water potential in guard cells so that water flows out of the guard cells by osmosis into adjacent cells. Guard cells become flaccid and are pushed closer together by the adjacent cells so that the stomatal pore closes.

> ★ **Exam tip**
>
> The pumping of protons out of the cell to stimulate the influx of ions is similar to the role of proton pumps in companion cells (see page 69). Do not confuse proton pumps in guard cells and companion cells with proton pumps in mitochondria and chloroplasts that use energy from the movement of electrons through the ETC.

 **Try this... 7**

Often the data included in questions are presented in composite form as in Figure 14.8.

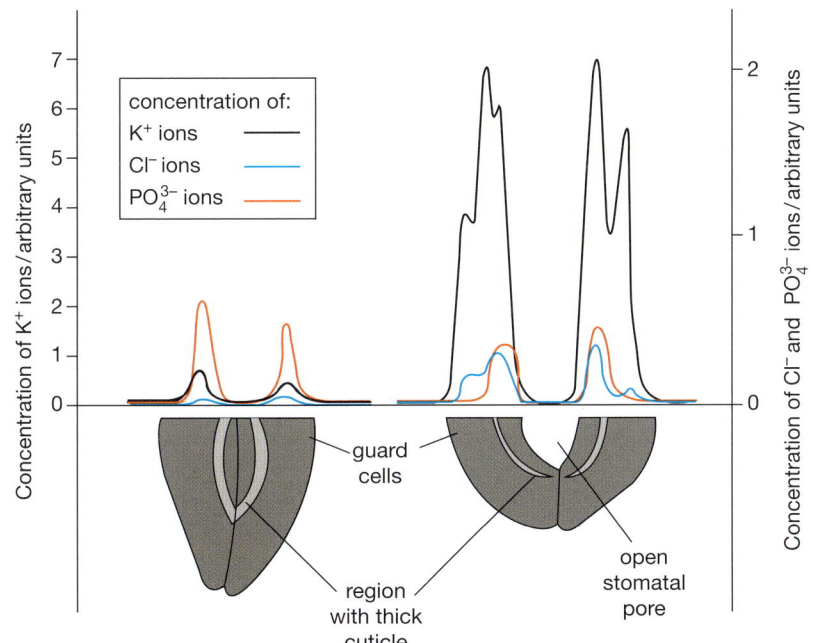

> ★ **Exam tip**
>
> In this graph, note that there are two vertical axes with very different scales.

▲ **Figure 14.8** Concentrations of three ions across guard cells of *Vicia faba* when a stoma is closed and when it is open

The concentrations of three ions, potassium, chloride and phosphate, were determined in guard cells of closed and open stomata. Figure 14.8 shows these concentrations measured in arbitrary units, which are the same for all three ions.

(a) Describe the results shown in Figure 14.8. [3]

(b) Explain how the difference in the concentrations of the ions may be responsible for the movement of guard cells when they open and close stomata. [5]

(c) Plasmodesmata are cytoplasmic connections between adjacent plant cells. Guard cells do not have plasmodesmata. Suggest how this helps guard cells function efficiently. [3]

(d) Abscisic acid (ABA) is produced by plants when there is a shortage of water. Explain how ABA stimulates the closing of stomata. [6]

↑ Raise your grade

The kidneys are one of the main excretory organs of the body. The diagram shows a vertical section of a kidney.

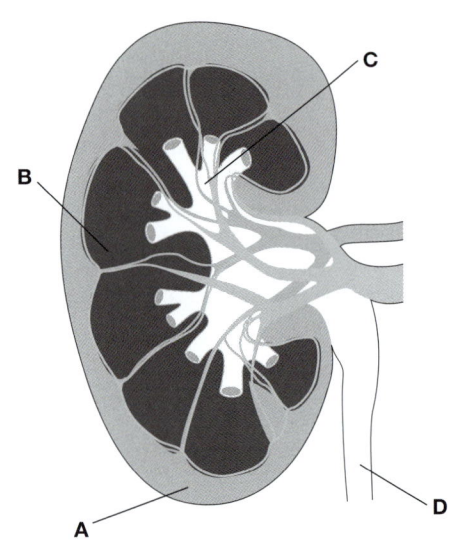

(a) (i) Identify the parts labelled **A** to **D**. [4]

A – cortex ✔ B – medulla ✔ C – pelvis ✔
D – ureter ✔

> All parts named correctly. These are easy marks if the candidate has made plenty of labelled drawings and diagrams when revising.

(ii) Describe briefly the functions of the parts labelled **C** and **D**. [2]

Urine passes into the pelvis from the collecting ducts and then passes down the ureter to the bladder. ✔ The ureter is a muscular tube that moves urine to the bladder by peristalsis. ✔

> Correct functions given for structures **C** and **D**.

(b) Selective reabsorption occurs in the proximal convoluted tubule of each nephron in the kidney.

Explain how cells in the proximal convoluted tubule are adapted for selective reabsorption. [5]

These cells have many microvilli that give a large surface area for absorbing substances from the filtrate in the proximal convoluted tubule. ✔ Some of these, like glucose and sodium, are absorbed by active transport. This needs ATP, which is supplied by the many mitochondria ✔ in the cells. Mitochondria have many cristae to give a large surface area for the protein carriers in the ETC and for many ATP synthase molecules. The membranes of PCT cells have many co-transporters for sodium and glucose.

> This is *not* a well-structured answer. The first sentence clearly links structure to function and the point about many mitochondria gains a mark. The adaptations of mitochondria are not relevant as they apply to all cells with high demands for ATP. The last sentence does not state that it is the *luminal* membranes that are the location of the co-transporters. Sodium *ions* are present in body fluids and in cells, not sodium.

(c) Explain the changes that occur to the volume and composition of the glomerular filtrate as it flows through the proximal convoluted tubule. [5]

The volume of filtrate decreases as most of the water is reabsorbed down a water potential gradient by osmosis into the blood. ✔ This happens because solutes are reabsorbed by active transport. All the glucose ✔ and amino acids ✔ and most of the sodium ions ✔ are reabsorbed too by carrier proteins in the membranes of the cells. This changes the composition of the filtrate so that it has no glucose and no amino acids and much less sodium ions. Some urea diffuses back in the blood so the filtrate has less urea. ✔

> All correct. Notice that it is necessary to include some description: 'volume decreases' and 'changes composition' even though the question says 'Explain'. In questions like this when asked to explain, keep any descriptions as short as necessary for the answer.

Exam-style questions

Structured questions (Paper 4)

1 The common vampire bat, *Desmodus rotundus*, is found in Trinidad and Central America. This bat feeds on the blood of sleeping mammals, ingesting about 60% of its body mass in blood with each meal. This protein-rich food has the same water potential as the bat's blood plasma but has a high volume. The stomachs of vampire bats concentrate the blood meals very quickly by absorbing water.

The rate of urine production and the concentration of urine produced by a captive common vampire bat were determined before and after one blood meal. The bat was provided with a blood meal during the second hour of the investigation. The results are shown in the graph.

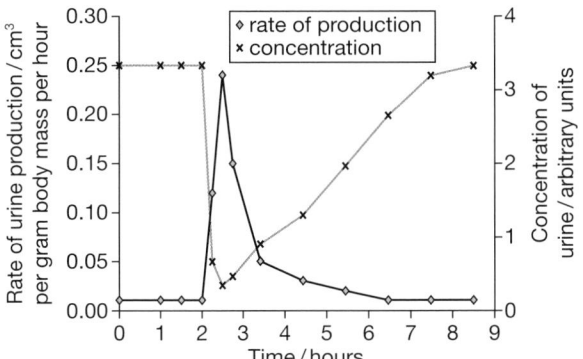

(a) Describe the immediate effect of feeding on the the rate of production of urine and the concentration of urine. [4]

(b) Explain the benefits to the bat of the effects you have described in (a). [3]

(c) Explain why *D. rotundus* excretes large quantities of urea. [3]

(d) Vampire bats are able to produce a much more concentrated urine than that produced by humans. Suggest how they are able to do this. [2]

2 The water potential of the blood of mammals is maintained within narrow limits. The flow chart below shows how the water potential of the blood is controlled when it decreases.

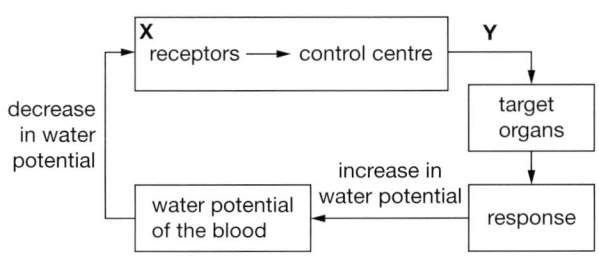

(a) Name:

   (i) the part of the brain shown by box **X** [1]

   (ii) the hormone shown by **Y** [1]

   (iii) the target organs. [1]

(b) Describe the response carried out by the target organs to increase the water potential of the blood. [3]

(c) Use this example to explain how negative feedback is used to maintain constant conditions in the body. [5]

Planning question (Paper 5)

3 Salicylic acid is a natural compound found in plants. It has been shown to stimulate the closure of stomata even at concentrations as low as $0.001\,mmol\,dm^{-3}$. *Tradescantia* makes good material for studying the structure and function of stomata as it is easy to tear off the lower epidermis from the leaves. Aspirin (acetyl salicylate) is a substance related to salicylic acid that has also been observed to stimulate stomatal closure.

Plan an investigation to find the lowest concentration of aspirin that causes all the stomata of *Tradescantia* leaves to close.

You are supplied with the following apparatus and materials:

Unlimited number of *Tradescantia* leaves.
Unlimited $1.0\,mol\,dm^{-3}$ solution of aspirin.

Microscope, microscope slides, cover slips, test-tubes, test-tube racks, Petri dishes, scalpel, forceps, glass rod, syringes, marker pen, timer and pipettes.

(a) State the independent variable and the dependent variable. [2]

(b) Describe a method for the investigation. Your method should be set out in a logical order and be detailed enough for another person to follow. [10]

(c) Explain how the results will be collected, analysed and presented on a graph. [3]

Before you attempt this question read pages 185 and 186.

One way to prepare for examinations is to identify the types of questions that are asked. This section deals with three types of question that you can expect to be asked on control and coordination in mammals and in plants:

- stating the names of structures
- describing sequences of events
- making comparisons.

The naming of parts

Here are some suggestions of ways to learn the structures that make up the nervous system.

1. Make your own drawings of a motor neurone and a sensory neurone. Use a variety of sources for your drawings and also look online for photomicrographs and electron micrographs. There are plenty to choose from. Label all the parts of each neurone and write notes around your drawings about the functions of each part that you have labelled. Do some research and add more notes based on your class notes and textbook.

2. Make your own drawing of the three neurones that form the reflex arc that functions to withdraw the hand from a painful object. Add the receptor and the effector involved in the reflex. Label and annotate your drawing to show the functions of each part of the reflex arc.

3. Draw a detailed diagram to show an interneuronal synapse. This should include the organelles in the presynaptic neurone and the membrane proteins that control the movement of ions across the pre- and post-synaptic membranes. Label and annotate.

4. Search online and in textbooks that you use for images of striated muscle. Make a series of drawings that show a whole muscle (e.g. a biceps muscle), a muscle fibre (striated muscle is composed of multinucleate 'cells' known as fibres), the internal structure of part of a muscle fibre showing the sarcolemma, transverse system tubules (T-tubule system), sarcoplasmic reticulum, myofibrils and mitochondria, and a sarcomere viewed in longitudinal and transverse sections.

> **★ Exam tip**
>
> Do not attempt to learn the details of muscle contraction without a really good understanding of the structure of muscle fibres, myofibrils and sarcomeres. Look at animations and also try making some models to show what happens in a sarcomere when a muscle contracts and then relaxes.

5. Make a labelled and annotated diagram of a neuromuscular junction. Base this on your drawing of the synapse, but the postsynaptic membrane is a sarcolemma and this is usually folded to increase surface area.

6. Make a careful drawing of a longitudinal section through a sarcomere with a minimum of three thick filaments in the non-contracted (relaxed) state. Use a ruler to draw the Z lines and the thick and thin filaments. Make sure that the thin filaments on either side are all the same length. Label and annotate your drawing. Find the actual length of the sarcomere and calculate the magnification of your drawing.

Also make several drawings to show what happens to the sarcomere during contraction (see Figure 15.3 on page 129).

> **★ Exam tip**
>
> If you read the syllabus carefully you should be able to write some questions of your own based on the wording of each learning outcome in Unit 15.

> **💡 Remember**
>
> 'There are no greater aids to learning than pen (or pencil) and paper'. The advice in this Unit is to continue making your own learning resources to help you gain the confidence you need to do well in the exams.

> **★ Exam tip**
>
> The long projection between the sensory dendrites and the cell body in a sensory neurone is sometimes labelled in textbooks as a 'dendron'. This term will not be used in exam questions or be expected in answers. The long projections either side of the cell body form the axon.

> **★ Exam tip**
>
> Exam questions may be set on the knee jerk reflex. The reflex arc that controls this is composed of only sensory and motor neurones. No intermediate neurones in the spinal cord are involved.

> **🔗 Link**
>
> There is a TEM of an interneuronal synapse in Question 1 on page 131. Use it to help with your drawing. Search online for other electron micrographs of synapses

Fact files

This unit has a large number of technical terms to learn and understand. As soon as you begin this Unit start making a list of these terms. As well as writing a glossary of these terms, make a fact file for each one. Each fact file can contain a concise definition, a diagram, some short notes, links to your textbook, any online resources that you use and examples of questions that test your knowledge and understanding of the term.

Telling stories

All good stories have a beginning, a middle and an end. Many exam questions ask you to describe a sequence of events. The stories that you should learn in this Unit are the sequences of events that occur in:

- impulse transmission along a neurone
- impulse transmission across an interneuronal synapse
- impulse transmission across a neuromuscular junction
- coupling depolarisation of the sarcolemma of muscle fibres with the contraction of sarcomeres in myofibrils
- sliding of thin filaments over thick filaments during muscle contraction.

Here are some suggestions of ways to help you learn how to write correct sequences.

1. Make a drawing of a chemoreceptor on the tongue and its sensory neurone. Write the sequence of events that occurs between the stimulation of the chemoreceptor and impulse generation in the sensory neurone.

 **Link**

Use the diagram in *Try this... 5* on page 128 to help tell the story of the chemoreceptor.

2. Use your fact file for impulse transmission to write the sequence of events that occurs as an impulse travels along a myelinated neurone. Make a storyboard first to show (a) a node at resting potential, (b) the same node at the height of an action potential and (c) the same node during the refractory period. The diagrams on pages 130 and 131 should help you make the storyboards.

3. Use your diagram of an interneuronal synapse to sequence the events that occur during synaptic transmission.

4. Use your diagram of a neuromuscular junction to sequence the events that occur when an impulse arrives at the end of a motor neurone.

5. Use your diagrams that show the structure of striated muscle to make a storyboard to sequence the events that occur after an impulse arrives at a motor neurone.

Making comparisons

The syllabus requires you to compare the endocrine system with the nervous system. You need to know about three hormones:

- antidiuretic hormone (ADH) from the posterior pituitary gland
- insulin and glucagon from the islets of Langerhans in the pancreas.

The stories you tell about these three hormones should include what happens when they reach their target organs (cell signalling from Units 4 and 14) and their roles in maintaining near constant conditions in homeostasis.

Link

There are drawings of sarcomeres in *Try this ... 6* on page 129. Each drawing shows only two thick filaments and two thin filaments – this is enough to help your learning of the sliding filament mechanism.

→ Try this... 1

The following are found at synapses:

presynaptic membrane, voltage-gated calcium ion channel proteins, vesicles, mitochondria, synaptic gap, postsynaptic membrane, chemical-gated sodium ion channel proteins, acetylcholinesterase

Make a 'fact file' for each of the structures. Use the fact files to write an answer to the question: Describe how an impulse is transmitted from one neurone to another.

★ Exam tip

An alternative to writing your sequences as bullet points is to make storyboards like those that film and video makers use. Search online for examples and also for templates that you can use to make storyboards – yet another type of graphic organiser – see Unit 1.

→ Try this... 2

Make a table to compare the features of the endocrine system with the features of the nervous system. First make a list of the features you will compare and then draw a table with three columns headed 'feature', 'endocrine system' and 'nervous system'. Leave space to add further features when you revise this topic.

Make a fact file for each of these hormones. Include information about the structure of the hormones, how they act in cell signalling and the effects that they have on the body.

Plants are not an afterthought

There are only three learning outcomes on control and coordination in plants, but that does not mean you should treat them superficially. Plants look deceptively simple. They may not have complex systems made of many different types of specialised cell, but they detect stimuli and coordinate their responses using electrical impulses and chemicals in much the same way as the nervous systems and endocrine systems of mammals.

The two plant hormones that you need to know about are auxin and gibberellin. The principles of cell signalling involving auxins are very similar to those of cell signalling in mammals, which are covered in Unit 14.

Gibberellins act on cells by altering the expression of genes. There is more about their mode of action in Unit 16. In this Unit you need to know about their role in germination of cereals, such as barley. Cereals produce one-seeded fruits, often known as grains, that have an endosperm that stores starch. During germination the starch is hydrolysed by α-amylase into maltose, which is hydrolysed to glucose that is respired to provide energy. Gibberellin is the substance that activates the production of α-amylase when the grain starts to absorb water at the start of germination.

Plants respond to changes in their environment. They do not have complex organs for detecting stimuli or for communication, but their responses can be just as sophisticated.

The Venus fly trap, *Dionaea muscipula*, has one of the fastest responses to stimuli in the plant kingdom. The plant has leaves that are modified for trapping and digesting insects. The internal surfaces of these leaves have sensory hair cells that are deflected when an insect walks over them. Deflection of the hair is a mechanical stimulus that activates calcium ion channel proteins at the base of the hair. Calcium ions enter the cells causing the cell membrane to depolarise. If two hairs are touched within 35 seconds then impulses spread over the leaf along cell surface membranes. The action potentials in the Venus fly trap are similar to those in neurones, but the ion flow is different and they last longer.

> **Remember**
>
> Plasmodesmata are thin cytoplasmic connections between plant cells. Impulses can spread from cell to cell via plasmodesmata because they are lined by cell surface membrane that is continuous with the cells on either side.

When the impulse reaches the hinge region of the trap, pump proteins in the cell surface membranes respond by pumping protons into the cell walls. The decrease in pH in the cell wall loosens the cross links between the cell wall components. Calcium ions enter the cell to decrease the water potential. Water enters through aquaporins and these cells become turgid. The rapid change in turgidity and a change in the tension within the cell walls of the hinge cells are thought to be responsible for rapid closure of the trap.

> ★ **Exam tip**
>
> You should be able to compare the roles of the endocrine and nervous systems in maintaining homeostatic equilibrium in the aspects described in Unit 14 – water potential of the blood and glucose concentration of the blood.

> 🔗 **Link**
>
> Details of cell signalling in plants are in the answer to part (e) of the Worked example on page 127.

> ➔ **Try this... 3**
>
> Make a flow chart to show the sequence of events to show how gibberellin controls the germination of barley grains.

▲ **Figure 15.1** The Venus flytrap. The rapid closing of the traps is coordinated by electrical impulses

> ✎ **Revision strategy**
>
> Calcium ions have many roles in animal and plant coordination and cell signalling. Research answers to this question: Describe the roles of calcium ions in plants and animals.

Worked Example

Shoots from seedlings of *Arabidopsis* were cut into sections and divided into six groups of ten (**A** to **F**). The sections in each group were placed into a Petri dish and treated as follows:

- groups **A** to **C** were treated with different concentrations of the auxin, IAA
- group **D** was treated with a solution of expansins isolated from cell walls
- group **E** was treated with expansins and the highest concentration of IAA
- group **F** was the control group.

The lengths of the sections were measured at 4 hours and 18 hours after the treatments started. The results are shown in Figure 15.2.

(a) Suggest a suitable treatment for group **F**. [1]

(b) State why the results are shown as percentage increases in length, rather than actual increases. [1]

(c) Use the data in the bar chart to describe how the effect of expansins (**D**) differs from the effect of the treatments with solutions of IAA (**A** to **C**). [3]

(d) The results show that there is no difference between the mean percentage increase of the sections in groups **D** and in group **E**.

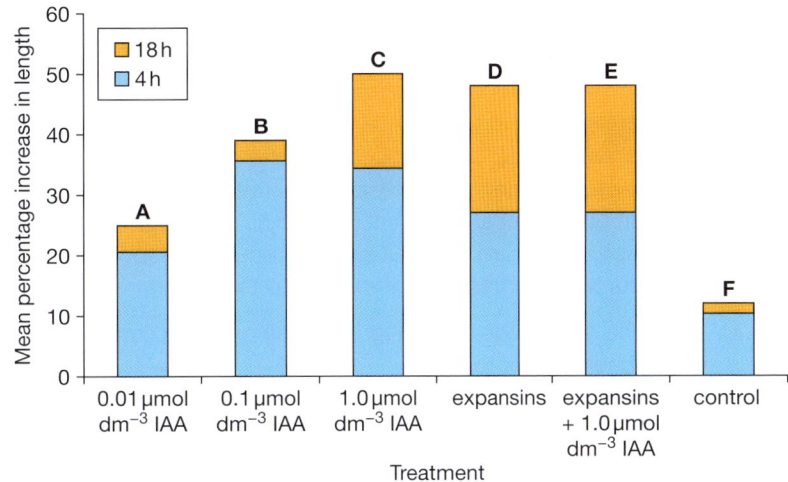

▲ **Figure 15.2**

Suggest why the results are the same even though both IAA and expansins stimulate elongation growth. [2]

(e) Outline the role of auxins in controlling elongation growth in plants. [5]

Answers

(a) The sections of shoot could be floated on water and kept in exactly the same conditions as the other groups.

(b) The initial lengths of the sections were not the same.

(c) Most of the increase in length with IAA occurs in the first 4 hours. For example, with $1.0\,\mu mol\,dm^{-3}$ there is a 33% increase after 4 hours, but at 18 hours the percentage increase is 50% – a change of 17%. The expansins cause an increase of 26% after 4 hours but an overall increase of 48% at 18 hours – a change of 22%.

(d) There may be a limit to the expansion that can occur in these sections. The sections are cut from the shoots and there are unlikely to be any new cells being produced by mitosis.

(e) The auxin indolyl acetic acid (IAA) is synthesised in growing shoot tips, from where it diffuses down the stem. IAA is thought to stimulate the phosphorylation of proton pump proteins in cell surface membranes so increasing their activity. Pumping out protons has the following effects:

- decreases the pH of cell walls – this acidification has the effect of breaking the bonds between cellulose microfibrils and the surrounding matrix made of hemicelluloses and pectins. It also activates cell wall proteins known as expansins that break hydrogen bonds between cell wall polymers
- changes the potential difference across the membrane stimulating potassium influx channels to open
- potassium ions diffuse into cells so decreasing water potential
- water enters by osmosis through aquaporins increasing turgor pressure
- the increase in turgor pressure causes the cell walls to stretch allowing plant cells to grow in size.

➔ Try this... 4

Longitudinal and transverse sections of muscle fibres were examined in a transmission electron microscope. Drawings of the structures visible in a sarcomere were made.

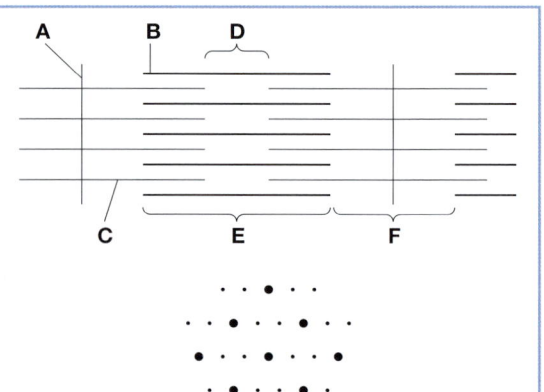

(a) Explain why an electron microscope rather than a light microscope was used to study these sections. [1]

(b) (i) Name the structures **A**, **B** and **C**. [3]

  (ii) Name the regions of the sarcomere labelled **D**, **E** and **F**. [3]

(c) State the region of the sarcomere where the transverse section was taken. [1]

(d) Explain how the sliding of filaments in a sarcomere leads to the contraction of a muscle fibre. [5]

➔ Try this... 5

Chemoreceptors in the tongue respond to five different tastes: sweet, sour, bitter, salt and umami (savoury). The diagram shows a chemoreceptor exposed to a salt solution and the response of the sensory neurone that transmits impulses to the brain.

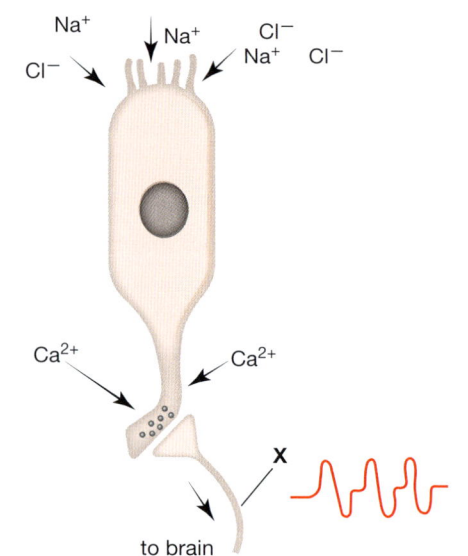

(a) State the advantage of having microvilli over the surface of the chemoreceptor. [1]

(b) Describe the function of calcium ions in the chemoreceptor. [3]

The supply of sensory neurones to chemoreceptors is complex. Some sensory neurones have dendrites on several different chemoreceptors. The graphs show the responses of two different sensory neurones (**A** and **B**) to stimulation by increasing concentrations of salt and sucrose. The recordings were made by placing electrodes on the sensory neurones at the position labelled **X** on the diagram.

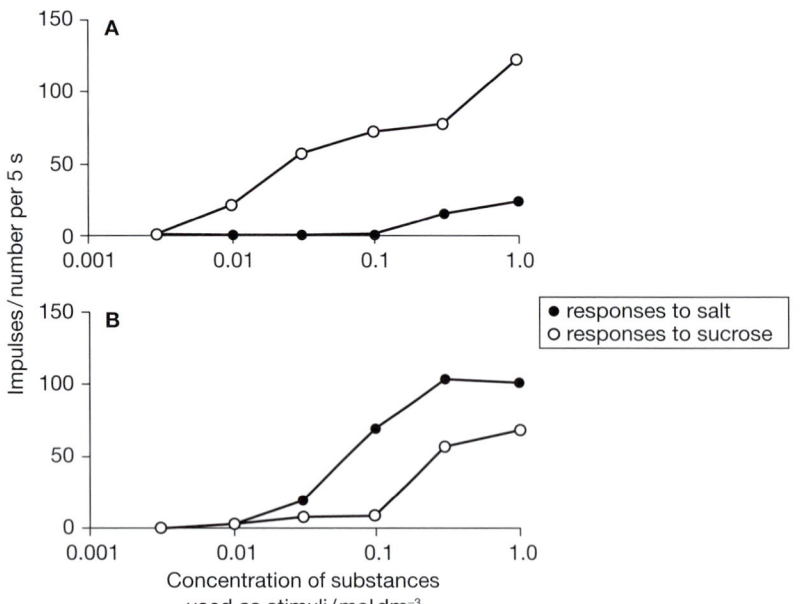

> ★ **Exam tip**
>
> Study each graph carefully. Use a ruler to move across each graph from left to right. Make a list of the differences between them on any white space on the exam paper.

(c) Use the information in the graphs to comment on the differences between the responses shown by neurones **A** and **B**. [4]

(d) Explain how sensory neurones send information about the different strengths of stimuli to the CNS. [4]

→ **Try this... 6**

An isometric muscle contraction is one in which a muscle develops tension, but the length of the muscle remains constant. In the 1960s, physiologists at the University of London investigated the tension developed during isometric contractions of striated muscle with different sarcomere lengths. The diagrams in Figure 15.3 show three arrangements of thick and thin filaments within the sarcomeres that were kept at different lengths.

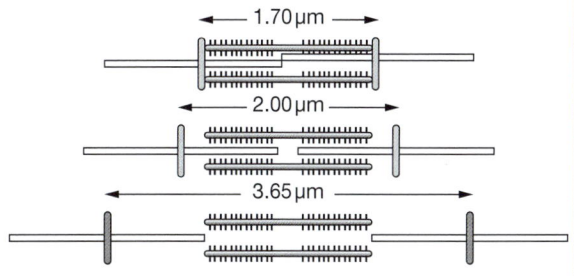

The table shows the forces generated by striated muscle as a percentage of the maximum force for a variety of sarcomere lengths.

▲ **Figure 15.3**

Sarcomere length / μm	Mean tension generated as a percentage of maximum
1.25	0
1.70	75
1.90	95
2.00	100
2.25	100
2.30	97
3.67	0

★ **Exam tip**

This question shows how important it is to read all the information provided before you read and start answering the questions.

(a) State the independent and dependent variables in this investigation. [2]

(b) Draw a graph to show the results of the investigation. [5]

(c) Describe the effect of increasing sarcomere length on the tension developed in the muscle. [3]

(d) Use the information in the diagrams and your graph to explain how these results provided evidence for the sliding filament theory. [4]

(e) Titin is a spring-like polypeptide that is found between the ends of the thick filaments and the Z lines in sarcomeres.

Suggest a role for titin in striated muscle. [3]

→ **Try this... 7**

α-Amylase catalyses the hydrolysis of starch to maltose, a reducing sugar. The production of α-amylase during germination of cereal grains, such as wheat and barley, can be investigated by placing germinating grains that have been soaked and cut in half onto starch agar plates. After at least 24 hours, iodine in potassium iodide solution is added to the starch agar plate. Clear areas around the grains indicate where the starch has been broken down.

In this question, you are required to consider some of the steps that you would take in an investigation to find the effect of soaking barley grains in different concentrations of gibberellin on the production of amylase. Before you start to answer the questions, read pages 185–186.

(a) The concentration of gibberellin in barley grains is approximately 346×10^{-6} g dm^{-3}, which is equivalent to 1.0 μmol dm^{-3}.

Explain how you would make up a wide range of concentrations of gibberellin from a stock solution of 1.0 μmol dm^{-3}. [5]

(b) State and explain two control experiments that should be included. [4]

(c) State the independent and dependent variables in this investigation. [2]

(d) Explain why it is important to maintain a constant temperature while the barley grains are on the starch agar plates. [2]

(e) Suggest how you would modify the procedure to find out how much maltose is produced by the action of amylase from the germinating grains. [7]

↑ Raise your grade

(a) Sodium and potassium ions are involved in the transmission of impulses in the nervous system.

State and explain the distribution of these ions when an axon is at resting potential. [5]

The concentration of sodium ions is higher outside the axon than inside. The concentration of potassium ions is higher inside the axon than outside. ✔ Sodium/ potassium pumps in the axon membrane pump three sodium ions out and two potassium ions in for every molecule of ATP used. ✔ Both ions are unable to diffuse through the hydrophobic core of the axon membrane ✔ and, at rest, the voltage-gated channel proteins are closed. ✔ Potassium ions can diffuse out through 'leak' channel proteins, ✔ but they are kept within the axon by negatively charged molecules, such as proteins. ✔

A very full explanation of a difficult question. The candidate makes good use of ideas from Unit 4. The answer gives you an idea of the detail needed to answer questions about how resting potential is maintained.

(b) The figure shows an action potential in the axon of a sensory neurone.

Explain what happens to change the membrane potential from:

(i) −65 mV to +40 mV (region A) [3]

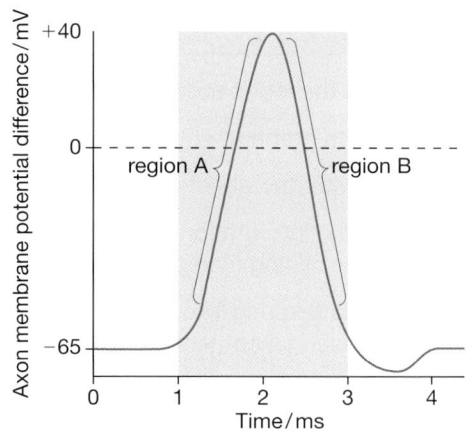

The axon membrane depolarises as voltage-gated sodium ion channel proteins open. ✔ There is a positive feedback so that more and more of these open. ✔ Sodium ions move through the membrane ✔ into the neurone down their electrochemical gradient as there is a high concentration outside and a negative charge inside. ✔

The candidate makes good use of the appropriate terminology.

(ii) +40 mV to −70 mV (region B). [3]

The membrane repolarises. ✔ Voltage-gated sodium ion channel proteins close so that sodium ions cannot diffuse in. ✔ Voltage-gated potassium ion channel proteins open ✔ and potassium ions diffuse out down their concentration gradient to restore the potential difference to resting potential. ✔

A good answer. The candidate explains that the diffusion of potassium ions out of the axon is responsible for the decrease in potential difference in the falling phase of the action potential.

These questions should show you how annotating graphs and diagrams during your revision can help you anticipate and prepare for questions like these on Paper 4.

Exam-style questions

Structured questions (Paper 4)

1 The electron micrograph shows a section through the junction between two neurones, **A** and **B**, in the spinal cord.

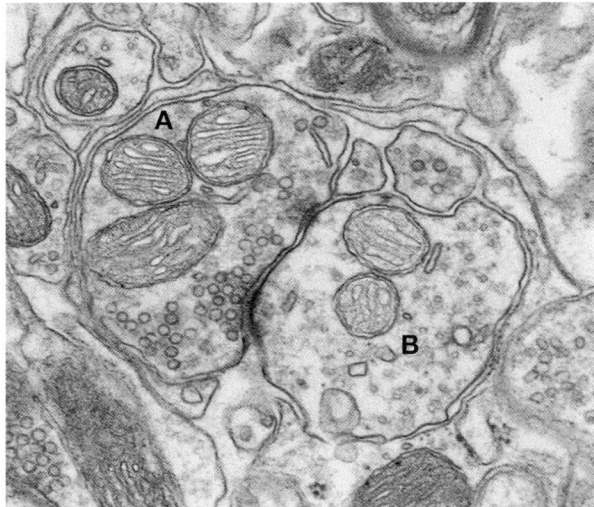

×30 000

(a) (i) The junction between the two neurones is a cholinergic synapse. State what this means. [1]

(ii) With reference to the electron micrograph, explain how the structure of a synapse ensures that impulses travel in one direction. [3]

(b) Stimulation of a relay neurone by a sensory neurone does not always result in impulse transmission.

Explain why a relay neurone may not respond to stimulation by a sensory neurone. [3]

(c) The speed of nerve impulses from touch receptors in the skin is about $80\,m\,s^{-1}$, but from some pain receptors it is about $1.0\,m\,s^{-1}$.

Suggest and explain what causes the difference in speed of impulses from these receptors. [3]

(d) Describe the role of calcium ions in the passage of impulses across a synapse. [3]

2 The leaves of the Venus fly trap catch and digest insects. The trap is a specialised leaf with two lobes either side of a central midrib, which acts as a hinge. The lobes are red inside and have sensitive hairs that respond when touched so causing the lobes to shut.

The sensitive hairs generate a receptor potential when they are stimulated. The trap only shuts if at least two hairs are stimulated within 35 s of each other. Once stimulated the trap shuts partially within one second. After a short while the trap closes tightly.

(a) Explain how the receptor potential is produced. [2]

(b) (i) Suggest the advantage of requiring two deflections of different hairs before closure of the trap. [1]

(ii) Suggest why the trap does not close tightly at first. [1]

(c) The Venus fly trap does not have specialised cells like neurones to conduct impulses. Explain how impulses travel across the leaf to the midrib. [3]

(d) Venus fly trap plants grow in nutrient-poor, waterlogged soils in the Carolinas in the USA.

Suggest how trapping insects benefits these plants in this habitat. [2]

3 The drawing was made from a transmission electron micrograph of a longitudinal section through the axon of a myelinated neurone.

(a) (i) Name the region of the neurone labelled **A**. [1]

(ii) State the name of the cell that makes myelin. [1]

(b) Explain the role of myelin in impulse transmission. [4]

(c) Describe the changes that occur at region **A** during the passage of an impulse in the direction shown by the arrow. [6]

(d) Explain the role of the refractory period in the transmission of impulses. [3]

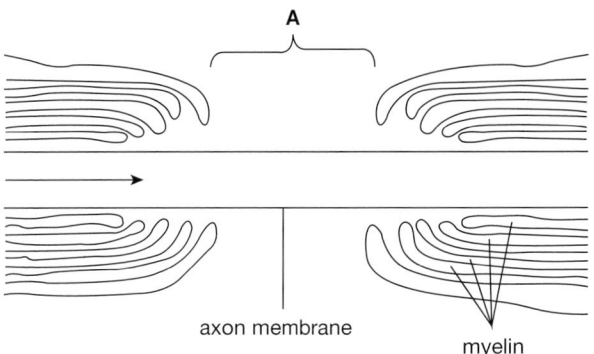

axon membrane

myelin

16 Inheritance

This Unit is about genes, how they are inherited and how they are controlled in prokaryotes and eukaryotes. Before starting you should spend time revising the structure of chromosomes, DNA structure and replication and the stages of the cell cycle (including mitosis) from Units 5 and 6. Ask yourself the question: 'What happens to individual chromosomes during the life of a cell?'

DNA replicates during the S phase of the cell cycle. Chromosomes become visible as double stranded structures under the light microscope during prophase of mitosis. Each chromosome now has two molecules of DNA packaged tightly to make two sister chromatids that are joined at the centromere.

As replication is precise, the two sister chromatids usually have identical sequences of base pairs and therefore are genetically identical. Figure 16.1 shows the chromosomes of a species of deer at metaphase of mitosis. There are three pairs of **homologous chromosomes** (2n = 6): two pairs are autosomes and one pair are the sex chromosomes (XX).

The two chromosomes that form a homologous pair have the same genes in exactly the same positions along the DNA. The genes on the two chromosomes may or may not have identical sequences of base pairs. If the sequences of base pairs are not identical for a particular gene, then the chromosomes have different alleles of that gene. This is the case in most species. Each homologous pair has one chromosome that was originally inherited from the male parent (paternal) and one chromosome that was originally inherited from the female parent (maternal).

Make sure you can define the terms gene and allele as follows:

- Gene – a length of DNA (sequence of nucleotides) that codes for a single polypeptide (structural gene) or controls the expression of other genes (regulatory gene). In genetic diagrams, letters are used to designate genes, for example, **A/a**, **B/b**.

- Allele – an alternative form (or variant) of a gene. There may be two alleles of a gene (e.g. **A** and **a**). Some genes have multiple alleles, for example, the ABO blood group gene, which has three (I^a, I^B and I^o).

Meiosis

Meiosis is important in life cycles as it halves the chromosome number and generates variation in the nuclei that are produced. Meiosis is carefully controlled so that each daughter cell gains one example of each type of chromosome. Each nucleus goes through two divisions in meiosis: homologous chromosomes separate in **meiosis I** and the chromatids of each chromosome separate in **meiosis II**. Each cell that divides by meiosis forms four haploid nuclei that are genetically different from each other.

> **→ Try this... 1**
>
> Make drawings of the chromosomes in Figure 16.1 to show the separation of homologous chromosomes during anaphase I and the separation of chromatids during anaphase II. Also make models using modelling pipe cleaners or pieces of string.

Random (independent) assortment and crossing over are two sources of genetic variation. The positioning of pairs of homologous chromosomes (known as bivalents) at metaphase I is entirely random. Use models of the muntjac chromosomes to show how meiosis can generate a mixture of paternal and maternal chromosomes as a result of how the pairs align at metaphase.

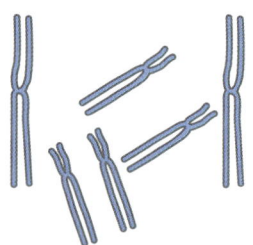

▲ **Figure 16.1** Chromosomes of a female Indian muntjac deer, *Muntiacus muntjak*, at metaphase of mitosis

Key terms

Homologous chromosomes: a pair of chromosomes that have the same shape, same position of the centromere and have the same genes in the same sequence. The alleles of the genes are often different on the two chromosomes.

Locus (plural **loci**): the position of a gene on a chromosome.

★ Exam tip

Use animations of meiosis to make sure that you can describe and explain what happens in meiosis. See John Kyrk's animation at johnkyrk.com and the McGraw-Hill animation on YouTube.

💡 Remember

During meiosis the chromosome number halves (diploid to haploid). The diploid number is restored when gametes fuse at fertilisation. These two events in the life cycle ensure that chromosome number remains constant from generation to generation.

The breakage and exchange of DNA between non-sister chromatids of homologous pairs that occurs early in prophase I is crossing over. As a result, a chromosome has one part that is maternal in origin and another that is paternal. This gives different combinations of alleles of different genes. Nucleotides are not gained or lost and each gene remains in the same position (**locus**) on the chromosome.

Genetic differences between individuals are caused by the different alleles they have inherited. The term **recombination** applies to the new combinations of alleles that have occurred as a result of meiosis. Further variation is introduced at fertilisation since males and females usually have different genotypes and show random mating. There is also random fusion of gametes at fertilisation which, with meiosis, increases the chances that rare, recessive alleles are expressed in organisms that are homozygous for the gene(s) concerned. Many genetic diseases are caused by recessive alleles (see Table 16.2).

Genetic diagrams

In a genetic diagram the **parental generation** are the first individuals to be crossed. The **F1 generation** is the first generation resulting from crossing two homozygotes in the parental generation. If the parents are not homozygous the term 'offspring 1' is used. The **F2 generation** is the second generation resulting from crossing individuals of the F1 generation. If the individuals in the parental generation were not homozygous, then the term 'offspring 2' is used.

Genetic diagrams are used to show how the genes for different features are inherited and should always be set out clearly so that examiners can follow your reasoning.

> 🔗 **Link**
>
> If you find random assortment a difficult concept to understand, use your models of muntjac chromosomes. Attach sticky labels to one pair of chromosomes to show the alleles of a gene (A/a) and sticky labels to another pair (B/b). Confirm that there is a 50% probability that two pairs of homologous chromosomes will align themselves at metaphase with the dominant alleles of the two genes together.

> → **Try this... 2**
>
> Explain how the events that occur in meiosis are responsible for generating variation. Use the drawings of the chromosomes in Figure 16.1 to illustrate your answer.

▼ **Table 16.1** The rules for making genetic diagrams

Step 1	Describe the gene or genes concerned.	State the feature or features controlled by the gene or genes.
Step 2	Identify the allelic features.	Two alleles or more for each gene. Use information provided to work out if alleles show dominance and recessiveness or if codominance is shown.
Step 3	Choose symbols for the alleles.	Capital letter for dominant allele; lowercase letter for the recessive allele. Use the *same* letter for both. For codominant alleles or multiple alleles, use a capital letter for the gene and superscripts for the alleles (see *Try this... 4* on page 134).
Step 4	Give the phenotype and genotype of the parents.	Genotype has two alleles for each gene, except X-linked genes, where a male will only have one allele. When writing a genetic diagram that shows sex linkage include the X and Y chromosomes in the genotypes (see the answer to Question 2(b) on page 136).
Step 5	State the genotype of the gametes.	Always write genotypes of gametes inside circles: monohybrid crosses will have one letter in each circle; dihybrid crosses will have two. Write down the different types of gamete. If they are all the same just write down one genotype in a circle. When writing a genetic diagram that shows sex linkage then include the X and Y chromosomes in the genotypes.
Step 6	Show all the possible genotypes that will result from fusion of gametes at fertilisation.	Use a Punnett square to show all the possible fusions whenever there are gametes with two or more different genotypes. The Punnett square gives the probability of each offspring genotype, not the actual numbers of offspring.
Step 7	Write out the different genotypes and give the phenotype of each one.	See how this is done in the genetic diagrams in the answers for this Unit provided on the support website.
Step 8	Write out the probability of each phenotype and express the answer as a ratio.	You may be given the numbers of offspring. Note that these are numbers for different categories (categorical data). Always divide the numbers by the smallest number to find the overall phenotypic ratio, for example, 66:33 is 2:1.

Worked Example

A student used test crosses to identify the genotypes of some male fruit flies with long wings. In some crosses (**A**) all the offspring had long wings. In other test crosses (**B**) 50% of the offspring had long wings and 50% had short (vestigial) wings.

(a) Use the symbols **W** and **w** to state the genotypes of the parent fruit flies for crosses **A** and **B**. [2]

(b) Use this example to explain the advantage of carrying out a test cross to identify unknown genotypes rather than crossing two long-winged fruit flies together. [4]

Answers

(a) Cross **A**: (males) **WW** and (females) **ww**. Cross **B**: (males) **Ww** and (females) **ww**.

(b) The offspring of a test cross always inherit a recessive allele (e.g. **w**) from the parent that is homozygous recessive. This means that the allele that the offspring inherit from the parent with the unknown genotype will always be expressed. If it is recessive, then the offspring will show the recessive phenotype (e.g. short wings); if dominant, then the offspring will show the dominant phenotype (e.g. long wings). If the female in this cross was long-winged, then she could be homozygous dominant and all the offspring would be long-winged and that would not tell us anything about the genotype of the male.

➡ Try this... 3

Make a genetic diagram to show how it is possible to work out the genotype of the male fruit fly in the worked example. Compare your diagram with the one provided on the support website.

➡ Try this... 4

Flower colour in the four o'clock plant, *Mirabilis jalapa*, is controlled by a single gene with two alleles. When red and white flowered plants are crossed together the offspring are all pink (Figure 16.2).

(a) Use the symbols C^R and C^W to state the genotypes of the parents and the offspring. [3]

(b) Explain why the phenotypic ratio among the offspring is the same as the genotypic ratio. [3]

(c) State the expected phenotypic ratio of each of the following crosses: red × pink, white × pink and pink × pink. [3]

▲ **Figure 16.2**

➡ Try this... 5

Almost all fruit flies have normal (straight) wings and grey bodies (known as wild type). Some are found with bent wings and black bodies. When these flies are crossed all the offspring have straight wings and grey bodies.

A test cross was set up with a male fruit fly with the wild type phenotype (normal wings, grey body) and a female fruit fly with bent wings and black body. This cross gave the following results:

wild type 78; normal wings and black body 82; bent wings and grey body 72; bent wings and black body 69.

In this question, use the following symbols for the alleles of the two genes:

G = allele for grey body, **g** = allele for black body

B = allele for normal (straight) wings, **b** = allele for bent wings

(a) State the genotypes of the fruit flies in this test cross and the gametes that they produced. [4]

(b) Draw a genetic diagram to explain these results. [8]

(c) State the ratio between the phenotypes. [1]

(d) Explain how events in meiosis are responsible for the results. You may use a diagram to illustrate your answer. [5]

(e) Draw a genetic diagram to show the results of crossing fruit flies that are heterozygous for both genes. [8]

Interactions between genes

Some features are controlled by two or more genes that interact with each other. The genes involved will show random assortment if they are on different chromosomes, but the ratio obtained in the F_2 generation may be different to the 9:3:3:1 of a dihybrid cross where genes do not interact.

Flower colour in blue-eyed Mary, *Collinsia parviflora*, is a good example, as the pigment that gives the petals their colour is produced by reactions that occur in series catalysed by two different enzymes (Figure 16.3).

Gene **A/a** codes for enzyme **1** and gene **B/b** codes for enzyme **2**. The flowers will be white if enzyme **1** is absent or non-functioning as in plants with genotypes **aabb**, **aaBB** and **aaBb**. The flowers will be magenta when enzyme **1** is present but enzyme **2** is absent or non-functioning, as in the genotypes **AAbb** and **Aabb**. If the genotype of the plant has dominant alleles of both genes, then the flowers are blue.

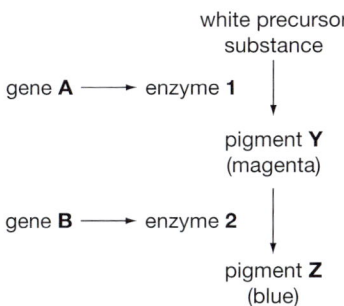

▲ **Figure 16.3** The two enzymes, **1** and **2**, catalyse reactions to produce a flower colour pigment. Gene **A/a** codes for enzyme **1** and gene **B/b** codes for enzyme **2**

 Try this... 6

Make a genetic diagram to show the expected phenotypic ratio when plants heterozygous for both genes, **A** and **B**, are crossed. Check your diagram with the one provided on the support website.

 Try this... 7

Marking exercise. Use the mark scheme that is provided online to mark the answers to these two questions. Look carefully to see how the student has written the answers and used technical terms.

1   A student carried out a genetic investigation with fruit flies, *Drosophila melanogaster*. Two characteristics were observed, body colour and wing shape. The dominant features were grey body and normal wings. The student carried out a test cross on fruit flies that were heterozygous for both genes. The results were as follows: grey body and normal wing 83; black body and normal wing 88; grey body and bent wing 78; black body and bent wing 74.

   (a)   Outline how the student would carry out a test cross.   [1]

   > Fruit flies that show the dominant phenotype (grey body and normal wings) were crossed with flies that were homozygous recessive for both genes (black body and bent wings).

   (b)   The student used the chi-squared test to analyse the results. The value of X^2 is 1.37. Use the table on page 196 to make a conclusion from this result.   [4]

   > There are four categories so the df = 3. The critical value at p = 0.05 is 7.82. The X^2 value of 1.37 is lower than this so the probability of this result by chance is much more than 0.05 (5%) so the null hypothesis is accepted. There is no significant difference between the observed and the expected results. The genes are on different chromosomes and are not linked. The results show that independent assortment has occurred in the formation of gametes in the heterozygous fruit flies.

2   A red-eyed male fruit fly was crossed with a white-eyed female fruit fly. The offspring were a mixture of both red-eyed females and white-eyed males in a ratio of 1:1.

   (a)   Use this example to explain the term *sex linkage*.   [3]

   > Sex linkage is the occurrence of a gene on a sex chromosome, usually the X chromosome. The gene for eye colour is on the X chromosome so males only have one copy (as they are XY) and always express the allele that they have.

> (b) The offspring were crossed together. Give the genotypes of the offspring and the
> phenotypic ratio. [2]
>
> X^RY (red-eyed males); X^RX^r (red-eyed females); X^rY (white-eyed males); X^rX^r
> (white-eyed females). The phenotypic ratio is 1:1:1:1.
>
> (c) Explain why male fruit flies cannot inherit their eye colour from their fathers. [3]
>
> A male inherits a Y chromosome from his father and the gene for eye colour is on
> the X, not the Y. His X chromosome is inherited from his mother.

Gene mutation

In biology, **mutation** is used to refer to changes in DNA to a gene (**gene mutation**) to a or to a chromosome (chromosome mutation). Changes to individual genes involve changing the sequence of nucleotide bases during replication.

DNA polymerase has a proofreading capacity and removes and replaces a nucleotide that is in the wrong place. However, this proofreading ability is not 100% accurate, and errors occur during replication.

Substitution. The change of one base pair for another.

Frameshift. The sequence of triplets in DNA changes by the **insertion** of one or more bases or the **deletion** of one or more bases. Changes that are not multiples of three bases will change the entire sequence of amino acids of the polypeptide formed, from the point of mutation onwards.

Neutral mutations are those that have no effect on the amino acid sequence and those that change the sequence, but have no effect on protein function.

DNA to protein to phenotype

Proteins have direct and indirect effects on the phenotype. We have discovered these effects when there are errors in metabolism. For example, if a mutation occurs in the *TYR* gene, either no tyrosinase is produced or a non-functional form is made. Tyrosine is not converted to melanin, so skin pigment (melanin) is not produced, leading to the condition known as albinism in people who are homozygous for the mutation. Table 16.2 lists the mutations that you need to know.

> ★ **Exam tip**
>
> For the exam you need to know only about gene mutation. Chromosome mutations are not on the syllabus.

> ★ **Exam tip**
>
> Frameshifts are likely to have a much greater effect on the protein formed than base substitution. However, a substitution mutation can have profound effects if it changes an amino acid in an important part of a protein (e.g. an active site of an enzyme).

> 💡 **Remember**
>
> Look back to the details of the genetic code in Unit 6 page 56 to help you to understand the effects of mutation.

▼ **Table 16.2** Five human genes, their most common mutations and the consequences. *The number in brackets is the chromosome where the gene is located

Gene*	Type of mutation	Polypeptide affected	Consequences of faulty gene (inheritance pattern)
HBB (11)	substitution in sixth codon recessive allele	β-globin (one of the polypeptides in haemoglobin – see Unit 2 page 21)	**sickle cell anaemia:** many effects, including sickle cell crises when blood cells get stuck in small blood vessels (autosomal recessive)
TYR (11)	substitution and frameshift recessive allele	enzyme: tyrosinase (transmembrane protein in melanin-producing cells)	**albinism:** no melanin in the skin or hair (autosomal recessive)
HTT (4)	repeated base pairs (stutter) dominant allele	production of abnormal protein that is cut into sections that bind together and accumulate in neurones	**Huntington's disease:** progressive degeneration of brain tissue (autosomal dominant)
F8 (X)	inversion (sequence of bases is turned around) recessive allele	blood clotting factor 8 (also called factor VIII)	**haemophilia:** slow clotting time (sex-linked recessive)

→ Try this... 8

You will need to use the genetic code to answer part (a). You could use Figure 6.4 on page 56, which shows the RNA codons. The bases in the DNA triplets on the transcribed strand are complementary to the bases on mRNA. Remember that A in RNA pairs with T in DNA and U in RNA pairs with A in DNA.

(a) The following is a sequence of DNA triplets on the transcribed (template) strand of the gene for an octapeptide:

CTA ATG TAC CCA ACC TAC CTA AAG

State what happens to the amino acid sequence of the peptide produced in translation if the following gene mutations occur to the second triplet:

(i) a deletion of the first base

(ii) the first base changes from A to T

(iii) the triplet is deleted

(iv) the addition of the base T at the beginning of the triplet

(v) the third base changes from G to C
In each case show your reasoning. [10]

(b) Classify the gene mutations you have described in **(a)** as substitution, frameshift or neutral. [5]

(c) (i) Explain the genetic cause of sickle cell anaemia. [4]

(ii) Explain how sickle cell anaemia is inherited. [4]

→ Try this... 9

The bacterium *Escherichia coli* can metabolise lactose as it can produce the enzyme β-galactosidase, which breaks down lactose to form glucose and galactose. The activity of β-galactosidase can be assessed by using the compound ONPG, which is a colourless compound that can be broken down by β-galactosidase into galactose and a yellow compound. The intensity of the yellow colour is an indication of the activity of the enzyme β-galactosidase.

Students investigated the ability of *E. coli* to metabolise ONPG by setting up seven test-tubes as shown in the table. The test-tubes were placed in a water bath at 35 °C and observed.

Test-tube	*E. coli*	*E. coli* incubated with 1% lactose solution	β-Galactosidase solution	1% Lactose solution	ONPG
1	✓			✓	✓
2	✓			✓	
3		✓			✓
4		✓			
5			✓		✓
6			✓	✓	
7				✓	✓

The students found that the contents of test-tubes **1**, **3** and **5** became yellow over time. Test-tube **5** was the first to become yellow, followed by **3** and then **1**.

(a) Explain why the students included the following pairs of test-tubes:

(i) **1** and **3** (ii) **2** and **4**

(iii) **5**, **6** and **7** [7]

(b) (i) State why there were colour changes in test-tubes **1**, **3** and **5**. [1]

(ii) Explain the sequence of colour changes as observed by the students. [4]

(c) Suggest how the students could improve their investigation by taking quantitative results. [3]

(d) The students decided to adapt their method to test the hypothesis:

The rate of breakdown of ONPG by E. coli is increased by adding higher concentrations of lactose.

Plan an investigation to test this hypothesis. Your method should be detailed enough for another person to follow. [5]

(e) Describe how the results could be analysed. [2]

↑ Raise your grade

In the bacterium *Escherichia coli* there is a short metabolic pathway involving three enzymes that synthesise the amino acid tryptophan. The bacterium only makes tryptophan when there is none available in its surroundings. The five genes that code for the enzymes required for tryptophan synthesis are part of the *trp* operon shown in the diagram.

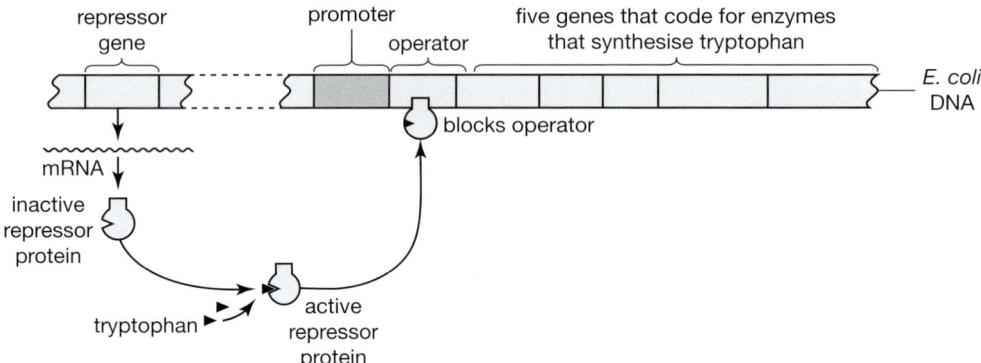

(a) State **two** advantages of regulating the production of enzymes. [2]

There is no need to produce enzymes if there is nothing for them to do. If tryptophan can be absorbed from the surroundings, *E. coli* does not need to make it as well. This saves energy in protein synthesis. ✔ It also saves using amino acids to make an enzyme that is not needed. ✔

> A well-worded answer with good use of unfamiliar information in the diagram.

(b) (i) State **two** ways in which the *trp* operon shown in the diagram differs from the *lac* operon. [2]

The repressor is inhibited by lactose in the *lac* operon, whereas tryptophan activates the repressor in the *trp* operon. ✔ There are five structural genes in the *trp* operon. In the *lac* operon there are only three. ✔

> This is good use of the information in the diagram. Be prepared to see unfamiliar examples like the *trp* operon in Paper 4. You are expected to use your knowledge to analyse the information provided. Always study all information, including diagrams, provided in questions like this.

(ii) Explain why the control of the *trp* operon differs from the control of the *lac* operon. [3]

The *lac* operon is activated by lactose because proteins are needed to metabolise it to gain energy. Lactose is a respiratory substrate that *E. coli* breaks down to gain energy. ✔ The default state for the *trp* operon is to be 'switched on' unless tryptophan is present. When it is present there is no need to make it. ✔ Tryptophan is used to make proteins, it is not broken down like lactose. ✔

> A very thorough answer clearly written in the candidate's own words (e.g. 'default state'). This shows good application of the principles learnt in this Unit.

Exam-style questions

Structured questions (Paper 4)

1 In shorthorn cattle there is a gene that controls coat colour. The allele C^R gives a red colour, the allele C^W gives white. Cattle that are heterozygous for this gene have a coat that is described as roan – a light red colour. Cattle with horns are homozygous for the allele, **p**. Cattle with the dominant allele, **P**, are hornless. Neither of these gene loci is sex linked. The two gene loci are on different chromosomes.

(a) (i) A white cow with horns is mated with a bull that has a red coat and is homozygous for the hornless condition. Draw a genetic diagram to predict what you would expect in the F_1 generation. [4]

(ii) Cattle in the F_1 generation were mated amongst themselves. Draw a genetic diagram to predict what you would expect in the F_2 generation. [6]

(b) Explain, using this example of shorthorn cattle, the effect of dominance and codominance on phenotypic variation. [4]

2 One of the roles of the plant hormone gibberellin (GA) is to control the growth of stems. There are three types of mutation that have been identified in thale cress, *Arabidopsis thaliana*, that affect the action of gibberellin on growth. Plants with each of these mutations were treated with gibberellin. The plants were grown from seed and were all the same age when they were treated with GA. The drawings show the plants before and after treatment with gibberellin. The drawings were made at the same time after application of GA. The wild type plants in group **A** do not have any of these mutations.

(a) (i) Compare the growth of the plants in groups **A** and **B**. [2]

(ii) Suggest an explanation for the response of the plants in group **B** to the supply of gibberellin. [3]

(b) Explain why the plants in group **C** do not respond to the gibberellin treatment in the same way as those in group **B**. [3]

(c) (i) Describe how the growth of plants in group **D** differs from group **A**. [2]

(ii) Suggest an explanation for the growth of plants in group **D**. [3]

Group **A**

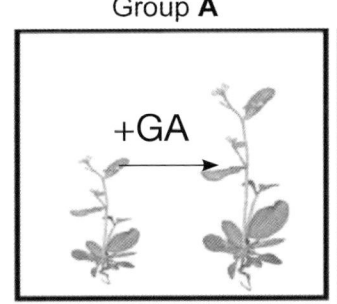

Group **B**

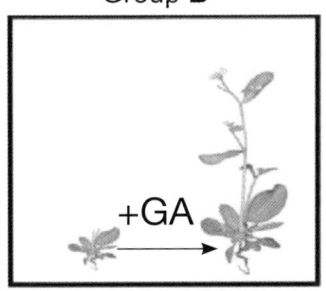

Group **C**

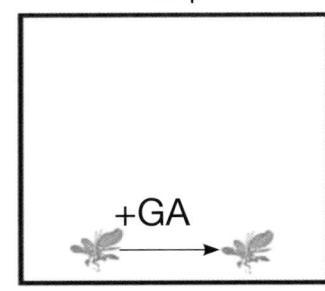

Group **D**

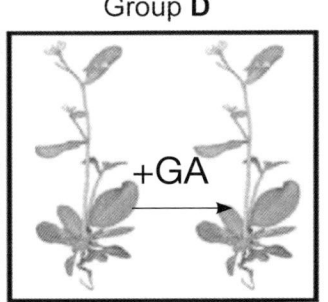

Planning question (Paper 5)

3 Plants of the species *Brassica rapa* normally grow a long stem, but one mutant is rosette as its stem does not grow at all. When pure bred long-stemmed plants are crossed with pure bred rosette plants, all the offspring have long stems. When these plants are interbred three quarters of the offspring are long-stemmed and one quarter of them are rosette. The plants also have a gene for determining production of anthocyanin pigments in the stem. When purple-stemmed plants are crossed with green-stemmed plants all the offspring have purple stems.

A student designed an investigation to find out if the genes for stem length and stem colour are linked on the same chromosome or not. The student had access to pure bred plants showing the dominant phenotype and pure bred plants showing the recessive phenotype.

(a) State the null hypothesis for the investigation. [1]

(b) Draw a genetic diagram to derive the phenotypic ratio predicted by the null hypothesis. [6]

(c) Describe a method to test the hypothesis. Your method should be detailed enough for another person to follow. [6]

(d) Explain how the results will be collected and analysed. [4]

17 Selection and evolution

This Unit shows you the importance of making links between different topics. To be fully confident of the topics in this Unit you will have to use information on meiosis, genetics and mutation from Unit 16, environmental biology from Unit 18 and genetic technology from Unit 19. Look for as many links as you can. Your understanding will improve hugely.

Population biology is a main theme running through this Unit. A population is formed of all the individuals of a particular species that live and breed together in a certain area.

Variation refers to differences between organisms. These are phenotypic and genotypic differences. Phenotypic variation is morphological, anatomical, physiological, biochemical and behavioural. Genotypic variation occurs because genes have two or more alleles and because there are differences in the DNA sequences that code for the same proteins in different organisms.

There are two types of phenotypic variation – **continuous** and **discontinuous**. Genetic factors and environmental factors, such as light, food, water and temperature, influence continuous variation. Genetic factors alone are responsible for discontinuous variation.

The **gene pool** of a population is formed of all the alleles of the genes in a population. A population with a wide gene pool has a great deal of genetic variation. The term is usually used when analysing the frequencies of different alleles in populations – see page 147.

Variation in populations is the raw material for selection. Agents of **natural selection** are abiotic and biotic features of the environment; humans are agents of **artificial selection**, which is also known as **selective breeding**. Selection changes the frequencies of alleles of genes in populations.

If part of a population migrates, selection may result in differences between populations to such an extent that they cannot breed together. **Speciation** has occurred as the two populations are reproductively isolated. The formation of new species is evidence of evolution occurring. Allele frequencies can also change when small populations are isolated and there are no opportunities for reproduction with other populations of the same species. This is another way in which speciation can occur.

Natural selection

Charles Darwin and Alfred Russel Wallace proposed the theory of natural selection in 1858 to explain how organisms evolve. A year later Darwin published *On the Origin of Species* in which he described evidence for a way in which evolution could occur. He started by describing four general observations that he had made:

- **Overpopulation** – all species have the ability to produce large numbers of young individuals. Not all of these live to maturity.

- The populations of many organisms remain fairly **stable** from year to year with only minor fluctuations.

- There is considerable phenotypic **variation** within most species (intraspecific variation).

- Offspring have phenotypes that resemble those of their parents.

▲ **Figure 17.1** Genetic corn – an example of discontinuous variation as there are grains of four different colours on this maize ear

> 💡 **Remember**
>
> Flower colour in the four o'clock plant and human blood groups are good examples of discontinuous variation. See Unit 16 for the genetics involved.

> ★ **Exam tip**
>
> An analogy helps to understand the idea of the gene pool. Imagine a vending machine that contains many balls of chewing gum that are covered in either red or blue paper. Each ball is an allele. Dispense two balls from the machine at random and you have the genotype of an individual.

> → **Try this... 1**
>
> Use bullet points to make a list of the features of continuous and discontinuous variation. Draw a histogram of an example of continuous variation and a bar chart of an example of discontinuous. Use your list and the two charts to summarise the differences between the two types of variation.

> ★ **Exam tip**
>
> Allele frequencies change as a result of selection. Remember this as you read the rest of this Unit. Selection does not change the frequencies of genes.

The theory of natural selection explains the role of the environment in determining which individuals survive to reproduce:

- There are limited resources available in the environment for each population. There is a **struggle for existence** as individuals **compete** for these resources. Animals compete for water, food, territories, nesting sites and mates; plants compete for space, water, ions, light, carbon dioxide and, in some cases, pollinators (e.g. insects). Individuals of the same species have the same features for obtaining those resources.

- Competition between members of the same species (intraspecific competition) for food leads to high death rates from starvation among young animals. They are also likely to be eaten by predators or die of disease. There is a similar high mortality among seedling plants that start growing in unsuitable places, do not absorb enough water, ions, light or carbon dioxide, are eaten by herbivores or are killed by disease.

- The individuals that are best **adapted** to obtain resources from their environment survive to reproduce and pass on their **alleles**. Those that do not survive to reproduce (or produce few offspring) and do not pass on their alleles are selected against.

- This **differential survival** means that populations mainly consist of individuals that are well adapted to the environmental conditions that exist at any one time.

Over very long periods of time, populations do not change very much – this is supported by studies of fossils. This type of selection is **stabilising selection**, in which there is selection against the extremes of a range of variation. For example, the mean length of wings in bird species does not change between generations.

When the environment changes, the struggle for existence may become much more intense for a population of a species. Selection pressures change and individuals with specific phenotypes that were selected against are now better able to find resources and survive. This is an example of **directional selection**.

Environmental conditions sometimes change so that individuals at either end of the range for one or more features are at a selective advantage and those in the middle of the range are not. When this happens, it may give rise to two populations by **disruptive selection**.

★ **Exam tip**

Competition between members of the same species is intraspecific competition – a useful term to use in an answer on natural selection.

★ **Exam tip**

Notice that this says alleles and not genes. All individuals of the same species have the same genes – they differ in the alleles of those genes. Some alleles give individuals the competitive edge that increases their chance of survival.

🔗 **Link**

The two populations formed by disruptive selection often change so much that they do not interbreed and are two separate species. See Table 17.5 on page 144, which shows the ways in which species are reproductively isolated from each other.

➡ **Try this... 2**

Peter and Rosemary Grant have studied a population of the medium ground finch, *Geospiza fortis*, on the island of Daphne Major in the Galápagos. In the mid-1970s, there was a drought and many of the plants that provide seeds for this species died; the only plants to survive produced harder seeds. The population of *G. fortis* decreased considerably after the drought. Table 17.1 shows data that the Grants collected on the birds that died and those that survived.

▼ **Table 17.1**

	Birds that died	Birds that survived
Mean beak length / mm	10.68	11.07
Mean beak depth / mm	9.42	9.66

▲ **Figure 17.2** A medium ground finch, *Geospiza fortis*, eating seeds

Only birds with beaks larger than 10.5 mm were able to eat the seeds. As the population of *G. fortis* increased in the years after the rains returned, the mean beak size and the mean body size of the population was greater than before the drought. It has been discovered that genes influence these two features.

Suggest a full explanation for the change in the two phenotypic features of the population of *G. fortis* using the terminology in the section on natural selection. [6]

Exam questions are often based on examples taken from scientific research. Some of these may be familiar to you, others may not. Always read **all** the information provided, even if the example is familiar, since aspects new to you may be included. Here are three examples of research on natural selection.

Kettlewell's experiments on peppered moths

Bernard Kettlewell investigated the effect of predation by birds as the selective agent in maintaining populations of peppered moths in the 1950s and 1970s. He trapped and reared melanic and non-melanic forms, marked them and then released them in a wood in an industrial area of Birmingham in the UK and a wood in a rural area nearby where the trees were covered in lichen, which gives the bark a grey, speckled appearance. After a few days he used a moth trap to recapture the moths. His results are in Table 17.2.

▲ **Figure 17.3** Non-melanic (top) and melanic (bottom) forms of *Biston betularia*

▼ **Table 17.2**

Site of woodland		Number of peppered moths		
		Non-melanics	Melanics	Total
non-polluted, rural area	number marked and released	496	473	969
	number recaptured	62	30	92
	% of marked moths recaptured	12.5	6.3	
polluted, industrial area	number marked and released	64	154	218
	number recaptured	16	82	98
	% of marked moths recaptured	25.0	52.3	

Kettlewell observed the behaviour of predatory birds and filmed them feeding on the peppered moths that were least well camouflaged against the bark of the trees. His observations provided evidence that visual predation by birds was the agent of selection in both areas.

Melanism is not unusual in animal species. An example is the variation within populations of the bananaquit, *Coereba flaveola*, a bird that lives on the islands of Grenada and St. Vincent in the Caribbean. The more common form is mainly yellow and black (Figure 17.4). Melanic forms are completely black and on Grenada and St. Vincent they are only found in moist forest at low and high altitudes whereas the yellow forms live on disturbed dry lowland habitat. Melanics have a stronger preference for shade than the yellow birds. There is no evidence for assortative mating in which each form mates with birds of the same colour.

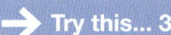 **Try this... 3**

Describe and explain the data shown in Table 17.2.

▲ **Figure 17.4** A non-melanic bananaquit feeding on the nectar of a *Helicornia* flower

Try this... 4

Suggest how you might investigate melanism in bananaquits to discover how it is inherited and how it is maintained in populations on Grenada and St. Vincent.

Banded snails

Banded snails, *Cepaea hortensis* and *C. nemoralis*, live on the ground amongst leaf litter and ground vegetation. They exist in three different colours: brown, pink and yellow. Some snails have bands, others do not (Figure 17.5). These two features are controlled by alleles at two separate loci on different chromosomes. In a survey, snails were collected from woodland where the leaf litter was dark brown and adjacent grassland where the background colour is more variable, but mostly yellow and green. Table 17.3 shows the percentage of yellow-shelled snails and unbanded snails in three samples from each area.

▲ **Figure 17.5** These snails with different shell colours and banding patterns are all members of the same species, *Cepaea hortensis*

▼ Table 17.3

Habitat	Sample	Percentage of yellow snails in sample	Percentage of unbanded snails in sample
woodland	1	12	88
	2	21	77
	3	12	70
grassland	1	79	21
	2	58	14
	3	83	22

These results are very similar to those obtained by surveys in similar habitats over many years.

Birds known as thrushes are common predators of *C. nemoralis*. The birds hold them in their beaks and strike them against a stone. Broken shells are found around the stones. Equal numbers of banded yellow and unbanded brown snails were collected and marked before being released into the centre of each habitat. A count was made after a few days of broken snail shells around the stones in each habitat. Table 17.4 shows the numbers of shells of each type found in the two habitats.

→ **Try this... 5**

Use the information to describe how selection acts to maintain different types of *C. nemoralis* in the two habitats.

▼ Table 17.4

Habitat	Banded yellow shells	Unbanded dark shells
grassland	23	76
woodland	68	30

Guppies in Trinidad

The guppy, *Poecilia reticulata,* is a small fish that originates from South America but has been introduced to habitats across the world (Figure 17.6). David Reznick studied the effects of predation on populations of these fish in the Aripo river system in Trinidad.

The guppies living in rivers with predators grow up faster, mature at smaller sizes and reproduce earlier; they need to breed as soon as possible because they can get eaten at any time. In rivers without predators the guppies grow more slowly and put more energy into their offspring. In a series of experiments fish were taken from each population and put into rivers that previously did not contain guppies. Some of these new rivers had predators in them, others did not. The experiment was set up so populations from rivers with predators were moved to rivers without predators and vice versa. As a control they also moved populations from rivers with predators to different rivers with predators, and the same for populations from rivers lacking predators.

The guppies were monitored for 11 years. Over that time the body size of the guppy population in rivers without predators had increased and sexual maturation occurred later; in rivers with predators the fish were smaller and matured earlier. This showed that the guppy populations had changed to maximise their chances of reproduction by adopting different strategies depending on the presence or absence of predators.

Key term

Natural selection: the survival of individuals with particular features that adapt them to the factors of the environment, for example, predators, competition and climate; these individuals have a greater chance of breeding and passing on their alleles than other individuals that are selected against.

🔗 **Link**

Another example of predation as the agent of natural selection is confirmed by research on populations of mosquito fish, *Gambusia hubbsi*, in freshwater ponds on Andros Island in the Bahamas.

→ **Try this... 6**

Suggest what type of selection has occurred in the populations of these three species:

B. betularia, C. nemoralis and *P. reticulata.*

▲ **Figure 17.6** Guppies, *P. reticulata*, show huge phenotypic variation when bred in captivity

Genetic drift

In small populations changes in allele frequency often occur at random rather than as a result of selection. It may be pure chance as to which individuals survive and breed when the population is small. Also mating is not at random as the numbers of individuals are so small. These changes in allele frequency are known as **genetic drift**.

There are two ways in which genetic drift occurs in small populations. In both cases there is considerable loss of genetic variation because of loss of alleles.

- A population is severely affected by some catastrophe (harmful event) so that there are very few survivors; the cheetah, *Acinonyx jubatus*, and the Northern Elephant seal, *Mirounga angustirostris* (Figure 17.7), are good examples.

- Small populations that migrate and colonise new areas, especially islands or other isolated ecosystems, are likely to have allele frequencies that are not representative of the main population from which they came. This is the **founder effect**.

A genetic bottleneck is the term used to describe the effect of near extinction that occurred to species like the cheetah. Many species are near extinction now and if they do survive will suffer from a severe loss of genetic variation. This lack of variation makes them very susceptible to extinction if the environment changes.

The changes described so far apply to changes in populations of a species. According to the definition of the term biological species (see Unit 18 page 150), these populations are all members of the same species because they can interbreed – they can reproduce with each other. With time a population may change significantly in other ways so that reproduction with other populations is not possible. Table 17.5 summarises the isolating mechanisms that act as barriers to reproduction between species.

▲ **Figure 17.7** A Northern elephant seal, one of the descendants of a very small population (about 20) that survived intense hunting at the end of the 19th century. Numbers have now recovered, but they only represent a small portion of the genetic diversity of the original population

Key terms

Genetic drift: the change in allele frequency that occurs by chance, not as a result of selection.

Founder effect: the loss of genetic diversity when a very small number of individuals colonise a new area.

→ Try this... 7

The island of Tristan da Cunha in the South Atlantic has a population of 262. The islanders are descendants of people who arrived on the island in the 19th century.

The prevalence of asthma among the population is higher than might be expected and is thought to be due to genetic factors rather than any environmental factors on the island.

Suggest an explanation for the high prevalence of asthma among the islanders of Tristan da Cunha.

▼ **Table 17.5** Isolating mechanisms that act as barriers to reproduction between species

Isolating mechanism	Explanation
Pre-zygotic – prevents fertilisation	
geographical	features such as rivers, lakes, mountains, lowlands, forests separate populations so they never or rarely meet
ecological	populations inhabit different habitats within the same area so individuals rarely meet
temporal	breeding occurs at different times
reproductive behaviour	courtship rituals are different so that males and females cannot mate
Post-zygotic – prevents the development of the embryo or the ability of the offspring to reproduce	
production of a hybrid prevented	fertilisation does not occur embryo fails to develop
breeding of hybrids prevented	offspring are sterile (often because homologous chromosomes cannot pair in meiosis) no viable individuals are produced

→ **Try this... 8**

Read the question and the answers. Use the mark scheme that is provided online to mark the answers. Look carefully to see how the student has written the answers and used technical terms.

The Ngorongoro crater in northern Tanzania is relatively isolated from the neighbouring Serengeti National Park. In the early 1960s, the population of lions in the crater numbered about 70. In 1962, the lions suffered a serious disease, reducing the population to nine females and one male. Seven more males migrated into the area and this population remained isolated for at least the next 25 years, recovering to between 75 and 125 animals. A study of the lion population in the crater in the late 1980s showed low genetic diversity, low reproductive rates and high proportions of abnormal sperm in the males' semen.

(a) Suggest the information that needs to be collected to make an assessment of the genetic diversity of a population. [3]

Identify the number of different alleles for each gene and then find out their frequencies in the population. Also find out how many lions are heterozygous for each gene.

(b) Explain why the lion population had such a low genetic diversity even though numbers had recovered from the crash in the 1960s. [3]

As there were only 17 lions left to breed, there cannot have been much genetic diversity amongst them and alleles of some genes would not be present. Inbreeding has occurred. Males and females are closely related so over time many in the population become homozygous for many genes. Changes in allele frequencies are likely to be due to genetic drift (non-random mating), rather than to natural selection.

Speciation

Speciation is the process by which a new species arises from an existing species.

Allopatric speciation. If individuals of a species migrate to occupy a new area, such as an island, they are exposed to different selection pressures compared with the area that they have left. Over time this may lead to changes in the isolated population to the extent that they cannot interbreed with the original population.

Sympatric speciation. This occurs within a population without physical separation. Sometimes this is an abrupt change in a species, so that individuals are not able to interbreed.

Scientists have described many examples of speciation. Some of these are:

* English cord grass, *Spartina anglica*, in the UK

* Midas cichlid fish, *Amphilophus* spp, in Lake Apoyo, Nicaragua

* apple maggot fly, *Rhagoletis pomonella*, in the USA

* snapping shrimps, *Alpheus* spp, in the waters off the coasts of Panama.

Selective breeding (artificial selection)

Crop improvement

Disease resistance in wheat and rice. Plant breeders have improved bread wheat, *Triticum aestivum*, by using techniques of selective breeding to incorporate the gene *Sr2*, responsible for resistance to stem rust disease, from the related species *T. turgidum* to produce a variety of bread wheat called Hope. *Sr2* has since been used in other varieties. Over 60 genes have been identified as improving resistance to disease in rice. Some of these act in the signalling pathway that activates the plant's defences against attack by pathogens.

✏ **Revision strategy**

Make a list of pairs of terms and their definitions that you find difficult to remember. You could start with allopatric and sympatric.

→ **Try this... 9**

Research these examples of speciation. Identify the type of speciation that has occurred or is thought to be occurring in each case. Record your sources so you can access them when you revise.

★ **Exam tip**

To answer questions on selective breeding it helps to know something about how cereal crops reproduce and how plant breeders make crosses between different varieties.

Inbreeding and hybridisation in maize. Breeders establish inbred varieties of maize that have some features they wish to incorporate, such as drought tolerance, by preventing cross-pollination and ensuring that only self-pollination occurs. After several generations plants become homozygous for most of their genes. The yield of these plants is low but when they are crossed with another inbred line the heterozygous offspring are highly vigorous, producing good yields of maize. This is known as **hybrid vigour**.

Improving the milk yield of cattle

The milk yield of dairy cattle is a feature that is influenced by environmental factors, such as quantity and quality of feed, and genetic factors. Yields have increased over the past 60 years or so by providing high-quality feed, controlling disease and providing shelter so that more energy can be devoted to making milk. Herds have also been improved by selective breeding and assisted reproduction, such as artificial insemination (AI), IVF and embryo splitting to produce clones.

Cows that produce large quantities of milk are inseminated with sperm from a high-quality bull that is known to have female offspring that produce high volumes of milk. By using AI, sperm from one bull may fertilise eggs in thousands of cows. Eggs from cows that show superior qualities may be harvested, fertilised *in vitro* and the embryos placed in surrogate cows. This protects the superior cow from the risks of pregnancy.

> ➡ **Try this... 10**
>
> M73 and Mo17 are two inbred varieties of maize, which have been used to breed high-performing hybrid maize. The table shows data from several studies that compared the performance of the two varieties and the hybrid obtained by cross breeding them.
>
> ▼ **Table 17.6**
>
> | Feature | Maize varieties | | |
> |---|---|---|---|
> | | **M73** | **Mo17** | **Hybrid M73×Mo17** |
> | Mean yield of grain / tonnes ha^{-1} | 6.32 | 4.06 | 10.41 |
> | Mean number of grains per ear | 430 | 271 | 628 |
> | Mean mass of grain / g ear^{-1} | 115 | 98 | 232 |
> | Mean ear length / mm | 127 | 143 | 212 |
>
> Heterosis is defined as the improvement of the hybrid variety over the better of the two parent varieties.
>
> (a) Calculate the percentage heterosis for the mean yield of grain. Show your working. [2]
>
> (b) Suggest two reasons why the hybrid variety shows heterosis. [2]
>
> (c) Crossing inbred varieties does not always lead to heterosis for all features. When a dwarf variety of garden pea is crossed with a tall variety, all the offspring resemble the tall variety. Explain this result with reference to the control of growth of plants. [4]
>
> (d) Explain why maize farmers who grow hybrid corn have to buy new grain each year to sow for the next crop, rather than keeping some of their crop for sowing. [3]

★ **Exam tip**

Make sure that you can distinguish between selective breeding (artificial selection) and genetic engineering.

★ **Exam tip**

Make a table to compare artificial selection (selective breeding) and natural selection to make sure that you understand the relevant similarities and differences.

★ **Exam tip**

You might be tested on your knowledge of meiosis by being asked why maize farmers cannot keep their seed from one year to the next. Instead, they have to buy seeds of hybrid corn from seed merchants. Think of how meiosis generates variation and the effect that this will have on subsequent crops. They may flower at different times and grow to different heights making harvesting very difficult.

★ **Exam tip**

Breeders of dairy cattle also select for other desirable features, such as docility (not aggressive), udder shape and high food conversion. You should read about the selective breeding of other livestock to make sure you can write about this topic with confidence.

✏ **Revision strategy**

Research some of the techniques of assisted reproduction used in cattle breeding, such as AI, IVF, surrogacy and reproductive cloning.

Maths Skills

Hardy–Weinberg principle

The Hardy–Weinberg principle is used to calculate the frequencies of alleles of a particular gene in a population. Equation 1 is for the alleles in the gene pool of the population and equation 2 is for genotypes in populations:

Equation 1 $\qquad\qquad p + q = 1$

where p = the frequency of the dominant allele, **A**, (or whatever allele you are investigating) in the population; and q = the frequency of the recessive allele, **a**, in the population.

Equation 2 $\qquad\qquad p^2 + 2pq + q^2 = 1$

where p^2 = the frequency of the genotype **AA**; $2pq$ = the frequency of the genotype **Aa**; and q^2 = the frequency of the genotype **aa**.

In a population of mice, 16% have the recessive phenotype with the genotype **aa**. Using Equation 2, 16% becomes 0.16, which is equivalent to q^2. This means that we can calculate the frequency of the recessive allele (**a**) as the square root of 0.16, which is 0.4. Using Equation 1, the frequency of the dominant allele (**A**) is therefore 0.6 ($p = 1 - q$).

▼ **Table 17.7** A modified Punnett square shows how equation 2 is derived if all individuals can mate *at random*

		Frequency of female gametes in the population	
		p (A)	q (a)
Frequency of male gametes in the population	p (A)	p^2 (AA)	pq (Aa)
	q (a)	pq (Aa)	q^2 (aa)

We can now put these allele frequencies into Equation 2 and calculate the frequencies of the homozygous dominant genotype and the heterozygous genotype as **AA** = 0.6^2 = 0.36 (36%) and **Aa** = $2 \times (0.6 \times 0.4)$ = 0.48 (48%).

We can analyse the population in this way because the homozygous recessive individuals in the population have a phenotype that is recognisable. We cannot count the number of homozygous dominant individuals to find p^2 because they have a phenotype indistinguishable from that of the heterozygotes. We can use the equations to calculate the frequency of allele **A** in the population and therefore the frequencies of **AA** and **Aa**.

There are several requirements of the Hardy–Weinberg principle. It assumes:

- the population is large
- mating occurs within a population at random (mating in a small population is non-random)
- no mutation
- no immigration or emigration
- no selective pressure operating against one of the phenotypes.

The Hardy–Weinberg equations can be used to see if allele frequencies change from generation to generation. If the frequencies of genotypes in one generation do not conform to the expected frequencies then one or more of the assumptions above does not apply. For example, It may be that selection is occurring so that the frequency of one allele is decreasing and the other is increasing.

→ Try this... 11

Red blood cells of humans often express the Rhesus antigen on the cell surface. People with this antigen are Rhesus positive (Rh⁺). Those who do not express the antigen are Rhesus negative (Rh⁻). The alleles of the gene that controls the expression of the antigen are **D** and **d**. The gene is not sex linked.

(a) A man who is Rh⁺ and his wife who is Rh⁻ have two children. One child is Rh⁺ and the other is Rh⁻. Each of their children has a partner who is Rh⁻.

     State the probability of each genotype in the first grandchild.   [2]

(b) Blood samples were taken from 700 people at random. Of these people 112 were found to be Rhesus negative.

     Use the Hardy–Weinberg equations (see above) to predict the number of people in the random sample who are heterozygous for this gene. Show all your working.   [4]

(c) In an adult population in a rural area of Africa affected by malaria the following genotypes are found: Hb^{A}Hb^A 605; Hb^{A}Hb^S 390; Hb^{S}Hb^S 5.

Use the Hardy–Weinberg principle to find out if this population is in equilibrium. Show all the steps in your working. [6]

↑ Raise your grade

1 (a) Describe two examples of the effects of the environment on the phenotype of named organisms. [2]

Animals will put on weight if they eat too much and may be burnt by the sun if it is very hot.

The candidate has not read the question carefully. There should be a named organism in the answer not just 'Animals'.

(b) Explain how the interaction of alleles can influence the phenotype of an organism when
   (i) the alleles are at one locus
   (ii) the alleles are at different loci. [5]

The alleles of a gene can be dominant, recessive or codominant. These can have important effects on the phenotype because sometimes the allele has an effect (dominant) and sometimes it does not (recessive). Both codominant alleles have an effect at the same time. ✔

A poor answer that should have detail about the interaction of dominant and recessive alleles. Recessive alleles have an effect on phenotype. This does not attempt an answer to part (ii). This shows the importance of knowing the syllabus so that you can anticipate the questions.

(c) The mean milk yield for cattle in the UK has increased from 4099 dm³ per cow per year in 1975 to 7968 dm³ per cow per year in 2019.
Explain how a cattle breeder can increase the milk yield of a herd of dairy cattle. [5]

The best cattle are crossed together producing cattle that will produce better milk. Then they will take the best cattle from the offspring and breed them together. And so on.

A very poor answer that overlooks the fact that male cattle (bulls) do not produce milk.

2 Cystic fibrosis (CF) is the most common genetic disease in Caucasian populations. In these populations, 1 in 2500 babies are born with the condition.

Use the Hardy–Weinberg principle to calculate the proportion of these populations that are carriers of the mutant allele, **f**, for cystic fibrosis. [4]

*p is the frequency of the dominant allele (**F**) and q is the frequency of the recessive allele (**f**). As 1 in every 2500 people are affected, the recessive allele q = 0.0004 and the dominant allele p = 0.9996. So the frequency of allele **f** = 0.0004 and that of **F** = 0.9996 in the population.*

Inserting these frequencies into the equation: $p^2 + 2pq + q^2 = 1$ ✔
So the frequency of carriers (**Ff**) = 2pq = 2 × (0.0004 × 0.9996) = 0.000799 = 0.08% ✔

This answer contains a serious error in the first step. The frequency of children with CF is $\frac{1}{2500}$ = 0.0004, but that is q^2 and **not** q. The frequency of allele **f** is the square root of 0.0004, which is 0.02. So p = 0.98 and the frequency of carriers (**Ff**) is 2pq = 2 × (0.98 × 0.02) = 0.0392 or 3.92% of the population. A mark can be awarded for calculating 2pq using the incorrect figures for p and q.

Exam-style questions

Structured questions (Paper 4)

1 (a) Explain why body mass is an example of continuous variation. [2]

(b) Three separate populations of mice on different islands across the world were studied over a long period of time. The researchers collected data on body mass. At the beginning, body mass of all the mice showed a normal distribution and the mean body mass of each population was about the same.

At the end of the study, these results were obtained:

Population **A**: the mean body mass remained the same, but the range in mass decreased

Population **B**: the mean mass increased, but with fewer small mice and more larger mice

Population **C**: there were many small mice and many much larger mice, but none with the mean mass of the original population.

(i) Draw graphs for populations **A**, **B** and **C** to show the variation in body mass at the beginning and at the end of the study. [7]

(ii) Name the type of selection that occurred to each population. [3]

2 (a) The table shows the sequence of bases in the non-transcribed strand of DNA that codes for the first four amino acids in a fibrous protein found in all mammals.

Mammal species	Amino acid position			
	1	2	3	4
A	ATG	ATC	CAG	TTT
B	ACC	ACT	CAG	TTA
C	TTG	ATC	CAG	TTT

(i) State the number of differences between the DNA sequences of species **A** and **B**, between **A** and **C**, and between **B** and **C**. [1]

(ii) State the cause of the differences between the three species. [2]

(b) The enzyme known as GAPDH catalyses a reaction in the glycolysis pathway. The gene *GAPDH* that codes for this enzyme has been sequenced in many organisms. The amino acid sequences of GAPDH in the different organisms have been derived from the gene sequences.

The table shows a comparison of the DNA sequences and amino acid sequences from four animals and humans.

Species	Percentage identical to base sequence of human gene *GAPDH*	Percentage identical to amino acid sequence of human enzyme GAPDH
chimpanzee	99.6	100.0
dog	91.3	95.2
fruit fly	72.4	76.7
roundworm	68.2	74.3

(i) Explain how the amino acid sequence of human GAPDH can be derived from the DNA sequence of the human gene *GAPDH*. [2]

(ii) Explain the advantage of deriving the amino acid sequence from a DNA sequence rather than deriving the DNA sequence from the amino acid sequence. [3]

(iii) Explain why the percentage similarity between the genes and human DNA is less than the percentage similarity between the proteins and the human protein. [2]

(iv) Yeast and bacteria also have the gene *GAPDH*. Predict their relative positions to each other and to the other organisms in the table. Explain your answer. [3]

3 The gene *LacZ* codes for the enzyme β-galactosidase in the bacterium *Escherischia coli*. Researchers investigated competition between two populations of bacteria, **M** and **O**, each with a different mutant allele of this gene when grown with a population having the normal (wild type) allele. Lactose was the only source of energy provided to the populations of *E. coli*.

Population **M** decreased in numbers compared with the normal population.

Population **O** increased in numbers compared with the normal population.

(a) Suggest one way in which the mutant alleles may differ from the normal allele of *LacZ*. [1]

(b) Explain why lactose was the only source of energy provided. [3]

(c) Explain the results for populations **M** and **O**. [5]

4 (a) With reference to a named organism, explain the differences between continuous and discontinuous variation. [4]

(b) Explain the roles of geographical isolation and small population size in the evolution of new species. [5]

Classification

Every known species has two unambiguous scientific names. The first or genus name begins with a capital letter and the second begins with a lowercase letter, for example, *Taraxacum officinale* for the dandelion plant. When a scientific name has been used once, it may be shortened, for example, *T. officinale*.

Classification is the organisation of living things into groups that are arranged in a hierarchy. The hierarchical classification system has large groups that are continually subdivided to the level of the species.

▼ **Table 18.1** The hierarchical classification of three species of mammals with prehensile tails

Taxonomic rank	Peruvian spider monkey	Brown howler monkey	Common spotted cuscus
Domain	Eukarya	Eukarya	Eukarya
Kingdom	Animalia	Animalia	Animalia
Phylum	Chordata	Chordata	Chordata
Class	Mammalia	Mammalia	Mammalia
Order	Primates	Primates	Diprotodontia
Family	Atelidae	Atelidae	Phalangeridae
Genus	*Ateles*	*Alouatta*	*Spilocuscus*
Species	*A. chamek*	*A. guariba*	*S. maculatus*

Biological species (biospecies) concept. The term species is applied to all the populations that interbreed, produce fertile offspring and so contribute to the same gene pool. All the members of the same species are reproductively isolated from populations of other species.

Morphological species concept. It is not possible to apply the biospecies concept to all populations; for example, individuals may never have been observed to reproduce. Some populations only reproduce asexually and some organisms are extinct and only known from fossils. In these cases, physical features, such as morphology (outward appearance) and anatomy, are used to distinguish between particular species.

Ecological species concept. Some populations have very similar physical features but occupy different ecological niches. Two populations of organisms with similar appearance are separated into separate species using ecological features.

⭐ **Exam tip**

The scientific name for each species is *both* names. The second name should not be used on its own.

▲ **Figure 18.1** *Spilocuscus maculatus* is found in Papua New Guinea. Superficially it looks a bit like monkeys from the Americas as it has a prehensile tail, but it is not closely related at all

🔗 **Link**

The features of prokaryotic and eukaryotic cells are described in Unit 1.

⭐ **Exam tip**

Table 18.1 shows the hierarchical arrangement of the taxonomic ranks beginning with the domain and ending with species. Each of the groups in the rest of the table (e.g. Eukarya, Primates) is a taxon (plural: taxa). The species of monkey are more closely related to each other than to the cuscus.

The three domains

The key features of the three domains are concerned with DNA, ribosomes, RNA polymerase and membrane lipids. The Archaea share features with the other two domains, but are considered to be a distinct group of prokaryotic organisms.

➡ **Try this... 1**

Research the features of the three domains and make a table to summarise the information you find. There should be four columns to your table. The features included in the first column must include membrane lipids, ribosomal RNA and cell wall components.

➡ **Try this... 2**

Research the characteristic features of the four kingdoms in the Eukarya and make a table to show the similarities and differences between them.

✏ **Revision strategy**

Many archaeans live in extreme environments. Search for information on extremophiles to read about their importance.

Viruses are not included in the three-domain classification. Each virus is composed of nucleic acid surrounded by a protein coat. As they do not have a cellular structure and have no form of metabolism, they cannot be classified with prokaryotes and eukaryotes. They are classified according to the type of nucleic acid (RNA or DNA) and whether the nucleic acid is single stranded or double stranded.

> **🔗 Link**
>
> See Units 1 and 10 for more about viruses. Search online for the Baltimore classification system to learn more about how they are classified.

> **➡ Try this... 3**
>
> Make a list of the viruses that you have heard or read about. You may know them by the diseases that they cause. Classify them using the Baltimore classification system.

Biodiversity

An ecosystem is a relatively self-contained unit, made up of biotic and abiotic components interacting and functioning together. An ecosystem includes the community of living organisms of all types in a given area and all the abiotic (physical and chemical) factors in their environment, linked together by energy flow and cycling of nutrients. Ecosystems may vary in size but always form a functional entity: for example, a decomposing log, a pond, a meadow, a coral reef, a forest or the open ocean. The environment provides habitats for different species. Each species within an ecosystem occupies a particular **niche** that it does not share with any other species. The niche occupied by any species is determined by the effect of biotic and abiotic factors in the ecosystem.

The **biodiversity** of an area, such as a country or a region, is a measure of:

- the different ecosystems and different habitats (aquatic and terrestrial)

- the number of different species

- the abundance of each species

- the genetic diversity within each species.

Tropical forests and coral reefs are two of the most species-rich areas on Earth.

Species diversity is considered important as it makes an ecosystem more able to resist changes than one with limited diversity. Generally, the further north you go from the equator, the more species diversity decreases.

Genetic diversity within a population considers factors that give different genetic characteristics, such as the number of different alleles in the genome and the number of loci that have multiple alleles. Different populations of the same species may be adapted differently, so could vary in their genetic diversity. Genetic diversity allows populations to adapt to changing environmental conditions.

Sampling biodiversity

To overcome any bias, **random sampling** is used to make sure that results are representative of a whole area. An area is marked out with tape measures to make a grid; random numbers are used to give coordinates and sampling is done where the coordinates intersect. Sampling communities is usually done with a **quadrat**:

- An open frame quadrat is a square frame made of wood, plastic or metal enclosing a known area – usually $0.25\,m^2$ or $1.0\,m^2$; larger areas can be marked out with tapes or string.

- A gridded quadrat is a frame quadrat divided into smaller sections (e.g. 10×10). Random samples within a small area can be taken rather than counting individual organisms in the whole quadrat.

> **★ Exam tip**
>
> Viruses are the ultimate parasites; they cannot replicate or spread without invading the cells of prokaryotes or eukaryotes. The host cells produce more viral particles that are released and spread to infect more cells.

> **★ Exam tip**
>
> A habitat is a place where a particular species lives and a community is all the populations of all the species in a given area at a given time. The term niche incorporates the habitat and all the interactions that a species has with other organisms and its physical environment.

> **Key term**
>
> **Niche:** the role of a species within a community including its position in the food web and its interactions with other species and its environment.

> **🔗 Link**
>
> There is more about genetic diversity in Units 17 and 19. You may be asked about the techniques to investigate genetic diversity (Unit 19) and the importance of genetic diversity for natural and artificial selection.

> **💡 Remember**
>
> You can illustrate answers on genetic diversity with examples from other Units. For example, it is estimated that there are about 900 different variants of the haemoglobin polypeptides in the human population – all with slightly different amino acid sequences.

A frame quadrat can be used to record the species that occur within it and the data used to calculate **species frequency** – the percentage of quadrats that contained each species.

The abundance of different species may be recorded by:

- counting individual plants and animals where this is possible and expressing results as **species density** – number of individuals per unit area

- estimating **percentage cover** (e.g. for organisms that are difficult to count individually) by finding the percentage of a quadrat that is occupied by each species

- using an **abundance scale** when species are far too numerous to count and, for plants, when it is difficult to isolate individuals (e.g. ACFOR).

Random sampling using quadrats is usually done in a uniform ecosystem, such as grassland or woodland. It is not appropriate if the physical environment is not the same across the whole area being sampled.

> ★ **Exam tip**
>
> Some biodiversity surveys are carried out in much larger areas. For example, ecosystem diversity in the Amazon region was assessed with quadrats that were 1000 km by 1000 km.

A line **transect** is useful for assessing non-uniform distribution, for example, an area where there is an abrupt change from one ecosystem to another, such as between grassland and a woodland. A long rope or tape measure marked at intervals is placed across an area. The species at each sampling point along the transect is recorded and the results used to make a drawing that shows the changes in **distribution** of species. Line transects are used to show how communities change along a gradient, which could be a slope or a change in an abiotic feature, such as exposure to the wind or change in soil moisture.

A **belt transect** is used to collect quantitative data along a transect. Quadrats are placed along the side of a line and used to assess species abundance in a **continuous belt transect**. Placing quadrats at intervals (e.g. every 5 m) gives an **interrupted belt transect**. Data may be collected as percentage cover and species density, and may be used to make a kite diagram.

> ★ **Exam tip**
>
> Look at the section on biological sampling under the Education tab at the Offwell Woodland & Wildlife Trust web site. There are plenty of examples of sampling techniques to read about.

Measuring abiotic factors

The distribution of species throughout ecosystems is determined by biotic and abiotic factors. Data on abiotic factors can be collected at sampling points along transects. Factors may include light intensity; temperature; humidity of air (measured with a hygrometer); wind speed; oxygen concentration, pH and salinity of water; and pH and water content of soil.

Abiotic factors must be collected consistently, for example, at the same height or depth. The results for the abiotic factors may be written on kite diagrams to see if there is any correlation. If this seems likely, then correlation coefficients can be calculated (see page 201). You should know how to calculate Spearman's rank and Pearson's linear correlation coefficients and, most importantly, interpret them in the context of examples given in exam questions.

> ★ **Exam tip**
>
> Make sure that you know the difference between the distribution of a species and the abundance of a species. Distribution is where the species occurs in an area – the spread of a species. Abundance is a measure of how many organisms of that species there are in a given area and can be in given terms of numbers, biomass or percentage of the area covered.

ACFOR – abundant, common, frequent, occasional, rare. Decide first how to apply each description; how much or how many plants or animals have to be present before you can record their abundance as 'common' or 'frequent', for example. Then you can make your recordings far quicker than making counts.

> **Key term**
>
> **Transect**: a tape or rope placed across an area so that samples are taken at regular intervals, for example, 0.5 m.

If field work is carried out on several occasions, then information about changes over time can be collected. Sensors and data loggers can be used to record abiotic factors over the long term.

▲ **Figure 18.2** Students measuring the infiltration rate – the speed at which a known volume of water enters a known area of soil. They compared the rates for soils in a palm oil plantation with soils in a rainforest

Maths Skills

Simpson's index of diversity

Expressing species diversity as one figure is simpler than looking at lists of species found in different ecosystems and their abundance. **Simpson's index of diversity** uses the number of species and their relative abundance to calculate a value between 0 and 1. The higher the number the greater the diversity (D).

The formula for calculating D is: $D = 1 - \left(\Sigma \left(\frac{n}{N} \right)^2 \right)$

★ **Exam tip**

There are many different indices of diversity and at least two ways to calculate Simpson's index. Learn the steps to follow when calculating this version.

where Σ = the sum of; n = the number of individuals of each type present in the sample (types may be species and/or higher taxa such as genera, families, etc.); and N = the total number of all individuals of all types present in the sample.

This index measures the probability that two individuals randomly selected from a sample will belong to the same species or group (e.g. genus or family).

Worked Example

Many plants that grow in waste ground can be counted as individual plants. Random sampling is used as counting all the plants in an area is too time-consuming. Some students studied the vegetation on an area of waste ground in Barbados. They recorded their results as follows:

thick-leaved grasses 40, thin-leaved grasses 150, Pride of Barbados 3, heart seed 5, Mexican poppy 18, wild cress 15, wild dolly 11, black sage 17.

(a) Use the formula above to calculate Simpson's index of diversity.

(b) State a conclusion that the students could make from their calculation.

(c) State **one** limitation of the data that the students collected.

Answers

A table showing how to calculate the index of diversity is in the answers to this Unit on the support website.

(a) $D = 1 - 0.3511 = 0.6489$

The index of diversity (D) is 0.65 (to 2 significant figures).

(b) When the index is small (near 0) there is a very low diversity. When the number is high (near 1) there is a very high diversity. This habitat is dominated by the thin-leaved grasses so does not have a very high diversity.

(c) They did not identify different species within the thin-leaved and thick-leaved grass species.

See page 171 for information about significant figures. In a question like this, you will often be told how many significant figures to use. If not, then look for any figures given in the question. For example, a question may ask you to calculate an index of diversity compared with another habitat. If so, express the answer to your calculation to the same number of significant figures.

Mark-release-recapture

One way to estimate numbers of a mobile population of animals is to catch a certain number and mark them – the first sample (S_1). Release these animals back into the environment and later catch a second sample (S_2). S_2 should contain both marked and unmarked individuals. The smaller the proportion of marked individuals, the larger the total population. Calculate an estimate of the population size by using the **Lincoln index**:

★ **Exam tip**

You should expect to plan a field work investigation in Paper 5 using the techniques of random or non-random sampling.

$$N \text{ (population size)} = \frac{n_1 \times n_2}{m_2}$$

where N = population estimate; n_1 = number of marked individuals released; n_2 = number of individuals (both marked and unmarked) captured; and m_2 = number of marked individuals recaptured.

Conservation

There are many threats to biodiversity. These threats are usually considered in relation to populations (local extinction) or to whole species (complete extinction). Threats can be summarised under these headings:

Climate change is happening at a rate that is more significant than would occur naturally because of human influences affecting the distribution and abundance of species, especially small populations (e.g. on isolated islands), those already under threat from disease (e.g. amphibians) and those with specific habitat requirements (e.g. alpine plants that live at high altitudes).

Competition, especially with livestock (e.g. cattle) and introduced or alien species. Red lionfish, *Pterois volitans* – voracious predators that originate in the Far East – have quickly spread throughout the Caribbean where they outcompete native fish and are having a detrimental effect on fish biodiversity. The Galápagos Islands have been severely affected by human activities. In the past, whalers killed huge numbers of marine mammals. Many mammals (e.g. pigs, dogs) and plant species were introduced to the islands. These have had a detrimental effect on indigenous (native) species.

Hunting by humans, which includes fishing and poaching of large mammals, for example, the African elephant and the five species of rhinoceros.

Degradation of land, such as deforestation with associated habitat loss. More humans means more land needed for housing, agriculture, industry, infrastructure, transport and recreation so reducing the space available for natural ecosystems.

Methods of protecting threatened ecosystems and species in danger of extinction

1. Conservation of species in their natural habitats (*in situ*) – national parks and marine parks. This is the best way to conserve a species as all the 'life support' systems are provided.

2. Conservation of species *ex situ*. Some species are so threatened in their habitat that they are removed to be kept somewhere else. Zoos and botanic gardens are the main examples of *ex situ* conservation.

> ★ **Exam tip**
>
> Any method of conservation that keeps whole organisms, gametes, embryos, seeds, tissues or any other part of an organism is known as a **gene bank**. It is not a store of bits of DNA but of whole genomes in one of the ways listed.

> ★ **Exam tip**
>
> If you know of any alien species in your country, find out where they came from and the reasons for controlling them. If not, read about cane toads, water hyacinth, Japanese knotweed and kudzu.

> ★ **Exam tip**
>
> Do not confuse **artificial insemination** (AI) with *in vitro* fertilisation (IVF). In AI the sperm are placed inside the female's reproductive tract so fertilisation is internal. IVF occurs outside the body in a lab.

→ **Try this... 4**

Make a series of fact files on different methods of conservation and use them to make a presentation, a series of posters or a storyboard for a documentary film on methods of conservation.

1. Read about National Parks in your country or region and marine parks. A good marine park to read about is Goat Island Marine Reserve in New Zealand. Find examples of species of plant and animal that are being saved from extinction by *in situ* conservation. A good example is the greater one-horned rhino in Chitwan National Park in Nepal.

2. Research the work of zoos in captive breeding programmes and reintroduction schemes. Go first to the web site of the World Association of Zoos and Aquariums: https://www.waza.org

   then read about the conservation work of the Durrell Wildlife Conservation Trust, based in Jersey in the Channel Islands: https://www.durrell.org/wildlife

   and the Cincinnati Zoo in the USA: https://cincinnatizoo.org/conservation/field-projects

   A 'must read' is the web site of the Frozen Zoo® at the Institute for Conservation Research at San Diego Zoo: https://institute.sandiegozoo.org/resources/frozen-zoo

3. Research different methods of assisted reproduction of mammals – *in vitro* fertilisation, embryo transfer and the use of surrogates. Draw flow charts to show the stages in assisted reproduction that might involve all three methods. Find examples of conservation programmes that use these methods.

4. Research the work of botanic gardens in propagating endangered and vulnerable species, and in reintroduction schemes and land reclamation. Start by using the web site of Botanic Gardens International: https://www.bgci.org

Then read about the conservation work of the Missouri Botanical Garden: http://www.missouribotanicalgarden.org/plant-conservation/plant-conservation/about-plant-conservation.aspx and The Royal Botanic Gardens Kew: https://www.kew.org

5. Find out about the role of seed banks in conservation. Make a flow chart to show how seeds of wild and cultivated plants are processed for storage and tested at intervals for viability.

The Convention in International Trade in Endangered Species of Wild Fauna and Flora (CITES) is an international treaty that protects animals and plants from various forms of exploitation, for example, illegal trade in animals for the pet trade and in animal materials, such as ivory. Find the criteria for allocating species at risk to the three Appendices and find 'How CITES works'. See: https://www.cites.org

The web site of the International Union of Nature Conservation will tell you about the conservation status of many species. See: https://www.iucn.org

The IUCN Red List is the most comprehensive source for information on the conservation status of animal, fungus and plant species. Each species that has been assessed is classified into one of nine categories. You should know about these categories: 'vulnerable', 'endangered', 'critically endangered', 'extinct in the wild' and 'extinct'.

→ Try this... 5

The giant river otter, *Pteronura brasiliensis*, is an endangered species that has a range that extends across South America, living along the Amazon River, its tributaries and in the Pantanal swamp. Numbers decreased partly as a result of hunting for its fur. Trade in otter skins was banned in 1975, so removing one threat to its survival.

▲ **Figure 18.3** The giant river otter

(a) The giant otter is a top carnivore in the Pantanal swamp. Explain why it is important for the biodiversity of ecosystems that top carnivores are conserved. [3]

(b) Explain the risks to a species of hunting and overexploitation. [4]

(c) DNA analysis suggests that there are four genetically distinct groups of giant river otters. Discuss the consequences of these results for conservation of the giant river otter. [3]

(d) The otter in the photograph lives in Budapest Zoo in Hungary. Outline the roles of zoos in the conservation of animal species, such as *P. brasiliensis*. [5]

(e) Explain why it is important to control the invasions of alien species into places like the Pantanal swamp. [6]

→ Try this... 6

In a study of a species of hawk moth, light traps were set up in a nature reserve. 80 hawk moths were caught on the first night, marked and released. The following night the traps were set up again. Of a total of 38 moths caught, 17 had been marked.

(a) Suggest two precautions that should be taken to ensure that animals are not harmed while carrying out the mark-release-recapture technique. [2]

(b) Use these results to estimate the number of hawk moths in the population. Show all your working. (See page 153 for the formula required.) [2]

(c) Suggest how this estimate of the population size of hawk moths could be improved. [2]

(d) The biodiversity of many terrestrial invertebrate animals, such as hawk moths, is not well catalogued for many regions of the world.

Explain why it is important to identify and catalogue the species of invertebrate animals in each region. [4]

▲ **Figure 18.4** The hummingbird hawk moth, *Macroglossum stellatarum*, which is distributed across North Africa, Europe and Asia

↑ Raise your grade

An island-endemic species is found on one particular island and nowhere else. There are many endemic species on the islands that make up Indonesia.

(a) Explain the difference between a biological species and a morphological species. [3]

A biological species consists of all the organisms that can breed together and have fertile offspring ✔ that can also reproduce. The organisms making up a morphological species share similar features, ✔ but have not been observed mating together. ✔

> A concise answer that could include some examples of features shared by individuals in a morphological species.

(b) Suggest why some islands have many endemic species. [5]

Many islands are surrounded by large areas of water that isolate them from the mainland or other islands and act as a barrier to movement of many organisms ✔. Any organisms that migrate to the island are likely to become isolated so that gene flow does not occur with other populations. ✔ Conditions on islands are likely to be different from other places, so selection pressures are different. ✔ Allele frequencies change in response to selection and allopatric speciation may occur. Also the founder effect and genetic drift might occur to help form new species.

> This answer has three correct ideas. The founder effect and genetic drift should be explained in the context of islands.

(c) Explain why it is important to conserve these endemic species. [3]

These species have evolved in response to the conditions on the island and the interdependence within the community depends on their specific adaptations. ✔ They may have products that could prove useful ✔ as may their genes for improvement of crops and livestock ✔ by selective breeding or by genetic engineering. ✔

> This question has been answered in two ways, both valid. One is the ecosystem approach and the other is to list the potential uses to humans of particular species.

(d) Endemic plant species are conserved in botanic gardens in Indonesia.
Suggest the difficulties that botanic gardens may have in conserving these species. [4]

The botanic gardens may not have the same conditions as in the island habitat of an endemic plant species so it doesn't grow at all. ✔ If it does grow, then over generations in the gardens it may change as a result of selection ✔ and then not fit back into the habitat if and when reintroduced. ✔

> The end of the last sentence could be improved. A better answer would refer to the absence of a niche.

(e) The Pantanal swamp is a huge wetland extending over nearly 200 000 km^2 in Brazil, Bolivia and Paraguay. Discuss the roles of international organisations in the conservation of areas of global importance, such as the Pantanal swamp. [5]

If trade is banned by CITES then poaching should decrease giving populations of otters a chance to recover. ✔ WWF is an important international organisation that could put pressure on countries to stop loss of habitat in the Pantanal swamp, such as drainage and deforestation. ✔ WWF can also fund research and/or habitat protection schemes. ✔

> The syllabus lists CITES and IUCN so it is best to refer to them if possible, but if you know of others then you should write about them.

Exam-style questions

Structured questions (Paper 4)

1 The black-faced grassquit, *Tiaris bicolor*, is a small bird found throughout the Caribbean and the coasts of Venezuela and Colombia. It is related to Darwin's finches of the Galápagos Islands in the Pacific Ocean.

(a) Outline how variation in wing length in a population of birds, such as *T. bicolor*, would be investigated, recorded and presented. [5]

(b) Explain how it is possible to determine if the population on a Caribbean island belongs to the same species as populations on the South American mainland. [3]

(c) It is thought that a small population of birds like *T. bicolor* colonised the Galápagos Islands. Explain how such a small population may have given rise to the 14 species of finch now found on the Galápagos Islands. [6]

Data analysis and evaluation (Paper 5)

2 Many farms have been abandoned across the United States and some of this farmland has been converted into nature reserves. Plant communities in the abandoned fields are composed of annuals that complete their life cycle within a year and die and perennials that survive through the winter and so persist from year to year.

Ecologists from the University of Minnesota have studied the changes in the composition of plant communities that have occurred on abandoned fields at the Cedar Creek Ecosystem Science Reserve, where the university has a field centre.

Initial research showed that recently abandoned fields appeared to have lower nitrate content and larger populations of annuals compared with fields abandoned many years ago. The ecologists wanted to see if there was a relationship between the soil nitrogen content and the composition of the plant communities on the abandoned fields.

The ecologists took 22 samples from the fields and assessed the percentage cover of annual and perennial plants. At each sampling point they took a soil sample and determined the nitrate content.

(a) Describe a procedure that the ecologists could use to collect the data on the plant communities. [5]

(b) The ecologists calculated Pearson's linear correlation coefficient (*r*) between the soil nitrate content and the percentage cover of the two types of plants. Their results were:

annual plants $r = -0.607$
perennial plants $r = +0.764$

(i) State one null hypothesis for this investigation. [1]

(ii) State two assumptions that the ecologists must have made about the data that they had collected in order to use the Pearson's linear correlation test. [2]

(iii) The table shows the critical values of *r* for $p = 0.05$ and $p = 0.01$.

Number of pairs of measurements	Critical values	
	$p = 0.05$ (5%)	$p = 0.01$ (1%)
20	0.444	0.561
21	0.433	0.549
22	0.423	0.537
24	0.404	0.515

Use the table and the calculated values of *r* for the annual and for the perennial plants to state and explain the conclusions that can be made from the investigation. [6]

(c) The ecologists investigated the species diversity of the plant communities. Outline a method to compare the species diversity of two fields with soils of different nitrate content. [4]

Planning question (Paper 5)

3 Grasslands are used for grazing livestock, such as sheep and cattle. Improved grasslands are treated with fertiliser to increase their productivity. Fertilisers tend to increase the growth rates of certain species of grass which outcompete slower growing plants so reducing species diversity. Students were asked to compare the biodiversity of improved and non-improved grasslands on fields in adjacent farms.

Plan a procedure that you would follow to compare the two types of grassland.

Include the following:

(a) independent and dependent variables [2]

(b) a hypothesis [1]

(c) a method and safety comments. [7]

(d) Explain how the data should be processed, presented and analysed to see if there are any differences between the two grasslands. [3]

This unit introduces some more ways to help you learn and revise.

The key to understanding much of this Unit is the structure and roles of nucleic acids that you learnt about in Unit 6. As that is likely to be some time ago, spend plenty of time studying the structure of DNA and the ways it is used in replication and transcription before you go any further.

> **💡 Remember**
>
> DNA is composed of two strands or **polynucleotides**. The monomers are four nucleotides, each with a purine or pyrimidine base, deoxyribose and a phosphate group.
>
> Adenine and guanine are the purine bases, thymine and cytosine are the pyrimidine bases.

> **🔗 Link**
>
> In 1953, Watson and Crick published a model of the structure of DNA beginning with the words: 'We wish to suggest a structure for … DNA. This structure has novel features which are of considerable biological interest.' Use your knowledge and understanding from Unit 6 to explain what they meant. Hint: think about base pairing.

> **➡ Try this... 1**
>
> Find a detailed image of a small length of DNA. The image should show details of the two polynucleotides with details of the phosphate–sugar 'backbone', base pairing and hydrogen bonding between the base pairs A–T and C–G. Indicate on the diagram the 3 prime (3′) and 5 prime (5′) ends of the two polynucleotides (strands). The 3′ end has the third carbon in the sugar-ring of the deoxyribose at its terminus and the 5′ end has the fifth carbon in the sugar-ring of the deoxyribose at its terminus. Draw a diagram of a molecule of the sugar deoxyribose and label the carbon atoms to help understand the directionality of each polynucleotide in DNA. Annotate your image of a DNA molecule to show the **antiparallel** arrangement of the two polynucleotides. Find diagrams of replication and transcription and show the direction taken by DNA polymerase in replication and RNA polymerase in transcription.
>
> Use your image of DNA to build up a resource that will help you to identify all the connections between the topics in this Unit and others (e.g. 6, 16 and 17).
>
> Make a list of all the terms related to DNA, RNA, replication, mitotic cell cycle, transcription, translation and mutation. Add more terms from genetics and gene control in Unit 16. You should add many more from this Unit. Write definitions of the terms in your list and make a 'mix and match' resource to test your learning of these topics (see page 10).
>
> Use your terms to build up a poster, chart or other type of graphic organiser showing the central role of DNA in information storage. Show how the information held in its sequence of nucleotide bases is used in cells – see Figure 1.5 on page 10 for an example.

> **★ Exam tip**
>
> Make sure your diagrams show that the 5′ carbon has a phosphate group attached to it and the 3′ carbon a hydroxyl (–OH) group.

> **★ Exam tip**
>
> Make sure you can use the terms **template strand** and **non-transcribed strand** correctly when describing what occurs during transcription.

Analysing questions

Questions in Papers 4 and 5 often draw on more than one Unit. You should always read through the whole of a question and analyse what you read before starting to answer part (a). One part of that analysis is identifying the parts of the syllabus that you will need to use in your answers. Read the question in *Try this... 2* and identify the learning outcomes that are being tested by each part. Then answer the questions.

The question on rice ends with a question about selective breeding. This is not to be confused with genetic engineering – the first topic in this Unit. As you revise you could spend some time on this topic, then stop and research and revise something different. This helps to make distinctions between different topics that might well be asked together in the same question. Topic switching happens both within questions (from part to part as in the question on rice) and between questions.

> **🔗 Link**
>
> You can check your analysis and your answers by looking at the answer file online.

> **★ Exam tip**
>
> Switching between topics is known as 'interleaving'. You can see from the analysis of questions that it could help you. There are many opportunities for interleaving in Unit 19.

→ **Try this... 2**

Questions do not usually have headings or first lines that say 'This question is about...' so that's what you have to ask yourself each time you start a new question in the exam.

Many varieties of rice, *Oryza sativa*, grow in fields that are flooded for part of the growing season. High-yielding varieties cannot survive flash flooding or lengthy submersion in water.

Low-yielding deep-water varieties of rice grow in Bangladesh. These varieties respond to flash flooding by growing very rapidly by as much as 250 mm a day to reach heights of up to 8 m. During growth of roots in flooded soils some cells in the cortex die to form large intercellular spaces.

Read the two paragraphs again and recall what you know from the syllabus about rice and the growth of stems and roots.

(a)   State the name of the tissue that is formed within the cortex by the death and breakdown of cells.   [1]

  This question shows the importance of making a glossary to help learn the technical terms.

(b)   Explain the advantages to rice plants of the two responses to flooding described in the passage.   [4]

  '...cannot survive flash flooding...' in the first paragraph is the clue that this question is about the survival of plants in adverse conditions. Think about what plants need to do in order to stay alive.

(c)   Gibberellin is involved in controlling elongation growth of stems.

  Explain the role of gibberellin in controlling elongation growth in rice.   [3]

  This shows the importance of making graphic organisers such as flow charts to help learn processes such as the control of elongation growth. See question 2 on page 139 for a structured question on gibberellin and elongation growth.

(d)   Recent research has discovered that two genes known as *SNORKEL-1 (S-1)* and *SNORKEL-2 (S-2)* are responsible for much of the response to flooding. Sequencing of the genes followed by computer modelling of the tertiary structure of the proteins coded by these two genes predicted that they both have DNA-binding regions.

  (i)   Outline the information needed to make predictions about tertiary structure from the base sequence of the DNA of a gene, such as *S-1* and *S-2*.   [3]

    This question needs an understanding of the genetic code from Unit 6.

  (ii)   Suggest a function for the proteins coded by *SNORKEL-1* and *SNORKEL-2*.   [3]

    'DNA-binding' is the clue that this question is about transcription factors.

(e)   High-yielding varieties of rice do not have the genes *S-1* and *S-2* and cannot survive where rice fields are likely to be submerged for long periods of time or at risk of flash flooding.

  Outline the steps that plant breeders would follow to incorporate genes that confer flood tolerance into high-yielding varieties.   [4]

  The key word in this question is 'breeder'. It says 'plant breeder', not 'genetic engineer', so needs information from Unit 17, not 19.

Genetic engineering to make recombinant DNA

Genetic engineering involves the removal of a gene or genes from one organism and placing them into another. This can involve removing a gene from one species and transferring it to another species (e.g. human insulin gene into a bacterium) or taking a gene from an individual of a species and transferring it into other individuals of the same species (e.g. gene therapy using the human gene *ADA* that codes for adenosine deaminase).

The DNA corresponding to a gene is obtained in one of a number of ways then inserted into a vector, such as a virus, plasmid or liposome (small phospholipid-bound vesicles), which is used to transfer the gene into host cells. DNA is universal so it is possible to make transfers between widely different species. The genetic code is also universal so all cells can 'read' a sequence of bases from a different species so that the protein encoded by a 'foreign' gene can be produced in any cell.

Key term

Recombinant DNA (rDNA): DNA from two sources (e.g. two different species) that are joined together.

💡 **Remember**

The term **vector** is also used for animals that transmit pathogens from one host to another. *Anopheles* mosquitoes are the vector for the causative organism of malaria.

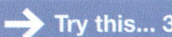

> ➜ **Try this... 3**

A genetic engineer requires a 'toolkit' that includes:

restriction endonucleases, plasmids, DNA polymerase, reverse transcriptase, fluorescent tags, genes that code for fluorescent products (e.g. GFP) and promoters.

Research each of the components of the 'toolkit' and write fact files for each of them. In each case find links to other Units, which will probably be 6 and 11. Search for examples of restriction enzymes (see question 1 on page 165) and plasmids used as vectors.

Make a graphic organiser to show how these different components of the 'toolkit' are used to produce a length of recombinant DNA. You may find a flow chart is best to use as you will be dealing with the steps in a process.

Make diagrams to show how DNA is cut and fragments of DNA are joined together. Show sticky ends, blunt ends, complementary base pairs and phosphodiester bonds. List three ways in which genes for use in genetic engineering are sourced and write a fact file for each way.

> ★ **Exam tip**
>
> Many monoclonal antibodies (see Unit 11) are prepared by recombinant DNA techniques. You could write a question of your own that uses this idea as the main theme. Try writing a question in the style of Paper 5.

Gene editing

Figure 19.1 shows the principles of gene editing using the Crispr/Cas9 system.

> 💡 **Remember**
>
> The genetic code is the sequence of three bases that code for different amino acids. It is *not* the sequence of bases in the structural genes that code for the amino acid sequences of polypeptides.

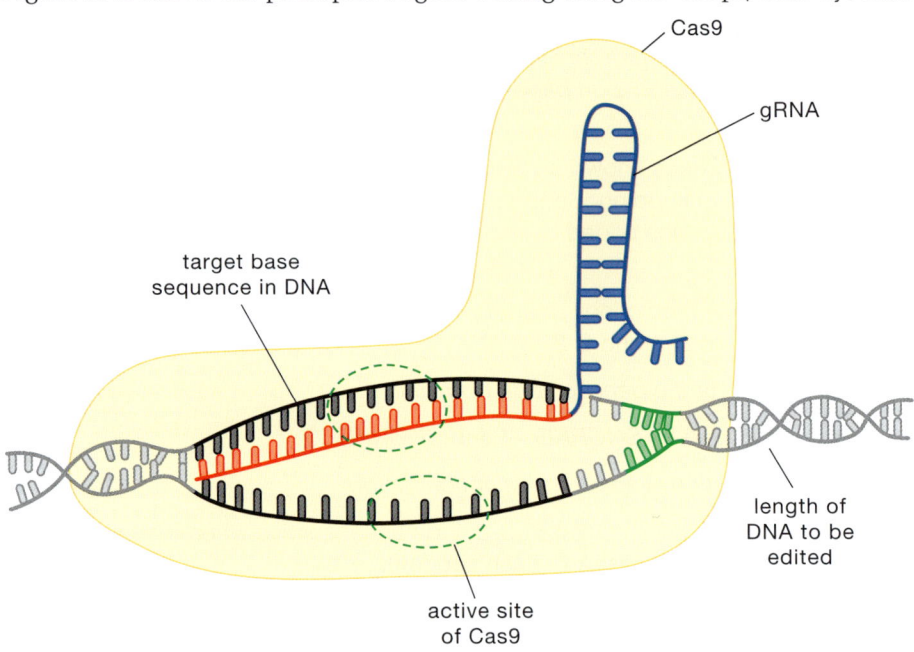

> **Key term**
>
> **Gene editing** involves the insertion, deletion or replacement of DNA at specific sites in the genome of organisms.

▲ **Figure 19.1** A diagram showing gene editing using the Crispr/Cas9 system

> ➜ **Try this... 4**

Make a copy of Figure 19.1 and use it to make revision notes on gene editing.

Research the details of gene editing and answer these questions:

- How is gene editing carried out by the Crispr/Cas9 system?

  Include the diagram in a graphic organiser, for example, a flow chart, to show how the system can change base sequences of DNA. You could adapt the diagram by writing a DNA target sequence of 20 base pairs and the complementary gRNA sequence. Show how the target sequence can be deleted, replaced, and silenced by inserting a stop triplet.

- What is gene editing used for?

  Search online for examples of how gene editing is being applied.

- What are the advantages of gene editing?

  The CRISPR-Cas9 system was first applied to editing the genomes of eukaryotes in 2013. Find out what is possible with gene editing that was not possible before 2013.

Microarrays

A microarray is based on a small piece of glass or plastic usually 2 cm² in size. Short lengths of single-stranded DNA probes are attached to this support with 10 000 or more different positions per cm². Each individual position has multiple copies of the same DNA probe. Figure 19.2 is an image of the results from a small region of a microarray. Two fluorescent tags were used – green and red. Yellow indicates where both tags are present.

Amplifying DNA

Samples of DNA are **amplified** in the **polymerase chain reaction** (PCR).

Primers are short sequences of DNA that bind to the single-stranded DNA that is being copied at the 3′ ends. This is necessary for DNA polymerase to start the process of replicating the existing polynucleotide using **deoxyribonucleotide triphosphates** (dNTPs). *Taq* polymerase is a **thermostable** DNA polymerase that is not denatured at the high temperatures needed to separate the two polynucleotides in PCR.

The four stages of each PCR cycle are denaturation, annealing and extension. Notice that at the end of one cycle, a length of double-stranded DNA has been amplified to give two lengths of double-stranded DNA. After another cycle, there are four lengths and so the number increases exponentially as the number of cycles increases.

Electrophoresis

Fragments of DNA (obtained using restriction endonucleases or PCR) are separated by **electrophoresis**. Samples are put into wells cut into a gel, which is in a tank filled with a buffer solution of an appropriate pH. A direct electric current is applied to the gel and fragments of DNA move towards an electrode. DNA is negatively charged so moves towards the anode. The distance moved by a fragment depends on size; smaller fragments move further per unit time than larger fragments.

DNA is invisible unless a blue or fluorescent stain is added. A radioactive DNA probe (with the isotope ^{32}P) may be used to locate specific sequences. These probes bind to complementary sequences in the DNA, making them show up as dark bands when exposed to X-ray film.

> ★ **Exam tip**
>
> Search for videos and animations that show the process of electrophoresis. Use the information you find to help answer Question 4 on page 165.

Search online for the genetic conditions that can be detected by genetic screening. You should find details of tests for Huntington's disease (HD), breast cancer (genes *BRCA1* and *BRCA2*) and cystic fibrosis (CF). You can also find details of *ADA* (for SCID), *F8* (haemophilia A), *HBB* (sickle cell anaemia), *TYR* (albinism) and *RPE65* (retinal dystrophy – an inherited eye disease).

The example in *Try this… 6* concerns genetic screening within a family. You should also consider the advantages of carrying out genetic tests for specific diseases in certain populations. These tests are helping to reduce the number of cases of these diseases. Read about the use of genetic screening – cases that you can research are:

- β-thalassaemia in countries surrounding the Eastern Mediterranean, for example, Cyprus

- sickle cell anaemia in Saudi Arabia

- CF and Tay–Sachs disease in Ashkenazi Jews.

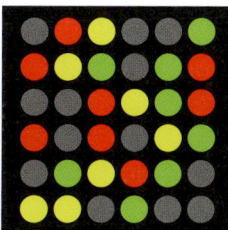

▲ **Figure 19.2** A small part of a microarray after use in a genetic test

> → **Try this... 5**
>
> Use Figure 19.2 to explain how microarrays are used to:
>
> - compare the genes present in complete genomes of two different species
>
> - find out which genes are being expressed in tissues or cells at any given time.

> 🔗 **Link**
>
> PCR is similar to semi-conservative replication of DNA, which occurs in the S phase of the cell cycle. See Unit 6.

> ★ **Exam tip**
>
> Watch some animations that show the PCR process. See the DNA Learning Center and Max Animations for examples.

> ★ **Exam tip**
>
> Search online for the Student guide for *The PCR and plant evolution* published by the National Centre for Biotechnology Education (NCBE). This gives you plenty of information about the use of PCR and electrophoresis in genome studies – in this case with chloroplast DNA (cpDNA). Use this to help answer Question 4 on page 165.

> 🔗 **Link**
>
> Use Genetic Home Reference (https://ghr.nlm.nih.gov) as a source of information about the human genetic conditions listed in Units 16 and 19.

Research the human diseases or conditions that can be treated by gene therapy including SCID and retinal dystrophy. Limit your research to conditions that have been successfully carried out to treat or cure the condition concerned. Make sure that you read reliable sources to prepare fact files with the information that you find. You can read more about the social and ethical issues surrounding genetic screening and gene therapy starting with two web sites that deal with these issues: www.beep.ac.uk and http://learn.genetics.utah.edu

Research the features of crop plants that have been improved by genetic engineering. Examples of crop plants are:

rice, soya, tobacco, sugar cane, maize, potato, papaya.

Make a list of the features that have been altered. You should be able explain the advantages to farmers and the environment from growing crops that are herbicide resistant and insect resistant.

> ★ **Exam tip**
>
> Information about GM crops may come from sources that are not impartial. If you read about GM crops and livestock on web sites, check which side of the GM debate they are on and treat their opinions and evidence accordingly.

Worked Example

The human gene *HTT* codes for the protein huntingtin. Mutation occurs in this gene with the insertion of multiple copies of the base sequence CAG that increase the length of the gene.

Explain how electrophoresis can distinguish between a person who is homozygous for the normal allele and a person who has the mutant allele.

Answer

If there is a single band, then the person who provided the sample is homozygous, **hh**.
If there are two bands then the person is heterozygous, **Hh**.

The full answer to this question is more complex. Read the answer on the support website before reading Try this… 6 about Huntington's disease.

→ **Try this... 6**

Huntington's disease (HD)

Analyse this question in the same way as on pages 158 and 159.

The text is taken from notes written by a genetic counsellor during a meeting with members of a family with a history of Huntingdon's disease (HD).

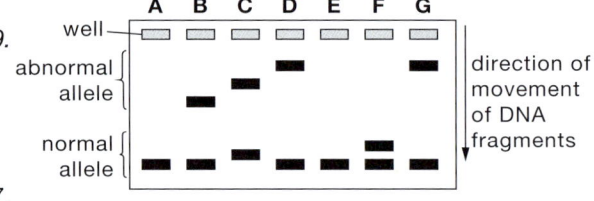

'Grandfather (**A**) has not developed symptoms and is now 87. Grandmother (**B**) developed symptoms of HD at age 58. Their daughter (**C**) developed symptoms of HD at age 40 and her eldest son (**D**) began to develop symptoms at age 29; C's husband (**E**), their youngest son (**F**) and daughter (**G**) have not developed any symptoms of HD. **E** comes from a family with no history of HD.'

DNA taken from each member of the family was prepared to give fragments of different lengths. The fragments were separated using gel electrophoresis.

(a) (i) Outline how the fragments of DNA would be prepared. [3]

(ii) Explain how the fragments of DNA are separated by gel electrophoresis. [4]

(b) The results of the analysis are shown in the electrophoretogram above. Both the normal allele and the abnormal allele exist in different lengths. The brackets indicate the range of lengths of the alleles.

The results show that the bands representing the normal allele and the bands representing the abnormal allele have not all travelled the same distance through the gel.

(i) Explain the results as shown in the electrophoretogram. [3]

(ii) Make a pedigree diagram to show the inheritance of Huntington's disease in the family. Show on the diagram the genotypes of the individual members of the family. Use the letters **H** for the dominant allele and **h** for the recessive allele. [6]

(iii) With reference to the family described in this question, discuss the benefits of genetic screening for Huntington's disease. [4]

→ **Try this... 7**

BRCA1 and *BRCA2*

BRCA1 and BRCA2 are proteins each composed of a single polypeptide. These two proteins are involved in the control of the cell cycle and in the repair of DNA.

Mutations to the genes *BRCA1* and *BRCA2* can cause changes to the proteins so that the cell cycle is not controlled correctly.

DNA sequencing has detected many mutations within both genes. Some of these are known to lead to cancer. Many are known to be harmless, but the effects of others are unknown.

BRCA1 is composed of 1863 amino acids. One of the many mutations that occur in *BRCA1* leads to a change in the amino acid at position 871 in the primary structure of the protein as shown below.

triplet (codon) in the non-transcribed strand of normal gene	CCA	amino acid in position 871 of normal BRCA1	proline
triplet (codon) in the non-transcribed strand of mutant variant	CAA	amino acid in position 871 of mutant BRCA1	glutamine

(a) (i) State the type of gene mutation that is shown above. [1]

   (ii) The amino acid proline has a non-polar R group (side chain) and glutamine has a polar side chain.

   Suggest the effect that this mutation may have on the structure of BRCA1. [2]

(b) Mutations to *BRCA1* are inherited as autosomal dominant disorders. Explain how the inheritance of this disorder differs from the inheritance pattern for an autosomal recessive disorder, such as cystic fibrosis. [3]

(c) Particular mutations are much more common in some groups of people; for example, Ashkenazi Jews are much more likely than other groups of people to have a deletion of two nucleotides that results in a premature stop signal at codon 39 in the *BRCA1* gene. This deletion is known as 185delAG.

   (i) Explain how particular mutations of *BRCA1*, such as 185delAG, are more likely to occur in particular groups of people. [3]

   (ii) Suggest the consequences of this for screening the human population for breast cancer. [3]

Right first time!

Most people who write for a living prepare notes and then write one or more drafts before they post their work online or send it to an editor for publication in a newspaper or in a book. You cannot do this when you answer questions in the exam papers. You must make your first answers the best you can. You do not get a second chance in the exam to rewrite all your answers.

Follow this advice and try applying it as you answer all the questions in this Unit and questions in other units that you have not yet attempted:

- Make some notes in the margin of points to make in your answer to each part question.

- Prepare the whole of your answer in your head.

- Make sure that you use knowledge of A level detail and standard.

- Do not see a trigger word in the question and think you need to write all you know about that subject or write an answer to a question you have practised.

- Read your answer after you have completed it.

In the exam, make any corrections by crossing out what you have already written and write your replacement answer somewhere on the paper where the examiner can find it. Do not write vertically in the margin or write between the lines.

★ **Exam tip**

These are the most important exam tips of all.

1. Read carefully all the information provided in each exam question before you start any of your answers.

2. Make sure you respond appropriately to the command words such as state, describe, outline and explain.

3. Answer the question that the examiner set, not the question that you would like to answer!

↑ Raise your grade

(a) The enzyme *Taq* polymerase is a DNA polymerase used in the polymerase chain reaction (PCR).

(i) Explain why *Taq* polymerase is used in PCR rather than human DNA polymerase. [2]

Taq polymerase is not denatured by the heat used in the separation stage of PCR as it comes from a heat-loving bacterium. ✔ *If a different enzyme was used it would have to be added after each stage of the process.* ✔

Some more terminology (e.g. thermostable) would help this answer.

(ii) Outline how the polymerase chain reaction (PCR) is used to produce 16 copies of a sample of DNA collected at the scene of a crime. [6]

The DNA is cut into fragments and specific DNA primers are used. ✔ *The primers bind to strands of the DNA* ✗ *so that Taq polymerase can build new strands using the existing strands as templates. The enzyme joins nucleotides together to make new strands that are complementary to the template strands (just like replication).* ✔ *This happens four times at high temperatures to make 16 copies of the DNA.* ✔

This answer is lacking in detailed knowledge of the process of PCR. The stages of each PCR cycle should be included: denaturation (separation of strands of DNA); annealing; extension by polymerase. In this answer, the denaturation stage is omitted and the whole process is said to occur at 'high temperatures'. It is only the denaturation stage that occurs at high temperature.

(b) Two problems with PCR are the high G–C composition of some fragments of DNA and the various substances present in test samples that inhibit PCR.

(i) Explain why high G–C composition of DNA should make PCR less effective. [3]

There are three hydrogen bonds between the base pair G–C compared with only two between A–T. ✔ *A piece of DNA with lots of C–G pairs takes more energy to break* ✔ *and not all the fragments may be denatured and the strands separate so can't be copied in PCR.* ✔

This answer has the right ideas. This shows how important it is in answering questions on this Unit to know the details of DNA structure.

(ii) Suggest how contaminating substances might inhibit PCR. [2]

These substances might be enzyme inhibitors. ✔ *The substance might enter the active site and be a competitive inhibitor of polymerase or attach to another part of the molecule and be a non-competitive inhibitor.* ✔

Correct use of information from Unit 3. These substances might also combine with DNA and inhibit progress of the reaction, for example, by binding to the primers.

(c) Explain how strands of DNA of different lengths are separated by gel electrophoresis. [4]

DNA is negatively charged so moves when an electric field is applied across a gel. ✔ *The samples of DNA are placed into wells and the current switched on. The DNA moves through the gel towards the cathode.* ✗ *Longer lengths of DNA are heavier than shorter lengths and they travel more slowly.* ✔ *All the DNA of the same length separates as a band. A DNA 'ladder' is used at the same time to identify the fragments of DNA.*

Again, detail is missing from the answer. DNA moves towards the anode (+ve) not the cathode (–ve). The way in which the DNA ladder is used should be explained.

Exam-style questions

Structured questions (Paper 4)

1 (a) Three restriction enzymes are *HindIII*, *EcoRI* and *HaeIII*.

   The diagram shows the restriction sites for these three enzymes.

   HindIII   5′...A A G C T T... 3′
              3′...T T C G A A... 5′

   EcoRI   5′...G A A T T C... 3′
              3′...C T T A A G... 5′

   HaeIII   5′...G G C C... 3′
              3′...C C G G... 5′

   Describe the features of the restriction sites shown in the diagram. [3]

   (b) Three identical lengths of DNA were treated *separately* with each of the restriction enzymes. The DNA has the following sequence of base pairs:

   5′ AGTTGAAAGGCCTTCATCGCACCCTTAATTCGTGGCCAAGCTT 3′

   3′ TCAACTTTCCGGAAGTAGCGTGGGAATTAAGCACCGGTTCGAA 5′

   (i) Use the information about these restriction endonucleases to state how many fragments of DNA will be present after treatment with each of the restriction enzymes. [3]

   (ii) Explain why some of the fragments need further treatment before they can be inserted into plasmid vectors. [2]

   (c) RNA can be incorporated into the genome of retroviruses to use as a vector for the genetic modification of animal cells. Suggest and explain how this approach to genetic engineering can lead to the production of transgenic animal cells. [3]

2 (a) Promoter sequences fulfil important roles in cells. State the role of promoters in genetically modified cells. [2]

   (b) Complex human proteins, such as antithrombin, cannot be produced by genetically modified bacteria. Suggest why bacteria are unable to produce complex human proteins such as antithrombin. [3]

   (c) Explain the advantages of using genetically modified cells to make proteins for use in human medicine. [4]

3 Several species of crop plant have been genetically engineered to express the gene *cry* from the bacterium, *Bacillus thuringiensis* (Bt). The gene codes for a protein that is toxic to some insect pests. GM varieties of soya, oil seed rape, cotton and maize are grown in countries such as the United States, China, Canada and Brazil.

   (a) Explain the advantages of growing varieties of these crop plants with the *cry* gene for the Bt toxin. [4]

   (b) Outline how crop plants, such as those listed above, are genetically modified to improve productivity. [4]

   (c) Outline the potential risks of growing GM crop varieties and suggest steps that can be taken to minimise them. [5]

4 Modern methods of identification and classification use PCR and electrophoresis to compare chloroplast DNA (cpDNA) including the genes that code for:

   • rbcL – a large polypeptide that forms part of RuBP

   • tRNA molecules.

   A strange plant is discovered growing in a botanical garden. Botanists think that it may be an alien species that has arrived as a contaminant of plant material collected in Asia. They plan to use PCR and electrophoresis to identify the family in which this plant is classified.

   Outline how the techniques of PCR and electrophoresis could be used to compare the cpDNA of this strange plant with the cpDNA of plant species with similar morphological features.

   You are supplied with the following apparatus and materials:

   • apparatus and reagents for carrying out PCR

   • agarose gels; electrophoresis tanks; a suitable buffer solution; DNA tracking dye; DNA staining solution; stem, root and leaves of the suspected alien species.

   Include the following in your answer: a method as a set of numbered points; safety precautions; an explanation of how the results will be interpreted. [10]

Biology is a practical subject. During your course you should do enough practical work to develop the skills needed to plan investigations, make careful observations, manipulate apparatus, take readings, record data in tables, draw graphs, analyse and interpret your findings, evaluate methods and data, and make conclusions. These skills cannot be practised simply by reading about them and interpreting observations and data collected and presented by other people. You have to carry out practical work in a lab.

There are two papers that test the practical skills that you develop during your course. Paper 3 is set on the AS syllabus and Paper 5 is set on the whole of the syllabus. These two papers are almost entirely concerned with assessing your practical skills. There are no questions that simply test your knowledge of biology. Many of the practicals listed in the syllabus are covered in the Practical skills boxes in Unit 1 through to Unit 19. This section of the book covers some of the skills that you need for Paper 3 and Paper 5. Obviously, it cannot help you with all of these skills – for this you need to work with laboratory apparatus. You also need to practise the microscope skills necessary for Paper 3.

It is a good idea to keep a lab book during your course to record all the practical work that you do. You should cross-check the practicals with the syllabus to make sure you have experienced all of them **and** kept some notes on each one. Also take photographs of the apparatus and results as that will help you remember what you did in the lab.

The laboratory skills required for Paper 3 are covered on pages 167–184. These skills are also relevant to Paper 5. The Planning skill is only assessed in Paper 5 and this is covered on pages 185–192. Paper 5 also tests your ability to use descriptive statistics and statistical tests and these are covered on pages 193–204. Statistics is also required for Paper 4.

You should get used to following instructions in Paper 3 and writing instructions for Paper 5. You can make your own learning resources for Papers 3 and 5 by using a drawing, diagram or photograph of some apparatus as a starting point to writing sets of instructions for the practicals that you should know.

✏ Revision strategy

You do not need to work in a lab to practise all of these skills. For example, You can analyse, interpret and evaluate the secondary data presented in this Unit. You can make drawings of biological material, such as stems and leaves of common plants.

🔗 Link

See page 12 for the first Practical skills box in the book.

★ Exam tip

It is highly likely that you will read something unfamiliar in Paper 3 and Paper 5. Prepare for the unexpected by learning how to make use of the information provided on the exam paper.

Learning resource

The hydrolysis of starch

In Unit 3 you study the role of enzymes in breaking down substrates. Amylase catalyses the hydrolysis of starch. Some of the apparatus that you would use to follow the reaction in which starch is hydrolysed is shown in Figure 20.1.

This investigation needs a 1% starch solution, a 1% amylase solution and a solution of iodine in potassium iodide (iodine in KI solution). Look carefully at the diagram and write down the steps involved in following the disappearance of starch.

Include the steps needed to record the data in a table. There are plenty of examples in this book for you to follow. Write a hypothesis and use it to make a prediction about the results.

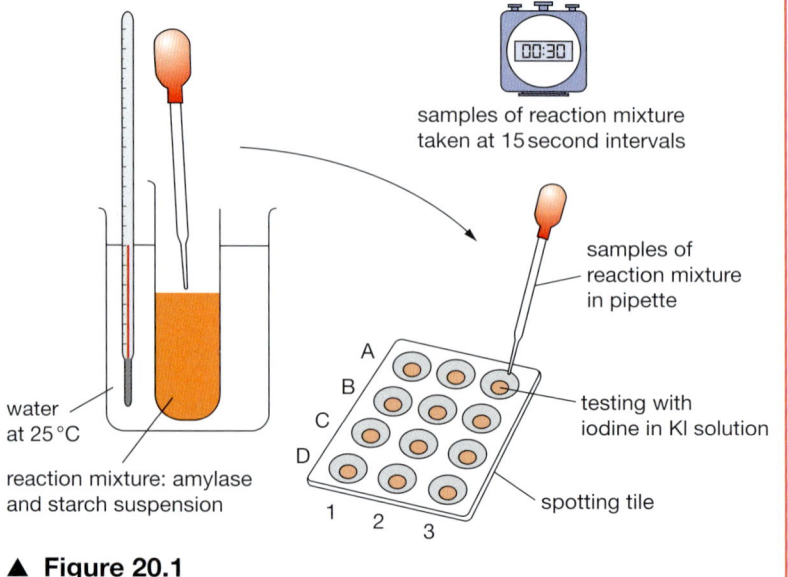

▲ Figure 20.1

Paper 3 (40 marks)

Paper 3 tests your ability to carry out practical work and is taken in a laboratory at your school or college or in a special centre (e.g. at a university). There are usually two, or sometimes three, questions: one question is usually an investigation in which you follow instructions and make decisions about the method and the recording and interpretation of results; a further question usually involves using a microscope and tests your drawing skills.

Marks are awarded for the following skills:

Skills	Breakdown of the skills	Marks
Manipulation, measurement and observation	Decisions relating to measurements and observations	15–17
	Collection of data and observations	
Presentation of data and observations	Recording data and observations	11–13
	Display of calculation and reasoning	
	Layout of data and observations	
Analysis, conclusions and evaluation	Interpreting data and observations	11–13
	Drawing conclusions	
	Identifying sources of error and suggesting improvements	

Maths skills, such as calculating percentages, percentage changes, means and magnifications, are also assessed.

Manipulation of apparatus, measurement and observation (MMO)

In Paper 3, you follow instructions and make decisions. You are instructed to read through the whole paper before starting any practical work. Read through each question and make notes on the paper. Highlight or underline the information given about the topics from the syllabus that provide the context for each question.

This section (pages 167–170) gives you some advice about decision making and implementing.

Working with solutions

In Paper 3, you may have to make up solutions from a stock solution. In Paper 5, you should also know how to make the stock solutions.

To make a stock solution of $100\,cm^3$ of $10\,g\,100\,cm^{-3}$ (a 10% solution) of glucose:

- use a balance to weigh $10\,g$ of glucose

- dissolve the glucose in about $50\,cm^3$ of warm water

- pour the solution into a measuring cylinder or volumetric flask and add water to the $100\,cm^3$ level (use a dropping pipette to add the last few cm^3 of water)

- pour into a labelled beaker and stir thoroughly.

★ **Exam tip**

Paper 3 is set on Units 1 to 11 only

★ **Exam tip**

Use this reading time to recall relevant aspects of your subject knowledge and to write down anything useful in the margin or on any white space.

💡 **Remember**

For a solution, use *volume* and *concentration* and avoid using 'amount', which is often used for concentration, volume or number.

🔗 **Link**

You can find examples of simple (proportional) and serial dilutions in Units 2.

To make a stock solution of $100\,cm^3$ of $1\,mol\,dm^{-3}$ sucrose:

- look up the relative molecular mass (RMM) of sucrose = $342\,g\,mol^{-1}$ (3 s.f.)

- use a balance to weigh $34.2\,g$ of sucrose (a tenth of the RMM)

- dissolve the sucrose in about $50\,cm^3$ of water

- pour the solution into a measuring cylinder or volumetric flask and proceed as above.

You should be able to describe how to make different percentage and molar concentrations using stock solutions and water.

You can make a range of concentrations from the $10\,g\,100\,cm^{-3}$ stock solution of glucose. For a wide range of concentrations, use **serial dilution**. For a narrower range with smaller intervals between the extremes of the range, use **simple (proportional) dilution**.

Serial dilution

1. Use a graduated pipette or syringe to remove $1\,cm^3$ of the stock glucose solution. Put it into a test-tube labelled with the appropriate concentration.

2. Add $9\,cm^3$ of water and stir or invert the test-tube to mix. This is now a $1.0\,g\,100\,cm^{-3}$ solution (1%).

3. Repeat this (see Figure 20.2) until you have a $0.0001\,g\,100\,cm^{-3}$ solution.

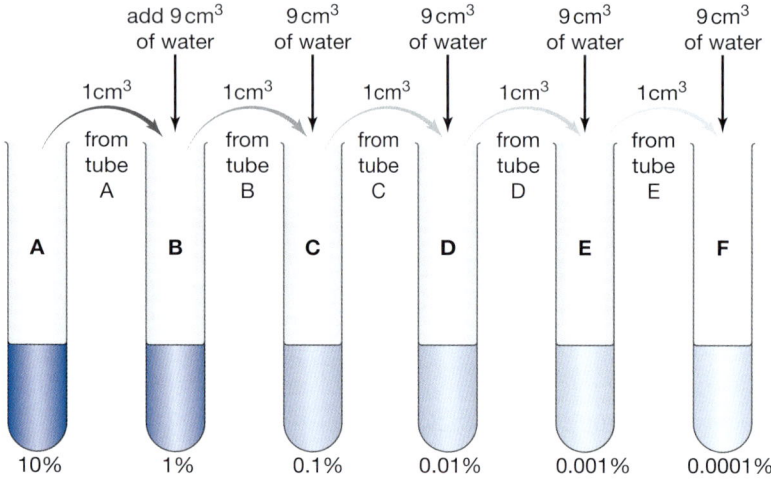

Simple (proportional) dilution

▼ **Table 20.1** Making glucose solutions by simple dilution. The volumes of a $10\,g\,100\,cm^{-3}$ (10%) stock solution of glucose and distilled water used to make four dilutions

Concentration of glucose / g 100 cm⁻³	Volume of 10 g 100 cm⁻³ glucose solution / cm³	Volume of distilled water / cm³
0	0	10
2	2	8
4	4	6
6	6	4
8	8	2
10	10	0

1. Use a syringe or graduated pipette to put certain volumes of the stock solution into test-tubes, each labelled with the appropriate concentration.

2. Add sufficient water to each test-tube to make the same *total* volume in each (Table 20.1).

To calculate the volume of stock solution you need in column 2, use this formula:

$$\text{volume of stock solution required} = \frac{\text{concentration wanted} \times \text{volume wanted}}{\text{concentration of stock solution}}$$

Investigations of enzyme activity often involve making different concentrations of an enzyme. Some enzymes are supplied as a liquid, not a powder. To make $100\,cm^3$ of a 1% solution, add $99\,cm^3$ of water to $1\,cm^3$ of the liquid enzyme.

Standardising variables

Standardised or controlled variables are variables that are kept constant to ensure that the results of the investigation are valid (see page 175).

Temperature is best controlled with a water bath. You will be provided with a thermometer and beaker(s) of water near to the temperature(s) you need to use. You may also be supplied with a means to heat the water. Follow these tips:

- stir the water with the thermometer before taking a reading

- put the bulb of the thermometer in the middle of the container of water when you take the reading

- keep checking the temperature to make sure it does not fluctuate too much

- record the temperatures on your exam paper as evidence of your attempt to keep the temperature constant.

pH can be controlled by using a buffer solution. You will be given pH papers (not pH meters) to monitor the pH of your reaction mixtures, so keep a record of the pH. Sometimes a *change* in pH is the dependent variable, for example, the breakdown of triglycerides to fatty acids by lipase; breakdown of urea to ammonia by urease.

Uncertainty in measuring

The scales on apparatus used for measuring linear dimensions and volumes are divided into sections. The **resolution** of each piece of apparatus is the smallest division on the scale: for a typical ruler it is $1\,mm$; for plastic syringes it varies, but for the one in Figure 20.3, it is $0.2\,cm^3$.

The **uncertainty of measurement** is half the smallest graduation on the apparatus. For example, for a plastic ruler with a smallest division of $1\,mm$, the uncertainty is ± 0.5 and this applies to both where you align on zero and where you take a measurement. If a drawing measures $50\,mm$ long, you can be certain that it is more than $49\,mm$ but less than $51\,mm$, so express the length as $50 \pm 1.0\,mm$.

When using a syringe to measure volumes, the smallest division for a $5\,cm^3$ syringe (Figure 20.3) is $0.2\,cm^3$. If the syringe is used to take up and deliver $5\,cm^3$ of water, the volume should be recorded as $5.0 \pm 0.1\,cm^3$ as you are only taking a reading from the scale at one place and do not have to look at the scale for zero. If, however, you are delivering $2\,cm^3$ of a liquid with the same syringe by moving the plunger from $5.0\,cm^3$ to $3.0\,cm^3$, then you are reading from the scale at *two* places and the volume should be recorded as $2.0 \pm 0.2\,cm^3$.

★ **Exam tip**

In simple dilution, it is best to increase the concentration using even intervals as in Table 20.1.

★ **Exam tip**

The range in the serial dilution shown in Figure 20.2 is $0.0001\,g\,100\,cm^{-3}$ to $10\,g\,100\,cm^{-3}$, which is an increase of a factor of 10^5. In the simple dilution in Table 20.1, the range is $2\,g\,100\,cm^{-3}$ to $10\,g\,100\,cm^{-3}$, which is an increase of a factor of 5.

Key term

Resolution: the smallest division on the scale of a piece of apparatus, e.g. a ruler or a plastic syringe. The smallest measurement possible with any digital apparatus.

★ **Exam tip**

When measuring with an eyepiece graticule, the uncertainty is half the smallest division on the graticule, whatever that is when you calibrate it (see Unit 1). If you do not calibrate the graticule, the uncertainty is 0.5 EPU (eyepiece unit).

★ **Exam tip**

A student calibrates an eyepiece graticule at a magnification of ×400 (high power). Each small division on the graticule scale = $2.5\,\mu m$, so the uncertainty is $\pm 1.25\,\mu m$. The width of a cell is measured as $45\,\mu m \pm 2.5\,\mu m$, as uncertainty applies at both sides of the cell where the scale is placed. The percentage error is 5.6% (2 s.f.).

▶ **Figure 20.3** To dispense $5\,cm^3$ of a liquid with this syringe, push the plunger to the bottom of the barrel. Put the nozzle into the liquid and raise and lower the plunger several times to make sure there are no air bubbles. Pull out the plunger slightly above the $5\,cm^3$ mark. Remove the syringe from the liquid and hold it at eye level. Push in the plunger till the part shown by the arrow is over the 5 mark. Then push the plunger right to the bottom of the barrel to expel $5\,cm^3$ of liquid

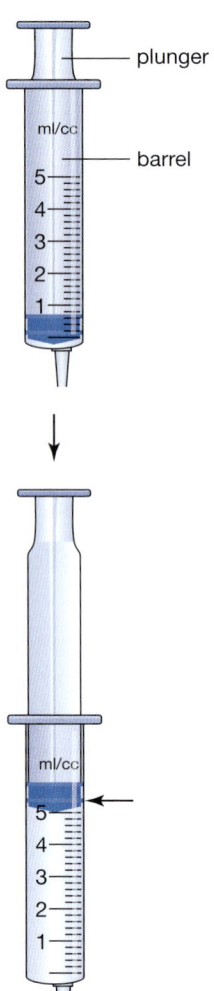

The uncertainty on any digital apparatus is the resolution of the apparatus in each measurement. For example, the uncertainty of a balance that reads to $0.01\,g$ is $\pm 0.01\,g$ for each measurement you take.

You can calculate the **percentage error** for apparatus used for measuring, both when setting up your experiment and when taking results. For example, $5\,cm^3$ of gas collected and measured with a gas syringe that has graduations every $1\,cm^3$ contains more than $4.5\,cm^3$ but less than $5.5\,cm^3$. Your error is $\pm 0.5\,cm^3$ in $5\,cm^3$. This gives:

$$\text{percentage error} = \frac{0.5}{5.0} \times 100 = 10\%$$

If $10\,cm^3$ of gas is collected, the percentage error is 5%.

Presentation of data and observations (PDO)

Processing data

Readings you record from your investigation are sometimes known as 'raw data'. You may have to process the data by calculating a percentage, a percentage change or a rate.

Calculating a percentage: Percentages are a way of making valid comparisons between items when the totals are different. For example, 20 in 200 cells near the root tip of garlic divide by mitosis (10%), but further up the root only 1 in 50 are dividing (2%). The percentage is the value divided by the total multiplied by 100.

Calculating a percentage change: Percentage change is a valid way to compare the change to the original value at the start. The percentage change is calculated as:

$$\text{percentage change} = \frac{\text{difference between original and final numbers}}{\text{original number}} \times 100$$

Calculating rates of reaction: If you collected a gas, then rates of reaction can be calculated as the volume collected per unit of time (e.g. seconds (s) or minutes (min)):

$$\text{Rate of reaction} = \frac{\text{volume of gas collected over a period of time}}{\text{time taken}}$$

The units will be $cm^3\,s^{-1}$ (cm^3 per second) or $cm^3\,min^{-1}$.

If you recorded the time taken to reach an end point (t), calculate the reciprocal of time taken $\left(\dfrac{1}{t}\right)$ and multiply by 10, 100 or 1000 to give a range of numbers greater than 1.

Calculating initial rates of reaction: Enzyme activity is often measured by determining the **initial rate** when substrate concentration is not limiting. You can find this by taking measurements over a short period of time, plotting them on a graph and using a tangent to calculate the rate, as shown in Figure 20.4. Use points to calculate the rate that are separated by at least half the length of the tangent you have drawn.

★ **Exam tip**

If the percentage error is large, increase the size of the measurements in your investigation to *reduce* the error as a proportion of the measurements that you take.

Key term

Percentage error: uncertainty in measurement expressed as a percentage of the total measurement.

★ **Exam tip**

If the percentage change is an increase, put a plus sign (+) in front of the answer; if it is a decrease put a minus sign (–).

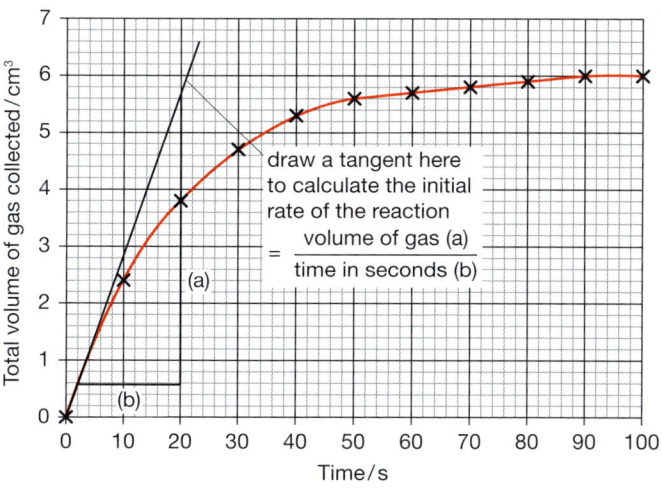

Figure 20.4 Calculating the initial rate of an enzyme-catalysed reaction

Significant figures

Express the results of any calculations to the same number of significant figures (s.f.) as the least accurate figure used, which will have the lowest number of significant figures.

All digits are significant except the zeros that are used to place the decimal point:

- zeros at the beginning of numbers are not significant, e.g. 0.032 has two s.f.

- zeros at the end of a whole number are significant, e.g. 7290 has four s.f.

- zeros between other numbers are significant, e.g. 601.4 has four s.f.

- trailing zeros after a decimal point are significant, e.g. 0.780 has three s.f.

If your input data has 3 s.f., your calculated answer should not have more than 3 s.f. If the numerator has 4 s.f. but the denominator has 2 s.f., your answer should only have 2 s.f.

If your calculation has more than one step, do not round up the number until after the last step in your calculation.

Calculations may generate numbers followed by many decimal places. Do not write down all the numbers from your calculator display. You must round them up or down and you must do this correctly. You should either round up to the closest whole number or to one or two decimal places to agree with the raw data. If you are carrying out a calculation on some data that you have collected or been given, then remember not to express the result to more decimal places than the data collected or provided. It is, however, acceptable to use one more decimal place for means and standard deviations.

A set of calculations gives answers to two decimal places, but the data collected was given to one decimal place. If the second decimal place is between 0 and 4, round down. If the second decimal place is ≥ 5 (greater than or equal to 5), then round up.

- 7.56 rounded to one decimal place is 7.6 (rounded up)

- 10.54 rounded to one decimal place is 10.5 (rounded down)

If there are three decimal places, then the same principle applies

- 9.546 rounded to one decimal place is 9.5 (rounded down)

Answers are usually followed by the number of decimal places that have been chosen, for example, 7.56 is rounded up and written as 7.6 (1 dp).

★ **Exam tip**

Devising a scale on a graph with figures that are much less than one can be difficult. That's why it is a good idea to multiply rates of reaction calculated as $\frac{1}{t}$ by 10^1, 10^2, 10^3, etc.

Remember

This graph shows the increase in the product over time. The concentration of the product eventually remains constant because there is no more substrate left.

★ **Exam tip**

The numerator is the number above the line in a calculation; the denominator is the number below the line.

★ **Exam tip**

If you have a large number of figures that are all X.5 and have to be rounded, then it is usual to round up half of them and round down the other half.

Recording results in tables

You will usually need to record the results of your practical work in tables:

- use the space provided and do not start right at the top of a page; draw table outlines (columns and rows) with a sharp pencil

- make the first column the **independent variable** and the second and subsequent columns the **dependent variable(s)**

- write brief but informative headings for each column and put units in the headings *not* in the body of the table

- use the appropriate SI unit for each column headed with a physical quantity, for example, g for mass; cm³ for volume

- use a solidus (/) or brackets to separate the physical quantity from the unit in which it is measured, for example, distance / m or distance (m); be consistent all the way through your answers

- use 'per' or the negative exponent, for example, cm^{-3}, in units; do *not* use a solidus to mean 'per', for example, for concentration use g per dm^3 or $g\,dm^{-3}$ *not* g/dm^3

- organise data so that patterns can be seen – arrange the values of the independent variable in ascending order, that is, values increase down the table

- make the body of the table brief – single words, short descriptive phrases, numbers, ticks or crosses, etc.

Presentation of data

Data can be presented as pie charts, bar charts, histograms, line graphs and scatter graphs. Use Figure 20.5 to help you decide the most appropriate way to present your data.

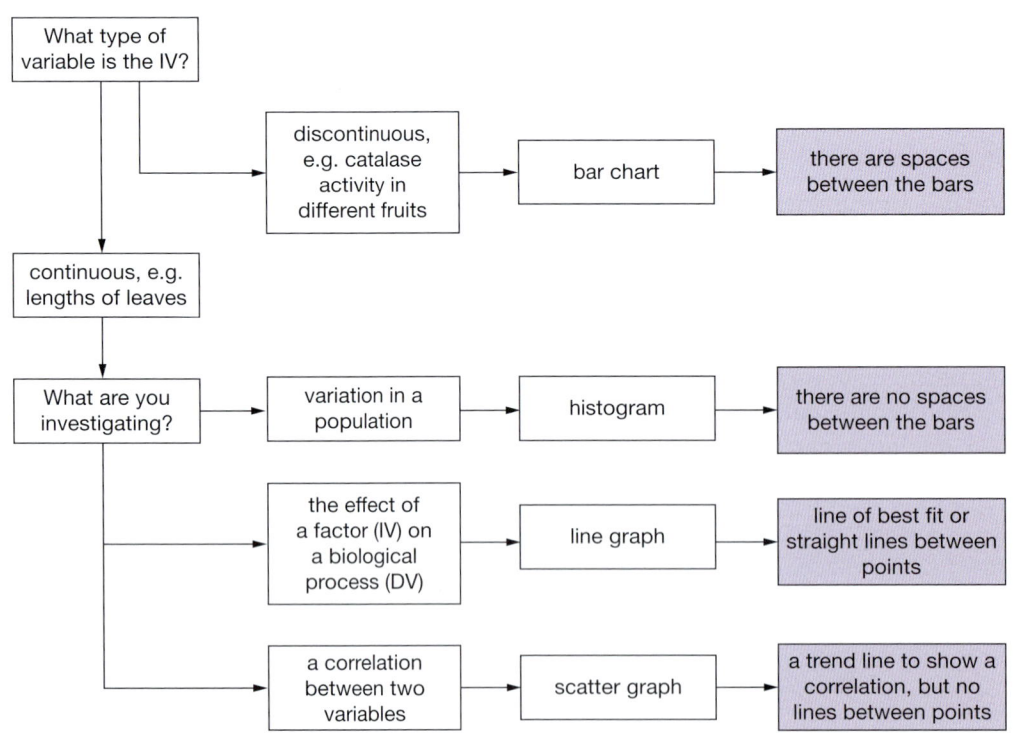

◀ **Figure 20.5** How to choose the correct way to present data; the shaded boxes show the key points about each graph or chart

Bar charts: Follow this guidance for drawing bar charts:

- use most of the grid provided – do not make the bar chart too small

- draw with a sharp pencil

- use lines or, more usually, blocks of equal width separated by spaces

- make the spaces between the bars on the *x*-axis equal

- scale the *y*-axis with equidistant intervals, usually starting at zero written at the base of the axis

- label the *y*-axis with the heading and unit taken from the table of results

- arrange the bars in the same order as in the table of results

- clearly identify each bar

- do not shade the blocks as it uses up valuable time.

Histograms: Follow the general guidance for bar charts and also:

- scale the *x*-axis with equidistant intervals as it represents continuous data; write these underneath, for example, '3.0–3.9' means that 3.0 is included in this class, but 4.0 is not; 4.0 will be included in the next class: 4.0–4.9

- label the *x*-axis and use the appropriate unit

- scale the *y*-axis properly; it can show percentage frequency; start the scale at zero written at the base of the axis

- label the *y*-axis as appropriate, for example, 'number' or 'percentage frequency'

- draw the blocks touching

- make the widths of the blocks equal as the *area* of each block is proportional to the size of the class and it is usual to have similar-sized classes.

Line graphs: The term *graph* applies to the whole representation and not just to the line. Line graphs are used to show relationships in data that are not immediately apparent from tables. The lines on graphs are straight trend lines, curved trend lines or straight lines between plotted points (dot-to-dot).

- Use at least half the grid provided, do not make the graph too small.

- Plot the independent variable on the *x*-axis.

- Plot the dependent variable on the *y*-axis; sometimes this is a **derived variable**, for example, rates or percentages (see Figure 4.3 on page 43).

- Use an appropriate scale for each axis; examine the data critically to decide whether to start the scale(s) at zero; if not, one or both axes may have a **displaced origin** (see page 178).

- Label each axis clearly with the quantity and SI unit or compound units as appropriate, for example, time / s and concentration / $g\,dm^{-3}$.

- Make the plotted points easily distinguishable from the grid lines; use encircled dots ($\odot$) or saltire crosses ($\times$), *not* dots on their own. If you need to plot three lines, vertical crosses ($+$) can also be used. Plot all points on the grid, *not* on the white space around the grid.

After plotting the points, decide if there are any **anomalous results** (outliers). Ask 'Do they fit the trend?'. Knowledge of the theory behind the investigation, will mean you are aware of the likely trend. Circle any results you think are anomalous. Make a key outside the graph to show that circled point(s) represent anomalous result(s). Then decide how to present the line.

- The points may lie on an obvious straight line. Decide whether to include the origin (0, 0) if it is not a datum point in your results. If it is, then place a clear plastic ruler on the grid and draw a straight line from the origin to give an even number of points on both sides of the line. If the origin is not a point or you are unsure, start the line at or near to the first plotted point. Do *not* continue the line past the last plotted point.

Link

Bar charts can be used to show mean results with error bars. Standard deviations, standard errors or 95% confidence intervals can be used as error bars. See page 194 for further information.

★ **Exam tip**

For ease of plotting, use 1, 2, 5 or 10 or multiples of these for scaling axes, not 3 or multiples of 3. If your scale is $20\,mm = 3\,cm^3$, each small square on the graph paper = $0.3\,cm^3$, which makes plotting points and interpolating (taking figures) from a line graph difficult.

Remember

The range of values should be divided into classes (also known as bins) when preparing a histogram.

Link

Line graphs are often used for extracting data. See Raise your grade on page 36 and Question 5(c) on page 81 for examples.

Key terms

Derived variable: variable produced by processing the data collected in an investigation.

Anomalous result: any result that does not agree with the trend of results (i.e., for any value of the independent variable) or any replicate result that is significantly different from most of the others.

Link

For examples of graphs and tables with derived variables, see Figures 3.5, 3.7 and 4.3, and Tables 4.4 and 12.2.

- Draw a smooth curve only if you know that the intermediate values fall on the curve. When you expect the relationship to be a curve and the points seem to fit on one, then draw it. Decide whether the origin is a point and, if not, start at the first plotted point. The curve should go through as many points as possible, but make sure there is an even number of points on either side of the curve. Do not continue past the last plotted point.

- When you are unsure if the relationship is a straight line or a curve, draw straight lines between the points. This indicates uncertainty about the results for values of the dependent variable between those plotted.

- When a graph shows more than one line or curve, label the curves or use a key to show what each line represents.

Analysis (interpretation of data or observations), conclusions and evaluation (ACE)

Accurate data

In an investigation, you may be asked to obtain values from samples prepared for the exam. For example, you may use the Benedict's test or the biuret test to estimate the concentration of reducing sugars or proteins in solutions given to you. The examiner and the technician who made up the samples will know these values. Your results can be compared with the true values to check the **accuracy** of your results.

During your investigation, you may not have time to take two or more results for each value of the independent variable – **replicate results** (replicates). **Repeatable results** are replicate results that are in close agreement. You can describe the variation in replicate results using maths (see pages 193–194).

Reproducible results are results obtained by someone else who has followed exactly the same procedure as you. In an exam, you can only comment on reproducibility if you are given some results to compare with yours.

Figure 20.6 shows some hypothetical results. Four students each carried out the same task and each took three readings. Student **A** has results with a high degree of precision as the three replicates are clustered together. The mean for these results is close to the true value and these results show good accuracy. Student **B** has a good cluster of results, but the mean is a long way from the true value so is inaccurate. Student **C** has two results that are close together and one, known as an anomalous result or an outlier that is far away. Student **C**'s outlier is closer to the true value than the other two readings. Student **D** has results that are widely scattered (poor precision) but the mean will be near the true value.

> **★ Exam tip**
>
> When there is no data for (0, 0), but the origin is obviously a point, include it.

> **★ Exam tip**
>
> There is no need to give a graph or a table a title on the exam paper as this wastes time and does not gain any marks.

> **★ Exam tip**
>
> You need to be able to use, analyse and interpret graphs that you draw and those given in any of the exam papers, not just those in Paper 3.

> **★ Exam tip**
>
> Take care using the term accuracy. Very few biology investigations can determine true value(s) exactly; for example, no-one will know the exact rates of reaction in an investigation into the effect of pH on the activity of catalase (pages 176–178).

> **Key terms**
>
> **Accuracy**: closeness between any measured value and the true value.
>
> **Replicate results**: repeated results for the same value of the independent variable.

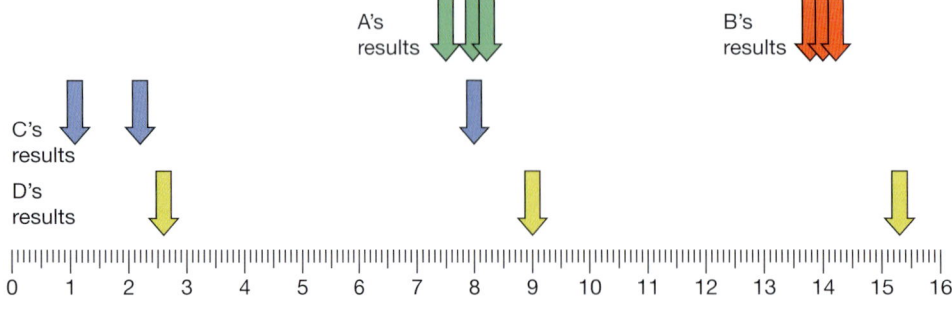

true result

range of replicate results obtained by the students

◀ **Figure 20.6** The concept of accuracy: results obtained by four students, A to D. Discuss with others possible reasons for these results. See some further comments on this figure in the answers to the questions in this Unit available on the support website.

Errors in measurement

You may have to identify any errors in your investigation:

Systematic errors are usually due to some fault with the measuring apparatus and have the same effect across the full range of measurements throughout an experiment. For example, a measuring device that is always wrong by a certain value, or a controlled variable that is always incorrect by the same quantity. When there are small systematic errors (that are always the same), the data may be precise but not accurate.

Random errors are caused by unknown and unpredictable changes in the experiment; the procedure is not exactly the same each time or the apparatus is read in a slightly differently way each time you take a reading. These errors often affect some results, but not all of them, and they do not always affect the results in the same way. Random errors can also be due to variation in biological material. These are not mistakes or due to poor technique. Their effect is reduced by repeating experiments and calculating mean results.

Evaluation

Identify the possible limitations of your method. Highlight on the question paper any aspects of the procedure that you found difficult or that needed extra care. For example, early results may be inaccurate if you were not confident at the start and didn't have time to repeat them. Also, timing may be a problem as you cannot start a stopwatch or bench timer at exactly the same time that you start another procedure. If you are always too slow starting the timer, you have a systematic error. If your timing method improved during the investigation, you have a random error that is more significant for the early readings.

Consider the effect of the limitations you have identified on the quality of your data. For example, starting your timer too early will make the time recorded too long and overestimate the time. Starting your timer too late will make the time recorded too short and underestimate the time. When you calculate rates of reaction, a longer time underestimates the rate and a shorter time overestimates the rate.

You can also expect to suggest an improvement for each limitation. Make suggestions for the investigation you have carried out. Do not plan a new investigation or devise a totally new procedure. For example, investigating the effect of pH on enzyme activity may not produce valid results if you did not use a thermostatically controlled water bath (limitation) as the temperature of the laboratory may fluctuate (temperature not controlled) and enzyme activity increases when the temperature increases (explanation). You could suggest repeating the investigation, this time using a thermostatically controlled water bath set to the same temperature for all pH values used (modification/improvement).

Making conclusions

There are only about three or four marks available in Paper 3 for using your knowledge to explain the results that you have obtained. As you practise past paper questions, learn to identify these questions and think about them as you carry out the practical work.

Validity refers to the confidence that you can have in your data and your conclusions. If you have a valid investigation then you have measured what your experiment was designed to measure. If asked about the validity of an investigation, consider the following:

- the limitations in the procedure
- any uncontrolled variables

Key terms

Systematic errors: are usually due to some fault with the measuring apparatus and have the same effect across the full range of measurements in an experiment.

Random errors: are caused by unknown and unpredictable changes in the experiment.

★ **Exam tip**

Terms such as **uncertainty** and **accuracy** are used when discussing experimental work. Make a list of these with their definitions and the contexts in which they are used.

Key term

Validity: the idea that an experiment really investigates the hypothesis that is being tested and whether the results really indicate what an experiment was designed to measure.

- the effects of errors (systematic and random) on the results
- the repeatability of the results
- the **precision** of the data collected
- the accuracy of the results.

Key term

Precision: closeness of repeated measurements (replicates) to each other.

★ **Exam tip**

Before you write your conclusion, look back to the beginning of the question to remind yourself of the topic from the syllabus that provides the context for the question.

Worked Example 1 for Paper 3

This is an example of a Question 1 on Paper 3.

Catalase is an enzyme that is present in many plant and animal tissues. The enzyme catalyses the breakdown of hydrogen peroxide as shown in the equation:

$$2H_2O_2 \longrightarrow 2H_2O + O_2$$

You will investigate the effect of pH on the rate of breakdown of hydrogen peroxide by the enzyme catalase.

★ **Exam tip**

Before you start, always read carefully through the **whole** of the question. Plan the use of your time to make sure that you finish everything.

You are provided with:

- cylinders freshly cut from a potato
- cylinders of potato that have been in boiling water for 3 min
- a flat-bottomed specimen tube
- five small beakers
- stop-clock or timer

- a beaker of hydrogen peroxide solution
- forceps, sharp scalpel, white tile and transparent plastic ruler
- two 5 cm³ plastic syringes
- five buffer solutions at different values of pH, each in a labelled beaker.

Proceed as follows:

Step 1   Use the scalpel to cut the unboiled potato cylinders into discs that are 2 mm thick.

Step 2   Put two discs into each of the beakers labelled pH 4, 5, 6, 7 and 8. Leave the discs in the buffer solutions for at least five minutes.

Step 3   Use a syringe to transfer 5 cm³ of hydrogen peroxide solution into the flat-bottomed specimen tube.

Step 4   Use a clean 5 cm³ syringe to put 5 cm³ of the buffer solution at pH 4 into the specimen tube.

Step 5   Use the forceps to place one of the discs from the beaker with the solution at pH 4 into the specimen tube.

Step 6   Start the stop-clock or timer as soon as the disc reaches the bottom of the tube. Stop timing as soon as any part of the disc starts to move up from the bottom of the tube. Record the time taken for the disc to rise.

Step 7   Remove the disc and repeat Steps 5 and 6 with the second disc at pH 4.

Step 8   Pour away the liquid from the specimen tube and wash it thoroughly.

Step 9   Repeat Steps 3 to 8 with the remaining discs at pH 5, 6, 7 and 8.

(a) Record all your results and any processed data in a table.   [5]

(b) Suggest two suitable controls **and** state why they are required to improve the validity of the investigation.   [4]

(c) Explain why the discs rise from the bottom of the tube.   [2]

(d) State **two** significant errors of the procedure that you have followed. For each error describe how you would improve the procedure. [4]

(e) A student carried out the same procedure and used the mean results to calculate the relative rate of reaction for each pH. The table shows the relative rate for each pH as a percentage of the maximum rate recorded.

pH of solution	Relative rate of reaction / percentage of maximum
3	21.5
4	55.2
5	85.0
6	92.5
7	100.0
8	98.0
9	89.0

Plot a graph of the student's results. [4]

(f) Use the information in the graph to describe **and** explain the effect of pH on the rate of breakdown of hydrogen peroxide. [5]

Answers

(a) *Some student results*

pH of solution	Time taken for discs to start to move from the bottom of the tube / s		
	Disc 1	Disc 2	Mean
4	36	37	36.5
5	16	13	14.5
6	12	10	11.0
7	9	10	9.5
8	10	10	10.0

(b) Control 1: a tube at pH 7 with no disc added to find out if any oxygen is produced when catalase is not present. Hydrogen peroxide decomposes in the light. Control 2: a tube at pH 7 and a disc cut from the boiled potato to find out if there is any oxygen produced when the enzyme is denatured. If no oxygen is produced in 1 and 2 by any non-enzymic reactions in the time taken by the slowest disc then it shows that the method is suitable for determining the rate of breakdown of hydrogen peroxide by catalase.

(c) Oxygen is not very soluble in water so forms bubbles that stick to the discs. The density of each disc decreases so it is less than water and the disc rises to the surface.

(d) With the apparatus supplied it is difficult to cut the discs so that they are all exactly the same thickness. Using a pair of calipers to measure the thickness would make sure that there is less variation in disc size. The concentration of hydrogen peroxide decreases after the first disc, so the concentration is not the same for the two replicates at each pH. The second disc should be put into a new specimen tube of hydrogen peroxide and buffer solution.

> ★ **Exam tip**
>
> A common random error in experiments like this one relates to timing. Read Step 6 again and consider how much variation there might be in starting and stopping the timer. Before giving this as a random error think carefully about the improvement you will suggest.

(e)

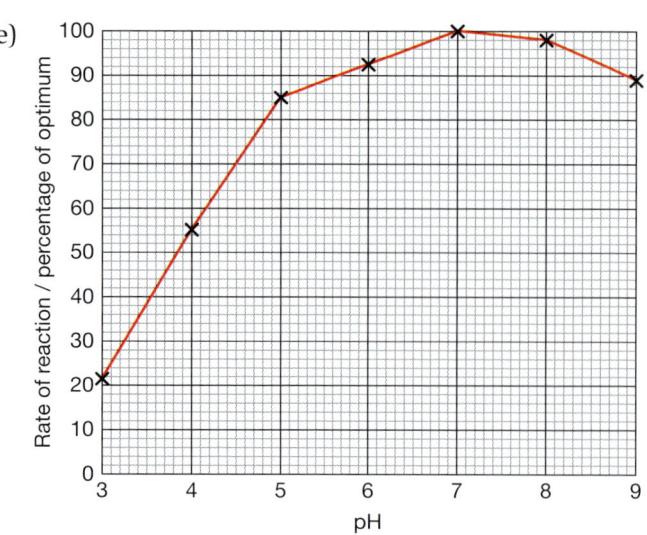

★ Exam tip

This graph has a displaced origin because there are no results for values of pH less than 3.

(f) Catalase functions over the range of pH between 3 and 9. The rate increases from 22% at pH 3 to 100% at pH 7 and then decreases. At pH 7 the active site is complementary to the substrate, but at lower and higher values of pH there are changes in tertiary structure as the concentration of hydrogen ions changes. There is a change in charge distribution as R groups gain or lose hydrogen ions and some of these will result in a change in shape of the active sites of catalase molecules so they do not accept the substrate so readily.

Microscopy

In the exam you may have to share a light microscope with another student. You may have to start with the microscopy question so the other student can use it for the second half of the exam. In the microscopy question, the examiners may ask you to:

- make a temporary preparation of a plant tissue (e.g. onion epidermis, see page 13) or some cells (e.g. yeast)
- use a microscope slide that has been prepared specially for the exam
- use photomicrographs or electron micrographs that are printed on the exam paper.

Temporary preparations of plant tissues may involve smearing material on a slide, cutting sections of stem, root or leaf, dissecting out plant tissues, pulling tissues from organs or breaking up tissues with a needle (macerating).

These are typical instructions to make a temporary preparation of the lower epidermis of a leaf.

1. Tear the leaf across and use your fingers or a pair of forceps to remove a piece of the lower epidermis.

2. Place the piece of epidermis with the external surface facing upwards in a drop of water on a slide. Use a mounted needle to gently lower a coverslip to cover the tissue.

3. Use absorbent paper to remove excess water from around the edge of the coverslip.

4. Dry the base of the slide before putting it on the stage of the microscope.

5. Observe the slide under the low and high powers of your microscope.

You may have to stain the preparation you have made by irrigating the slide. Place a drop of the stain (usually methylene blue or iodine) on one side of the coverslip and a piece of absorbent paper on the opposite side. As the paper absorbs water from underneath the coverslip, the stain spreads through. When the stain has spread right across the specimen, put a drop of water on the side of the coverslip and absorb the excess stain with absorbent paper. Wipe the base of the slide and check that the coverslip is dry.

★ Exam tip

Practise making temporary preparations and viewing them with a microscope. This will improve your manipulative skills.

🔗 Link

Look at the Practical skills section 'Resolution and magnification' in Unit 1 and 'Observing the mitotic cell cycle' in Unit 5.

★ Exam tip

You can also use a smartphone to take photos of the microscope slides that you look at. You can also find photographs of them on the internet, but it is much easier to take them yourself as you can label and annotate them with the information you need.

Question 2 often involves making plan diagrams to show the distribution of tissues in a structure and making drawings of cells observed through the high-power objective lens of a microscope.

When you make a plan diagram, follow these rules:

- hold up the slide and look at it with the naked eye and/or a hand lens to see the specimen before placing it on the stage of the microscope

- make the drawing fill at least half the space provided; leave space around the drawing for labels and annotations

- use a sharp HB pencil (never use a pen)

- use dots or faint lines to plan how you will make your drawing

- use thin, single, unbroken drawing lines ('clear and continuous lines'), *not* 'feathery' lines

- use lines to show the boundaries between the tissues

- make the proportions of tissues in the diagram the same as in the section

- do *not* include drawings of cells

- do *not* use any shading or colouring.

Add labels and annotations (notes) to your drawing *only* if you are asked for these in the question. Use a pencil and a ruler to draw straight lines from the drawing to your labels and notes. Write labels and notes in pencil so you can alter your answer if necessary.

You may be asked to make drawings of plant cells, such as epidermal cells, xylem vessel elements, companion cells or phloem sieve tube elements. If so, follow the general advice above and:

- search the slide to find a suitable group of cells to draw to answer the question

- if not told how many cells to draw, choose three or four

- plan on the paper where you will draw the cells and put short lines to indicate the width and length of one of the cells

- draw a line to represent the *inside* of one of these cells

- look carefully at the thickness of the cell wall between the cells

- make some faint dots on the paper to indicate where to draw the inside of the adjacent cells and then draw these with clear, continuous lines

- draw in the middle lamella, which is where the cell walls of adjacent cells are joined together

- look carefully at the question to see what you are required to do; if you are not asked to label your drawing, no marks will be gained for including labels.

Question 2 often asks for comparisons between two structures: usually the specimen you have drawn from a slide and a photograph. Comparisons are best shown in a table.

When drawing, make sure that you are not drawing something that you remember should be present and bear in mind the resolution of the light microscope.

🔗 **Link**

There are some plan diagrams in the Practical skills sections of Unit 7 (pages 64–66) and Unit 8 (pages 74–75). These plan diagrams have been shaded to help show the different tissues. Your plan diagrams should **not** be shaded – see the answer to (a) on page 83 (Unit 9).

⭐ **Exam tip**

The prepared slide is likely to be unfamiliar. Do not panic. Look carefully for the tissues you should be able to recognise, e.g. epidermis, xylem and phloem.

◀ **Figure 20.7** A student using a microscope correctly to make drawings. She is right-handed so has placed her paper on her right-hand side. If you are left-handed, then place your paper on the left of the microscope when drawing

⭐ **Exam tip**

Make sure that your label lines, labels and annotations are horizontal. Do not draw label lines that cross each other.

⭐ **Exam tip**

When you make a table of comparison, put similarities running across the columns and differences in separate columns. Make direct comparisons when giving differences.

Worked Example 2 for Paper 3

This is an example of a Question 2 on Paper 3.

Marram grass, *Ammophila arenaria*, is a xerophytic plant common on sand dunes. In dry weather, the leaves roll up to form vertical tubes. All the stomata are on the inner epidermis, where additional protection is provided by stiff interlocking hairs known as trichomes.

Figure 1 shows a transverse section of a leaf taken from marram on a dry day. Figure 2 is a view of part of the section at higher magnification.

> ★ **Exam tip**
>
> In the examination you will be given a microscope slide of marram grass and will be expected to draw a plan diagram and high power details from the slide not from photographs as in this question.

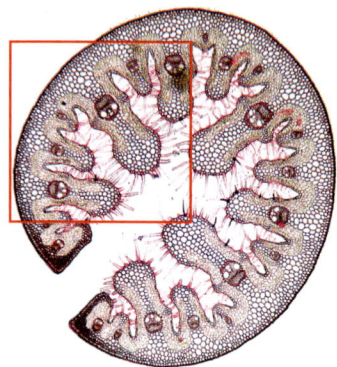

▲ **Figure 1** (×18)

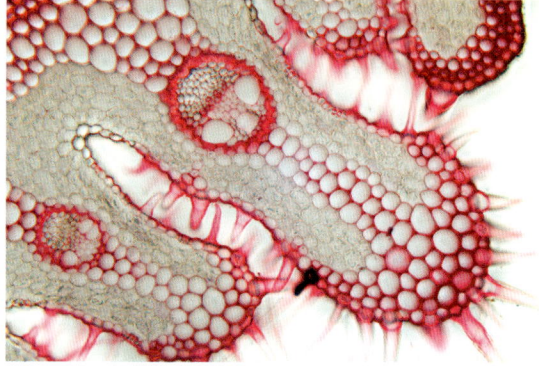

▲ **Figure 2** (×70)

(a) (i) Draw a large plan diagram of the region of the marram leaf in Figure 1 within the red rectangle. Do **not** include the trichomes in your plan diagram.

Use a sharp pencil. [4]

(ii) On your plan diagram, use ruled label lines and labels to indicate:

- xylem
- phloem
- the lower epidermis
- the upper epidermis. [2]

The photomicrographs show that one surface of the the leaf is covered in trichomes. Figure 3 shows some trichomes from marram grass and Figure 4 shows some trichomes from a leaf of loosestrife, *Lysimachia* sp.

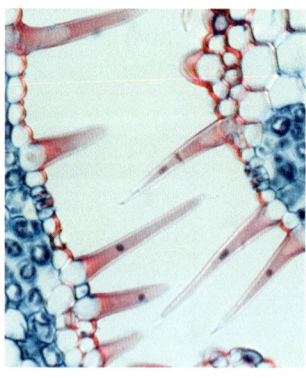

▲ **Figure 3** (×130)

▲ **Figure 4** (×40)

(b) (i) Make a drawing of one of the trichomes and the three adjacent cells from Figure 3. [3]

(ii) Calculate the actual size of the trichome. Show your working. [2]

(c) Identify two observable differences, other than size and colour, between the trichome of marram grass and the trichome of loosestrife.

Record your observations in a table. [3]

(d) Suggest the role of trichomes on the leaves of marram grass. [2]

Answers

(a) (i) and (ii)

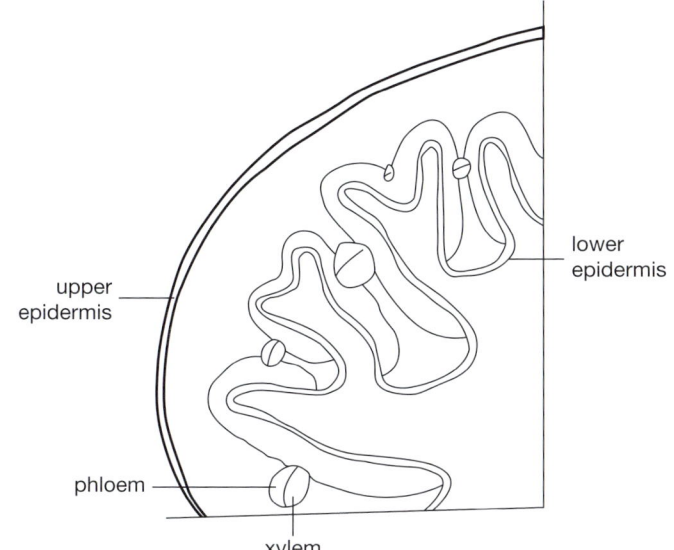

(b) (i)

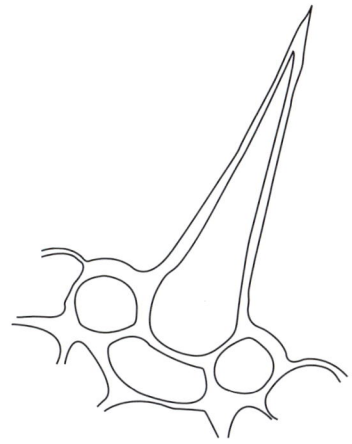

(ii) Length of trichome in Figure 3 is 17 mm.

Actual length = 17 / 130

Actual length = 130 μm.

(c)

Feature	Trichomes	
	Marram grass	**Loosestrife**
number of cells	one	many
shape	pointed	swollen at tip

(d) Trichomes reduce the movement of air inside the rolled leaf so it remains humid. This reduces the water potential gradient between the inside of the leaf and the air so that less water is lost by transpiration.

Advice for Paper 3

Remember these tips for taking Paper 3:

- read through each question carefully before you start any practical work

- annotate the questions as you read them and highlight the topic areas from the syllabus so you know what knowledge to use when answering questions that ask you to interpret and conclude

- keep one area of the lab bench for your exam paper and keep it dry; do not put any liquids near the paper

- look at the time to make sure that you spend about one hour on each question (assuming that there are two questions on the paper)

- prepare any tables in pencil and plan what you are putting into the columns and rows carefully before you start

- write your experimental results directly into a table; do not write them down somewhere else on the paper and copy them in later

- leave yourself enough time to look through your paper to double check your calculations and make sure that you have answered all the questions.

★ **Exam tip**

When you take Paper 3, make sure that you have: a calculator, two sharpened HB pencils, a pencil sharpener, a clean eraser and a clean, complete plastic ruler.

★ **Exam tip**

As you read through Question 1 when in the exam, imagine you are carrying out the practical and look for all the apparatus you will use that should be set out on the lab bench for you.

→ **Try this... 1 (for Paper 3)**

You can try this example of Question 1 from Paper 3 in a school or college laboratory or at home. All the materials and apparatus that you need are listed below.

Instructions for making the 1.0 mol dm⁻³ solution of sucrose are on page 168.

1   The water potential of a plant tissue is a function of the solute potential and the pressure potential of the cells. The water potential gradient between a plant tissue and any solution in which it is immersed determines the net movement of water between the tissue and the solution.

You are required to investigate the effect of immersing pieces of potato, *Solanum tuberosum*, in different sucrose solutions.

You are provided with the following:

- 600 cm³ of 1.0 mol dm⁻³ sucrose solution in a suitable container
- water for diluting the sucrose solution in a suitable container
- two large potatoes
- a sharp knife and board for cutting
- a transparent, plastic ruler and one piece of 2 mm graph paper

- a measuring cylinder or measuring beaker or cup with graduations every 20 cm³
- seven beakers, mugs, plastic cups or polystyrene cups as containers for immersion of potato strips
- a marker pen
- paper towels.

Proceed as follows:

Step 1   Use the 1 mol dm⁻³ sucrose solution to prepare five different concentrations of sucrose by **simple (proportional) dilution**. You will need to prepare *at least* 200 cm³ of each concentration.

(a)   Make a table to show how you will make the solutions.   [4]

Step 2   Put *at least* 200 cm³ of each sucrose solution into the containers.

Step 3   Use the sharp knife to cut the potato into strips with the dimensions shown in the diagram. You will need *at least* 10 strips. Make sure that there is no peel left on the strips of potato and that the ends of each strip are cut square.

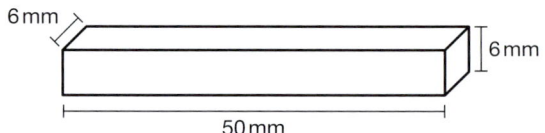

Step 4   Place *at least* two strips of potato into each solution of sucrose. Make sure that the strips are completely immersed. Put the beakers or plastic cups to one side for 30 minutes. While you are waiting continue with the rest of the questions starting from **(f)**.

Step 5   After 30 minutes remove the strips of potato from the solutions of sucrose and measure their lengths.

★ **Exam tip**

As you carry out the practical, identify any likely errors in measurement and any limitations of the procedure (see pages 174–176). Write down any ideas on any white space in your exam paper so you can use them in your answers.

(b)   Record all your results and any processed data in a table.   [4]

(c)   State the uncertainty of the measurements that you have taken and explain your answer.   [2]

(d)   Explain how you could use your results to estimate the water potential of the potato tissue.   [3]

(e)   State **two** main sources of error in your investigation and explain the effect that each has on the results.   [2]

The solute potential is one of the factors that determines the water potential of plant tissues. In an investigation a student peeled the epidermis from some onion scale leaves. The epidermal peels were cut into pieces and placed in solutions of different concentration of sodium chloride. The pieces were immersed for 10 minutes and then placed on microscope slides in the same bathing solutions and covered by cover slips.

The number of cells showing signs of plasmolysis in 100 cells chosen at random was counted. The results are shown in the table.

Concentration of sodium chloride solution / mol dm^{-3}	Water potential / kPa	Percentage of plasmolysed cells
0.00	0	0
0.10	−440	7
0.20	−850	43
0.30	−1260	67
0.40	−1680	87
0.50	−2120	100

(f) Plot a graph of these results. [4]

> ★ **Exam tip**
>
> Make sure you follow the rules for plotting graphs (see page 173); use a sharp pencil to make small saltire crosses. If you decide to put straight lines between the points use a ruler to draw the lines.

(g) The solute potential of plant cells is estimated as the value when 50% of the cells are plasmolysed.

    (i) State the water potential at which 50% of the cells are plasmolysed. [1]

    (ii) Explain why the epidermal cells became plasmolysed in some of the solutions of sodium chloride. [3]

➡ **Try this... 2 (for Paper 3)**

The photomicrographs show transverse sections through two muscular arteries.

Figure 1 was viewed with low power and Figure 2 is a sector of a muscular artery viewed with high power.

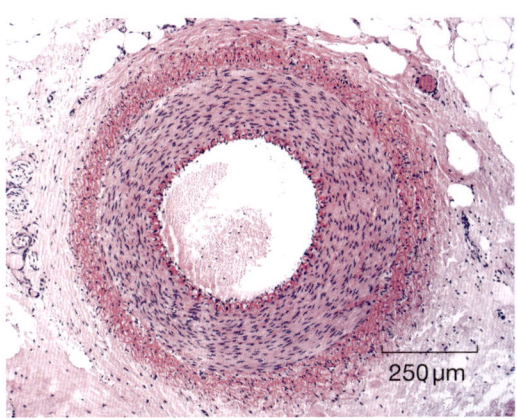

250 µm

▲ **Figure 1**　　　　　　　　▲ **Figure 2**

(a) (i) Draw a large plan diagram of the muscular artery as shown in Figure 1. Use a sharp pencil. [5]

    (ii) Label the tissues that you have shown in your plan diagram. [3]

(b) Use Figures 1 and 2 to describe the two features of muscular arteries:

    (i) the lining of the artery [2]

    (ii) the distribution of smooth muscle tissue. [2]

(c) Draw a line on Figure 1 to show the diameter of the artery.

Use the line and the scale bar to calculate the actual diameter of the artery.

Show all the steps in your calculation. [5]

(d) Use the line that you drew in (c) to calculate the ratio between the thickness of the wall of the artery in Figure 1 and the lumen.

Show your working. [3]

↑ Raise your grade (for Paper 3)

A student investigated the effect of increasing surface area to volume ratio (SA:V) on diffusion into agar blocks that had been stained with the pH indicator cresol red. The student cut six blocks of agar into cubes of decreasing size, beginning with a cube with sides of 6 mm. The blocks were immersed into hydrochloric acid and the time taken for the indicator to change from red to yellow throughout each block was recorded. The student repeated the investigation twice and recorded the results in a table.

Cube size / mm	Surface area / mm²	Volume / mm³	SA:V	Time for acid to diffuse to centre of cube / s			
				1	2	3	Mean
1	6	1	6.0	8	11	10	9.7
2	24	8	3.0	26	26	29	27.0
3	54	27	2.0	43	45	40	42.7
4	96	64	1.5	65	80	73	72.7
5				112	122	130	
6	216	216	1.0	216	216	210	198.3

(a) Complete the table by calculating the missing figures for the cube of size 5 mm. [2]

The missing figures that were added to the table are: 150, 125, 1.2 ✔ and 121.3 ✔

When you complete a table look carefully at the figures in the rest of the table. Ask yourself two questions – 'do my answers match the trend(s)' and 'how many decimal places are used for any of the calculations'. If an answer does not fit the trend then check your working. You can always calculate one of the results already in the table. For example, calculate SA:V for one of the other rows and see if you get the same answer. Always give your answer to the same number of decimal places as in this table.

(b) Draw a graph to show the effect of increasing SA:V on the mean time for diffusion of acid into the agar blocks. Use a sharp pencil. [5]

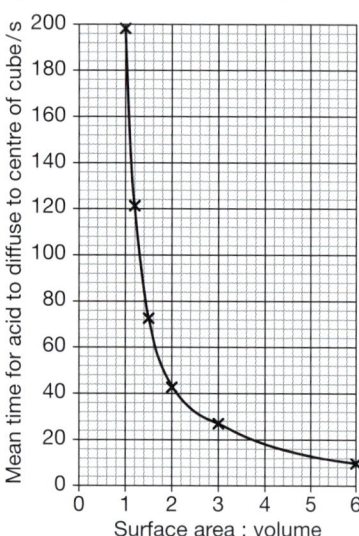

- The student has drawn a graph with the independent variable (SA:V ratio) on the x-axis and the dependent variable (time taken) on the y-axis.

- The student has chosen sensible scales – 10 mm on the x-axis to represent 1 'unit' and 10 mm on the y-axis to represent 20 s.

- Both axes are labelled in full and the unit (s for seconds) is added after a solidus on the y-axis.

- The points are plotted with small saltire crosses using a sharp pencil.

- The line is a smooth curve of best fit that does not extend beyond the first and last plotted points. The line is one continuous line without breaks and is drawn with a sharp pencil.

(c) Use the results of this investigation to explain why most human cells are very small. [5]

Small cells have a large SA:V ratio so it does not take very long for molecules of oxygen to diffuse to all parts of the cell. The cell of size 1 mm has the shortest mean time for diffusion of the acid (9.7 s). ✔ If animal cells were larger they would have a small SA:V ✔ and it would take longer for oxygen to diffuse throughout the cell. ✔ The surface of a large cell would not provide enough area for oxygen to diffuse ✔ into the cell and supply all the mitochondria. If mitochondria do not receive enough oxygen for aerobic respiration, ✔ then they will not provide enough ATP to keep the cell alive. ✔

A thorough answer to part (c) that refers to some of the data from the table and also uses information from Unit 1 as well as Unit 4.

Paper 5 (30 marks)

This paper is set on the whole syllabus. The questions involve aspects of planning, analysis and evaluation. There is no practical work, so the paper is not taken in a lab. The paper is set so that marks are awarded for the following skills:

Skills	Breakdown of the skills	Marks
Planning	Defining the problem	14–16
	Methods	
Analysis, conclusions and evaluation	Dealing with data	14–16
	Evaluation	
	Conclusions	

All the sections in this book that are about practical skills are relevant to Paper 5. The only skill not so far discussed in detail is the Planning skill.

Paper 5 tests your ability to devise hypotheses, make predictions, plan experiments, interpret results and evaluate procedures and data. Planning and implementing your own plans during your course will provide you with good practice at these skills. The contexts of questions in Paper 5 may involve unfamiliar experiments or biological materials. Do not panic: if you have revised thoroughly all the topics in the syllabus and practised writing and implementing your own plans, then you have the experience to answer confidently.

Planning

You will be expected to plan a logical procedure as part of an investigation that someone else could carry out following your instructions.

Here is some advice about answering the planning question on Paper 5.

Step 1 Identify the independent, dependent and control variables for the investigation.

The IV is the variable that the experimenter will change during the investigation. The DV is the variable that is not known at the beginning. In the example on page 102 the IV is temperature of the yeast suspension and the DV is the time taken for the methylene blue solution to go colourless. There is no need to state these variables in answer to the planning question if you have already answered a question about these variables – see Raise your grade on page 192.

Step 2 Choose the **range for the independent variable** (IV) and the **intermediate values** across the range. On page 102, the range is 10 °C to 60 °C and there are 4 intermediate values at intervals of 10 °C.

Step 3 Choose **apparatus and materials** that are appropriate. Only choose apparatus that is available in a school or college lab. You could choose a colorimeter or apparatus required to carry out electrophoresis as both are included in the syllabus. Do not forget ecological investigations, which are in Unit 18. You could be asked to design an investigation to measure the distribution and/or abundance of organisms.

Step 4 Decide which variables should be kept **constant** throughout the investigation. These variables are known as **controlled** or **standardised variables**. In an enzyme experiment it is important to keep the temperature and pH constant if another variable (e.g. enzyme concentration) is the IV. In your method you should state how at least one variable should be kept constant.

★ **Exam tip**

In the examination, the planning question will be based on a topic that you have studied from Units 1 to 19 and some practical work that you should have done. If the context of the investigation or apparatus required is unfamiliar then sufficient details will be provided.

🔗 **Link**

See Unit 18 and pages 188, 190, 191 and 203 for questions on ecological investigations.

Step 5 Decide whether any **control experiments** are needed. For example, you may need a control experiment to show that the presence of an organism is responsible for the changes that you measure. A control experiment is set up in exactly the same way but uses inert material of the same volume or mass to replace the living organism. For example, a control experiment should always be set up when using a respirometer like that on page 103. Boiled mung seeds or small pieces of stone of the same mass as the living seeds would be appropriate material to use.

★ **Exam tip**

Do not confuse control experiments with controlled (or standardised) variables.

Step 6 Decide where to start the method and the sequence of steps that should be followed. Your method should include a detailed explanation of how:

- the IV will be changed

- the apparatus will be used to measure the DV

- at least one important control variable should be kept constant.

Step 7 Carry out a risk assessment. Identify the main hazard(s) and state appropriate safety precautions for each one.

Step 8 Write the **method** using **numbered steps** as a set of instructions; do not use continuous prose. This allows you to include instructions such as 'repeat Step 5'. The procedure must be written in a logical sequence of steps. The best way to do this is to think about being in a lab. Ask yourself, what are the steps I would follow?

You should be aware of the principles of precision, accuracy and repeatability. Your method should include steps that refer to:

- using apparatus that measures to an appropriate level of precision, for example, mass to 0.1 g, time to the nearest second, volume to the nearest $1.0\,cm^3$

- stating clearly what precautions should be taken to ensure results are taken carefully and in the same way each time

- repeating the whole experiment using fresh materials at least twice to obtain replicate results.

★ **Exam tip**

There are plenty of examples in the Practical skills sections of this book that are written in this way. Make sure that you use them to help you write instructions in a logical sequence. See Units 3, 4, 12 and 13 for examples. Practise writing methods for different investigations.

Step 9 Complete the answer by identifying at least one hazard for the experiment and giving an appropriate precaution. You should choose the most significant risk to anyone who follows your method. Avoid statements such as 'low risk', 'tie hair back' or 'wear a lab coat'.

★ **Exam tip**

Not sure which statistical test is appropriate? Use the decision tree on page 195.

Step 10 Planning questions are often followed by questions that ask how the results should be processed. For example, the planning question on page 192 could be followed by a question asking how the results should be processed. The effect of glucose concentration on rates of respiration can be plotted on a graph. The results are given as 'time for the blue colour to disappear'. The rates can therefore be calculated as $1/t$, where t = time taken to go colourless. It may be appropriate to say that the results should be analysed by carrying out a statistical test. If you know which test is appropriate then name it.

Analysis, conclusions and evaluation

All the information given for Paper 3 (see pages 174–176) is relevant to Paper 5. In addition, you should know how to use descriptive statistics and how and when to use four statistical tests. You should also know the criteria for using each of these four tests:

- chi-squared test

- *t*-test

- Spearman's rank correlation coefficient test

- Pearson's linear correlation coefficient test.

Worked Example 1 for Paper 5

A group of students investigated the effects of light intensity and temperature on the rate of photosynthesis of discs cut from young leaves of *Coleus* sp. The discs were placed in a side arm test-tube of water and all the air inside the leaf discs was removed by using a vacuum pump.

All the discs were transferred into a flask of dilute sodium hydrogencarbonate solution. All the discs sank to the bottom of the flask. The disks were kept in the dark. At intervals, ten discs were removed and placed in separate specimen tubes containing dilute sodium hydrogencarbonate solution. The specimen tubes were positioned at different distances from a light source. After a while, the discs moved to the surface and floated on the solution.

The time taken for the first five of the discs to move towards the surface was recorded. The investigation was repeated with freshly cut discs at a higher temperature. All the results are in the table.

Distance of leaf discs from light source / mm	Time taken for five discs to float at 20 °C / s	Time taken for five discs to float at 30 °C / s
50	275	125
100	390	210
150	410	360
200	620	600
250	none of the discs moved from the bottom of the tube	none of the discs moved from the bottom of the tube

(a) Explain why the leaf discs sank to the bottom of the tube and why they floated. [3]

(b) Describe and explain the trend shown by the discs kept at 30 °C. [4]

(c) The leaf discs left in the dark remained on the bottom of the tube and did not float.

Explain why the leaf discs did not float. [3]

(d) Explain why the leaf discs kept at 20 °C took longer to float than those at 30 °C. [3]

(e) The students investigated the effect of light intensity and temperature on the rate of photosynthesis of leaf discs cut from young leaves of *Coleus* sp.

(i) Explain how the data in the table should be processed so that the students can draw a graph to present the results of their investigation. [2]

(ii) Another group of students used the same procedure to find out if the results are repeatable. They decided that the description given above was not detailed enough for them to repeat the procedure in the same way.

State **four** improvements to the description of the procedure described above so that others can find out if the results are repeatable. [4]

Answers

(a) The density of the discs is greater than water. They have had all the gas removed from the internal air spaces. When the leaves absorb light they use the energy to split water (photolysis) to provide electrons to the ETC. Oxygen is produced as a by-product. It forms bubbles in the water inside the leaf and makes the leaf less dense than water so it floats.

(b) As the distance of the lamp increases, the time taken for discs to float increases. At 30 °C the time increases by a factor of 4.8 (50 mm to 200 mm). The light intensity is highest when it is closest to the leaf discs (50 mm). The discs photosynthesise at the fastest rate as light provides energy for the light- dependent stage which is where photolysis occurs. As the distance increases the light intensity decreases and so the rate of photolysis decreases and it takes longer to make enough oxygen to reduce the density of the leaves so that they float. At 250 mm there is not enough light energy for the leaf cells to produce enough oxygen.

(c) The discs do not photosynthesise in the dark so no oxygen is made in photolysis. The cells still carry out respiration so they will use any dissolved oxygen and make carbon dioxide, which is much more soluble in water than oxygen so stays in solution.

(d) Temperature is a limiting factor of photosynthesis. The activity of the enzymes in chloroplasts will be much less so less ATP and reduced NADP needs to be produced by the light-dependent stage, so the rate of photolysis decreases and less oxygen is produced. When light intensity is not limiting (50 mm and 100 mm) the rate of photosynthesis at 30 °C is about double that at 20 °C. This suggests that the reason is due to enzyme activity.

(e) (i) Light intensity is proportional to $\frac{1}{d^2}$. This means that the highest light intensity can be calculated as 0.0004 units. This can be expressed by multiplying by 10 000 to give whole numbers to plot.

The rates of photosynthesis can be calculated as $\frac{1}{t}$, where t = the time taken for the first five discs to move to the surface. This will be plotted as light intensity on the x-axis and rate of photosynthesis on the y-axis.

(ii) 1 The concentration of sodium hydrogencarbonate solution.

2 The type of light source used.

3 The volume of sodium hydrogencarbonate solution in the specimen tubes.

4 The diameter of the leaf discs.

Worked Example 2 for Paper 5

Researchers in the Czech Republic investigated the effect of soil moisture on the species diversity of plants in a nature reserve that includes an area of wetland. They used quadrats to sample the vegetation and used a soil probe to record the moisture in each quadrat. The results are shown in the table.

Quadrat	1	2	3	4	5	6	7	8	9	10
Species diversity / number of species	23	41	27	34	43	46	33	38	35	35
Percentage soil moisture	20	30	38	40	50	60	70	35	45	43

The researchers calculated the Spearman's rank correlation coefficient (r_s) as 0.60 (2 dp).

(a) (i) State a null hypothesis for this investigation. [1]

(ii) Explain why it was important that the quadrats were positioned randomly across the wetland. [2]

(iii) Using Table 20.8 on page 202 and the value of r_s, state and explain the conclusion that can be made from these results. [4]

(b) The researchers planned to compare the species diversity in an area of woodland with an area of grassland in the nature reserve.

Describe how the researchers could collect data so that they could determine the Simpson's index of diversity for the two areas in the nature reserve.

Your method should be set out in a logical order and be detailed enough to allow another person to follow it.

Details of calculating the diversity index should **not** be included. [6]

Answers

(a) (i) There is no correlation between species diversity (number of species) and the percentage soil moisture.

(ii) This shows that there was no bias on the part of the researchers in choosing the positions of the quadrats. If the researchers chose where to put the quadrats the statistical test would not be valid. One of the criteria for the Spearman's rank correlation coefficient is that results are taken at random.

(iii) The value of r_s is 0.60. This is less than the critical value for 10 pairs of measurements which is 0.648. As it is less, the chance of this result is greater than 0.05 (5%) so the correlation is not significant and the null hypothesis is accepted.

(b) This can be done by using quadrats positioned randomly and the species identified within each quadrat and the numbers of individuals of each species counted.

1   Mark out a rectangular area within the grassland with measuring tapes.

2   Use a random number app to find coordinates, for example, 10 m on one axis and 5.5 m on the other.

3   Position each quadrat on the randomly selected coordinates. Use a key to identify the different species in the quadrat and count the number of individuals of each species. Enter the results on a spreadsheet – list of species and abundance of each species.

4   Put the quadrat at 10 to 20 different positions within the rectangular area.

5   Repeat Steps 1 to 4 in the woodland area.

6   Use the results to calculate the Simpson's index of diversity for the two areas.

The people doing the sampling must take care not to damage the two habitats and if it is hot and there is a chance of sunburn they should take a hat and use sun cream.

→ **Try this... 1 (for Paper 5)**

A student investigated the effect of different wavelengths of light on the rate of the light-dependent stage of photosynthesis.

Dichlorophenolindophenol (DCPIP) is a redox dye that is used to determine the activity of the light-dependent stage of photosynthesis. The blue colour of DCPIP disappears as it is reduced:

electrons and hydrogen ions + DCPIP → reduced DCPIP

                                (blue)   (colourless)

The student prepared a suspension of chloroplasts in a cold, sucrose solution buffered at pH 7.

Samples of the chloroplast suspension were mixed with a DCPIP solution and kept in the dark.

A short length of capillary tubing was dipped into the mixture of chloroplast suspension and DCPIP so that the mixture was taken up. The capillary tubing was placed on a bench beneath a coloured filter as shown in the diagram.

> ★ **Exam tip**
>
> The investigations described in Paper 5 may be familiar or unfamiliar. Read through carefully and try to imagine carrying them out in the lab or in the field. This should help you answer questions like Question (c).

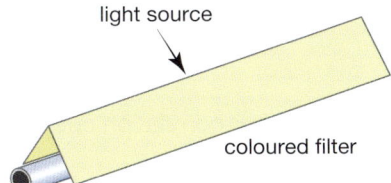

light source

coloured filter

The student timed how long it took for the DCPIP to decolourise. The student then repeated the procedure using filters of different colours.

(a) Identify the independent and dependent variables in this investigation. [2]

(b) Explain why the chloroplast suspension was prepared in a sucrose solution. [2]

(c) Suggest **two** suitable controls to include and explain why you think each is necessary. [4]

(d) Explain how the student would calculate the rate of the light-dependent stage of photosynthesis from the results collected. [1]

(e) The student decided to use the same procedure to investigate the effect of light intensity on the rate of the light-dependent stage of photosynthesis.

(i) State a hypothesis that the student could test. [1]

(ii) Write a plan that the student could follow to test the hypothesis and gain valid, high-quality data.

Your method should be set out in a logical way and be detailed enough to allow another person follow it. [7]

→ Try this... 2 (for Paper 5)

The marine iguana, *Amblyrhynchus cristatus*, is endemic to the Galápagos Islands. On the island of Santa Cruz, many female iguanas congregate at one site on the coast to lay their eggs. This site provides the right conditions for egg laying, but is not colonised by adults as it provides them with little protection. The young iguanas begin to hatch from the eggs during May and June each year and feed on the algae that are exposed at low tide.

Researchers used the mark-release-recapture method to estimate the numbers of young iguanas on four occasions during May and June 1995. Each marking period lasted for two days, followed by one day of recapture.

(a) Suggest **two** factors that the researchers should consider when using mark-release-recapture to estimate the population of the young marine iguanas. [2]

The table shows the results.

Date	Number marked and released	Number recaptured	Number marked recaptured	Population estimate
10 May	237	232	101	544
25 May	539	354	214	892
10 June	195	169	100	
25 June	128	124	103	154

(b) Complete the table by calculating the population estimate for the 10 June.

Write out the formula that you will use for calculating the population and give your answer to the nearest whole number. Show your working. [3]

(c) Suggest possible reasons why the estimated population on the 25 June was much less compared with the other estimates. [2]

Adult marine iguanas swim out to sea to feed on algae growing on rocks down to a depth of 15 m. Researchers investigated the relationship between food availability and the maximum size of adult iguanas on 16 of the islands in the Galápagos. They measured the height of the algae around each island and the body length of a sample of the largest adults.

The researchers tested the hypothesis that there was a correlation between the mean height of algae and the maximum length of adult iguanas by calculating the Pearson's linear correlation coefficient (r).

(d) Pearson's correlation coefficient can only be used if the data satisfies certain criteria. State **two** of these criteria. [2]

(e) The researchers calculated the value of r as 0.86.

The table shows some of the critical values for Pearson's linear correlation coefficient.

Number of pairs of measurements	Critical values	
	$p = 0.05$ (5%)	$p = 0.01$ (1%)
14	0.532	0.661
15	0.514	0.641
16	0.497	0.623

★ **Exam tip**

This question shows why it is important to know *when* you can use the different statistical tests and *how* you interpret the results.

(i) State what the value of r indicates about the relationship between the mean height of algae and the maximum length of adult iguanas. [1]

(ii) Describe how the researchers used this table to find out if the value for $r = 0.76$ is significant. [3]

→ **Try this... 3 (for Paper 5)**

Students went on a field course to the Pyrenees, which is the mountain range between Spain and France. They discovered that European beech, *Fagus sylvatica*, grows at altitudes between sea level and 1800 m above sea level. Temperatures decrease with altitude and they thought that leaves would become smaller, so less likely to be damaged by the wind. They decided to measure the areas of leaves of beech trees along a road up into the mountains.

The students planned an investigation to find the effect of altitude on leaf area.

(a) State a hypothesis for their investigation. [1]

(b) State the independent and dependent variables for their investigation. [2]

(c) Write a method that the students could use to collect data from the beech trees between sea level and 1800 m.

Your method should be set out in a logical order and be detailed enough for another person to follow. [7]

(d) The students were told that they should use a statistical test to see if there was a relationship between leaf area of the beech trees and altitude.

  (i) State the name of a statistical method that they could use to analyse their results. [1]

  (ii) State the assumptions that the students must make about the data to justify their choice. [2]

→ **Try this... 4 (for Paper 5)**

The survival of mammals in habitats where there is very little water is thought to be due to their ability to produce highly concentrated urine. This is thought to be related to having nephrons with long loops of Henle which require a relatively wide medullary region in the kidney. Many scientists have published data on the sizes of kidneys from individual animals of different species. They have also kept them without water for a period of time to determine the maximum concentration of their urine.

In 1990, a researcher collected data on 25 rodent species from many different studies to find out if there is any correlation between relative medullary thickness (RMT) and the maximum concentration of urine that each rodent could produce. The RMT for each species was calculated by dividing the thickness of the medulla by the volume of the kidney.

(a) State the null hypothesis for this investigation. [1]

The data was analysed using the Spearman's rank correlation test.

(b) The Spearman's rank correlation coefficient (r_s) for the data on the 25 rodent species is 0.77.

Part of the Spearman's rank probability table is shown below.

Number of pairs of measurements	Critical values		
	$p = 0.10$ (10%)	$p = 0.05$ (5%)	$p = 0.01$ (1%)
25	0.337	0.398	0.511

Use the value of r_s and the probability table to state the conclusions that the researcher can make from this investigation. [3]

(c) Explain why the researcher chose to analyse the results using the Spearman's rank correlation coefficient test rather than the Pearson's linear correlation test. [2]

(d) Suggest and explain a limitation of the study published in 1990. [2]

⬆ Raise your grade – Paper 5 Question 1

A student was investigating the effect of different variables on the rate of respiration of a yeast suspension. The student used the redox dye methylene blue.

The student investigated the effect of different concentrations of glucose using a 0.5 mol dm⁻³ solution.

(a) State the independent and dependent variables in the student's investigation. [2]

Independent variable concentration of glucose ✔

Dependent variable time ✗

> Always be more precise when 'time' is a variable in an experiment. Here the DV should be 'time for methylene blue to go colourless' or 'time for yeast suspension to lose its blue colour'.

(b) Plan a method to find out the effect of changing the concentration of glucose on the rate of respiration in yeast using the redox dye, methylene blue.

You are provided with the following apparatus and materials:

a stirring rod, a beaker of water to use as a water bath, hot and cold water, a thermometer, a timer, an unlimited supply of: test-tubes and syringes, 0.5 mol dm⁻³ glucose solution, 20% yeast suspension, 0.005% methylene blue solution, distilled water.

Your method should be set out in a logical order and be detailed enough for another person to follow. [8]

1. Use the glucose solution and the distilled water to make some different concentrations in labelled test-tubes:
   0, 0.1, 0.2, 0.3, 0.4, 0.5 mol dm⁻³. ✔
2. Put the same volume of glucose solution into each test-tube and add a known volume of yeast suspension to each test-tube. Stir the yeast suspension each time before taking up into the syringe.
3. Put the test-tubes in the water bath at 30 °C. ✔
4. Add 1 cm³ of methylene blue solution to each test-tube and start the timer. ✔
5. Watch the test-tubes and record the time when the blue colour disappears. ✔
6. Take care when using the water bath and wear gloves.

Good points in the answer.

- Numbered points make it easy for someone to follow the method.

- Five separate values of the IV are used.

- A specific temperature is given for the investigation.

These points should be included in a good method.

- A statement to explain how the apparatus is used to keep the temperature constant.

- Actual volumes for the glucose solutions and yeast suspension should be given. The student should have experience of this practical (see page 102).

- Details of how to do the timing should be included. The test-tubes could be set up in sequence and each one timed separately.

- Repeats should be included. The whole experiment beginning with Step 1 should be repeated at least twice to give three replicate readings for each concentration.

- The specific hazard associated with water baths should be given.

Descriptive statistics

These are used to summarise data you have collected about a continuous variable.

You should know how to calculate and use the following:

- range (difference between largest and smallest)

- mean ($\bar{x}$) calculated as: $\dfrac{\Sigma x}{n}$

  where Σ = 'the sum of', x = data values, n = number of readings

- sample standard deviation (s)

- standard error (SE)

- median.

🔗 Link

Table 20.6 in *Try this... 2* on page 199 shows the mean lengths of two samples of 30 leaves. Linear dimensions, such as lengths and widths of leaves, are continuous variables.

> **★ Exam tip**
>
> Other symbols are also used for standard deviation and standard error. The two shown here are those used in the exam papers and are the ones you should use in your calculations and as abbreviations in your answers.

The **range** is the difference between the largest result and the smallest. You can express this in two ways, for example, for the length of leaves as 71 to 113 mm or as the difference between them, which is 42 mm. The range is one way to show the spread of results about the mean.

The term **average** is often used to refer to the 'centre of a distribution' which can be the **mean**, the **mode** or the **median**.

> **★ Exam tip**
>
> Avoid the word 'average' as it is ambiguous unless you specify whether you are using mean, median or mode.

Variables such as length and mass may be distributed normally so that the mean is in the middle of the range. A histogram of continuous data that gives a bell-shaped curve indicates a **normal distribution**. When the data are like this, you can calculate how much spread there is about the mean.

The **variance** is the difference between each result and the mean. All these differences are squared to remove the negative signs. The sum of these is divided by one less than the number of readings:

$$\text{variance } (s^2) = \frac{\Sigma(x - \bar{x})^2}{n - 1}$$

> **★ Exam tip**
>
> Never calculate a mean from numbers that are themselves means. Always calculate means directly from the raw data.

Variance is used in calculations, but rarely used on its own as a descriptive statistic because the units are not the same as the raw data.

The **sample standard deviation (s)** is the square root of the variance:

$$s = \sqrt{\frac{\Sigma(x - \bar{x})^2}{n - 1}}$$

The standard deviation shows how widely the sample data is dispersed. Figure 20.8 shows that 68.2% of results are within 1 s of the mean, 95.4% are within 2 s of the mean and 99.7% are within the mean $\pm 3\ s$. This pattern applies to all data that show a normal distribution whatever the investigation. If the standard deviation is large relative to the mean, then the results are widely dispersed and you cannot have much confidence in the value of the mean.

Variance is calculated by squaring the differences and so the unit for variance is the square of the unit of measurement, e.g. mm^2 for linear measurements and $(cm^3)^2$ for volumes. These are not useful in the context of showing the variation in results about a mean, which is why we calculate standard deviation.

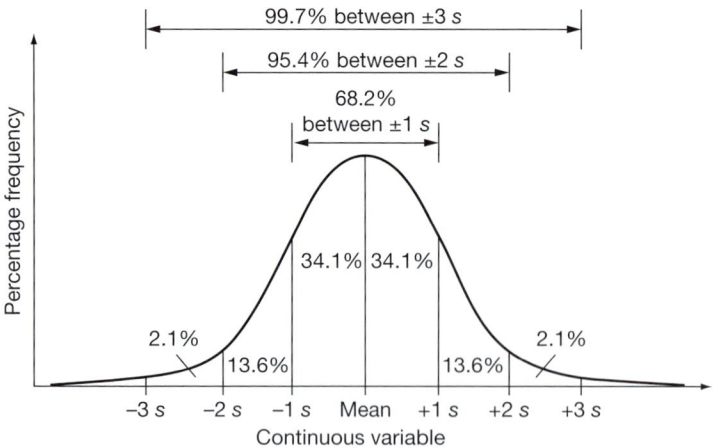

▲ **Figure 20.8** A normal distribution showing the proportions of the population that are enclosed by $\bar{x} \pm 1\,s$, $\bar{x} \pm 2\,s$ and $\bar{x} \pm 3\,s$

Standard error tells you about the mean of the **population** from which the sample has come. It is calculated by dividing the sample standard deviation by the square root of the number of readings:

$$\text{standard error } (SE) = \frac{s}{\sqrt{n}}$$

This value is used to calculate the **95% confidence interval** (95% CI). There is a 95% probability that the population mean can be found within the range $\bar{x} \pm$ CI. The 95% CI may be estimated for samples of ≥ 20 by:

$$95\%\,\text{CI} = \bar{x} \pm 2 \times SE$$

The 95% confidence limits are the upper and lower values of this range. The 95% CI is the best measure of the dispersal of the results around the mean and the best to use for error bars on graphs.

For data that are not distributed normally (the graph is not a bell-shaped curve) the best 'average' to use is the **median**, which is the middle value of a distribution. The median divides the data into two equal halves; for example, 35 is the median of 46, 44, 37, 35, 31, 28 and 25. Quartiles divide the data into quarters. The interquartile range contains all the results within the range 25% below and 25% above the median.

The total range may include the outliers that are often discounted because of errors. The total range (including outliers) gives the idea that the real variation is greater than it really is. The interquartile range gives most of the data, but with standard deviation and standard error the extent of each of the deviations from the mean is taken into account.

Error bars are drawn on bar charts and line graphs as shown in Figure 20.9.

Standard error and the 95% confidence interval are the best to use for error bars, but you can also use standard deviation.

A vertical line is drawn above and below each bar or plotted point. If SE is used, the upper error bar is drawn 1 SE above the mean and the lower error bar is drawn 1 SE below the mean. The lower error bar is often omitted on bar charts, especially when shading is used, as shown in Figure 20.9.

A line of best fit should go through error bars. You can expect to put error bars on graphs in Paper 5 and refer to them in your answers.

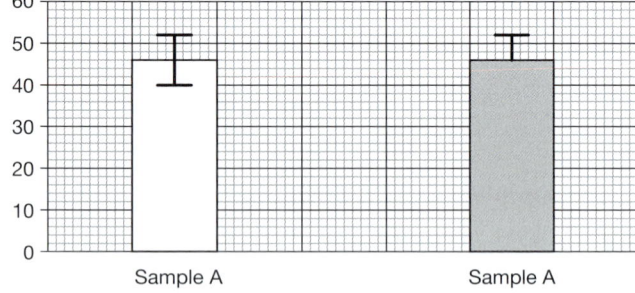

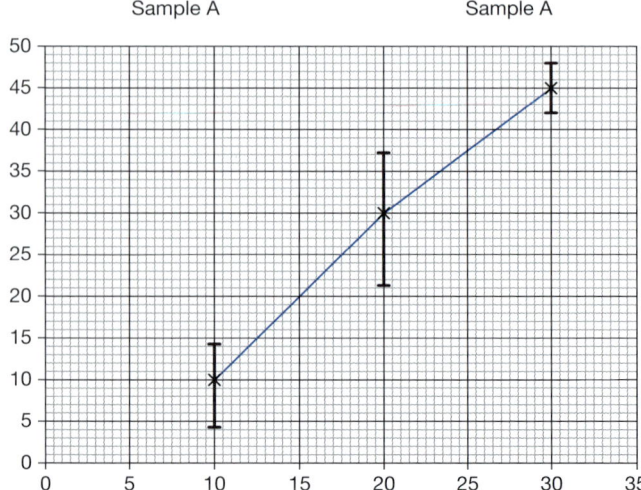

▲ **Figure 20.9** Error bars on a bar chart and a line graph

Statistical tests

There are different statistical tests for the different types of data that you may collect. Two types of variable are **qualitative** and **quantitative** as shown in Table 20.2.

▼ **Table 20.2** Types of variable and types of data with examples from this book

Type of variable	Type of data	Example(s) in this book
Qualitative: Categorical	nominal	presence or absence of starch; fruit flies with long or very small wings; people with different blood groups
Ordered	ordinal (ranked)	degrees of cloudiness on a scale of 0–10; abundance scales (e.g. ACFOR)
Quantitative: Continuous	interval – having any value (e.g. 1.0, 2.5)	mass of potato pieces; length of leaves
	interval – integers only (e.g. 1, 2, 3)	numbers of different species on a rocky shore

To make a correct choice of statistical test, you need to know what sort of variables you have investigated, the type of data you have collected and what you are trying to achieve with a statistical test (Figure 20.10).

You may have to:

- select which statistical test is appropriate for analysing the results of an investigation

- use the test to calculate the test statistic (e.g. χ^2, t, r_s or r)

- use a table of probabilities to make conclusions from the result of a statistical test.

★ **Exam tip**

You should know when to use these tests and the assumptions that we make when using them. Make sure that you read carefully the introduction to each of the statistical tests over the next few pages.

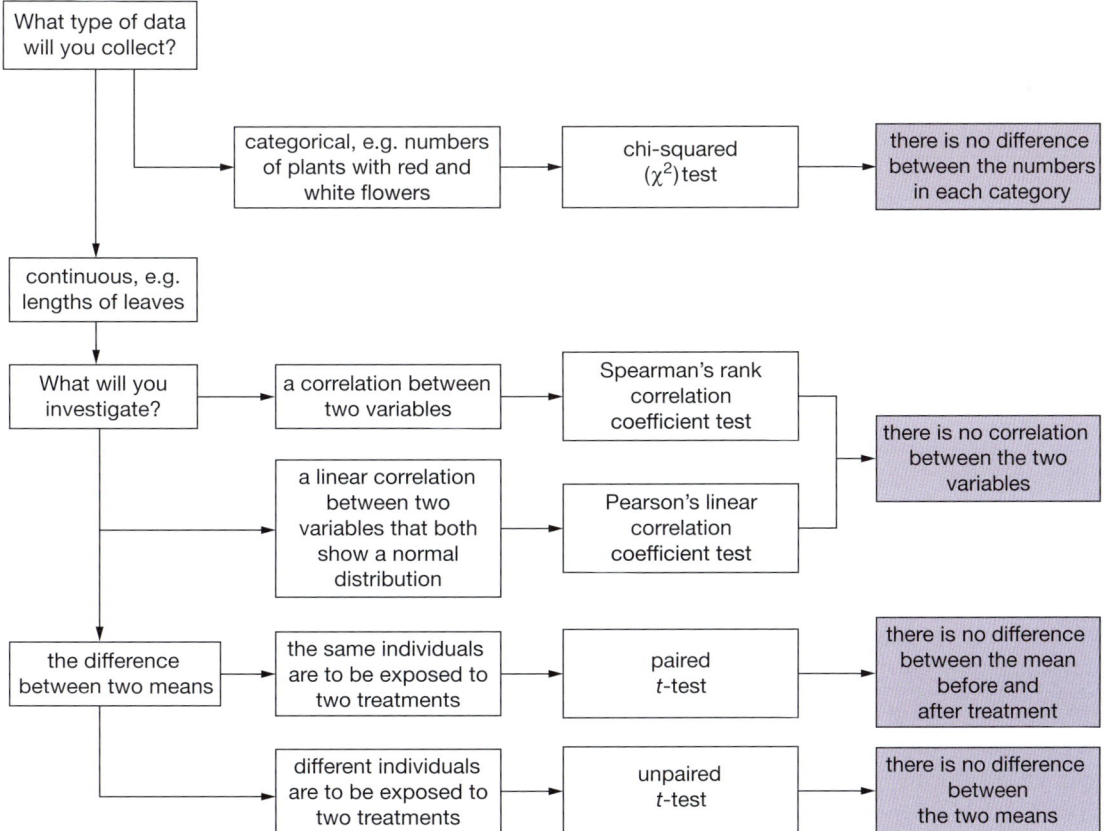

▲ **Figure 20.10** A decision tree for which statistical test to use when planning an investigation or analysing results; the shaded boxes give examples of the null hypotheses to use

Maths Skills

The chi-squared test

The chi-squared test is a 'goodness of fit' test to check the significance of differences between observed and expected results when using categorical data. You are most likely to use the test to analyse results from experiments on genetics (Unit 16).

The chi-squared test should only be used when: data is categorical; the outcomes of an experiment can be predicted from theory; it can be assumed that they will be random events; and the number for all the expected outcomes is > 5.

These are the steps to follow in carrying out a chi-squared test.

Step 1   Analyse the information to find the type of inheritance pattern.

Step 2   Calculate the ratio of phenotypes **expected** in the offspring.

Step 3   Write a **null hypothesis**. This states that there is no difference between the observed results and the expected results.

Step 4   Make or complete a table to calculate the value of χ^2 as shown opposite in Table 20.4.

The formula for calculating χ^2 is:

$$\chi^2 = \sum \frac{(O - E)^2}{E}$$

where $\sum$ = sum of...; O = observed value; E = expected value; and degrees of freedom (df) = number of categories − 1.

To find out if the χ^2 value is significant or not, you need to look at a table of probabilities. You will be given a table of probabilities in the examination.

> **Link**
>
> The type of data collected in genetic studies is called categorical data (see Unit 16). This is because you count the number of individuals in different categories.

▼ **Table 20.3** Table of probabilities for chi-squared test. The additional table shows how to interpret the probabilities – see Steps 6 and 7.

Degrees of freedom	Distribution of χ^2							
	← Increasing values of *p* Decreasing values of *p* →							
	Probability, *p*							
	0.99	0.90	0.50	0.10	0.05	0.02	0.01	0.001
1	0.00016	0.016	0.46	2.71	3.84	5.41	6.64	10.83
2	0.02	0.21	1.39	4.61	5.99	7.82	9.21	13.82
3	0.12	0.58	2.37	6.25	7.82	9.84	11.35	16.27
4	0.30	1.06	3.36	7.78	9.49	11.67	13.28	18.47

$p > 0.90$	$p > 0.05$	$p < 0.05$	$p < 0.01$	$p < 0.001$
result is highly unlikely = too good!	result is not significantly different from expected outcome	result is significantly different from expected outcome	highly significant	very highly significant

Tomato plants usually have indented leaves, known as 'cut'. Some tomato plants have leaves shaped like those of potatoes, known as 'potato'. Pure-bred tomato plants with cut leaves and purple stems were crossed with pure-bred plants with potato leaves and green stems. All the F1 generation had cut leaves and purple stems. These F1 plants were test crossed against tomato plants showing the recessive phenotype – potato leaves and green stems. The test cross offspring showed the following numbers of plants in each of four phenotypes:

purple, cut	purple, potato	green, cut	green, potato
70	91	86	77

Table 20.4 shows how to calculate the chi-squared value for the test cross data. The expected ratio is 1:1:1:1 assuming that random assortment occurs during meiosis to produce gametes in the F1 tomato plants.

The number of columns is always six, but the number of rows depends on the number of classes of data. For a monohybrid cross with two phenotypes among the offspring you need three rows; for a dihybrid cross with four phenotypes among the offspring you need five rows in your table. (One row is needed for the headings of the columns.)

▼ **Table 20.4** Table to show how to calculate chi-squared values

Insert the categories and observed numbers

Enter the expected numbers based on the expected ratio

Subtract the expected numbers from the observed

Square the difference to remove the negative sign

Categories	O	E	O – E	$(O – E)^2$	$(O – E)^2 / E$
purple cut	70	81	−11	121	1.49
purple potato	91	81	10	100	1.23
green cut	86	81	5	25	0.31
green potato	77	81	−4	16	0.20
totals	324	324		$\chi^2 =$	3.23

Total the expected numbers to check the calculation

Total this column to give value of χ^2

The calculated value of χ^2 is 3.23 in this example. To find out if this is significant or not, we need to look at a table of probabilities.

Step 5 To use the table of probabilities we need to know how many degrees of freedom (df) there are. In this example, there are four possible phenotypes and therefore the degrees of freedom is 4 − 1 = 3.

Step 6 Read across the table at the appropriate df until you come to the column for $p = 0.05$. This is the probability that we will get this result 5% of the time or once in every 20 times we carry out the investigation. This value is the **critical value**.

Step 7 Write a conclusion based on the critical value. In this case, the column and row intersect at 7.82. Our result, 3.23, is less than this critical value, which means that the result is not significantly different from the expected outcome and we can accept the null hypothesis.

> ★ **Exam tip**
>
> In the chi-squared test, remember that df = number of categories − 1.

> ★ **Exam tip**
>
> The decision to use a probability of 0.05 or 5% is now an accepted value in biological investigations that many researchers use.

It is more correct to say that the value of p is greater than 0.1 and less than 0.5. The probability of getting this result is therefore between 10% and 50% which means that the difference between observed and expected results is due to chance effects such as random fertilisation. The difference is not *statistically significant* and so the null hypothesis can be accepted. This means that the results support the idea that random assortment has occurred during meiosis in the F1 tomato plants. The two genes – for leaf shape and stem colour – are on different chromosomes.

If the value for χ^2 is greater than the critical value, then the probability of the results is *less than 0.05* and there is a *significant difference* between observed and expected. If so, the null hypothesis is rejected.

> ★ **Exam tip**
>
> These instructions assume that you are carrying out all the steps of a chi-squared test, but exam questions may ask you to state the type of statistical test to analyse categorical data or ask you to make conclusions based on the results of a chi-squared test.

➡️ **Try this... 1**

Curled wings and spineless bristles are autosomal recessive features in the fruit fly *Drosophila melanogaster*. Pure-breeding wild-type flies with straight wings and normal bristles were crossed with pure-breeding flies with curled wings and spineless bristles. All the F1 fruit flies had straight wings and normal bristles. In a test cross, female flies from the F1 were crossed with males homozygous for both gene loci. The results were:

straight wings, normal bristles = 186; straight wings, spineless bristles = 18; curled wings, normal bristles = 16; curled wings, spineless bristles = 180.

The ratio of phenotypes expected in a cross such as this is 1:1:1:1 assuming that random assortment occurs during meiosis to produce gametes in the F1 fruit flies.

(a) State a null hypothesis for this investigation. [1]

(b) Use the formula on page 196 to calculate the value of χ^2 for the results of the cross. [5]

(c) Make a conclusion from the results of the chi-squared test. [4]

📐 Maths Skills

The *t*-test

The **unpaired *t*-test** is used to find out whether the means of **two sets** of data are significantly different from each other. It answers the question, 'Are the differences due to chance or not?'

⭐ **Exam tip**

You cannot conclude anything about the difference between means by looking at error bars that are plotted using standard deviation or standard error. If the 95% CI error bars overlap you cannot be certain that there is a significant difference between the means, so you need to carry out the *t*-test to find out; if they do not overlap and the sample sizes are equal, there is a significant difference at a probability of less than 5% ($p < 0.05$).

You should only use the *t*-test when

- interval data have been collected (see Table 20.2)

- you want to see if there is a significant difference between the means of **two sets of unpaired data**, that is, from two different populations of plants or animals

- the data in each set shows a normal distribution

- the total number in each sample may be different, for example, 10 and 15.

The formula for calculating the value of *t* is:

$$t = \frac{|\bar{x}_1 - \bar{x}_2|^2}{\sqrt{\left(\frac{s_1^2}{n_1} + \frac{s_2^2}{n_2}\right)}}$$

where $\bar{x}_1$ and $\bar{x}_2$ are the means of the two samples; s_1 and s_2 are the standard deviations of the two samples; and n_1 and n_2 are the numbers of individual measurements in the two samples. The vertical lines either side of the numerator indicate that the sign can be ignored; use the absolute difference between the two means.

The formula for calculating the degrees of freedom is:

$$df = (n_1 - 1) + (n_2 - 1)$$

Here are the steps to follow when using the t-test for unpaired data.

Step 1 Write a null hypothesis (NH). This is usually written in this form: 'there is no difference between the mean of ... and the mean of ...'

Step 2 Calculate $\bar{x}_1$ and $\bar{x}_2$ and find the difference between them (ignore the sign).

Step 3 Calculate s_1 and square it, then divided by n_1; repeat for the other data set and then add the two calculated values together.

⭐ **Exam tip**

If you write your NH as shown in Step 1, you have a **two-tailed test**. If, for example, you write 'the mean of A is greater than the mean of B' then you have a **one-tailed test**. The tables of probability that you will be given for the *t*-test will assume that you are using a two-tailed test.

Step 4   Calculate t by dividing the value obtained in Step 2 by the value obtained in Step 3.

Step 5   Calculate the total degrees of freedom (df) for all the data, using the formula given earlier. (You are expected to know how to calculate the degrees of freedom for the t-test.)

Step 6   Find the critical value at $p = 0.05$ (p_{crit}) for the degrees of freedom that you have calculated.

> 💡 **Remember**
>
> The probability value that is used for the four statistical tests in the syllabus is $p = 0.05$ (5%). If the value for χ^2 and for t is greater than the critical value at $p = 0.05$, you can say that there is a significant difference.

▼ **Table 20.5** Examples of critical values for the t-test

Degrees of freedom	Decreasing values of $p \longrightarrow$			
	0.10 (10%)	0.05 (5%)	0.01 (1%)	0.001 (0.1%)
5	2.02	2.57	4.03	6.87
10	1.81	2.23	3.17	4.59
20	1.72	2.09	2.85	3.85
30	1.70	2.04	2.75	3.65
>30	1.64	1.96	2.58	3.29
	$p > 0.05$ results are not significantly different	$p < 0.05$ results are significantly different	$p < 0.01$ results are highly significant	$p < 0.001$ results are very highly significant

> ★ **Exam tip**
>
> You do not need to memorise the formulae for the statistical tests as they will be provided. Tables of critical values will also be provided and are likely to show only a few rows.

The result of the t-test cannot prove that a particular hypothesis is correct. The result, however, can provide support for the hypothesis if $p < 0.05$.

➡ **Try this... 2**

A student was investigating the effect of pollution on the growth of holly, *Ilex aquifolium*. Trees of this species grow at the edge of a road and also within nearby woodland, 100 m away from the road. The student measured 30 leaves from trees growing in each location.

▼ **Table 20.6** Lengths of 30 holly leaves collected from trees growing alongside a busy road and inside nearby woodland

Site	Mean length of leaves / mm	Standard deviation (SD)	Standard error (SE)	95% CI
Side of road	45.8	8.3	1.51	3.02
Woodland	80.0	12.7	2.32	4.64

The student used the t-test to find out if pollution from traffic had any effect on the growth of the leaves.

(a) Two terms can be used to describe the type of variation that the student has investigated. Name these types of variation. [2]

(b) State the independent **and** dependent variables for the investigation. [2]

(c) State a null hypothesis for the investigation. [1]

(d) Explain how the data needs to be presented to check that the t-test is appropriate for analysing the data from this investigation. [2]

(e) The student calculated the value of t as 12.35.

    (i) State the degrees of freedom for the data collected. [1]

    (ii) Use Table 20.5 to make a conclusion from this result. [4]

(f) State two limitations of the investigation as described above. [2]

> ★ **Exam tip**
>
> Pollution is not the independent variable because the student has not measured any aspect of pollution. The student could have wiped the surfaces of the leaves to collect the dust, dirt and grime to compare pollution in the two sites.

→ Try this... 3

Conservationists studied populations of Bojer's skink, *Gongylomorphus bojerii*, a species of lizard that is now extinct on the main island of Mauritius but survives on smaller islands close by (Figure 20.11). The researchers found that the population of Bojer's skinks on Round Island appeared to be much larger than the skinks on Gunner's Quoin. They measured the body lengths of random samples of skinks from both islands. Their results and calculations are shown in Table 20.7.

▼ Table 20.7

Population	Number sampled (*n*)	Mean length ($\bar{x}$) / mm	Standard deviation (*s*)	Standard error (*SE*)	Mean ± 95% CI
Gunner's Quoin	30	35.33	7.124	1.30	35.33 ± 2.60
Round Island	30	56.50	7.714		56.50 ±

★ Exam tip

Read the entry for this lizard species in the IUCN Red List of Threatened Species – see www.iucnredlist.org and use the search facility. The Red list is a source of useful information for Unit 18.

(a) Copy and complete Table 20.7 by calculating the standard error and the 95% confidence interval (CI) for the population on Round Island. [2]

(b) Plot the data shown in the table in an appropriate format. [5]

(c) Explain the advantages of calculating the standard deviation, standard error and 95% CI. [3]

(d) State what the graph shows about the two populations. [2]

(e) Rats live on Gunner's Quoin, but not on Round Island. Discuss how rats may be responsible for the difference in body size of these two populations of skink. [4]

▲ Figure 20.11 Bojer's skink

★ Exam tip

You may need to read pages 193, 194 and 198 to help you answer parts (a) to (d).

→ Try this... 4

Sexual dimorphism is the difference in appearance of males and females. Scientists investigating a population of the tri-spine horseshoe crab, *Tachypleus tridentatus*, in waters around Sabah, Malaysia, wanted to see if there was any evidence for sexual dimorphism in this species. They took measurements of the bodies of male and female horseshoe crabs (see photograph of a related species). Their results are shown in the table.

Sex	Mean maximum width (±SD) / mm	Mean total length of body (±SD) / mm
male (*n* = 154)	257 ± 16	538 ± 46
female (*n* = 67)	312 ± 23	667 ± 56

The researchers used the *t*-test to analyse their results.

They calculated the value of *t* for the difference between the mean maximum width of the bodies as 17.79.

(a) (i) State a suitable null hypothesis for the investigation into total length of the bodies. [1]

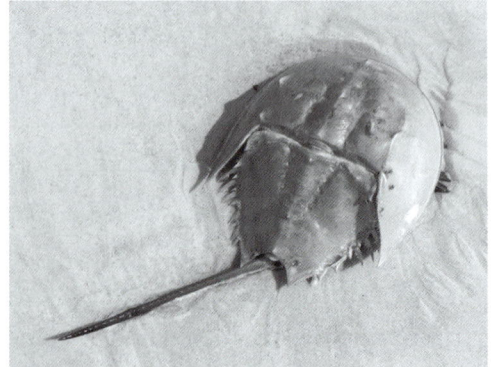

▲ Figure 20.12 Horseshoe crab

(ii) Calculate the value for *t* for total length of the body. Show all your working.

(See page 198 for the formula to calculate the value of *t*.) [5]

(b) Use Table 20.5 on page 199 to make a full conclusion from the results of this investigation. [5]

(c) State the assumption that the scientists have made about their data before using the *t*-test. [1]

Corrections

Field work often involves investigating the relationship between the distribution and/or abundance of two species or the effect of an abiotic factor on the distribution and/or abundance of a particular species. You should calculate a correlation coefficient as part of the analysis of results of these investigations.

The relationship between two variables, such as the abundance of species A and species B, may be positive, negative or non-existent, as shown in the scatter graphs in Figure 20.13.

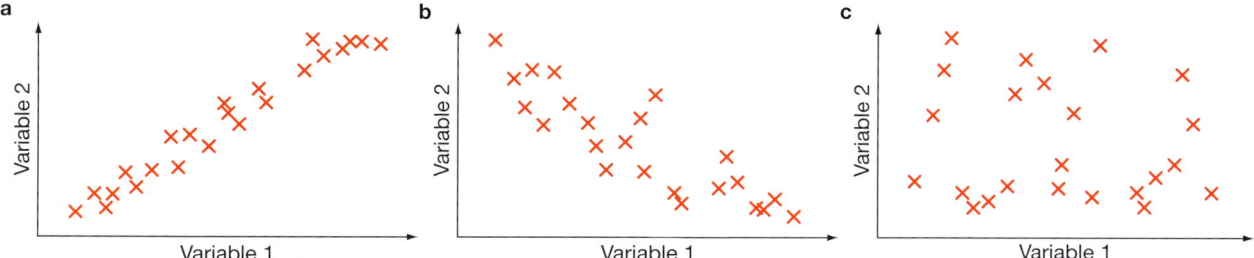

▲ **Figure 20.13** Scatter graphs: **a** positive correlation; **b** negative correlation; **c** no correlation

The strength of the correlation can be assessed by calculating a correlation coefficient. A coefficient of +1 indicates there is a perfect positive correlation (all the points are on a straight line) and −1 indicates that there is a perfect negative correlation. A coefficient of 0 means the points are scattered at random on the graph and there is no correlation.

Maths Skills

Correlation coefficients

Use a correlation coefficient test if:

- The number of paired observations is ideally between 10 and 30. You can, however, use these tests if there are more than five paired observations.

- All individual results must be selected at random from a population; each individual must have an equal chance of being selected.

- Each data point (pair of readings) on a scatter graph is independent of all the others and the data is paired.

Choose **Spearman's rank correlation test** if:

- interval data or ordinal data has been collected (see Table 20.2 on page 195)

> ★ **Exam tip**
>
> Abundance scales, such as ACFOR, and data that is expressed using an arbitrary scale, such as 0–10, are examples of ordinal data.

- a scatter graph indicates the possibility of an increasing or a decreasing relationship. This does not have to be a linear relationship, it could be one that increases and then levels out (but it must not decrease after levelling out). It cannot be used if the relationship increases and then decreases or decreases and then increases.

Choose **Pearson's linear correlation test** if:

- interval data has been collected (do **not** use for ordinal data)

- a scatter graph indicates the possibility of an increasing or a decreasing **linear** relationship.

Spearman's rank correlation

The formula to calculate the Spearman's rank correlation coefficient, r_s, is:

$$r_s = 1 - \left(\frac{6 \times \Sigma D^2}{n^3 - n} \right)$$

where ΣD^2 = sum of differences between ranks; and n is the number of pairs of items in the sample.

These are the steps to follow when calculating the Spearman's rank correlation coefficient.

Step 1 Plot the results as a scatter graph to see if there may be a correlation. The easiest way to do this is to enter the figures in a spreadsheet and choose the scatter graph function.

Step 2 Write a null hypothesis. This is usually going to say 'there is no significant correlation between …'

Step 3 Rank each set of data. The largest number in each set of data is given the rank of 1. If two or more items have the same rank, then calculate the mean rank for all of them. The best way to do this is in a table or by using a spreadsheet. You can see one in the answers to the next *Try this*.

Step 4 Calculate the differences in the ranks, D, by subtraction.

Step 5 Square the differences in the ranks to give D^2. This removes the negative signs.

Step 6 Add all the values for D^2 to calculate ΣD^2.

Step 7 Calculate the Spearman's rank correlation coefficient by inserting the values for ΣD^2 and n into the formula above.

Step 8 Interpret the value of r_s. The value of r_s may range from -1 to $+1$. A positive value indicates a positive correlation in which the values of variable y increase as the values of variable x increase. A negative value indicates a negative correlation in which the values of variable y decrease as the values of variable x increase. The closer the number is to 1, the stronger the correlation. A coefficient of 0 indicates that there is no correlation.

Step 9 Interpret the significance of the value of r_s. The sign is ignored when comparing r_s to the critical value. Now look up the Spearman's rank coefficient in the table of critical values that correspond to the number of pairs of measurements in the results table (see Table 20.8).

Step 10 Accept or reject the null hypothesis. If the value of r_s is equal to or greater than the critical value, then the null hypothesis is rejected. If the value of r_s is less than the critical value then the null hypothesis is accepted.

Step 11 Write a conclusion that includes the type of correlation (positive or negative), the strength of the correlation (the value of r_s) and the degree of significance.

▼ **Table 20.8** The critical values of the Spearman's rank correlation coefficient (r_s) at $p = 0.05$ and $p = 0.01$

Number of pairs of measurements	Critical values	
	$p = 0.05$ (5%)	$p = 0.01$ (1%)
5	1.000	
6	0.886	1.000
7	0.786	0.929
8	0.738	0.881
9	0.700	0.833
10	0.648	0.794
11	0.618	0.755
12	0.587	0.727
14	0.538	0.697
16	0.503	0.635
18	0.472	0.600
20	0.447	0.570
30	0.362	0.467

→ **Try this... 5**

Dung beetles feed on the dung produced by large herbivores, such as cattle, sheep, deer and other animals. Students have collected data on the species diversity of dung beetles in the Cusuco National Park in Honduras for many years. The data from one such collecting trip is shown in the table.

The students wanted to know if there was a correlation between species diversity and altitude. They used Spearman's rank correlation test to find out.

(a) State the null hypothesis for this investigation. [1]

(b) Calculate the Spearman's rank correlation coefficient (r_s) using the formula given earlier. Show all your working. [5]

(c) Using Table 20.8 and the value for r_s, state and explain the conclusion that can be made from the results. [5]

Altitude range / m	Species diversity / mean number of species of dung beetle
600–799	7.3
800–999	5.8
1000–1199	5.4
1200–1399	6.5
1400–1599	4.7
1600–1799	5.3
1800–1999	4.9
2000–2199	4.7

⌐ Maths Skills

Pearson's linear correlation

The formula for calculating Pearson's linear correlation, r, is:

$$r = \frac{\Sigma xy - n\bar{x}\bar{y}}{(n-1)s_x s_y}$$

where $\bar{x}$ equals the mean of sample X; $\bar{y}$ equals the mean of sample Y; s_x is the standard deviation of sample X; s_y is the standard deviation of sample Y; and n is the total number of samples.

Step 1 Plot a scatter graph to see if there is a linear relationship.

Step 2 Write a null hypothesis.

Step 3 Calculate the mean and standard deviation for each variable.

Step 4 Multiply each pair of values together to give their product, xy.

Step 5 Calculate the sum of the products xy, to give Σxy.

Step 6 Insert the appropriate figures into the formula given above.

Step 7 Interpret the value of r as for the Spearman's rank correlation coefficient (see Step 8 on page 202).

Step 8 Interpret the significance of the value of r. The sign is ignored when comparing r to the critical value. Use the table of critical values that correspond to the number of pairs of measurements in the results table (see Table 20.9 on page 204).

Step 9 Accept or reject the null hypothesis. If the value of r is equal to or greater than the critical value, then the null hypothesis is rejected. If the value of r is less than the critical value then the null hypothesis is accepted.

Step 10 Write a conclusion that includes the type of correlation (positive or negative), the strength of the correlation (the value of r) and the degree of significance.

▼ **Table 20.9** Some critical values of the Pearson's linear correlation coefficient (r) at $p = 0.05$ and $p = 0.01$

Number of pairs of measurements	Critical values	
	$p = 0.05$ (5%)	$p = 0.01$ (1%)
5	0.878	0.959
6	0.811	0.917
7	0.754	0.874
8	0.707	0.834
9	0.666	0.798
10	0.632	0.765
11	0.602	0.735
12	0.576	0.708
20	0.444	0.561
30	0.361	0.463
40	0.312	0.403

→ **Try this... 6**

Researchers in Brazil tested the hypothesis that there is a relationship between the height of trees and various aspects of leaf morphology including stomatal density.

The table shows the results for a random sample of 12 taken from all the trees that the researchers measured.

Tree	Height / m	Mean stomatal density / number mm^{-2}
1	18.8	284
2	23.6	288
3	33.0	213
4	16.8	285
5	32.3	406
6	23.7	477
7	31.2	314
8	24.2	110
9	35.0	588
10	31.6	175
11	19.4	150
12	17.8	367

The researchers calculated the value for Pearson's linear correlation coefficient, r, as 0.266.

(a) State a null hypothesis for this investigation. [1]

(b) Explain why the researchers chose to use Pearson's correlation coefficient. [2]

(c) Using Table 20.9 and the value of r that the researchers calculated, make a suitable conclusion. [5]

Index

Headings in **bold** indicate key terms..